ITIL® Service Transition

London: TSO

information & publishing solutions

Published by TSO (The Stationery Office) and available from:

Online
www.tsoshop.co.uk

Mail, Telephone, Fax & E-mail
TSO
PO Box 29, Norwich, NR3 1GN
Telephone orders/General enquiries: 0870 600 5522
Fax orders: 0870 600 5533
E-mail: customer.services@tso.co.uk
Textphone 0870 240 3701

TSO@Blackwell and other Accredited Agents

First edition Crown copyright 2007
Second edition Crown copyright 2011

Third impression 2014

ISBN 9780113313068

Printed in the United Kingdom for The Stationery Office
Material is FSC certified and produced using ECF pulp, sourced from fully sustainable forests.

P002581448   c6   10/13

Contents

List of figures   v

List of tables   vii

Foreword   viii

Preface   ix

Acknowledgements   xi

1   Introduction   1
    1.1   Overview   3
    1.2   Context   6
    1.3   ITIL in relation to other publications
          in the Best Management Practice
          portfolio   8
    1.4   Why is ITIL so successful?   10
    1.5   Chapter summary   10

2   Service management as a practice   13
    2.1   Services and service management   15
    2.2   Basic concepts   22
    2.3   Governance and management
          systems   27
    2.4   The service lifecycle   30

3   Service transition principles   35
    3.1   Policies for service transition   37
    3.2   Optimizing service transition
          performance   45
    3.3   Service transition inputs and outputs   46

4   Service transition processes   49
    4.1   Transition planning and support   51
    4.2   Change management   60
    4.3   Service asset and configuration
          management   89
    4.4   Release and deployment
          management   114
    4.5   Service validation and testing   150

4.6   Change evaluation   175
4.7   Knowledge management   181

5   Managing people through service
    transitions   197
    5.1   Managing communications and
          commitment   199
    5.2   Managing organization and
          stakeholder change   203
    5.3   Stakeholder management   215

6   Organizing for service transition   219
    6.1   Organizational development   221
    6.2   Functions   221
    6.3   Organizational context for
          transitioning a service   222
    6.4   Roles   223
    6.5   Responsibility model – RACI   234
    6.6   Competence and training   234
    6.7   Service transition relationship with
          other lifecycle stages   236

7   Technology considerations   239
    7.1   Knowledge management tools   242
    7.2   Collaboration   242
    7.3   Configuration management system   243

8   Implementing service transition   245
    8.1   Key activities in the introduction of
          service transition   247
    8.2   An integrated approach to service
          transition processes   250
    8.3   Implementing service transition in
          a virtual or cloud environment   250

9   Challenges, critical success factors
    and risks   253
    9.1   Challenges   255
    9.2   Critical success factors   255

9.3 Risks   256

9.4 Service transition under difficult
     conditions   256

Afterword   **261**

Appendix A: Description of asset types   **265**

A.1 Management   267

A.2 Organization   267

A.3 Process   267

A.4 Knowledge   267

A.5 People   268

A.6 Information   268

A.7 Applications   268

A.8 Infrastructure   268

A.9 Financial capital   269

**Appendix B: Risk assessment
and management**   **271**

B.1 Definition of risk and risk
     management   273

B.2 Management of Risk (M_o_R)   273

B.3 ISO 31000   274

B.4 ISO/IEC 27001   275

B.5 Risk IT   276

Appendix C: Related guidance   **279**

C.1 ITIL guidance and web services   281

C2   Quality management system   281

C.3 Risk management   282

C.4 Governance of IT   282

C.5 COBIT   282

C.6 ISO/IEC 20000 service management
     series   283

C.7 Environmental management and
     green/sustainable IT   283

C.8 ISO standards and publications for IT   284

C.9 ITIL and the OSI framework   284

C.10 Programme and project
      management   285

C.11 Organizational change   285

C.12 Skills Framework for the
      Information Age   286

C.13 Carnegie Mellon: CMMI and
      eSCM framework   286

C.14 Balanced scorecard   286

C.15 Six Sigma   287

**Appendix D: Examples of inputs and
outputs across the service lifecycle**   **289**

References and further reading   **293**

Abbreviations and glossary   **297**

Index   **339**

List of figures

Figure 1.1   The ITIL service lifecycle   3

Figure 1.2   The scope of service transition   5

Figure 1.3   ITIL's relationship with other Best Management Practice guides   9

Figure 2.1   Conversation about the definition and meaning of services   16

Figure 2.2   Logic of value creation through services   20

Figure 2.3   Sources of service management practice   21

Figure 2.4   Examples of capabilities and resources   23

Figure 2.5   Process model   23

Figure 2.6   The service portfolio and its contents   27

Figure 2.7   Architectural layers of an SKMS   28

Figure 2.8   Plan-Do-Check-Act cycle   29

Figure 2.9   Integration across the service lifecycle   32

Figure 2.10   Continual service improvement and the service lifecycle   33

Figure 4.1   Scope of change management and release and deployment management for services   62

Figure 4.2   Example of a process flow for a normal change   70

Figure 4.3   Example of a process flow for standard deployment request   71

Figure 4.4   Example of a process flow for a standard operational change request   71

Figure 4.5   Example of a change authorization model   78

Figure 4.6   Interfaces between change management and service asset and configuration management   87

Figure 4.7   Example of a logical configuration model   93

Figure 4.8   Example of relationships between the CMS and SKMS   94

Figure 4.9   Example of the application of the architectural layers of the CMS   96

Figure 4.10   The relationship between the definitive media library and the configuration management system   99

Figure 4.11   Typical service asset and configuration management activity model   101

Figure 4.12   Example of a configuration breakdown for an end-user computing service   103

Figure 4.13   Example of a configuration breakdown for a managed virtual system   103

Figure 4.14   Example of service lifecycle configuration levels and baseline points   108

Figure 4.15   Simplified example of an IT infrastructure   108

Figure 4.16   Example of a configuration item lifecycle   110

Figure 4.17   Simplified example of release units for an IT service   116

Figure 4.18   Architecture elements to be built and tested   117

Figure 4.19   Example of a release package   118

Figure 4.20   Coordinating the deployment of service components   119

Figure 4.21   Options for 'big bang' and phased deployment   120

Figure 4.22   Phased deployment across geographical locations   121

Figure 4.23   Phases of release and deployment management   123

Figure 4.24   Example of service testing through service transition   134

Figure 4.25 Example of a set of
deployment activities   138

Figure 4.26 Example of early life support
activities   144

Figure 4.27 Illustration of the benefits of
targeted early life support   145

Figure 4.28 Dynamics of a service model   153

Figure 4.29 Design constraints driven by
strategy   154

Figure 4.30 Designing tests to cover a range
of service assets, utilities and
warranties   162

Figure 4.31 Example of a validation and
testing process   169

Figure 4.32 Performing test activities – an
example   171

Figure 4.33 Change evaluation process flow   177

Figure 4.34 Context for qualification and
validation activities   179

Figure 4.35 The flow from data to wisdom   184

Figure 4.36 Relationship of the CMDB, the
CMS and the SKMS   185

Figure 4.37 Examples of data and information
in the service knowledge
management system   186

Figure 4.38 Contribution of knowledge to
effectiveness of support staff   195

Figure 5.1   Example of a communication
strategy and plan contents   201

Figure 5.2   Example of a communication
path   202

Figure 5.3   Example of service transition
steps for outsourcing   203

Figure 5.4   The emotional cycle of change   204

Figure 5.5   Potential stakeholders   216

Figure 5.6   Example of a stakeholder map   217

Figure 5.7   Power impact matrix   217

Figure 5.8   Example of a commitment
planning chart   218

Figure 6.1   Example of service transition
organizational structure for a
small organization   222

Figure 6.2   Example of service transition
organizational structure for a
larger organization   222

Figure 6.3   Example of service transition
organization and its interfaces   223

Figure 6.4   Organizational interfaces for a
service transition   224

Figure 6.5   Flow of experience   236

Figure 8.1   Steps to improving the service
transition processes   247

Figure 8.2   An example of a path through the
processes that might be required
for a single service transition   251

Figure B.1   The M_o_R framework   274

Figure B.2   ISO 31000 risk management
process flow   275

Figure B.3   ISACA Risk IT process framework 277

List of tables

Table 2.1	The processes described in each core ITIL publication	31
Table 3.1	Service transition inputs and outputs by lifecycle stage	46
Table 4.1	Example of a responsibility matrix for release points during service transition	53
Table 4.2	Extract from a service release policy for a retail organization	55
Table 4.3	Example of types of request by service lifecycle stage	66
Table 4.4	Example of contents of change documentation	72
Table 4.5	Example of a change impact and risk categorization matrix	75
Table 4.6	Change priority examples	76
Table 4.7	Configuration documentation for assets and responsibilities through the service lifecycle	106
Table 4.8	Levels of configuration for build and testing	125
Table 4.9	Questions to be answered when planning deployment	128
Table 4.10	Examples of service test models	157
Table 4.11	Service requirements, 1: improve user accessibility and usability	158
Table 4.12	Examples of service management manageability tests	165
Table 4.13	Key terms that apply to the change evaluation process	176
Table 4.14	Factors to consider when assessing the effect of a service change	178
Table 5.1	Job characteristics that motivate people	203
Table 5.2	Understanding the culture of the parties involved	207
Table 5.3	Example of a RACI matrix for managing change	209
Table 5.4	Organizational role and skills assessment checklist	210
Table 5.5	Example of a feedback survey	211
Table 5.6	Tips for managing change	212
Table 5.7	J. P. Kotter's 'eight steps to transform your organization'	213
Table 6.1	An example of a simple RACI matrix	234

Foreword

Back in the 1980s no one truly understood IT service management (ITSM), although it was clear that it was a concept that needed to be explored. Hence a UK government initiative was instigated and ITIL® was born. Over the years, ITIL has evolved and, arguably, is now the most widely adopted approach in ITSM. It is globally recognized as the best-practice framework. ITIL's universal appeal is that it continues to provide a set of processes and procedures that are efficient, reliable and adaptable to organizations of all sizes, enabling them to improve their own service provision.

In the modern world the concept of having a strategy to drive the business forward with adequate planning and design transitioning into day-to-day operation is compelling. The aim of service transition is to make the move into the live business environment as smooth as possible. This vital step in the service lifecycle ensures that processes and procedures are in place to protect the live operational environment, ensuring that only tested and planned services are enabled for the business, in accordance with an agreed and communicated business timescale and with adequate fallback provision.

The principles contained within *ITIL Service Transition* have been proven countless times in the real world. We encourage feedback from business and the ITSM community, as well as other experts in the field, to ensure that ITIL remains relevant. This practice of continual service improvement is one of the cornerstones of the ITIL framework and the fruits of this labour are here before you in this updated edition.

There is an associated qualification scheme so that individuals can demonstrate their understanding and application of the ITIL practices. So whether you are starting out or continuing along the ITIL path, you are joining a legion of individuals and organizations who have recognized the benefits of good quality service and have a genuine resolve to improve their service level provision.

ITIL is not a panacea to all problems. It is, however, a tried and tested approach that has been proven to work.

I wish you every success in your service management journey.

Frances Scarff

Head of Best Management Practice
Cabinet Office

Preface

'They always say that time changes things, but you actually have to change them yourself.'
Andy Warhol

This is the third book in the series of five ITIL core publications containing advice and guidance around the activities and processes associated with the five stages of the service lifecycle. The primary purpose of the service transition stage of the service lifecycle is to ensure that any modifications or transitions to the live operational environment – affecting either new, modified, retiring or retired services – meet the agreed expectations of the business, customers and users. This means that all modifications to operational environments should be managed, planned and coordinated through service transition processes and activities to facilitate a smooth transition to live operation. This will ensure that a new, modified, retiring or retired service fulfils its operational expectation and has no or minimal adverse impact on customers, users and the business.

Successful service transition does not happen until an organization recognizes the need for it and the benefits it will bring. Effective service transition is necessary because business operations and processes are in a constant state of transition. The quest for competitive advantage, best-of-breed innovation, agility and self-preservation are eternal catalysts for changes that must ultimately be delivered.

Service transition ensures that the requirements of service strategy encoded in service design are effectively realized through to the delivery of live services within the service operation stage of the service lifecycle. Service transition takes the outputs from service design, the preceding stage of the lifecycle, and uses them to ensure that service solutions are smoothly migrated to live operation, fulfilling agreed customer and business requirements. The trigger for this transition activity is the production of a service design package produced by the processes and activities of service design. Service transition takes this new business requirement contained within the service design package and, using the five aspects of design, creates services and their supporting practices that meet business demands for functionality, security, performance, reliability and flexibility. The service design package facilitates the build, test, and release and deployment activities of service transition, and the operation, support and improvement activities within the service operation and continual service improvement stages of the service lifecycle.

ITIL Service Transition is the IT service management (ITSM) professional's guide to delivering those changes through transition lifecycle steps, which help them to manage change in a broader context. Large-scale IT change is often driven through project or programme initiatives. These are mistakenly seen to be outside 'change management' and too often not considered to be a service management concern until it is time to implement them. Experience teaches us that this approach rarely yields the best possible benefit to the business.

Service transition also requires the effective management of knowledge, organizational culture and transition in difficult or unusual circumstances. Every IT professional knows that the major part of any change – that can make or break its success – is related to the human factor, especially cultural aversion to change.

ITIL Service Transition supplies guidance on managing service transition from designed specifications, dealing with change, configuration, test, release and deployment and every step in between. Effective service transition ensures that meeting business need, cost and efficiency are achieved with minimal risk, maximum optimization and the highest degree of confidence possible.

Contact information

Full details of the range of material published under the ITIL banner can be found at:

www.best-management-practice.com/IT-Service-Management-ITIL/

If you would like to inform us of any changes that may be required to this publication, please log them at:

www.best-management-practice.com/changelog/

For further information on qualifications and training accreditation, please visit

www.itil-officialsite.com

Alternatively, please contact:

APM Group – The Accreditor Service Desk
Sword House
Totteridge Road
High Wycombe
Buckinghamshire
HP13 6DG
UK

Tel: +44 (0) 1494 458948

Email: servicedesk@apmgroupltd.com

Acknowledgements

2011 EDITION

Authors and mentors

Stuart Rance (HP)   Author
Colin Rudd (IT Enterprise Management Service Ltd (ITEMS))   Mentor
Shirley Lacy (ConnectSphere)   Project mentor
Ashley Hanna (HP)   Technical continuity editor

Other members of the ITIL authoring team

Thanks are due to the authors and mentors who have worked on all the publications in the lifecycle suite and contributed to the content in this publication and consistency across the suite. They are:

David Cannon (HP), Lou Hunnebeck (Third Sky), Vernon Lloyd (Fox IT), Anthony T. Orr (BMC Software), Randy Steinberg (Migration Technologies Inc.) and David Wheeldon (David Wheeldon IT Service Management).

Project governance

Members of the project governance team included:

Jessica Barry, APM Group, project assurance (examinations); Marianna Billington, itSMFI, senior user; Emily Egle, TSO, team manager; Janine Eves, TSO, senior supplier; Phil Hearsum, Cabinet Office, project assurance (quality); Tony Jackson, TSO, project manager; Paul Martini, itSMFI, senior user; Richard Pharro, APM Group, senior supplier; Frances Scarff, Cabinet Office, project executive; Rob Stroud, itSMFI, senior user; Sharon Taylor, Aspect Group Inc., adviser to the project board (technical) and the ATO sub-group, and adviser to the project board (training).

For more information on the ATO sub-group see:

www.itil-officialsite.com/News/ATOSubGroupAppointed.aspx

For a full list of acknowledgements of the ATO sub-group at the time of publication, please visit: www.itil-officialsite.com/Publications/PublicationAcknowledgements.aspx

Wider team

Change advisory board

The change advisory board (CAB) spent considerable time and effort reviewing all the comments submitted through the change control log and their hard work was essential to this project. Members of the CAB involved in this review included:

David Cannon, Emily Egle, David Favelle, Ashley Hanna, Kevin Holland, Stuart Rance, Frances Scarff and Sharon Taylor.

Once authors and mentors were selected for the 2011 update, a revised CAB was appointed and now includes:

Emily Egle, David Favelle, Phil Hearsum, Kevin Holland and Frances Scarff.

Reviewers

Claire Agutter, IT Training Zone; Niels Backx, Quint Wellington Redwood; Ernest R. Brewster, Independent; David M. Brink, Solutions3; Jeroen Bronkhorst, HP; Tony Brough, DHL Supply Chain; Erin Casteel, Veridity Pty Ltd; Janaki Chakravarthy, Independent; Christiane Chung Ah Pong, NCS Pte Ltd, Singapore; Patrick Connelly, Gartner Consulting; Barry Corless, Global Knowledge; Federico Corradi, Cogitek; Jenny Dugmore, Service Matters; Frank Eggert, MATERNA GmbH; Robert Falkowitz, Concentric Circle Consulting; David Favelle, UXC Consulting/Lucid IT; Ryan Fraser, HP; Anne Goddard, Goddard Service Management Consulting; Vawns Guest, Pink Elephant; Kevin Holland, NHS Connecting for Health; Steve Ingall, iCore-ltd; Randy Johnson, IBM; George Kinnear, The Grey Matters Education Ltd; Brad Laatsch, HP; Chandrika Labru, Tata Consultancy Services; Zoe Lambert, HP; Reginald Lo, Third Sky; Jane McNamara, Lilliard Associates Ltd; Jeroen Moolhuijsen, Getronics Consulting; Judit Pongracz, ITeal Consulting; Arvind Raman, Infosys Technologies Ltd.; Peter Ravnholt, UXC Consulting/Lucid IT; Claudio Schicht, Independent; Noel Scott, Symantec; Arun Simha, L-3 Communications STRATIS; Hon P Suen, The Hong Kong Jockey

Club; Helen Sussex, Logica; J.R. Tietsort, Micron Technology; Claudia Tropp, Technology Partners International, Inc.; Ken Turbitt, Service Management Consultancy (SMCG) Ltd; Deborah Wagner, Booz Allen Hamilton; Chuck Wysocki, McKesson Corporation

2007 EDITION

Chief architect and authors

Thanks are still due to those who contributed to the 2007 edition of *Service Transition*, upon which this updated edition is based.

Sharon Taylor (Aspect Group Inc)   Chief architect
Shirley Lacy (ConnectSphere)   Author
Ivor Macfarlane (Guillemot Rock)   Author

All names and organizations were correct at publication in 2007.

For a full list of all those who contributed to the 2007 and 2011 editions of *Service Strategy*, *Service Design*, *Service Transition*, *Service Operation* and *Continual Service Improvement*, please go to

www.itil-officialsite.com/Publications/ PublicationAcknowledgements.aspx

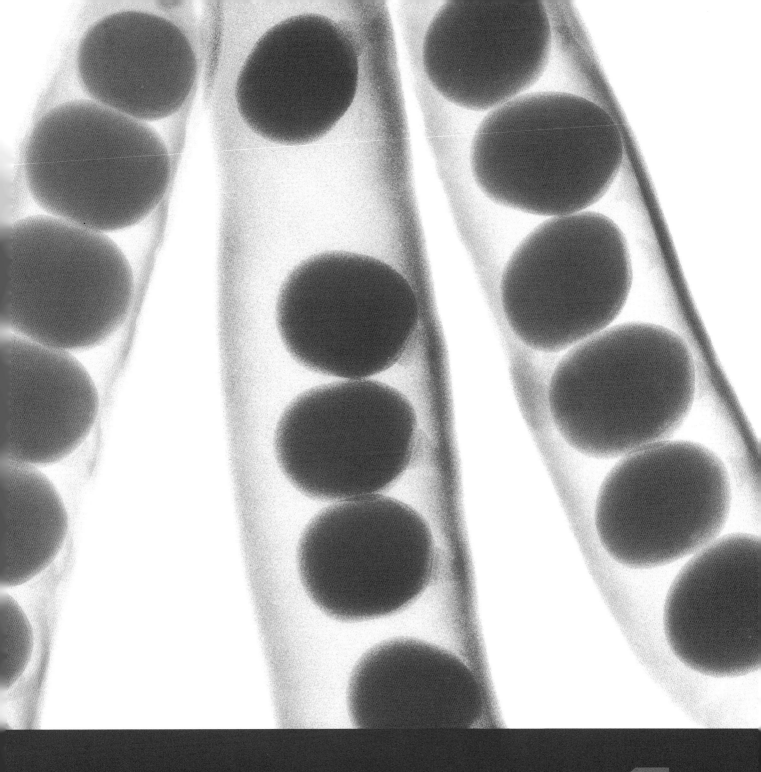

Introduction

1

1 Introduction

ITIL is part of a suite of best-practice publications for IT service management (ITSM).[1] ITIL provides guidance to service providers on the provision of quality IT services, and on the processes, functions and other capabilities needed to support them. ITIL is used by many hundreds of organizations around the world and offers best-practice guidance applicable to all types of organization that provide services. ITIL is not a standard that has to be followed; it is guidance that should be read and understood, and used to create value for the service provider and its customers. Organizations are encouraged to adopt ITIL best practices and to adapt them to work in their specific environments in ways that meet their needs.

ITIL is the most widely recognized framework for ITSM in the world. In the 20 years since it was created, ITIL has evolved and changed its breadth and depth as technologies and business practices have developed. ISO/IEC 20000 provides a formal and universal standard for organizations seeking to have their service management capabilities audited and certified. While ISO/IEC 20000 is a standard to be achieved and maintained, ITIL offers a body of knowledge useful for achieving the standard.

In 2007, the second major refresh of ITIL was published in response to significant advancements in technology and emerging challenges for IT service providers. New models and architectures such as outsourcing, shared services, utility computing, cloud computing, virtualization, web services and mobile commerce have become widespread within IT. The process-based approach of ITIL was augmented with the service lifecycle to address these additional service management challenges. In 2011, as part of its commitment to continual improvement, the Cabinet Office published this update to improve consistency across the core publications.

The ITIL framework is based on the five stages of the service lifecycle as shown in Figure 1.1, with a core publication providing best-practice guidance for each stage. This guidance includes key principles, required processes and activities, organization and roles, technology, associated challenges, critical success factors and risks. The service lifecycle uses a hub-and-spoke design, with service strategy at the hub, and service design, transition and operation as the revolving lifecycle stages or 'spokes'. Continual service improvement surrounds and supports all stages of the service lifecycle. Each stage of the lifecycle exerts influence on the others and relies on them for inputs and feedback. In this way, a constant set of checks and balances throughout the service lifecycle ensures that as business demand changes with business need, the services can adapt and respond effectively.

In addition to the core publications, there is also a complementary set of ITIL publications providing guidance specific to industry sectors, organization types, operating models and technology architectures.

1.1 OVERVIEW

ITIL Service Transition provides best-practice guidance for the service transition stage of the ITIL service lifecycle. Although this publication can be

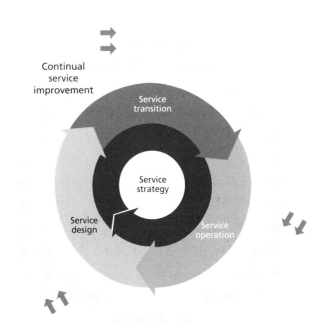

Figure 1.1 The ITIL service lifecycle

---

1 ITSM and other concepts from this chapter are described in more detail in Chapter 2.

read in isolation, it is recommended that it is used in conjunction with the other core ITIL publications.

1.1.1 Purpose and objectives of service transition

The purpose of the service transition stage of the service lifecycle is to ensure that new, modified or retired services meet the expectations of the business as documented in the service strategy and service design stages of the lifecycle.

The objectives of service transition are to:

- Plan and manage service changes efficiently and effectively
- Manage risks relating to new, changed or retired services
- Successfully deploy service releases into supported environments
- Set correct expectations on the performance and use of new or changed services
- Ensure that service changes create the expected business value
- Provide good-quality knowledge and information about services and service assets.

In order to achieve these objectives, there are many things that need to happen during the service transition lifecycle stage. These include:

- Planning and managing the capacity and resources required to manage service transitions
- Implementing a rigorous framework for evaluating service capabilities and risk profiles before new or changed services are deployed
- Establishing and maintaining the integrity of service assets
- Providing efficient repeatable mechanisms for building, testing and deploying services and releases
- Ensuring that services can be managed, operated and supported in accordance with constraints specified during the service design stage of the service lifecycle.

1.1.2 Scope

ITIL Service Transition provides guidance for the development and improvement of capabilities for transitioning new and changed services into supported environments, including release

planning, building, testing, evaluation and deployment. The publication also considers service retirement and transfer of services between service providers. The guidance focuses on how to ensure that the requirements from service strategy, developed in service design, are effectively realized in service operation while controlling the risks of failure and subsequent disruption.

Consideration is given to:

- Managing the complexity associated with changes to services and service management processes
- Allowing for innovation while minimizing the unintended consequences of change
- Introducing new services
- Changes to existing services, e.g. expansion, reduction, change of supplier, acquisition or disposal of sections of user base or suppliers, change of requirements or skills availability
- Decommissioning and discontinuation of services, applications or other service components
- Transferring services to and from other service providers.

Guidance on transferring the control of services includes transfer in the following circumstances:

- Out to a new supplier, e.g. outsourcing
- From one supplier to another
- Back in from a supplier, e.g. insourcing
- Moving to a partnership or co-sourcing arrangement (e.g. partial outsourcing of some processes)
- Multiple suppliers, e.g. co-sourcing or multi-sourcing
- Joint venture
- Down-sizing, up-sizing (right-sizing) and off-shoring
- Merger and acquisition.

In reality, circumstances generate a combination of several of the above options at any one time and in any one situation.

The scope also includes the transition of changes in the service provider's service management capabilities that will impact on the ways of working, the organization, people, projects and third parties involved in service management.

1.1.2.1 Processes within service transition

The processes described in *ITIL Service Transition* can be categorized into two groups, based on the extent to which process activities take place within the service transition stage of the service lifecycle.

Processes with significant activities throughout the service lifecycle

The first group are processes that are critical during the service transition stage but influence and support all stages of the service lifecycle. These comprise:

■ Change management
■ Service asset and configuration management
■ Knowledge management.

Processes which have most of their activities in the service transition stage of the service lifecycle

The second group are processes that are strongly focused within the service transition stage:

■ Transition planning and support
■ Release and deployment management

■ Service testing and validation
■ Change evaluation.

Some activities of all service transition processes may be carried out during the service design stage of the service lifecycle – for example, design of a release package or planning of a service transition.

Figure 1.2 shows all of the processes described in *ITIL Service Transition*. Processes that are largely within the service transition stage of the service lifecycle are shown within the central rectangle; the other stages of the service lifecycle that come before and after these processes are shown in the smaller darker rectangles.

Figure 8.2 in Chapter 8 gives an example of how the many processes involved in service transition might interact.

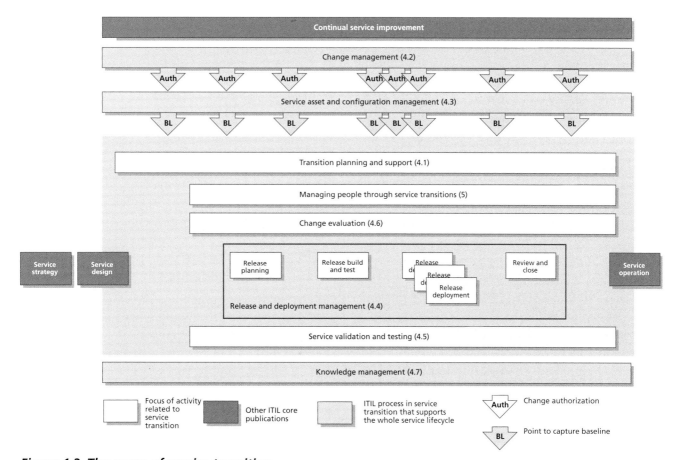

Figure 1.2 The scope of service transition

1.1.3 Usage

ITIL Service Transition provides access to proven best practice based on the skill and knowledge of experienced industry practitioners in adopting a standardized and controlled approach to service management. Although this publication can be used and applied in isolation, it is recommended that it is used in conjunction with the other core ITIL publications. All of the core publications need to be read to fully appreciate and understand the overall lifecycle of services and IT service management.

1.1.4 Value to business

Selecting and adopting the best practice as recommended in this publication will assist organizations in delivering significant benefits. It will help readers to set up service transition and the processes that support it, and to make effective use of those processes to facilitate the effective transitioning of new, changed or decommissioned services.

Adopting and implementing standard and consistent approaches for service transition will:

- Enable projects to estimate the cost, timing, resource requirement and risks associated with the service transition stage more accurately
- Result in higher volumes of successful change
- Be easier for people to adopt and follow
- Enable service transition assets to be shared and re-used across projects and services
- Reduce delays from unexpected clashes and dependencies – for example, if multiple projects need to use the same test environment at the same time
- Reduce the effort spent on managing the service transition test and pilot environments
- Improve expectation setting for all stakeholders involved in service transition including customers, users, suppliers, partners and projects
- Increase confidence that the new or changed service can be delivered to specification without unexpectedly affecting other services or stakeholders
- Ensure that new or changed services will be maintainable and cost-effective
- Improve control of service assets and configurations.

1.1.5 Target audience

ITIL Service Transition is relevant to organizations involved in the development, delivery or support of services, including:

- Service providers, both internal and external
- Organizations that aim to improve services through the effective application of service management and service lifecycle processes to improve their service quality
- Organizations that require a consistent managed approach across all service providers in a supply chain or value network
- Organizations that are going out to tender for their services.

The publication is also relevant to IT service managers and to all those working in service transition or areas supporting the objectives of service transition, including:

- Staff working in programmes and projects who are responsible for delivering new or changed services and the service environment
- Transition managers and staff
- Testing managers and testing practitioners, including test environment and test data managers and librarians
- Quality assurance managers
- Service asset and configuration management staff
- Change management staff
- Release and deployment management staff
- Procurement staff
- Relationship managers and supplier managers
- Suppliers delivering services, support, training etc.

1.2 CONTEXT

The context of this publication is the ITIL service lifecycle as shown in Figure 1.1.

The ITIL core consists of five lifecycle publications. Each provides part of the guidance necessary for an integrated approach as required by the ISO/IEC 20000 standard specification. The five publications are:

- *ITIL Service Strategy*
- *ITIL Service Design*
- *ITIL Service Transition*

- *ITIL Service Operation*
- *ITIL Continual Service Improvement*

Each one addresses capabilities having direct impact on a service provider's performance. The core is expected to provide structure, stability and strength to service management capabilities, with durable principles, methods and tools. This serves to protect investments and provide the necessary basis for measurement, learning and improvement. The introductory guide, *Introduction to the ITIL Service Lifecycle*, provides an overview of the lifecycle stages described in the ITIL core.

ITIL guidance can be adapted to support various business environments and organizational strategies. Complementary ITIL publications provide flexibility to implement the core in a diverse range of environments. Practitioners can select complementary publications as needed to provide traction for the ITIL core in a given context, in much the same way as tyres are selected based on the type of vehicle, purpose and road conditions. This is to increase the durability and portability of knowledge assets and to protect investments in service management capabilities.

1.2.1 Service strategy

At the centre of the service lifecycle is service strategy. Value creation begins here with understanding organizational objectives and customer needs. Every organizational asset including people, processes and products should support the strategy.

ITIL Service Strategy provides guidance on how to view service management not only as an organizational capability but as a strategic asset. It describes the principles underpinning the practice of service management which are useful for developing service management policies, guidelines and processes across the ITIL service lifecycle.

Topics covered in *ITIL Service Strategy* include the development of market spaces, characteristics of internal and external provider types, service assets, the service portfolio and implementation of strategy through the service lifecycle. Business relationship management, demand management, financial management, organizational

development and strategic risks are among the other major topics.

Organizations should use *ITIL Service Strategy* to set objectives and expectations of performance towards serving customers and market spaces, and to identify, select and prioritize opportunities. Service strategy is about ensuring that organizations are in a position to handle the costs and risks associated with their service portfolios, and are set up not just for operational effectiveness but for distinctive performance.

Organizations already practising ITIL can use *ITIL Service Strategy* to guide a strategic review of their ITIL-based service management capabilities and to improve the alignment between those capabilities and their business strategies. *ITIL Service Strategy* will encourage readers to stop and think about why something is to be done before thinking of how.

1.2.2 Service design

For services to provide true value to the business, they must be designed with the business objectives in mind. Design encompasses the whole IT organization, for it is the organization as a whole that delivers and supports the services. Service design is the stage in the lifecycle that turns a service strategy into a plan for delivering the business objectives.

ITIL Service Design provides guidance for the design and development of services and service management practices. It covers design principles and methods for converting strategic objectives into portfolios of services and service assets. The scope of *ITIL Service Design* is not limited to new services. It includes the changes and improvements necessary to increase or maintain value to customers over the lifecycle of services, the continuity of services, achievement of service levels, and conformance to standards and regulations. It guides organizations on how to develop design capabilities for service management.

Other topics in *ITIL Service Design* include design coordination, service catalogue management, service level management, availability management, capacity management, IT service continuity management, information security management and supplier management.

1.2.3 Service transition

ITIL Service Transition (this publication) provides guidance for the development and improvement of capabilities for introducing new and changed services into supported environments. It describes how to transition an organization from one state to another while controlling risk and supporting organizational knowledge for decision support. It ensures that the value(s) identified in the service strategy, and encoded in service design, are effectively transitioned so that they can be realized in service operation.

ITIL Service Transition describes best practice in transition planning and support, change management, service asset and configuration management, release and deployment management, service validation and testing, change evaluation and knowledge management. It provides guidance on managing the complexity related to changes to services and service management processes, preventing undesired consequences while allowing for innovation.

ITIL Service Transition also introduces the service knowledge management system, which can support organizational learning and help to improve the overall efficiency and effectiveness of all stages of the service lifecycle. This will enable people to benefit from the knowledge and experience of others, support informed decision-making, and improve the management of services.

1.2.4 Service operation

ITIL Service Operation describes best practice for managing services in supported environments. It includes guidance on achieving effectiveness and efficiency in the delivery and support of services to ensure value for the customer, the users and the service provider.

Strategic objectives are ultimately realized through service operation, therefore making it a critical capability. *ITIL Service Operation* provides guidance on how to maintain stability in service operation, allowing for changes in design, scale, scope and service levels. Organizations are provided with detailed process guidelines, methods and tools for use in two major control perspectives: reactive and proactive. Managers and practitioners are provided with knowledge allowing them to make better decisions in areas such as managing the availability of services, controlling demand, optimizing capacity utilization, scheduling of operations, and avoiding or resolving service incidents and managing problems. New models and architectures such as shared services, utility computing, web services and mobile commerce to support service operation are described.

Other topics in *ITIL Service Operation* include event management, incident management, request fulfilment, problem management and access management processes; as well as the service desk, technical management, IT operations management and application management functions.

1.2.5 Continual service improvement

ITIL Continual Service Improvement provides guidance on creating and maintaining value for customers through better strategy, design, transition and operation of services. It combines principles, practices and methods from quality management, change management and capability improvement.

ITIL Continual Service Improvement describes best practice for achieving incremental and large-scale improvements in service quality, operational efficiency and business continuity, and for ensuring that the service portfolio continues to be aligned to business needs. Guidance is provided for linking improvement efforts and outcomes with service strategy, design, transition and operation. A closed loop feedback system, based on the Plan-Do-Check-Act (PDCA) cycle, is established. Feedback from any stage of the service lifecycle can be used to identify improvement opportunities for any other stage of the lifecycle.

Other topics in *ITIL Continual Service Improvement* include service measurement, demonstrating value with metrics, developing baselines and maturity assessments.

1.3 ITIL IN RELATION TO OTHER PUBLICATIONS IN THE BEST MANAGEMENT PRACTICE PORTFOLIO

ITIL is part of a portfolio of best-practice publications (known collectively as Best Management Practice or BMP) aimed at helping organizations and individuals manage projects, programmes and services consistently and effectively (see Figure 1.3). ITIL can be used in harmony with other BMP products, and international or internal organization standards. Where appropriate, BMP guidance is supported by a qualification scheme and accredited training and consultancy services. All BMP guidance is intended to be tailored for use by individual organizations.

BMP publications include:

■ **Management of Portfolios (MoP™)** Portfolio management concerns the twin issues of how to do the 'right' projects and programmes in the context of the organization's strategic objectives, and how to do them 'correctly' in terms of achieving delivery and benefits at a collective level. MoP encompasses consideration of the principles upon which effective portfolio management is based; the key practices in the portfolio definition and delivery cycles, including examples of how they have been applied in real life; and guidance on how to implement portfolio management and sustain progress in a wide variety of organizations. Office of Government Commerce (2011). *Management of Portfolios*. TSO, London.

■ **Management of Risk (M_o_R®)** M_o_R offers an effective framework for taking informed decisions about the risks that affect performance objectives. The framework allows organizations to assess risk accurately (selecting the correct responses to threats and opportunities created by uncertainty) and thereby improve their service delivery. Office of Government Commerce (2010). *Management of Risk: Guidance for Practitioners*. TSO, London.

■ **Management of Value (MoV™)** MoV provides a cross-sector and universally applicable guide on how to maximize value in a way that takes account of organizations' priorities, differing stakeholders' needs and, at the same time, uses resources as efficiently and effectively as possible. It will help organizations to put in place effective methods to deliver enhanced value across their portfolio, programmes, projects and operational activities to meet the challenges of ever-more competitive and resource-constrained environments. Office of Government Commerce (2010). *Management of Value*. TSO, London.

■ **Managing Successful Programmes (MSP®)** MSP provides a framework to enable the achievement of high-quality change outcomes and benefits that fundamentally affect the way in which organizations work. One of the core

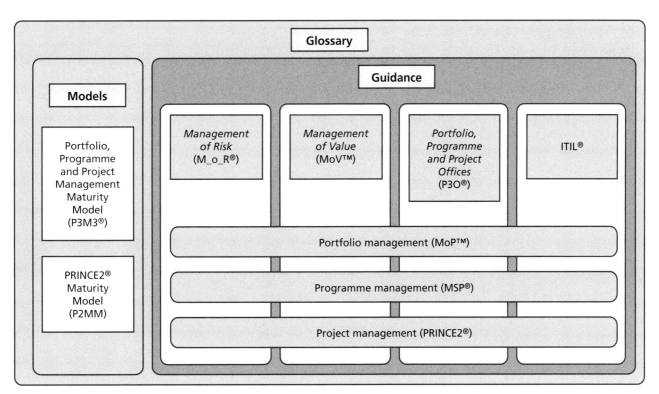

Figure 1.3 ITIL's relationship with other Best Management Practice guides

themes in MSP is that a programme must add more value than that provided by the sum of its constituent project and major activities.
Cabinet Office (2011). *Managing Successful Programmes*. TSO, London.

■ *Managing Successful Projects with PRINCE2®*
PRINCE2 (PRojects IN Controlled Environments, V2) is a structured method to help effective project management via clearly defined products. Key themes that feature throughout PRINCE2 are the dependence on a viable business case confirming the delivery of measurable benefits that are aligned to an organization's objectives and strategy, while ensuring the management of risks, costs and quality.
Office of Government Commerce (2009). *Managing Successful Projects with PRINCE2*. TSO, London.

■ *Portfolio, Programme and Project Offices (P3O®)* P3O provides universally applicable guidance, including principles, processes and techniques, to successfully establish, develop and maintain appropriate support structures. These structures will facilitate delivery of business objectives (portfolios), programmes and projects within time, cost, quality and other organizational constraints.
Office of Government Commerce (2008). *Portfolio, Programme and Project Offices*. TSO, London.

1.4 WHY IS ITIL SO SUCCESSFUL?

ITIL embraces a practical approach to service management – do what works. And what works is adapting a common framework of practices that unite all areas of IT service provision towards a single aim – that of delivering value to the business. The following list defines the key characteristics of ITIL that contribute to its global success:

■ **Vendor-neutral** ITIL service management practices are applicable in any IT organization because they are not based on any particular technology platform or industry type. ITIL is owned by the UK government and is not tied to any commercial proprietary practice or solution.

■ **Non-prescriptive** ITIL offers robust, mature and time-tested practices that have applicability to all types of service organization. It continues to be useful and relevant in public and private sectors, internal and external service providers, small, medium and large enterprises, and within any technical environment. Organizations should adopt ITIL and adapt it to meet the needs of the IT organization and their customers.

■ **Best practice** ITIL represents the learning experiences and thought leadership of the world's best-in-class service providers.

ITIL is successful because it describes practices that enable organizations to deliver benefits, return on investment and sustained success. ITIL is adopted by organizations to enable them to:

■ Deliver value for customers through services
■ Integrate the strategy for services with the business strategy and customer needs
■ Measure, monitor and optimize IT services and service provider performance
■ Manage the IT investment and budget
■ Manage risk
■ Manage knowledge
■ Manage capabilities and resources to deliver services effectively and efficiently
■ Enable adoption of a standard approach to service management across the enterprise
■ Change the organizational culture to support the achievement of sustained success
■ Improve the interaction and relationship with customers
■ Coordinate the delivery of goods and services across the value network
■ Optimize and reduce costs.

1.5 CHAPTER SUMMARY

ITIL Service Transition comprises:

■ Chapter 2 Service management as a practice This chapter explains the concepts of service management and services, and describes how these can be used to create value. It also summarizes a number of generic ITIL concepts that the rest of the publication depends on.

- Chapter 3 Service transition principles
  This chapter describes some of the key principles of service transition that will enable service providers to plan and implement best practice in service transition. These principles are the same irrespective of the organization; however, the approach may need to be tailored to circumstances, including the size of the organization, geographic distribution, culture and available resources. It concludes with a table showing the major inputs and outputs for the service transition lifecycle stage.

- Chapter 4 Service transition processes
  Chapter 4 sets out the processes and activities on which effective service transition depends and how they integrate with the other stages of the lifecycle.

- Chapter 5 Managing people through service transitions
  Chapter 5 deals with the management of organizational and stakeholder change, and communications. These critical aspects of service transition are key to the success of any transition, and must be carefully managed.

- Chapter 6 Organizing for service transition
  This chapter identifies the organizational roles and responsibilities that should be considered to manage the service transition lifecycle stage and processes. These roles are provided as guidelines and can be combined to fit into a variety of organizational structures. Examples of organizational structures are also provided.

- Chapter 7 Technology considerations
  ITIL service management practices gain momentum when the right type of technical automation is applied. This chapter provides recommendations for the use of technology in service transition and the basic requirements a service provider will need to consider when choosing service management tools.

- Chapter 8 Implementing service transition
  For organizations new to ITIL, or those wishing to improve their maturity and service capability, this chapter outlines effective ways to implement the service transition lifecycle stage.

- Chapter 9 Challenges, risks and critical success factors
  It is important for any organization to understand the challenges, risks and critical success factors that could influence their success. This chapter discusses typical examples of these for the service transition lifecycle stage.

- Appendix A Description of asset types
  This appendix describes the key asset types of management, organization, process, knowledge, people, information, applications, infrastructure and financial capital.

- Appendix B Risk assessment and management
  This appendix contains basic information about several commonly used approaches to the assessment and management of risk.

- Appendix C Related guidance
  This contains a list of some of the many external methods, practices and frameworks that align well with ITIL best practice. Notes are provided on how they integrate into the ITIL service lifecycle, and when and how they are useful.

- Appendix D Examples of inputs and outputs across the service lifecycle
  This appendix identifies some of the major inputs and outputs between each stage of the service lifecycle.

- References and further reading
  This provides a list of other sources of information that both informed the writing of this publication and can be used for further study and exploration by readers.

- Abbreviations and glossary
  This contains a list of abbreviations and a selected glossary of terms.

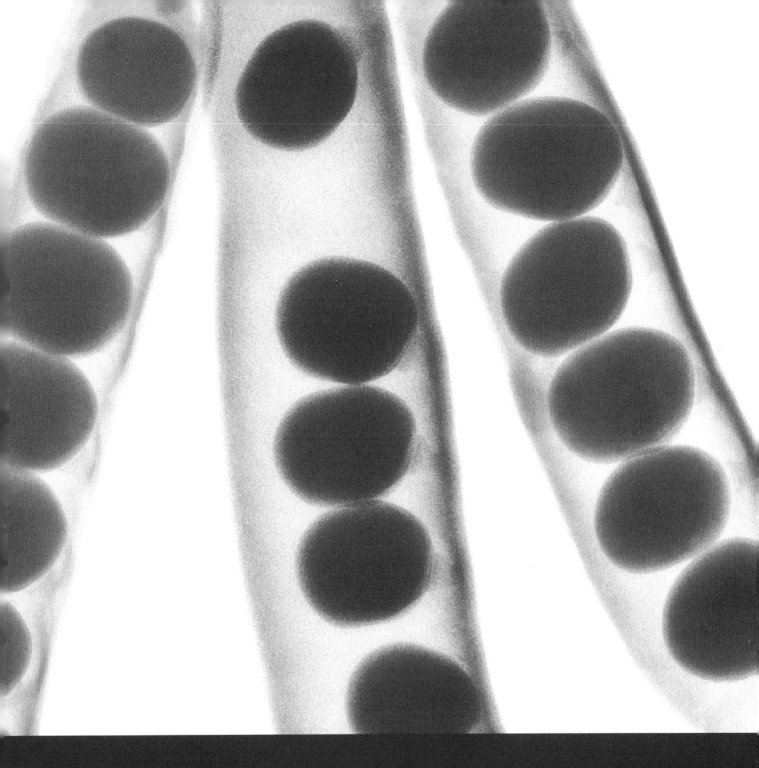

Service management as a practice

2

2 Service management as a practice

2.1 SERVICES AND SERVICE MANAGEMENT

2.1.1 Services

Services are a means of delivering value to customers by facilitating the outcomes customers want to achieve without the ownership of specific costs and risks. Services facilitate outcomes by enhancing the performance of associated tasks and reducing the effect of constraints. These constraints may include regulation, lack of funding or capacity, or technology limitations. The end result is an increase in the probability of desired outcomes. While some services enhance performance of tasks, others have a more direct impact – they perform the task itself.

The preceding paragraph is not just a definition, as it is a recurring pattern found in a wide range of services. Patterns are useful for managing complexity, costs, flexibility and variety. They are generic structures useful to make an idea applicable in a wide range of environments and situations. In each instance the pattern is applied with variations that make the idea effective, economical or simply useful in that particular case.

Definition: outcome

The result of carrying out an activity, following a process, or delivering an IT service etc. The term is used to refer to intended results, as well as to actual results.

An outcome-based definition of service moves IT organizations beyond business–IT alignment towards business–IT integration. Internal dialogue and discussion on the meaning of services is an elementary step towards alignment and integration with a customer's business (Figure 2.1). Customer outcomes become the ultimate concern of business relationship managers instead of the gathering of requirements, which is necessary but not sufficient. Requirements are generated for internal coordination and control only after customer outcomes are well understood.

Customers seek outcomes but do not wish to have accountability or ownership of all the associated costs and risks. All services must have a budget when they go live and this must be managed. The service cost is reflected in financial terms such as return on investment (ROI) and total cost of ownership (TCO). The customer will only be exposed to the overall cost or price of a service, which will include all the provider's costs and risk mitigation measures (and any profit margin if appropriate). The customer can then judge the value of a service based on a comparison of cost or price and reliability with the desired outcome.

Definitions

Service: A means of delivering value to customers by facilitating outcomes customers want to achieve without the ownership of specific costs and risks.

IT service: A service provided by an IT service provider. An IT service is made up of a combination of information technology, people and processes. A customer-facing IT service directly supports the business processes of one or more customers and its service level targets should be defined in a service level agreement. Other IT services, called supporting services, are not directly used by the business but are required by the service provider to deliver customer-facing services.

Customer satisfaction is also important. Customers need to be satisfied with the level of service and feel confident in the ability of the service provider to continue providing that level of service – or even improving it over time. The difficulty is that customer expectations keep shifting, and a service provider that does not track this will soon find itself losing business. *ITIL Service Strategy* is helpful in understanding how this happens, and how a service provider can adapt its services to meet the changing customer environment.

Services can be discussed in terms of how they relate to one another and their customers, and can be classified as core, enabling or enhancing.

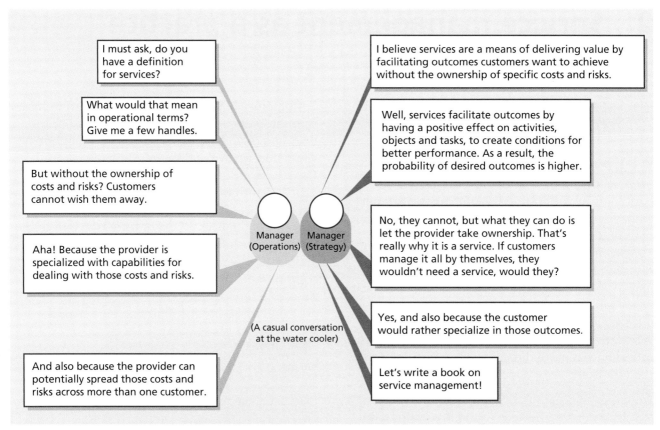

Figure 2.1 Conversation about the definition and meaning of services

Core services deliver the basic outcomes desired by one or more customers. They represent the value that the customer wants and for which they are willing to pay. Core services anchor the value proposition for the customer and provide the basis for their continued utilization and satisfaction.

Enabling services are services that are needed in order for a core service to be delivered. Enabling services may or may not be visible to the customer, but the customer does not perceive them as services in their own right. They are 'basic factors' which enable the customer to receive the 'real' (core) service.

Enhancing services are services that are added to a core service to make it more exciting or enticing to the customer. Enhancing services are not essential to the delivery of a core service, and are added to a core service as 'excitement' factors, which will encourage customers to use the core service more (or to choose the core service provided by one company over those of its competitors).

Services may be as simple as allowing a user to complete a single transaction, but most services are complex. They consist of a range of deliverables and functionality. If each individual aspect of these complex services were defined independently, the service provider would soon find it impossible to track and record all services.

Most service providers will follow a strategy where they can deliver a set of more generic services to a broad range of customers, thus achieving economies of scale and competing on the basis of price and a certain amount of flexibility. One way of achieving this is by using service packages. A service package is a collection of two or more services that have been combined to offer a solution to a specific type of customer need or to underpin specific business outcomes. A service package can consist of a combination of core services, enabling services and enhancing services.

Where a service or service package needs to be differentiated for different types of customer, one or more components of the package can be changed, or offered at different levels of utility and warranty, to create service options. These different service options can then be offered to customers and are sometimes called service level packages.

2.1.2 Service management

When we turn on a water tap, we expect to see water flow from it. When we turn on a light switch, we expect to see light fill the room. Not so many years ago, these very basic things were not as reliable as they are today. We know instinctively that the advances in technology have made them reliable enough to be considered a utility. But it isn't just the technology that makes the services reliable. It is how they are managed.

The use of IT today has become the utility of business. Business today wants IT services that behave like other utilities such as water, electricity or the telephone. Simply having the best technology will not ensure that IT provides utility-like reliability. Professional, responsive, value-driven service management is what brings this quality of service to the business.

Service management is a set of specialized organizational capabilities for providing value to customers in the form of services. The more mature a service provider's capabilities are, the greater is their ability to consistently produce quality services that meet the needs of the customer in a timely and cost-effective manner. The act of transforming capabilities and resources into valuable services is at the core of service management. Without these capabilities, a service organization is merely a bundle of resources that by itself has relatively low intrinsic value for customers.

Definitions

Service management: A set of specialized organizational capabilities for providing value to customers in the form of services.

Service provider: An organization supplying services to one or more internal or external customers.

Organizational capabilities are shaped by the challenges they are expected to overcome. An example of this is provided by Toyota in the 1950s when it developed unique capabilities to overcome the challenge of smaller scale and financial capital compared to its American rivals. Toyota developed new capabilities in production engineering, operations management and managing suppliers to compensate for its inability to afford large inventories, make components, produce raw materials or own the companies that produced them (Magretta, 2002).

Service management capabilities are similarly influenced by the following challenges that distinguish services from other systems of value creation, such as manufacturing, mining and agriculture:

- Intangible nature of the output and intermediate products of service processes: they are difficult to measure, control and validate (or prove)
- Demand is tightly coupled with the customer's assets: users and other customer assets such as processes, applications, documents and transactions arrive with demand and stimulate service production
- High level of contact for producers and consumers of services: there is little or no buffer between the service provider's creation of the service and the customer's consumption of that service
- The perishable nature of service output and service capacity: there is value for the customer from assurance on the continued supply of consistent quality. Providers need to secure a steady supply of demand from customers.

Service management is more than just a set of capabilities. It is also a professional practice supported by an extensive body of knowledge, experience and skills. A global community of individuals and organizations in the public and private sectors fosters its growth and maturity. Formal schemes exist for the education, training and certification of practising organizations, and individuals influence its quality. Industry best practices, academic research and formal standards contribute to and draw from its intellectual capital.

The origins of service management are in traditional service businesses such as airlines, banks, hotels and phone companies. Its practice has grown with the adoption by IT organizations of a service-oriented approach to managing IT applications, infrastructure and processes. Solutions to business problems and support for business models, strategies and operations are increasingly in the form of services. The popularity of shared services and outsourcing has contributed to the increase in the number of organizations that behave as service providers, including internal IT organizations. This in turn has strengthened the practice of service management while at the same time imposed greater challenges.

2.1.3 IT service management

Information technology (IT) is a commonly used term that changes meaning depending on the different perspectives that a business organization or people may have of it. A key challenge is to recognize and balance these perspectives when communicating the value of IT service management (ITSM) and understanding the context for how the business sees the IT organization. Some of these meanings are:

- IT is a collection of systems, applications and infrastructures which are components or sub-assemblies of a larger product. They enable or are embedded in processes and services.
- IT is an organization with its own set of capabilities and resources. IT organizations can be of various types such as business functions, shared services units and enterprise-level core units.
- IT is a category of services utilized by business. The services are typically IT applications and infrastructure that are packaged and offered by internal IT organizations or external service providers. IT costs are treated as business expenses.
- IT is a category of business assets that provide a stream of benefits for their owners, including, but not limited to, revenue, income and profit. IT costs are treated as investments.

Every IT organization should act as a service provider, using the principles of service management to ensure that they deliver the outcomes required by their customers.

Definitions

IT service management (ITSM): The implementation and management of quality IT services that meet the needs of the business. IT service management is performed by IT service providers through an appropriate mix of people, process and information technology.

IT service provider: A service provider that provides IT services to internal or external customers.

ITSM must be carried out effectively and efficiently. Managing IT from the business perspective enables organizational high performance and value creation.

A good relationship between an IT service provider and its customers relies on the customer receiving an IT service that meets its needs, at an acceptable level of performance and at a cost that the customer can afford. The IT service provider needs to work out how to achieve a balance between these three areas, and communicate with the customer if there is anything which prevents it from being able to deliver the required IT service at the agreed level of performance or price.

A service level agreement (SLA) is used to document agreements between an IT service provider and a customer. An SLA describes the IT service, documents service level targets, and specifies the responsibilities of the IT service provider and the customer. A single agreement may cover multiple IT services or multiple customers.

2.1.4 Service providers

There are three main types of service provider. While most aspects of service management apply equally to all types of service provider, other aspects such as customers, contracts, competition, market spaces, revenue and strategy take on different meanings depending on the specific type. The three types are:

- **Type I – internal service provider** An internal service provider that is embedded within a business unit. There may be several Type I service providers within an organization.
- **Type II – shared services unit** An internal service provider that provides shared IT services to more than one business unit.
- **Type III – external service provider** A service provider that provides IT services to external customers.

ITSM concepts are often described in the context of only one of these types and as if only one type of IT service provider exists or is used by a given organization. In reality most organizations have a combination of IT service providers. In a single organization it is possible that some IT units are dedicated to a single business unit, others provide shared services, and yet others have been outsourced or depend on external service providers.

Many IT organizations who traditionally provide services to internal customers find that they are dealing directly with external users because of the online services that they provide. *ITIL Service Strategy* provides guidance on how the IT organization interacts with these users, and who owns and manages the relationship with them.

2.1.5 Stakeholders in service management

Stakeholders have an interest in an organization, project or service etc. and may be interested in the activities, targets, resources or deliverables from service management. Examples include organizations, service providers, customers, consumers, users, partners, employees, shareholders, owners and suppliers. The term 'organization' is used to define a company, legal entity or other institution. It is also used to refer to any entity that has people, resources and budgets – for example, a project or business.

Within the service provider organization there are many different stakeholders including the functions, groups and teams that deliver the services. There are also many stakeholders external to the service provider organization, for example:

- **Customers** Those who buy goods or services. The customer of an IT service provider is the person or group who defines and agrees the service level targets. This term is also sometimes used informally to mean user – for example, 'This is a customer-focused organization.'
- **Users** Those who use the service on a day-to-day basis. Users are distinct from customers, as some customers do not use the IT service directly.
- **Suppliers** Third parties responsible for supplying goods or services that are required to deliver IT services. Examples of suppliers include commodity hardware and software vendors, network and telecom providers, and outsourcing organizations.

There is a difference between customers who work in the same organization as the IT service provider, and customers who work for other organizations. They are distinguished as follows:

- **Internal customers** These are customers who work for the same business as the IT service provider. For example, the marketing department is an internal customer of the IT organization because it uses IT services. The head of marketing and the chief information officer both report to the chief executive officer. If IT charges for its services, the money paid is an internal transaction in the organization's accounting system, not real revenue.
- **External customers** These are customers who work for a different business from the IT service provider. External customers typically purchase services from the service provider by means of a legally binding contract or agreement.

2.1.6 Utility and warranty

The value of a service can be considered to be the level to which that service meets a customer's expectations. It is often measured by how much the customer is willing to pay for the service, rather than the cost to the service provider of providing the service or any other intrinsic attribute of the service itself.

Unlike products, services do not have much intrinsic value. The value of a service comes from what it enables someone to do. The value of a service is not determined by the provider, but by the person who receives it – because they decide what they will do with the service, and what type of return they will achieve by using the service. Services contribute value to an organization only when their value is perceived to be higher than the cost of obtaining the service.

From the customer's perspective, value consists of achieving business objectives. The value of a service is created by combining two primary elements: utility (fitness for purpose) and warranty (fitness for use). These two elements work together to achieve the desired outcomes upon which the customer and the business base their perceptions of a service.

Utility is the functionality offered by a product or service to meet a particular need. Utility can be summarized as 'what the service does', and can be used to determine whether a service is able to meet its required outcomes, or is 'fit for purpose'. Utility refers to those aspects of a service that contribute to tasks associated with achieving outcomes. For example, a service that enables a business unit to process orders should allow sales people to access customer details, stock availability, shipping information etc. Any aspect of the service that improves the ability of sales people to improve the performance of the task of processing sales orders would be considered utility. Utility can therefore represent any attribute of a service that removes, or reduces the effect of, constraints on the performance of a task.

Warranty is an assurance that a product or service will meet its agreed requirements. This may be a formal agreement such as a service level agreement or contract, or a marketing message or brand image. Warranty refers to the ability of a service to be available when needed, to provide the required capacity, and to provide the required reliability in terms of continuity and security. Warranty can be summarized as 'how the service is delivered', and can be used to determine whether a service is 'fit for use'. For example, any aspect of the service that increases the availability or speed of the service would be considered warranty. Warranty can therefore represent any attribute of a service that increases the potential of the business to be able to perform a task. Warranty refers to any means by which utility is made available to the users.

Utility is *what* the service does, and warranty is *how* it is delivered.

Customers cannot benefit from something that is fit for purpose but not fit for use, and vice versa. The value of a service is therefore only delivered when both utility and warranty are designed and delivered. Figure 2.2 illustrates the logic that a service has to have both utility and warranty to create value. Utility is used to improve the performance of the tasks required to achieve an outcome, or to remove constraints that prevent the task from being performed adequately (or both). Warranty requires the service to be available, continuous and secure and to have sufficient capacity for the service to perform at the required level. If the service is both fit for purpose and fit for use, it will create value.

It should be noted that the elements of warranty in Figure 2.2 are not exclusive. It is possible to define other components of warranty, such as usability, which refers to how easy it is for the user to access and use the features of the service to achieve the desired outcomes.

The warranty aspect of the service needs to be designed at the same time as the utility aspect in order to deliver the required value to the business. Attempts to design warranty aspects after a service has been deployed can be expensive and disruptive.

Information about the desired business outcomes, opportunities, customers, utility and warranty of the service is used to develop the definition of a service. Using an outcome-based definition helps to ensure that managers plan and execute all aspects of service management from the perspective of what is valuable to the customer.

2.1.7 Best practices in the public domain
Organizations benchmark themselves against peers and seek to close gaps in capabilities. This enables them to become more competitive by improving their ability to deliver quality services that meet the needs of their customers at a price their customers can afford. One way to close such gaps is

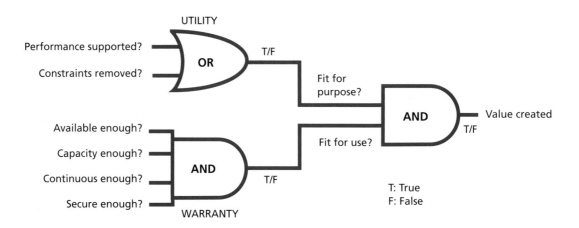

Figure 2.2 Logic of value creation through services

the adoption of best practices in wide industry use. There are several sources for best practice including public frameworks, standards and the proprietary knowledge of organizations and individuals (Figure 2.3). ITIL is the most widely recognized and trusted source of best-practice guidance in the area of ITSM.

Public frameworks and standards are attractive when compared with proprietary knowledge for the following reasons:

■ Proprietary knowledge is deeply embedded in organizations and therefore difficult to adopt, replicate or even transfer with the cooperation of the owners. Such knowledge is often in the form of tacit knowledge which is inextricable and poorly documented.

■ Proprietary knowledge is customized for the local context and the specific needs of the business to the point of being idiosyncratic. Unless the recipients of such knowledge have matching circumstances, the knowledge may not be as effective in use.

■ Owners of proprietary knowledge expect to be rewarded for their investments. They may make such knowledge available only under commercial terms through purchases and licensing agreements.

■ Publicly available frameworks and standards such as ITIL, LEAN, Six Sigma, COBIT, CMMI, PRINCE2, PMBOK®, ISO 9000, ISO/IEC 20000 and ISO/IEC 27001 are validated across a diverse set of environments and situations rather than the limited experience of a single organization. They are subject to broad review across multiple organizations and disciplines, and vetted by diverse sets of partners, suppliers and competitors.

■ The knowledge of public frameworks is more likely to be widely distributed among a large community of professionals through publicly available training and certification. It is easier for organizations to acquire such knowledge through the labour market.

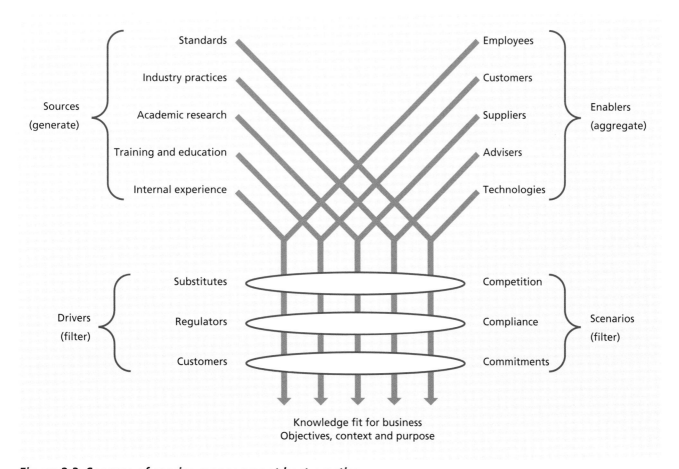

Figure 2.3 Sources of service management best practice

Ignoring public frameworks and standards can needlessly place an organization at a disadvantage. Organizations should cultivate their own proprietary knowledge on top of a body of knowledge based on public frameworks and standards. Collaboration and coordination across organizations become easier on the basis of shared practices and standards. Further information on best practice in the public domain is provided in Appendix C.

2.2 BASIC CONCEPTS

2.2.1 Assets, resources and capabilities

The service relationship between service providers and their customers revolves around the use of assets – both those of the service provider and those of the customer. Each relationship involves an interaction between the assets of each party.

Many customers use the service they receive from a service provider to build and deliver services or products of their own and then deliver them on to their own customers. In these cases, what the service provider considers to be the customer asset would be considered to be a service asset by their customer.

Without customer assets, there is no basis for defining the value of a service. The performance of customer assets is therefore a primary concern for service management.

Definitions

Asset: Any resource or capability.

Customer asset: Any resource or capability used by a customer to achieve a business outcome.

Service asset: Any resource or capability used by a service provider to deliver services to a customer.

There are two types of asset used by both service providers and customers – resources and capabilities. Organizations use them to create value in the form of goods and services. Resources are direct inputs for production. Capabilities represent an organization's ability to coordinate, control and deploy resources to produce value. Capabilities are typically experience-driven, knowledge-intensive, information-based and firmly embedded within an organization's people, systems, processes

and technologies. It is relatively easy to acquire resources compared to capabilities (see Figure 2.4 for examples of capabilities and resources).

Service providers need to develop distinctive capabilities to retain customers with value propositions that are hard for competitors to duplicate. For example, two service providers may have similar resources such as applications, infrastructure and access to finance. Their capabilities, however, differ in terms of management systems, organization structure, processes and knowledge assets. This difference is reflected in actual performance.

Capabilities by themselves cannot produce value without adequate and appropriate resources. The productive capacity of a service provider is dependent on the resources under its control. Capabilities are used to develop, deploy and coordinate this productive capacity. For example, capabilities such as capacity management and availability management are used to manage the performance and utilization of processes, applications and infrastructure, ensuring service levels are effectively delivered.

2.2.2 Processes

Definition: process

A process is a structured set of activities designed to accomplish a specific objective. A process takes one or more defined inputs and turns them into defined outputs.

Processes define actions, dependencies and sequence. Well-defined processes can improve productivity within and across organizations and functions. Process characteristics include:

- **Measurability** We are able to measure the process in a relevant manner. It is performance-driven. Managers want to measure cost, quality and other variables while practitioners are concerned with duration and productivity.
- **Specific results** The reason a process exists is to deliver a specific result. This result must be individually identifiable and countable.
- **Customers** Every process delivers its primary results to a customer or stakeholder. Customers may be internal or external to the organization, but the process must meet their expectations.

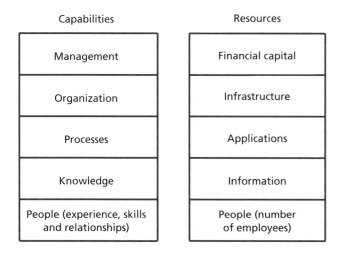

Figure 2.4 Examples of capabilities and resources

■ **Responsiveness to specific triggers** While a process may be ongoing or iterative, it should be traceable to a specific trigger.

A process is organized around a set of objectives. The main outputs from the process should be driven by the objectives and should include process measurements (metrics), reports and process improvement.

The output produced by a process has to conform to operational norms that are derived from business objectives. If products conform to the set norm, the process can be considered effective (because it can be repeated, measured and managed, and achieves the required outcome). If the activities of the process are carried out with a minimum use of resources, the process can also be considered efficient.

Inputs are data or information used by the process and may be the output from another process.

A process, or an activity within a process, is initiated by a trigger. A trigger may be the arrival of an input or other event. For example, the failure of a server may trigger the event management and incident management processes.

A process may include any of the roles, responsibilities, tools and management controls required to deliver the outputs reliably. A process may define policies, standards, guidelines, activities and work instructions if they are needed.

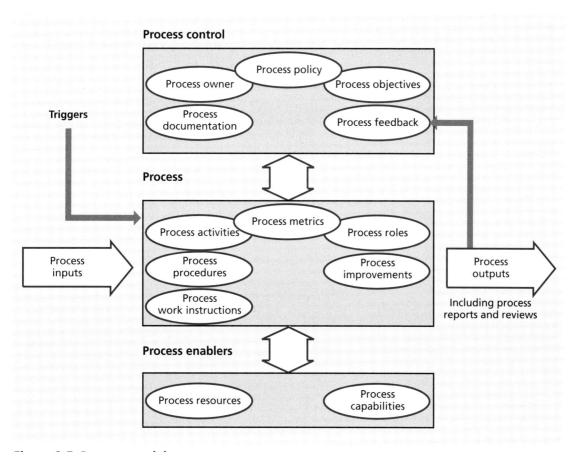

Figure 2.5 Process model

Processes, once defined, should be documented and controlled. Once under control, they can be repeated and managed. Process measurement and metrics can be built into the process to control and improve the process as illustrated in Figure 2.5. Process analysis, results and metrics should be incorporated in regular management reports and process improvements.

2.2.3 Organizing for service management

There is no single best way to organize, and best practices described in ITIL need to be tailored to suit individual organizations and situations. Any changes made will need to take into account resource constraints and the size, nature and needs of the business and customers. The starting point for organizational design is strategy. Organizational development for service management is described in more detail in *ITIL Service Strategy* Chapter 6.

2.2.3.1 Functions

A function is a team or group of people and the tools or other resources they use to carry out one or more processes or activities. In larger organizations, a function may be broken out and performed by several departments, teams and groups, or it may be embodied within a single organizational unit (e.g. the service desk). In smaller organizations, one person or group can perform multiple functions – for example, a technical management department could also incorporate the service desk function.

For the service lifecycle to be successful, an organization will need to clearly define the roles and responsibilities required to undertake the processes and activities involved in each lifecycle stage. These roles will need to be assigned to individuals, and an appropriate organization structure of teams, groups or functions will need to be established and managed. These are defined as follows:

- **Group** A group is a number of people who are similar in some way. In ITIL, groups refer to people who perform similar activities – even though they may work on different technologies or report into different organizational structures or even different companies. Groups are usually not formal organizational structures, but are very useful in defining common processes across the organization – for example, ensuring that all people who resolve incidents complete the incident record in the same way.
- **Team** A team is a more formal type of group. These are people who work together to achieve a common objective, but not necessarily in the same organizational structure. Team members can be co-located, or work in multiple locations and operate virtually. Teams are useful for collaboration, or for dealing with a situation of a temporary or transitional nature. Examples of teams include project teams, application development teams (often consisting of people from several different business units) and incident or problem resolution teams.
- **Department** Departments are formal organizational structures which exist to perform a specific set of defined activities on an ongoing basis. Departments have a hierarchical reporting structure with managers who are usually responsible for the execution of the activities and also for day-to-day management of the staff in the department.
- **Division** A division refers to a number of departments that have been grouped together, often by geography or product line. A division is normally self-contained.

ITIL Service Operation describes the following functions in detail:

- **Service desk** The single point of contact for users when there is a service disruption, for service requests, or even for some categories of request for change. The service desk provides a point of communication to users and a point of coordination for several IT groups and processes.
- **Technical management** Provides detailed technical skills and resources needed to support the ongoing operation of IT services and the management of the IT infrastructure. Technical management also plays an important role in the design, testing, release and improvement of IT services.
- **IT operations management** Executes the daily operational activities needed to manage IT services and the supporting IT infrastructure. This is done according to the performance standards defined during service design. IT operations management has two sub-functions

that are generally organizationally distinct. These are IT operations control and facilities management.

- **Application management** Is responsible for managing applications throughout their lifecycle. The application management function supports and maintains operational applications and also plays an important role in the design, testing and improvement of applications that form part of IT services.

The other core ITIL publications do not define any functions in detail, but they do rely on the technical and application management functions described in *ITIL Service Operation*. Technical and application management provide the technical resources and expertise to manage the whole service lifecycle, and practitioner roles within a particular lifecycle stage may be performed by members of these functions.

2.2.3.2 Roles

A number of roles need to be performed during the service lifecycle. The core ITIL publications provide guidelines and examples of role descriptions. These are not exhaustive or prescriptive, and in many cases roles will need to be combined or separated. Organizations should take care to apply this guidance in a way that suits their own structure and objectives.

Definition: role

A role is a set of responsibilities, activities and authorities granted to a person or team. A role is defined in a process or function. One person or team may have multiple roles – for example, the roles of configuration manager and change manager may be carried out by a single person.

Roles are often confused with job titles but it is important to realize that they are not the same. Each organization will define appropriate job titles and job descriptions which suit their needs, and individuals holding these job titles can perform one or more of the required roles.

It should also be recognized that a person may, as part of their job assignment, perform a single task that represents participation in more than one process. For example, a technical analyst who submits a request for change (RFC) to add memory to a server to resolve a performance problem is participating in activities of the change

management process at the same time as taking part in activities of the capacity management and problem management processes.

See Chapter 6 for more details about the roles and responsibilities described in *ITIL Service Transition*.

2.2.3.3 Organizational culture and behaviour

Organizational culture is the set of shared values and norms that control the service provider's interactions with all stakeholders, including customers, users, suppliers, internal staff etc. An organization's values are desired modes of behaviour that affect its culture. Examples of organizational values include high standards, customer care, respecting tradition and authority, acting cautiously and conservatively, and being frugal.

High-performing service providers continually align the value network for efficiency and effectiveness. Culture through the value network is transmitted to staff through socialization, training programmes, stories, ceremonies and language.

Constraints such as governance, capabilities, standards, resources, values and ethics play a significant role in organizational culture and behaviour. Organizational culture can also be affected by structure or management styles resulting in a positive or negative impact on performance. Organizational structures and management styles contribute to the behaviour of people, process, technology and partners. These are important aspects in adopting service management practices and ITIL.

Change related to service management programmes will affect organizational culture and it is important to prepare people with effective communication plans, training, policies and procedures to achieve the desired performance outcomes. Establishing cultural change is also an important factor for collaborative working between the many different people involved in service management. Managing people through service transitions is discussed at more length in Chapter 5 of this publication.

2.2.4 The service portfolio

The service portfolio is the complete set of services that is managed by a service provider and it represents the service provider's commitments and investments across all customers and market spaces.

It also represents present contractual commitments, new service development, and ongoing service improvement plans initiated by continual service improvement. The portfolio may include third-party services, which are an integral part of service offerings to customers.

The service portfolio represents all the resources presently engaged or being released in various stages of the service lifecycle. It is a database or structured document in three parts:

■ **Service pipeline** All services that are under consideration or development, but are not yet available to customers. It includes major investment opportunities that have to be traced to the delivery of services, and the value that will be realized. The service pipeline provides a business view of possible future services and is part of the service portfolio that is not normally published to customers.

■ **Service catalogue** All live IT services, including those available for deployment. It is the only part of the service portfolio published to customers, and is used to support the sale and delivery of IT services. It includes a customer-facing view (or views) of the IT services in use, how they are intended to be used, the business processes they enable, and the levels and quality of service the customer can expect for each service. The service catalogue also includes information about supporting services required by the service provider to deliver customer-facing services. Information about services can only enter the service catalogue after due diligence has been performed on related costs and risks.

■ **Retired services** All services that have been phased out or retired. Retired services are not available to new customers or contracts unless a special business case is made.

Service providers often find it useful to distinguish customer-facing services from supporting services:

■ **Customer-facing services** IT services that are visible to the customer. These are normally services that support the customer's business processes and facilitate one or more outcomes desired by the customer.

■ **Supporting services** IT services that support or 'underpin' the customer-facing services. These are typically invisible to the customer, but are essential to the delivery of customer-facing IT services.

Figure 2.6 illustrates the components of the service portfolio, which are discussed in detail in *ITIL Service Strategy*. These are important components of the service knowledge management system (SKMS) described in section 2.2.5.

2.2.5 Knowledge management and the SKMS

Quality knowledge and information enable people to perform process activities and support the flow of information between service lifecycle stages and processes. Understanding, defining, establishing and maintaining information is a responsibility of the knowledge management process.

Implementing an SKMS enables effective decision support and reduces the risks that arise from a lack of proper mechanisms. However, implementing an SKMS can involve a large investment in tools to store and manage data, information and knowledge. Every organization will start this work in a different place, and have their own vision of where they want to be, so there is no simple answer to the question 'What tools and systems are needed to support knowledge management?' Data, information and knowledge need to be interrelated across the organization. A document management system and/or a configuration management system (CMS) can be used as a foundation for implementation of the SKMS.

Figure 2.7 illustrates an architecture for service knowledge management that has four layers including examples of possible content at each layer. These are:

■ **Presentation layer** Enables searching, browsing, retrieving, updating, subscribing and collaboration. The different views onto the other layers are suitable for different audiences. Each view should be protected to ensure that only authorized people can see or modify the underlying knowledge, information and data.

■ **Knowledge processing layer** Is where the information is converted into useful knowledge which enables decision-making.

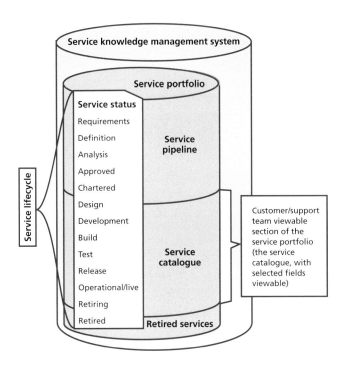

Figure 2.6 The service portfolio and its contents

- **Information integration layer** Provides integrated information that may be gathered from data in multiple sources in the data layer.
- **Data layer** Includes tools for data discovery and data collection, and data items in unstructured and structured forms.

In practice, an SKMS is likely to consist of multiple tools and repositories. For example, there may be a tool that provides all four layers for the support of different processes or combinations of processes. Various tools providing a range of perspectives will be used by different stakeholders to access this common repository for collaborative decision support.

This architecture is applicable for many of the management information systems in ITIL. A primary component of the SKMS is the service portfolio, covered in section 2.2.4. Other examples include the CMS, the availability management information system (AMIS) and the capacity management information system (CMIS).

2.3 GOVERNANCE AND MANAGEMENT SYSTEMS

2.3.1 Governance

Governance is the single overarching area that ties IT and the business together, and services are one way of ensuring that the organization is able to execute that governance. Governance is what defines the common directions, policies and rules that both the business and IT use to conduct business.

Many ITSM strategies fail because they try to build a structure or processes according to how they would like the organization to work instead of working within the existing governance structures.

> **Definition: governance**
>
> Ensures that policies and strategy are actually implemented, and that required processes are correctly followed. Governance includes defining roles and responsibilities, measuring and reporting, and taking actions to resolve any issues identified.

Governance works to apply a consistently managed approach at all levels of the organization – first by ensuring a clear strategy is set, then by defining the policies whereby the strategy will be achieved. The policies also define boundaries, or what the organization may not do as part of its operations.

Governance needs to be able to evaluate, direct and monitor the strategy, policies and plans. Further information on governance and service management is provided in Chapter 5 of *ITIL Service Strategy*. The international standard for corporate governance of IT is ISO/IEC 38500, described in Appendix C.

2.3.2 Management systems

A system is a number of related things that work together to achieve an overall objective. Systems should be self-regulating for agility and timeliness. In order to accomplish this, the relationships within the system must influence one another for the sake of the whole. Key components of the system are the structure and processes that work together.

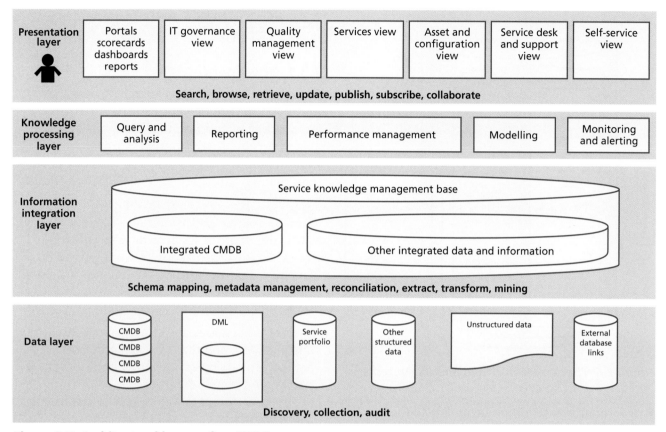

Figure 2.7 Architectural layers of an SKMS

A systems approach to service management ensures learning and improvement through a big-picture view of services and service management. It extends the management horizon and provides a sustainable long-term approach.

By understanding the system structure, the interconnections between all the assets and service components, and how changes in any area will affect the whole system and its constituent parts over time, a service provider can deliver benefits such as:

■ Ability to adapt to the changing needs of customers and markets
■ Sustainable performance
■ Better approach to managing services, risks, costs and value delivery
■ Effective and efficient service management
■ Simplified approach that is easier for people to use
■ Less conflict between processes
■ Reduced duplication and bureaucracy.

Many businesses have adopted management system standards for competitive advantage and to ensure a consistent approach in implementing service management across their value network. Implementation of a management system also provides support for governance (see section 2.3.1).

Definition: management system (ISO 9001)

The framework of policy, processes, functions, standards, guidelines and tools that ensures an organization or part of an organization can achieve its objectives.

A management system of an organization can adopt multiple management system standards, such as:

■ A quality management system (ISO 9001)
■ An environmental management system (ISO 14000)
■ A service management system (ISO/IEC 20000)
■ An information security management system (ISO/IEC 27001)
■ A management system for software asset management (ISO/IEC 19770).

Service providers are increasingly adopting these standards to be able to demonstrate their service management capability. As there are common elements between such management systems, they should be managed in an integrated way rather than having separate management systems. To meet the requirements of a specific management system standard, an organization needs to analyse the requirements of the relevant standard in detail and compare them with those that have already been incorporated in the existing integrated management system. Appendix C provides further information on these standards.

ISO management system standards use the Plan-Do-Check-Act (PDCA) cycle shown in Figure 2.8. The ITIL service lifecycle approach embraces and enhances the interpretation of the PDCA cycle. You will see the PDCA cycle used in the structure of the guidance provided in each of the core ITIL publications. This guidance recognizes the need to drive governance, organizational design and management systems from the business strategy, service strategy and service requirements.

> **Definition: ISO/IEC 20000**
>
> An international standard for IT service management.

ISO/IEC 20000 is an internationally recognized standard that allows organizations to demonstrate excellence and prove best practice in ITSM. Part 1 specifies requirements for the service provider to plan, establish, implement, operate, monitor, review, maintain and improve a service management system (SMS). Coordinated integration and implementation of an SMS, to meet the Part 1 requirements, provides ongoing control, greater effectiveness, efficiency and opportunities for continual improvement. It ensures that the service provider:

■ Understands and fulfils the service requirements to achieve customer satisfaction
■ Establishes the policy and objectives for service management
■ Designs and delivers changes and services that add value for the customer
■ Monitors, measures and reviews performance of the SMS and the services
■ Continually improves the SMS and the services based on objective measurements.

Service providers across the world have successfully established an SMS to direct and control their service management activities. The adoption of an SMS should be a strategic decision for an organization.

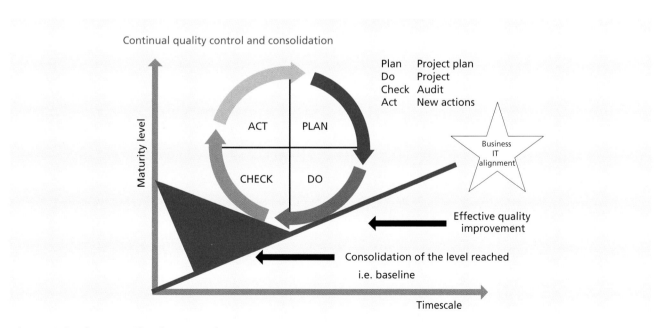

Figure 2.8 Plan-Do-Check-Act cycle

One of the most common routes for an organization to achieve the requirements of ISO/IEC 20000 is by adopting ITIL service management best practices and using the ITIL qualification scheme for professional development.

Certification to ISO/IEC 20000-1 by an accredited certification body shows that a service provider is committed to delivering value to its customers and continual service improvement. It demonstrates the existence of an effective SMS that satisfies the requirements of an independent external audit. Certification gives a service provider a competitive edge in marketing. Many organizations specify a requirement to comply with ISO/IEC 20000 in their contracts and agreements.

2.4 THE SERVICE LIFECYCLE

Services and processes describe how things change, whereas structure describes how they are connected. Structure helps to determine the correct behaviours required for service management.

Structure describes how process, people, technology and partners are connected. Structure is essential for organizing information. Without structure, our service management knowledge is merely a collection of observations, practices and conflicting goals. The structure of the service lifecycle is an organizing framework, supported by the organizational structure, service portfolio and service models within an organization. Structure can influence or determine the behaviour of the organization and people. Altering the structure of service management can be more effective than simply controlling discrete events.

Without structure, it is difficult to learn from experience. It is difficult to use the past to educate for the future. We can learn from experience but we also need to confront directly many of the most important consequences of our actions.

See Chapter 1 for an introduction to each ITIL service lifecycle stage.

2.4.1 Specialization and coordination across the lifecycle

Organizations need a collaborative approach for the management of assets which are used to deliver and support services for their customers.

Organizations should function in the same manner as a high-performing sports team. Each player in a team and each member of the team's organization who are not players position themselves to support the goal of the team. Each player and team member has a different specialization that contributes to the whole. The team matures over time taking into account feedback from experience, best practice, current process and procedures to become an agile high-performing team.

Specialization and coordination are necessary in the lifecycle approach. Specialization allows for expert focus on components of the service but components of the service also need to work together for value. Specialization combined with coordination helps to manage expertise, improve focus and reduce overlaps and gaps in processes. Specialization and coordination together help to create a collaborative and agile organizational architecture that maximizes utilization of assets. Coordination across the lifecycle creates an environment focused on business and customer outcomes instead of just IT objectives and projects. Coordination is also essential between functional groups, across the value network, and between processes and technology.

Feedback and control between organizational assets helps to enable operational efficiency, organizational effectiveness and economies of scale.

2.4.2 Processes through the service lifecycle

Each core ITIL lifecycle publication includes guidance on service management processes as shown in Table 2.1.

Service management is more effective if people have a clear understanding of how processes interact throughout the service lifecycle, within the organization and with other parties (users, customers, suppliers).

Process integration across the service lifecycle depends on the service owner, process owners, process practitioners and other stakeholders understanding:

■ The context of use, scope, purpose and limits of each process

Table 2.1 The processes described in each core ITIL publication

Core ITIL lifecycle publication	Processes described in the publication
ITIL Service Strategy	Strategy management for IT services Service portfolio management Financial management for IT services Demand management Business relationship management
ITIL Service Design	Design coordination Service catalogue management Service level management Availability management Capacity management IT service continuity management Information security management Supplier management
ITIL Service Transition	Transition planning and support Change management Service asset and configuration management Release and deployment management Service validation and testing Change evaluation Knowledge management
ITIL Service Operation	Event management Incident management Request fulfilment Problem management Access management
ITIL Continual Service Improvement	Seven-step improvement process

- The strategies, policies and standards that apply to the processes and to the management of interfaces between processes
- Authorities and responsibilities of those involved in each process
- The information provided by each process that flows from one process to another; who produces it; and how it is used by integrated processes.

Integrating service management processes depends on the flow of information across process and organizational boundaries. This in turn depends on implementing supporting technology and management information systems across organizational boundaries, rather than in silos. If service management processes are implemented, followed or changed in isolation, they can become a bureaucratic overhead that does not deliver value for money. They could also damage or negate the operation or value of other processes and services.

As discussed in section 2.2.2, each process has a clear scope with a structured set of activities that transform inputs to deliver the outputs reliably. A process interface is the boundary of the process. Process integration is the linking of processes by ensuring that information flows from one process to another effectively and efficiently. If there is management commitment to process integration, processes are generally easier to implement and there will be fewer conflicts between processes.

Stages of the lifecycle work together as an integrated system to support the ultimate objective of service management for business value realization. Every stage is interdependent as shown in Figure 2.9. See Appendix D for examples of inputs and outputs across the service lifecycle.

The SKMS, described in section 2.2.5 enables integration across the service lifecycle stages. It provides secure and controlled access to the knowledge, information and data that are needed to manage and deliver services. The

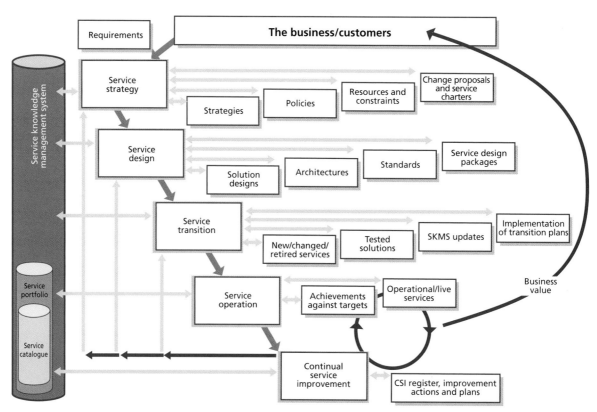

Figure 2.9 Integration across the service lifecycle

service portfolio represents all the assets presently engaged or being released in various stages of the lifecycle.

Chapter 1 provides a summary of each stage in the service lifecycle but it is also important to understand how the lifecycle stages work together.

Service strategy establishes policies and principles that provide guidance for the whole service lifecycle. The service portfolio is defined in this lifecycle stage, and new or changed services are chartered.

During the service design stage of the lifecycle, everything needed to transition and operate the new or changed service is documented in a service design package. This lifecycle stage also designs everything needed to create, transition and operate the services, including management information systems and tools, architectures, processes, measurement methods and metrics.

The activities of the service transition and service operation stages of the lifecycle are defined during service design. Service transition ensures that the requirements of the service strategy, developed in

service design, are effectively realized in service operation while controlling the risks of failure and disruption.

The service operation stage of the service lifecycle carries out the activities and processes required to deliver the agreed services. During this stage of the lifecycle, the value defined in the service strategy is realized.

Continual service improvement acts in tandem with all the other lifecycle stages. All processes, activities, roles, services and technology should be measured and subjected to continual improvement.

Most ITIL processes and functions have activities that take place across multiple stages of the service lifecycle. For example:

■ The service validation and testing process may design tests during the service design stage and perform these tests during service transition.
■ The technical management function may provide input to strategic decisions about technology, as well as assisting in the design and transition of infrastructure components.

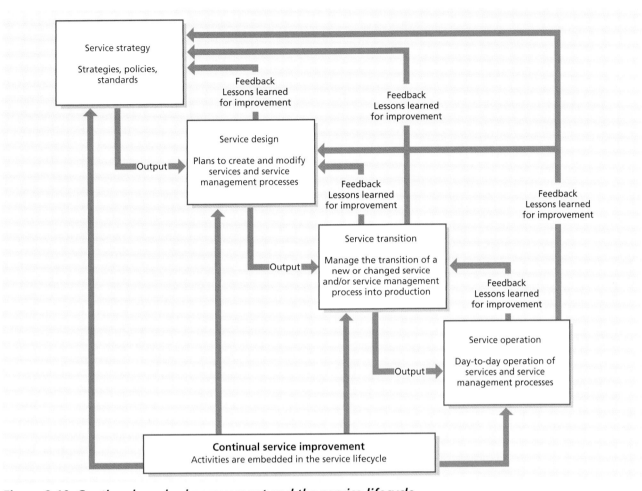

Figure 2.10 Continual service improvement and the service lifecycle

■ Business relationship managers may assist in gathering detailed requirements during the service design stage of the lifecycle, or take part in the management of major incidents during the service operation stage.

■ All service lifecycle stages contribute to the seven-step improvement process.

Appendix D identifies some of the major inputs and outputs between each stage of the service lifecycle. Chapter 3 of each core ITIL publication provides more detail on the inputs and outputs of the specific lifecycle stage it describes.

The strength of the service lifecycle rests upon continual feedback throughout each stage of the lifecycle. This feedback ensures that service optimization is managed from a business perspective and is measured in terms of the value the business derives from services at any point in time during the service lifecycle. The service lifecycle is non-linear in design. At every point in the service lifecycle, the process of monitoring, assessment and feedback

between each stage drives decisions about the need for minor course corrections or major service improvement initiatives.

Figure 2.10 illustrates some examples of the continual feedback system built into the service lifecycle.

Adopting appropriate technology to automate the processes and provide management with the information that supports the processes is also important for effective and efficient service management.

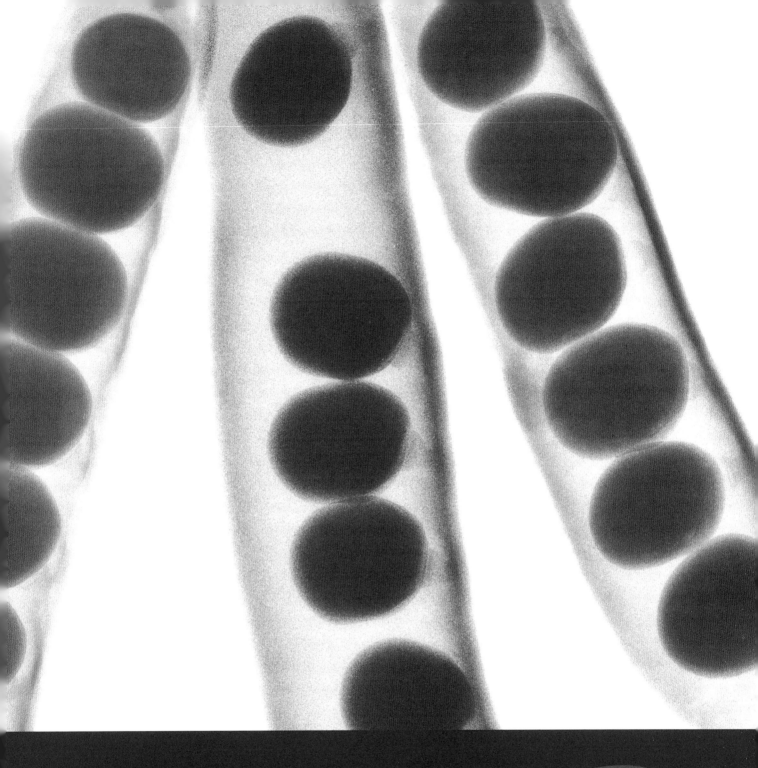

Service transition
principles

3

3 Service transition principles

This chapter describes the key policies and principles that will enable service providers to plan and implement service transition best practice. These principles are the same irrespective of the organization; however, the approach may need to be tailored to circumstances, including size, distribution, culture and resources.

3.1 POLICIES FOR SERVICE TRANSITION

The following are examples of policies for service transition. Every service provider should agree and document policies that are appropriate for their circumstances. Endorsement and visible support from senior management contribute to the overall effectiveness. Each policy is explicitly stated and its suggested application and approach are illustrated by applicable principles and best practices that help an organization to deliver that principle. Examples of these policies include:

- Define and implement a formal policy for service transition
- Implement all changes to services through service transition
- Adopt a common framework and standards
- Maximize re-use of established processes and systems
- Align service transition plans with the business needs
- Establish and maintain relationships with stakeholders
- Establish effective controls and disciplines
- Provide systems for knowledge transfer and decision support
- Plan release packages
- Anticipate and manage course corrections
- Proactively manage resources across service transitions
- Ensure early involvement in the service lifecycle
- Provide assurance of the quality of the new or changed service
- Proactively improve quality during service transition.

3.1.1 Define and implement a formal policy for service transition

3.1.1.1 Policy

- A formal policy for service transition should be defined, documented and approved by the management team, who ensure that it is communicated throughout the organization and to all relevant suppliers and partners.

3.1.1.2 Principles

- Policies should clearly state the objectives, and any non-compliance with the policy must be remedied.
- Policies should be aligned with the overall governance framework, organization and service management policies, with appropriate auditing and enforcement. This should include alignment with ISO/IEC 20000, ISO/IEC 38500 and COBIT where these have been adopted.
- Sponsors and decision makers involved in developing the policy must demonstrate their commitment to adapting and implementing the policy. This includes the commitment to deliver predicted outcomes from any change in the services.
- Processes should integrate teams, blending competencies while maintaining clear lines of accountability and responsibility.
- Changes should be delivered in releases, except for standard changes and some emergency changes.
- Deployment must be addressed early in the release design and release planning stages.

3.1.1.3 Best practice

- Obtain formal sign-off from the management team, sponsors and decision makers involved in developing the policy.

3.1.2 Implement all changes to services through service transition

3.1.2.1 Policy

- All service changes must be managed by the service transition lifecycle stage, except for standard changes that follow a procedure defined during the service transition lifecycle stage.
- The scope of service change must be documented. This scope should include all changes to the service portfolio or service catalogue and should normally exclude business process changes and some minor operational changes.

3.1.2.1 Principles

- There should be a single focal point for changes to supported services, to minimize the probability of conflicting changes and potential disruption.
- People who do not have the authority to make a change or release into the supported environment should be prevented from having access.
- Each release will be designed and governed by a request for change raised via the change management process to ensure effective control and traceability.
- All standard changes, normal changes and emergency changes must follow policy, principles and processes defined by service transition.
- Standardized methods and procedures are used for efficient and prompt handling of all changes in order to minimize the impact of change-related incidents on business continuity, service quality and re-work.
- All updates to changes and releases are recorded against service assets and/or configuration items (CIs) in the configuration management system.

3.1.2.2 Best practice

- The definition of a change is clearly explained.
- Internal and external changes are differentiated.
- Changes are justified through the development of a clear business case. This may be provided as part of the documentation for the change,

or in the case of a standard change it may be predefined.

- Changes to services are defined in a service design package, which can be used by service transition to measure the actual versus predicted progress and performance.
- The change management process should be standardized and enforced.
- Management commitment to enforcing the process is essential, and it must be clearly visible to all stakeholders.
- Configuration auditing aims to identify unauthorized changes.
- Late requests for changes that cannot be properly managed should not be accepted.

3.1.3 Adopt a common framework and standards

3.1.3.1 Policy

- Base service transition on a common framework of standard re-usable processes and systems to improve integration of the parties involved in service transition and reduce variations in the processes.

3.1.3.2 Principles

- Implement industry best practice as the basis of standardization to enable integration across the supply chain.
- Control the service transition framework and standards under the direction of change management and service asset and configuration management.
- Ensure that processes are adopted consistently by scheduling regular reviews and audits of the service management processes.

3.1.3.3 Best practice

- Publish standards and best practices for service transition.
- Provide a framework for establishing consistent processes for assuring and evaluating the service capability and risk profile before and after a release is deployed. A flowchart such as that shown in Figure 8.2 can be helpful for identifying how the various service transition processes work together to achieve this.
- Provide supporting systems to automate standard processes in order to reduce resistance to adoption.

- Ensure that there is management understanding of the need for standard ways of working by developing and delivering improvements based on a sound business case.
- Establish the level of management and stakeholder commitment and take action to close any gaps.
- Continually plan how to improve the buy-in to adopting a common framework and standards.

3.1.4 Maximize re-use of established processes and systems

3.1.4.1 Policy

- Service transition processes are aligned with the organization's processes and related systems to improve efficiency and effectiveness, and where new processes are required they are developed with re-use in mind.

3.1.4.2 Principles

- Re-use established processes and systems wherever possible.
- Capture data and information from the original source to reduce errors and aid efficiency.
- Develop re-usable standard service transition models to build up experience and confidence in the service transition activities.
- Implement industry standards and best practice as the basis of standardization to enable integration of deliverables from many suppliers.

3.1.4.3 Best practice

- Integrate the service transition processes into the overall service management system.
- Use the organization's programme and project management practices (typically based on PRINCE2 or PMBOK).
- Use existing communications channels for service transition communication.
- Follow human resources, training, finance and facilities management processes and common practices.
- Design service transition models that enable easy customization to suit specific circumstances.
- Structure models such that a consistent approach is repeated for each target service unit or environment with local variation as required.

3.1.5 Align service transition plans with the business needs

3.1.5.1 Policy

- Align service transition plans and new or changed service with the customer's and business organization's requirements in order to maximize the value delivered by a change.

3.1.5.2 Principles

- Set customer and user expectations during transition as to how the new or changed service can be used effectively to enable business change.
- Provide information and establish processes to enable business change projects and customers to integrate a release into their business processes and services.
- Ensure that the service can be used in accordance with the requirements and constraints specified within the service requirements in order to improve customer and stakeholder satisfaction.
- Communicate and transfer knowledge to the customers, users and stakeholders in order to increase their capability to maximize use of the new or changed service.
- Monitor and measure the use of the services and underlying applications and technology solutions during deployment and early life support in order to ensure that they are well established before transition closure.
- Compare the actual performance of services after a transition against the predicted performance defined in service design with the aim of reducing variations in service capability and performance.

3.1.5.3 Best practice

- Adopt programme and project management best practices to plan and manage the resources required to package, build, test and deploy a release successfully within the predicted cost, quality and time estimates. These practices will typically be based on PRINCE2 or PMBOK.
- Provide clear and comprehensive plans that enable the customer and business change projects to align their activities with the service transition plans.
- Manage stakeholder commitment and communications.

3.1.6 Establish and maintain relationships with stakeholders

3.1.6.1 Policy
- Establish and maintain relationships with customers, customer representatives, users and suppliers throughout service transition in order to set their expectations about the new or changed service.

3.1.6.2 Principles
- Set stakeholder expectations on how the performance and use of the new or changed service can be used to enable business change.
- Communicate changes to all stakeholders in order to improve their understanding and knowledge of the new or changed service.
- Provide good-quality knowledge and information so that stakeholders can find information about the service transition easily, e.g. release and deployment plans, and release documentation.

3.1.6.3 Best practice
- Stakeholders should verify that the new or changed service can be used in accordance with the requirements and constraints specified within the service requirements.
- Share service transition and release plans and any changes with stakeholders.
- Work with business relationship management and service level management to build customer and stakeholder relationships during service transition.
- Work with supplier management to ensure commitment and support from key suppliers during and following transition.

3.1.7 Establish effective controls and disciplines

3.1.7.1 Policy
- Establish suitable controls and disciplines throughout the service lifecycle to enable the smooth transition of service changes and releases.

3.1.7.2 Principles
- Establish and maintain the integrity of all identified service assets and configurations as they evolve through the service transition stage.
- Automate audit activities, where beneficial, in order to increase the detection of unauthorized changes and discrepancies in the configurations.
- Clearly define 'who is doing what, when and where' at all handover points to increase accountability for delivery against the plans and processes.
- Define and communicate roles and responsibilities for handover and acceptance through the service transition activities (e.g. build, test, deployment) to reduce errors resulting from misunderstandings and lack of ownership.
- Establish transaction-based processes for configuration, change and problem management to provide an audit trail and the management information necessary to improve the controls.
- Ensure that benefits realization for the business is measured and reported for every service transition.

3.1.7.3 Best practice
- Ensure that roles and responsibilities are well defined, maintained and understood by those involved and are mapped to any relevant processes for current and foreseen circumstances.
- Assign people to each role and maintain the assignment in the service knowledge management system (SKMS) or configuration management system (CMS) to provide visibility of the person responsible for particular activities.
- Implement integrated incident, problem, change, service asset and configuration management processes with service level management to measure the quality of configuration items throughout the service lifecycle.
- Ensure that the service can be managed, operated and supported in accordance with the requirements and constraints specified within the service design by the service provider organization.

- Ensure that only competent staff can implement changes to controlled test environments and supported services.
- Perform configuration audits and process audits to identify configuration discrepancies and non-conformance that may impact service transitions.

3.1.8 Provide systems for knowledge transfer and decision support

3.1.8.1 Policy

- Service transition develops systems and processes to transfer knowledge for effective operation of the service and enable decisions to be made at the right time by competent decision makers.

3.1.8.2 Principles

- Provide quality data, information and knowledge at the right time to the right people to reduce effort spent waiting for decisions and consequent delays.
- Ensure that there is adequate training and knowledge transfer to users to maximize the business value created by the new or changed service and to reduce the number of training calls that the service desk handles.
- Improve the quality of information and data to enhance user and stakeholder satisfaction while optimizing the cost of production and maintenance.
- Improve the quality of release and deployment documentation to reduce the number of incidents and problems caused by poor-quality user documentation, support or operational documentation time between changes being implemented and the documentation being updated.
- Provide easy access to quality information to reduce the time spent searching for information, particularly during critical activities such as handling a major incident.
- Establish the definitive source of knowledge and share information across the service lifecycle and with stakeholders in order to maximize the quality of information and reduce the overhead in maintaining it.
- Provide consolidated information to enable change and release and deployment management to expedite effective decisions

about promoting a release through the test environments and into a supported environment.

3.1.8.3 Best practice

- Provide easy access, presentation and reporting tools for the SKMS and CMS.
- Provide quality user interfaces to the SKMS and CMS for different people and roles to make decisions at appropriate times.
- After each transition is complete, publish a summary of the predicted and unpredicted effects of the change and deviations of actual from predicted capability and performance together with the risk profile.
- Ensure that service asset and configuration management information is accurate to trigger approval and notification transactions for decision-making via workflow tools, e.g. changes and acceptance of deliverables.
- Provide knowledge, information and data for deployment, service desk, operations and support teams to resolve incidents and errors.

3.1.9 Plan release packages

3.1.9.1 Policy

- Releases are planned and designed to be built, tested, delivered, distributed and deployed into the live environment in a manner that provides the agreed levels of traceability, in a cost-effective and efficient way.

3.1.9.2 Principles

- A release policy is agreed with the business and all relevant parties.
- Releases are planned well in advance.
- Resource utilization is optimized across service transition activities to reduce costs.
- Resources are coordinated during release and deployment management.
- Release and distribution mechanisms are planned to ensure that the integrity of components during installation, handling, packaging and delivery is maintained.
- Emergency releases are managed in line with the emergency change procedure and are reported to management as appropriate.
- The risks of remediating a failed release are assessed and managed.

■ The success and failure of the release package is measured with the aim of improving effectiveness and efficiency while optimizing costs.

3.1.9.3 Best practice

■ All updates to releases are recorded in the configuration management system.
■ Definitive versions of electronic media, including software, are captured in a definitive media library prior to release into the service operation readiness test environment.
■ Records are kept of planned release and deployment dates and deliverables with references to related change requests and problems.
■ Proven procedures are followed for handling, distribution and delivery of release packages, including verification.
■ Prerequisites and corequisites for a release are documented and communicated to the relevant parties, e.g. technical requirements for a test environment.

3.1.10 Anticipate and manage course corrections

Course corrections

When plotting a long route for a ship or aircraft, assumptions will be made about prevailing winds, weather and other factors, and plans for the journey prepared. Checks along the way – observations based on the actual conditions experienced – will require (usually minor) alterations to ensure the destination is reached.

Successful transition is also a journey – from the 'as is' state within an organization towards the 'as-required' state. In the dynamic world within which IT service management functions, it is very often the case that factors arise between initial design of a changed or new service and its actual transition. This means that 'course corrections' to that service transition journey will be required, altering the original course of action planned by service design in order to reach the destination agreed with the customer.

3.1.10.1 Policy

■ Use risk assessment and management to identify and document the range of course corrections that staff are allowed to implement.
■ Train staff to recognize the need for course corrections and empower them to apply necessary variations within prescribed and understood limits.

3.1.10.2 Principles

■ Encourage stakeholders to expect changes to plans and understand that these are necessary and beneficial.
■ Learn from previous course corrections to predict future ones and re-use successful approaches.
■ Debrief and propagate knowledge through end-of-transition debriefing sessions, and make conclusions available through the service knowledge management system.
■ Manage course corrections through appropriate change management, project management and baseline procedures.

3.1.10.3 Best practice

■ Use project management practices and the change management process to manage course corrections.
■ Document and control changes but without making the process bureaucratic. (It should be easier to do it correctly than to cope with the consequences of doing it wrong.)
■ Provide information on changes that were applied after the configuration baseline was established.
■ Involve stakeholders with changes when appropriate, but manage issues and risks within service transition when appropriate.

3.1.11 Proactively manage resources across service transitions

3.1.11.1 Policy

■ Provide and manage shared and specialist resources across service transition activities to eliminate delays and optimize utilization of resources.

3.1.11.2 Principles

- Recognize the resources, skills and knowledge required to deliver service transition within the organization.
- Develop a team (including externally sourced resources if required) capable of successful implementation of the service transition strategy, service design package and release. This team should have the ability to manage all required organizational change management before, during and after the service transition.
- Establish dedicated resources to perform critical activities to reduce delays.
- Establish and manage shared resources to improve the effectiveness and efficiency of service transition.
- Automate repetitive and error-prone processes to improve the effectiveness and efficiency of key activities, e.g. distribution, build and installation.

3.1.11.3 Best practice

- Work with human resources (HR), supplier management etc. to identify, manage and make use of competent and available resources.
- Recognize and use competent and specialist resources outside the core ITSM team to deliver service transition.
- Proactively manage shared resources to minimize the impact that delays in one transition have on another transition.
- Measure the impact of using dedicated versus non-dedicated resources on delays, e.g. the impact on service transition of using operations staff who get diverted to fix major incidents.

3.1.12 Ensure early involvement in the service lifecycle

3.1.12.1 Policy

- Establish suitable controls and disciplines to check at the earliest possible stage in the service lifecycle that a new or changed service will be capable of delivering the value required.

3.1.12.2 Principles

- Use a range of techniques to maximize fault detection early in the service lifecycle in order to reduce the cost of rectification. (The later in the lifecycle that an error is detected, the higher the cost of rectification.)
- Identify changes that will not deliver the expected benefits, and either change the service requirements or stop the change before resources are wasted.

3.1.12.3 Best practice

- Involve customers or customer representatives in service acceptance test planning and test design to understand how to validate that the service will add value to the customer's business processes and services.
- Involve users in test planning and design whenever possible. Base testing on how the users actually work with a service – not just on how the designers intended it to be used.
- Use previous experience to identify errors in the service design.
- Build in – at the earliest possible stage – the ability to check for and to demonstrate that a new or changed service will be capable of delivering the value required of it.
- Use a formal evaluation of the service design and internal audits to establish whether the risks of progressing are acceptable.

3.1.13 Provide assurance of the quality of the new or changed service

3.1.13.1 Policy

- Verify and validate that the proposed changes to the operational services defined in the service and release definitions, service model and service design package can deliver the required service requirements and business benefits.

3.1.13.2 Principles

- Service transition is responsible for assuring that the proposed changes to the operational services can be delivered according to the agreements, specifications and plans within agreed confidence levels.
- Service transition teams should understand what the customers and business actually require from a service to improve customers' and users' satisfaction.
- Quality assurance and testing practices provide a comprehensive method for assuring the quality and risks of new or changed services.

- Test environments need to reflect the live environment to the greatest degree possible in order to optimize the testing efforts. A cost benefit analysis should be performed to prioritize investments in the test environments. Change management should consider the potential impact of changes on the effectiveness of test environments.
- Test design and execution should be managed and delivered independently from the service designer and developer in order to increase the effectiveness of testing and meet any 'segregation of duty' requirements.
- Formal evaluations of the service design and the new or changed service should be performed to identify the risks that need to be managed and mitigated during build, test, deployment and use of the service – see section 4.6.
- Problem management and service asset and configuration management processes should be carried out across the service lifecycle in order to measure and reduce the known errors caused by implementing releases into supported environments.

3.1.13.3 Best practice
- Understand the business value that the service helps to create and the quality criteria for the business processes and products that may be affected by the new or changed service.
- Understand the business's process and priorities – this often requires an understanding of its culture, language, customs and customers.
- Comprehensive stakeholder involvement is important both for effective testing and for building stakeholder confidence, and so should be visible across the stakeholder community.
- Understand the differences between the build, test and live environments in order to manage any differences and improve the ability to predict a service's behaviour.
- Test environments are maintained under the control of change management and service asset and configuration management, and their continued relevance is considered directly as part of any change.
- Establish the current service baseline and the service design baseline prior to change evaluation.

- Evaluate the predicted capability, quality and costs of the service design taking into account the results of previous experience and stakeholder feedback prior to deployment.
- Consider the circumstances that will actually be in place when service transition is complete, not just what was expected at the design stage.

3.1.14 Proactively improve quality during service transition

3.1.14.1 Policy
- Proactively plan and improve the quality of the new or changed service during transition.

3.1.14.2 Principles
- Detect and resolve incidents and problems during transition to reduce the likelihood of errors occurring during the operational stage of the service lifecycle and adversely affecting business operations.
- Proactively manage and reduce incidents, problems and errors detected during service transition to reduce costs, re-work and the impact on the user's business activities.
- Align the management of incidents, problems and errors during transition with the processes used during the service operation stage of the service lifecycle, in order to facilitate measurement and management of the impact and cost of errors across the service lifecycle.

3.1.14.3 Best practice
- Compare actual versus predicted service capability, performance and costs during pilots and early life support in order to identify any deviations and risks that can be removed prior to service transition closure.
- Perform a formal evaluation of the new or changed service to identify the risk profile and prioritize the risks that need to be mitigated before transition closure, e.g. security risks that may impact the warranties.
- Use the risk profile from the evaluation of the service design to develop risk-based tests.
- Provide and test the diagnostic tools and aids with the service desk, operations and support staff to ensure that if something goes wrong in testing or live use, it is relatively simple to

obtain key information that helps to diagnose the problem without impacting too much on the user.

- Encourage cross-fertilization of knowledge between service transition and service operation stages to improve problem diagnoses and resolution time, e.g. workarounds and fixes.
- Establish transition incident, problem, error and resolution procedures and measures that reflect those in use in the live environment.
- Fix known errors and resolve incidents in accordance with their priority for resolution.
- Document any resolution, e.g. workarounds so that the information can be analysed.
- Proactively analyse the root cause of high-priority and repeat incidents.
- Record, classify and measure the number and impact of incidents and problems against each release in the test, deployment and live service operation stages in order to identify early opportunities to fix errors.
- Compare the number and impact of incidents and problems between deployments in order to identify improvements and fix any underlying problems that will improve the user experience for subsequent deployments.
- Update incident and problem management with workarounds and fixes identified in transition.

3.2 OPTIMIZING SERVICE TRANSITION PERFORMANCE

In order to be effective and efficient, service transition must focus on delivering what the business requires as a priority and doing so within financial and other resource constraints.

3.2.1 Metrics for alignment with the business and IT plans

The service transition lifecycle stage and release plans need to be aligned with the business, service management and IT strategies and plans.

Typical metrics that can be used in measuring this alignment are:

- Increased percentage of service transition plans that are aligned with the business, IT, service management strategies and plans

- Percentage of customer and stakeholder organizations or units that have a clear understanding of the service transition practice and its capabilities
- Percentage of service lifecycle budget allocated to service transition activities
- Quality rating of the plans including adherence to a structured approach, compliance with the plan templates and completeness of the plans
- Percentage of planning meetings where stakeholders have participated
- Percentage of service transition plans that are aligned with the service transition policies
- Percentage of strategic and tactical projects that adopt the service transition service practices
- Percentage of release planning documents that are quality assured by staff working in service transition roles.

3.2.2 Metrics for service transition

Measuring and monitoring the performance of the service transition lifecycle stage should focus on the delivery of the new or changed service against the predicted levels of warranty, service level, resources and constraints within the service design or release package. Metrics should therefore be aligned with the metrics for service design, and may include the variation in predicted versus actual measures for:

- Resource utilization against capacity
- Capabilities (where these can be measured)
- Warranties
- Service levels
- Cost against approved budget
- Time
- Quality of service, e.g. satisfaction rating or service levels met, breached and near misses
- Value
- Errors and incidents
- Risks.

Examples of other metrics for optimizing the performance of service transition are:

- Cost of testing and evaluation versus cost of live incidents
- Delays caused by service transition, e.g. due to a lack of service transition resources
- Operational problems that could have been identified by the service transition processes

Table 3.1 Service transition inputs and outputs by lifecycle stage

Lifecycle stage	Service transition inputs (from the lifecycle stages in the first column)	Service transition outputs (to the lifecycle stages in the first column)
Service strategy	Vision and mission Service portfolio Policies Strategies and strategic plans Priorities Change proposals, including utility and warranty requirements and expected timescales Financial information and budgets Input to change evaluation and change advisory board (CAB) meetings	Transitioned services Information and feedback for business cases and service portfolio Response to change proposals Service portfolio updates Change schedule Feedback on strategies and policies Financial information for input to budgets Financial reports Knowledge and information in the SKMS
Service design	Service catalogue Service design packages, including: ■ Details of utility and warranty ■ Acceptance criteria ■ Service models ■ Designs and interface specifications ■ Transition plans ■ Operation plans and procedures Requests for change (RFCs) to transition or deploy new or changed services Input to change evaluation and CAB meetings Designs for service transition processes and procedures Service level agreements, operational level agreements and underpinning contracts	Service catalogue updates Feedback on all aspects of service design and service design packages Input and feedback on transition plans Response to RFCs Knowledge and information in the SKMS (including the CMS) Design errors identified in transition for re-design Evaluation reports
Service operation	RFCs to resolve operational issues Feedback on quality of transition activities Input to operational testing Actual performance information Input to change evaluation and CAB meetings	New or changed services Known errors Standard changes for use in request fulfilment Knowledge and information in the SKMS (including the CMS) Change schedule
Continual service improvement	Results of customer and user satisfaction surveys Input to testing requirements Data required for metrics, key performance indicators (KPIs) and critical success factors (CSFs) Input to change evaluation and CAB meetings Service reports RFCs for implementing improvements	Test reports Change evaluation reports Knowledge and information in the SKMS Achievements against metrics, KPIs and CSFs Improvement opportunities logged in the continual service improvement register

■ Stakeholder satisfaction with the transition stage
■ Cost savings by targeted testing of changes to the service design
■ Reduction in emergency, urgent or late changes and releases – reducing unplanned work
■ Reduced cost of transitioning services and releases – by type. For example, the cost of implementing minor infrastructure changes, or the cost of retiring customer-facing services

■ Increased productivity of staff
■ Increased re-use and sharing of service assets and service transition process assets
■ More motivated staff and improved job satisfaction, where this can be measured
■ Improved communications and inter-team working (IT, customer, users and suppliers), where this can be measured
■ Enhanced performance of service transition processes.

3.3 SERVICE TRANSITION INPUTS AND OUTPUTS

The main input to service transition is a service design package, which includes all of the information needed to manage the entire lifecycle of a new or changed service. The main output is the deployment into live use of a new or changed service, with all the supporting knowledge and information, tools and processes required to support the service. Table 3.1 shows the major service transition inputs and outputs, by lifecycle stage. Appendix D provides a summary of the major inputs and outputs between each stage of the service lifecycle.

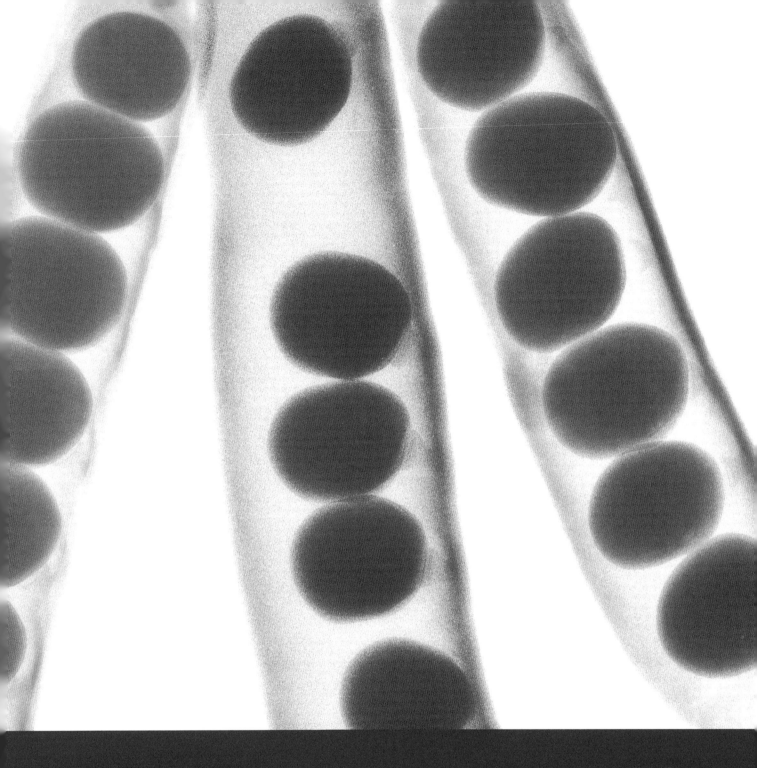

Service transition
processes

4

4 Service transition processes

This chapter sets out the processes and activities on which effective service transition depends. These comprise both lifecycle processes and those almost wholly contained within service transition. Each is described in detail, setting out the key elements of that process or activity.

The processes and activities and their relationships are set out in Figure 1.2 and the topics specifically addressed in this chapter are:

- Transition planning and support
- Change management
- Service asset and configuration management
- Release and deployment management
- Service validation and testing
- Change evaluation
- Knowledge management.

Some of these processes are used throughout the service lifecycle, but they are addressed in this publication since they are central to effective service transition.

The other processes and activities are mostly contained within the service transition stage of the lifecycle, but are also made use of in other stages; for example, change evaluation of the service design, and performance testing within service operation.

The purpose and scope of service transition as a whole are set out in section 1.1.

Figure 8.2 gives an example of how the many processes involved in service transition might interact.

Note that this chapter does not cover strategic planning for business transformation or organizational change, although the interfaces to these processes do need to be managed. Guidance on organizational change is addressed in Chapter 5. Business transformation is the subject of many publications aimed at the general business manager.

4.1 TRANSITION PLANNING AND SUPPORT

4.1.1 Purpose and objectives

The purpose of the transition planning and support process is to provide overall planning for service transitions and to coordinate the resources that they require.

The objectives of transition planning and support are to:

- Plan and coordinate the resources to ensure that the requirements of service strategy encoded in service design are effectively realized in service operation.
- Coordinate activities across projects, suppliers and service teams where required.
- Establish new or changed services into supported environments within the predicted cost, quality and time estimates.
- Establish new or modified management information systems and tools, technology and management architectures, service management processes, and measurement methods and metrics to meet requirements established during the service design stage of the lifecycle.
- Ensure that all parties adopt the common framework of standard re-usable processes and supporting systems in order to improve the effectiveness and efficiency of the integrated planning and coordination activities.
- Provide clear and comprehensive plans that enable customer and business change projects to align their activities with the service transition plans.
- Identify, manage and control risks, to minimize the chance of failure and disruption across transition activities; and ensure that service transition issues, risks and deviations are reported to the appropriate stakeholders and decision makers.
- Monitor and improve the performance of the service transition lifecycle stage.

4.1.2 Scope

The scope of transition planning and support includes:

- Maintaining policies, standards and models for service transition activities and processes
- Guiding each major change or new service through all the service transition processes
- Coordinating the efforts needed to enable multiple transitions to be managed at the same time
- Prioritizing conflicting requirements for service transition resources
- Planning the budget and resources needed to fulfil future requirements for service transition
- Reviewing and improving the performance of transition planning and support activities
- Ensuring that service transition is coordinated with programme and project management, service design and service development activities.

Transition planning and support is not responsible for detailed planning of the build, test and deployment of individual changes or releases; these activities are carried out as part of change management and release and deployment management.

4.1.3 Value to business

Effective transition planning and support can significantly improve a service provider's ability to handle high volumes of change and releases across its customer base. An integrated approach to planning improves the alignment of the service transition plans with the customer, supplier and business change project plans.

4.1.4 Policies, principles and basic concepts

This section sets out basic concepts for effective transition planning and support.

Service design coordination will – in collaboration with customers, external and internal suppliers and other relevant stakeholders – develop the service design and document it in a service design package (SDP). The SDP includes the following information that is required by the service transition teams:

- The service charter, which includes a description of the expected utility and warranty, as well as outline budgets and timescales

- The service specifications
- The service models
- The architectural design required to deliver the new or changed service, including constraints
- The definition and design of each release
- The detailed design of how the service components will be assembled and integrated into a release package
- Release and deployment management plans
- The service acceptance criteria.

Service design packages will be created (or updated) for all major changes. This could include implementation of new service management processes or tools, or replacement of old infrastructure components, as well as release of new or changed services and decommissioning or retiring assets or services.

4.1.4.1 Service transition policy

Policies that support service transition are provided in Chapter 3.

Policies for change management, service asset and configuration management, release and deployment management, service validation and testing, change evaluation and knowledge management also support service transition and examples of these are provided in sections 4.2, 4.3, 4.4, 4.5, 4.6 and 4.7.

4.1.4.2 Release policy

The release policy should be defined for one or more services and include:

- The unique identification, numbering and naming conventions for different types of release together with a description
- The roles and responsibilities at each stage in the release and deployment management process
- The requirement to only use software assets from the definitive media library
- The expected frequency for each type of release
- The approach for accepting and grouping changes into a release, e.g. how enhancements are prioritized for inclusion
- The mechanism to automate the build, installation and release distribution processes to improve re-use, repeatability and efficiency

■ How the configuration baseline for the release is captured and verified against the actual release contents, e.g. hardware, software, documentation and knowledge

■ Exit and entry criteria and authority for acceptance of the release into each service transition stage and into the controlled test, training, disaster recovery and other supported environments

■ Criteria and authorization to exit early life support and handover to the service operation functions.

A release that consists of many different types of service assets may involve many people, often from different organizations. The typical responsibilities for handover and acceptance of a release should be defined and then they can be modified as required for specific transitions. The main roles and responsibilities at points of handover should be defined to ensure that everyone understands their role and level of authority and those of others involved in the release and deployment management process.

An example of a responsibility matrix for an organization that supports client–server applications is shown in Table 4.1. Such a matrix will help to identify gaps and overlaps, and typical roles can be planned for the future.

All releases should have a unique identifier that can be used by service asset and configuration management and the documentation standards. The types of release should be defined, as this helps to set customer and stakeholder expectations about the planned releases. A typical example is:

■ **Major releases** Normally contain large areas of new functionality, some of which may eliminate temporary fixes to problems. A major upgrade or release usually supersedes all preceding minor upgrades, releases and emergency fixes.

Table 4.1 Example of a responsibility matrix for release points during service transition

	Development	Controlled test	Release to production	Live
Class of object	Released from	Accepted by	Authority to release to live	Accepted and supported by
Purchased package	Application development manager	Test manager	Change manager/change authority	Operations manager
Customized modules	Application development manager	Test manager	Change manager/change authority	Operations manager
Physical database changes	Application development manager	Database administrator	Change manager/change authority	Database administrator
Server	Server builder	Server manager	Change manager/change authority	Server manager
Desktop build (e.g. a new application)	Desktop development manager	Test manager	Change manager/change authority	Desktop support manager
Desktop application (already built and within operational constraints)	Desktop development manager	Desktop support manager	Desktop support manager, change manager/change authority	Desktop support manager
Desktop computers	Logistics	Desktop support	Desktop support manager, change manager/change authority	Desktop support manager
Desktop service	Service development	Desktop support	Service level management, desktop support manager, change manager/change authority	Service level management, desktop support manager
Release/change authorization	Development manager, change manager/change authority	Test manager, change manager/change authority	Release manager, test manager, operations manager, desktop support service, desk user at each site, customer stakeholder, change manager/change authority	Service desk users

- **Minor releases** Normally contain small enhancements and fixes, some of which may already have been issued as emergency fixes. A minor upgrade or release usually supersedes all preceding emergency fixes.
- **Emergency releases** Normally contain corrections to a small number of known errors, or sometimes an enhancement to meet a high-priority business requirement.

A release policy may specify, for example, that only strict 'emergency fixes' will be issued between formally planned releases of enhancements and non-urgent corrections.

An extract from a release policy is shown in Table 4.2, which shows how different types of release can be defined. In this table the following naming/numbering conventions have been used:

- Characters **before** the underscore (for example SS, ESWnnn, ESDnnn) identify the **service.**
- Characters **after** the underscore (for example x, 1.x, 1.1.x) identify the **specific release**. Characters to the right of decimal points represent successively minor releases.

4.1.5 Process activities, methods and techniques

4.1.5.1 Transition strategy

The organization should decide the most appropriate approach to service transition based on the size and nature of the services, the number and frequency of releases required, and any special needs of the users – for example, if a phased deployment is usually required over an extended period of time.

The service transition strategy defines the overall approach to organizing service transition and allocating resources. The aspects to consider are:

- Purpose and objectives of service transition
- Context, e.g. service customer, contract agreement portfolio
- Scope – inclusions and exclusions
- Applicable standards, agreements, legal, regulatory and contractual requirements:
  - Internal standards
  - Interpretation of legislation, industry guidelines and other externally imposed requirements and standards
  - Agreements and contracts that apply to service transition
- Organizations and stakeholders involved in transition:
  - Third parties, strategic partners, suppliers and service providers
  - Customers and users
  - Service management
  - Service provider
  - Transition organization (see section 6.2)
- Framework for service transition:
  - Policies, processes and practices applicable to service transition including process service provider interfaces (SPIs)
  - Integration with policies and methods used for programme and project management
  - Roles and responsibilities
  - Transition resource planning and estimation
  - Transition preparation and training requirements
  - The release and change authorization
  - Re-using the organization's experience, expertise, tools, knowledge and relevant historical data
- Criteria:
  - Entry and exit criteria for each release stage
  - Criteria for stopping or re-starting transition activities
  - Success and failure criteria
- Identification of requirements and content of the new or changed service:
  - Services to be transitioned with target locations, customers and organizational units
  - Release definitions
  - Applicable SDP including architectural design
  - Requirements for environments to be used, locations, organizational and technical
  - Planning and management of environments, e.g. commissioning and decommissioning
- People:
  - Assigning roles and responsibilities for all activities, including authorization
  - Assigning and scheduling training and knowledge transfer
- Approach:
  - Transition model including service transition lifecycle stages
  - Plans for managing changes, assets, configurations and knowledge

Table 4.2 Extract from a service release policy for a retail organization

Service	Release definition*	Naming/numbering	Frequency/occurrence	Release window
Store service	Type A	SS_x	Annual (Feb)	Wednesday 01.00–04.00 hours
	Type B or C	SS_1.x or SS_1.1.x	Quarterly	Not holiday weekends
	Emergency	SS_1.1.1.x	As required	Not 1 September to 31 January
E-store web service	Type A	ESWnnn_x	6 months	01.00–02.00 hours
	Type B or C	ESWnnn_1.x	Monthly	Not holiday weekends
	Emergency	ESWnnn_1.1.x	As required	Not 1 October to 10 January
E-store delivery service	Type A	ESDnnn_x	6 months	01.00–02.00 hours
	Type B	ESDSnnn_1.x	Quarterly	Highest level of authorization
	Type C	ESDnnn_1.1.x	Monthly	required during holiday
	Emergency	ESDnnn_1.1.1.x	As required	weekends

*Release definitions

Type A	Something that impacts the whole system/service.
Type B	A release that will impact part of the system, e.g. single sub-system or sub-service.
Type C	Correction to a single function.
Emergency	A change required to restore or continue service to ensure that the service level agreement (SLA) is maintained.

- Baseline and evaluation points
- Configuration audit and verification points
- Points where change authorization is needed
- Use of change windows
- Transition estimation, resource and cost planning
- Preparation for service transition
- Change evaluation and change authorization
- Release planning, build, test, deployment and early life support
- Error handling, correction and control
- Management and control – recording, progress monitoring and reporting
- Service performance and measurement system
- Key performance indicators (KPIs) and improvement targets

■ Deliverables from transition activities, including mandatory and optional documentation for each stage:
  - Transition plans
  - Change management and service asset and configuration management (SACM) plans
  - Release policy, plans and documentation
  - Test plans and reports
  - Build plans and documentation
  - Evaluation plan and report
  - Deployment plans and reports
  - Transition closure report

■ Schedule of milestones
■ Financial requirements – budgets and funding.

4.1.5.2 Service transition lifecycle stages

The SDP should define the lifecycle stages for the service transition, and the move from one stage to the next should be subject to formal checks. Typical stages in the life of a transition might include:

■ Acquire and test new configuration items (CIs) and components
■ Build and test
■ Service release test
■ Service operational readiness test
■ Deployment
■ Early life support
■ Review and close service transition.

For each stage there will be exit and entry criteria and a list of mandatory deliverables from the stage. These criteria are often implemented as 'quality gates' at specific stages in the design and transition of a new or changed service. Each quality gate will define a standard set of criteria which must be met before the service can move to the next stage.

4.1.5.3 Prepare for service transition

The service transition preparation activities include:

■ Review and acceptance of inputs from the other service lifecycle stages

- Review and check the input deliverables, e.g. change proposal, SDP, service acceptance criteria and evaluation report (see section 4.6.6)
- Identifying, raising and scheduling requests for change (RFCs)
- Checking that the configuration baselines are recorded in the configuration management system (CMS) before the start of service transition (see section 4.3.4.2)
- Checking transition readiness.

The configuration baselines help to fix a point in history that people can reference and apply changes to in a manner that is understandable. Any variance in the proposed service scope, service strategy requirements and service design baseline must be requested and managed through change management.

At a minimum, it should be accepted (by people responsible for service design and service transition, and other stakeholders) that the service design and all the release units can be operated and supported within the predicted constraints and environment. The change evaluation activity described in section 4.6 performs the evaluation of the SDP and service acceptance criteria and provides a report to change management with recommendations on whether the change should be authorized.

4.1.5.4 Planning and coordinating service transition

Planning an individual service transition

The release and deployment management activities should be planned in stages as details of the deployment might not be known in detail initially. Each service transition plan should be developed from a proven service transition model wherever possible. Although service design provides the initial plan, the planner will allocate specific resources to the activities and modify the plan to fit in with any new circumstances (e.g. a test specialist may have left the organization).

A service transition plan describes the tasks and activities required to release and deploy a release into the test environments and into production, including:

- Work environment and infrastructure for the service transition

- Schedule of milestones, handover and delivery dates
- Activities and tasks to be performed
- Staffing, resource requirements, budgets and time-scales at each stage
- Issues and risks to be managed
- Lead times and contingency.

Allocating resources to each activity and factoring in resource availability will enable the service transition planner to work out whether the transition can be deployed by the required date. If resources are not available, it may be necessary to review other transition commitments and consider changing priorities. Such changes need to be discussed with people responsible for change management and release and deployment management as this may affect other changes that could be dependent on or prerequisites for the release.

Integrated planning

Good planning and management are essential for successful deployment of a release into production across distributed environments and locations. It is important to maintain an integrated set of transition plans that are linked to lower-level plans such as release build and test plans. These plans should be integrated with the change schedule and release and deployment management plans. Establishing good-quality plans at the outset enables service transition to manage and coordinate the service transition resources, e.g. resource allocation, utilization, budgeting and accounting.

An overarching service transition plan should include the milestone activities to acquire the release components, package the release, build, test, deploy, evaluate and proactively improve the service through early life support. It will also include the activities to build and maintain the services and IT infrastructure, systems and environments and the measurement system to support the transition activities.

Adopting programme and project management best practice

It is best practice to manage several releases and deployments as a programme, with each significant deployment run as a project. This will typically be based on PRINCE2 or PMBOK. The actual deployment may be carried out by dedicated staff as part of broader responsibilities such as operations or through a team brought together for the purpose. Elements of the deployment may be delivered through external suppliers, and suppliers may deliver the bulk of the deployment effort, for example in the implementation of a commercial off-the-shelf system such as an ITSM support tool.

Significant deployments will be complex projects in their own right. The steps to consider in planning include the range of elements comprising that service, e.g. people, application, hardware, software, documentation and knowledge. This means that the deployment will contain sub-deployments for each type of element comprising the service.

Reviewing the plans

All service transition and release and deployment plans should be reviewed. Wherever possible, lead times should include an element of contingency and be based on experience rather than merely supplier assertion. This applies even more for internal suppliers where there is no formal contract. Lead times will typically vary seasonally, and they should be factored into planning, especially for long time-frame transitions, where the lead times may vary between stages of a transition, or between different user locations.

Before starting the release, the service transition planning role should verify the plans and ask appropriate questions such as:

■ Are these service transition and release plans up to date?
■ Have the plans been agreed and authorized by all relevant parties, e.g. customers, users, operations and support staff?
■ Do the plans include the release dates and deliverables and refer to related change requests, known errors and problems?
■ Have the impacts on costs, organizational, technical and commercial aspects been considered?
■ Have the risks to the overall services and operations capability been assessed?
■ Has there been a compatibility check to ensure that the configuration items that are to be released are compatible with each other and with configuration items in the target environments?

■ Have circumstances changed such that the approach needs amending?
■ Were the rules and guidance on how to apply it relevant for current service and release?
■ Do the people who need to use the plans understand and have the requisite skills to use them?
■ Is the service release within the SDP and the scope of the issues addressed by the transition model?

Example: Anticipating changed business circumstances

A new version of a retail organization's point-of-sale system was designed and ready for transition to the live environment. Although the new version offered added features, most improvements related to ease of use, ease of support and maintainability of the software.

The transition was originally scheduled for installation in September, but due to delays in third-party suppliers the service was not ready for test and subsequent deployment until late November. The initially planned approach of involving 20% of user staff in acceptance trials and store disruption across the user base was no longer appropriate. With the Christmas sales boom imminent, such disruption would have been prevented by the annual change freeze. Instead, a longer, slower but less resource-intensive acceptance-testing approach was selected with deployment to stores rescheduled for late January.

Where the transition approach does require rethinking and probable alteration, this should be delivered through the formal change management process, since the consideration of alternatives and agreement of the revised transition approach must be properly documented. However, for foreseeable scenarios, where the path of action is documented as an accepted reaction to the circumstances, authority to record and proceed with a change may be delegated to service transition or another appropriate party for authorization, e.g. customer or project. For example, where the service transition milestone dates and release dates can be achieved with the same cost and resources and with no impact on the service definition.

- Has the service design altered significantly such that it is no longer appropriate?
- Have potential changes in business circumstances been identified? (An example of anticipating changed business circumstances is shown.)

4.1.5.5 Provide transition process support

Advice

Service transition should provide support for all stakeholders to enable them to understand and follow the service transition framework of processes and supporting systems and tools. Although the transition planning and support team may not have the specialist resources to handle some issues, it is important that they are able to identify relevant resources that can help projects – e.g. experts who can set up the configuration management system or testing tools.

Projects should implement service transition activities and tasks in accordance with applicable service transition standards, policies and procedures, which should be documented by each organization based on best practice as described in this publication. However, project managers are not always aware of the need to adopt these standards, policies and procedures. When new projects start up, transition planning and support should proactively seek opportunities for establishing the service transition processes into the project quickly – before alternative methods are adopted. Another approach is to work closely with the programme or project support and offer support to projects via this route.

Administration

Transition planning and support should provide administration for:

- Managing service transition changes and work orders
- Managing issues, risks, deviations and waivers
- Managing support for tools and service transition processes
- Monitoring the service transition performance to provide input into continual service improvement.

Changes that affect the agreed baseline configuration items are controlled through change management.

Communication

Managing communication throughout a service transition is absolutely critical to success. A communication plan should include:

- Objectives of the communication
- Defined stakeholders, including users, customers, IT staff, suppliers and customers of the business (if appropriate)
- Communication content for each type of stakeholder
- Communication frequency (daily, weekly etc.), which may vary for each stakeholder group at different stages of the transition
- Channel and format (newsletters, posters, emails, reports, presentations etc.)
- How the success of the communication will be measured.

Plans and progress should be communicated and made available to relevant stakeholders. The stakeholder list is defined in the service design package received from the service design stage of the lifecycle, and people working in the service transition stage should establish the continued relevance of that list and update it as necessary.

Progress monitoring and reporting

Service transition activities should be monitored against the intentions set out in the transition model and plan. Measuring and monitoring the release and deployment will establish whether the transition is proceeding according to plan.

Maintaining an oversight of the actual transitions against the integrated service transition plans, release and change schedules is essential. This includes monitoring the progress of each transition periodically and at milestone or baseline points as well as receiving and chasing updates.

Management reports on the status of each transition will help to identify when there are significant variances from plan so that, for example, project management and the service management organization can make decisions and take action.

In many cases the transition plans will require amendment to bring them into line with a reality that has changed since design. This is not synonymous with bad design or error in selecting transition models, but merely a reflection of a dynamic environment.

4.1.6 Triggers, inputs, outputs and interfaces

4.1.6.1 Trigger

The trigger for planning a single transition is an authorized change. Longer-term planning may be triggered by receipt of a change proposal from service portfolio management. Budgeting for future transition requirements will be triggered by the organization's budgetary planning cycle.

4.1.6.2 Inputs

The inputs to transition planning and support are:

- Change proposal
- Authorized change
- Service design package, which includes:
  - Release package definition and design specification
  - Test plans
  - Deployment plans
  - Service acceptance criteria (SAC).

4.1.6.3 Outputs

The outputs from transition planning and support are:

- Transition strategy and budget
- Integrated set of service transition plans.

4.1.6.4 Interfaces

Transition planning and support has interfaces to almost every other area of service management:

- Demand management should provide long-term information about likely resource requirements.
- The service portfolio management process should engage transition planning and support to provide input to their planning and decision-making.
- Service portfolio management will submit a change proposal to trigger longer-term planning within transition planning and support.
- Business relationship management will help to manage appropriate two-way communication with customers.
- Key inputs to transition planning and support come from the service design stage of the lifecycle in the form of a service design package. It is common for some design work to actually be carried out by personnel who work within

service transition teams – especially in the areas of release build and test and release deployment. Key inputs to this SDP will come from service level management, information security management, IT service continuity management, availability management and capacity management.

- Supplier management will work during the service transition to ensure that appropriate contracts are in place.
- All service transition processes are coordinated by transition planning and support, so service transition planning and support must have interfaces to change management, SACM, release and deployment management, service validation and testing, change evaluation and knowledge management.
- Pilots, handover and early life support must be coordinated with the service operation functions.
- Technical management and application management will provide the personnel needed to carry out many aspects of service transition, for example to review changes or plan deployments.

There are also interfaces with project and programme management teams, which have to work very closely with transition planning and support, and with customers who must be involved in many aspects of service transition.

4.1.7 Information management

The transition planning and support process makes heavy use of the service knowledge management system, to provide access to the full range of information needed for short-, medium- and long-range planning.

Transition planning and support needs access to information about new or changed services to create and manage plans. This information may be found in many structured and unstructured documents, such as guidelines, standards, models and plans, as well as in documents created and maintained by other processes such as service design packages, contracts and operational level agreements (OLAs) and process documentation. Timely access to up-to-date versions of these documents is essential so that transition plans can be created and managed. All of these documents should be stored in the service knowledge management system (SKMS) and managed via change management and the CMS.

4.1.8 Critical success factors and key performance indicators

The following list includes some sample critical success factors (CSFs) for transition planning and support. Each organization should identify appropriate CSFs based on its objectives for the process. Each sample CSF is followed by a small number of typical KPIs that support the CSF. These KPIs should not be adopted without careful consideration. Each organization should develop KPIs that are appropriate for its level of maturity, its CSFs and its particular circumstances. Achievement against KPIs should be monitored and used to identify opportunities for improvement, which should be logged in the continual service improvement (CSI) register for evaluation and possible implementation.

- **CSF** Understanding and managing the trade-offs between cost, quality and time
  - **KPI** Increase in the number of releases implemented that meet the customer's agreed requirements in terms of cost, quality, scope and release schedule (expressed as a percentage of all releases)
  - **KPI** Reduced variation of actual versus predicted scope, quality, cost and time
- **CSF** Effective communication with stakeholders
  - **KPI** Increased customer and user satisfaction with plans and communications
  - **KPI** Reduced business disruption due to better alignment between service transition plans and business activities
- **CSF** Identifying and managing risks of failure and disruption
  - **KPI** Reduction in number of issues, risks and delays
  - **KPI** Improved service transition success rates
- **CSF** Coordinating activities of multiple processes involved in each transition
  - **KPI** Improved efficiency and effectiveness of the processes and supporting systems, tools, knowledge, information and data to enable the transition of new and changed services, e.g. sharing tool licences

- **KPI** Reduction in time and resource to develop and maintain integrated plans and coordination activities
- **CSF** Managing conflicting demands for shared resources
  - **KPI** Increased project and service team satisfaction with the service transition practices
  - **KPI** Reduced number of issues caused by conflicting demands for shared resources.

4.1.9 Challenges and risks

4.1.9.1 Challenges

The biggest challenge for transition planning and support is building up the relationships needed to manage and coordinate the many stakeholders who may be involved in service transition. Often the relationships are not hierarchical and require careful negotiation.

Coordinating and prioritizing many new or changed services can be a big challenge, especially if there are delays or test failures that cause projects to slip. Transition planning and support needs to understand the risks and issues for each project in order to proactively manage resource planning.

4.1.9.2 Risks

Risks to transition planning and support include:

- Lack of information from demand management and service portfolio management resulting in a reactive transition planning and support process with insufficient long-term planning
- Poor relationships with project and programme teams resulting in sudden and unexpected service transition requirements
- Delays to one transition having a subsequent effect on future transitions, due to resource constraints
- Insufficient information to prioritize conflicting requirements.

4.2 CHANGE MANAGEMENT

Changes are made for a variety of reasons and in different ways – for example:

- Proactively, e.g. when organizations are seeking business benefits such as reduction in costs, improved services or increased ease and effectiveness of support
- Reactively as a means of resolving errors and adapting to changing circumstances.

Changes should be managed in order to:

- Optimize risk exposure (supporting the risk profile required by the business)
- Minimize the severity of any impact and disruption
- Achieve success at the first attempt
- Ensure that all stakeholders receive appropriate and timely communication about the change so that they are aware and ready to adopt and support the change.

Such an approach will improve the bottom line for the business by delivering early realization of benefits (or removal of risk) while saving money and time.

An appropriate response to all requests for change entails a considered approach to assessment of risk and business continuity, change impact, resource requirements, change authorization and especially to the realizable business benefit. Risk assessment should consider the risk of not implementing the change as well as any risks that the change might introduce. This considered approach is essential to maintain the required balance between the need for change and the impact of that change.

This section provides information on the change management process and provides guidance that is scalable for:

- Different kinds and sizes of organization
- Small and large changes required at each lifecycle stage
- Changes with major or minor impact
- Changes in a required time frame
- Different levels of budget or funding available to deliver change.

4.2.1 Purpose and objectives

The purpose of the change management process is to control the lifecycle of all changes, enabling beneficial changes to be made with minimum disruption to IT services.

The objectives of change management are to:

- Respond to the customer's changing business requirements while maximizing value and reducing incidents, disruption and re-work.
- Respond to the business and IT requests for change that will align the services with the business needs.
- Ensure that changes are recorded and evaluated, and that authorized changes are prioritized, planned, tested, implemented, documented and reviewed in a controlled manner.
- Ensure that all changes to configuration items are recorded in the configuration management system.
- Optimize overall business risk – it is often correct to minimize business risk, but sometimes it is appropriate to knowingly accept a risk because of the potential benefit.

4.2.2 Scope

Change can be defined in many ways. The ITIL definition of a change is 'the addition, modification or removal of anything that could have an effect on IT services'. The scope should include changes to all architectures, processes, tools, metrics and documentation, as well as changes to IT services and other configuration items.

All changes must be recorded and managed in a controlled way. The scope of change management covers changes to all configuration items across the whole service lifecycle, whether these CIs are physical assets such as servers or networks, virtual assets such as virtual servers or virtual storage, or other types of asset such as agreements or contracts. It also covers all changes to any of the five aspects of service design:

- Service solutions for new or changed services, including all of the functional requirements, resources and capabilities needed and agreed
- Management information systems and tools, especially the service portfolio, for the management and control of services through their lifecycle
- Technology architectures and management architectures required to provide the services
- Processes needed to design, transition, operate and improve the services
- Measurement systems, methods and metrics for the services, the architectures, their constituent components and the processes.

Each organization should define the changes that lie outside the scope of its change management process. Typically these might include:

■ Changes with significantly wider impacts than service changes, e.g. departmental organization, policies and business operations – these changes would produce RFCs to generate consequential service changes.
■ Changes at an operational level such as repair to printers or other routine service components.

Figure 4.1 shows the typical scope of a change management process for an IT organization and how it interfaces with the business and suppliers at strategic, tactical and operational levels. It covers interfaces to internal and external service providers where there are shared assets and configuration items that need to be under change management. Change management must interface with business change management (to the left in Figure 4.1) and with the supplier's change management (to the right in the figure). This may be an external supplier within a formal change management system, or the project change mechanisms within an internal development project.

The service portfolio provides a clear definition of all current, planned and retired services. Understanding the service portfolio helps all parties involved in the service transition to understand the potential impact of the new or changed service on current services and other new or changed services.

Strategic changes are brought in via service strategy and the service portfolio management process in the form of change proposals. Changes to a service will be brought in via service design, continual service improvement, service level management and service catalogue management. Corrective change, resolving errors detected in services, will be initiated from service operation and may route via support or external suppliers into a formal RFC.

Change management is not responsible for coordinating all of the service management processes to ensure the smooth implementation of projects. This activity is carried out by transition planning and support.

4.2.3 Value to business
Reliability and business continuity are essential for the success and survival of any organization. Service and infrastructure changes can have a negative impact on the business through service disruption and delay in identifying business requirements, but change management enables the service provider to add value to the business by:

■ Protecting the business, and other services, while making required changes
■ Implementing changes that meet the customers' agreed service requirements while optimizing costs

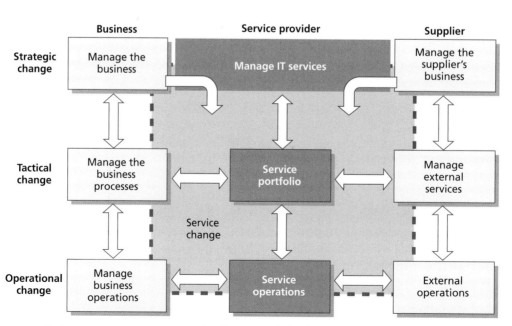

Figure 4.1 Scope of change management and release and deployment management for services

- Contributing to meet governance, legal, contractual and regulatory requirements by providing auditable evidence of change management activity. This includes better alignment with ISO/IEC 20000, ISO/IEC 38500 and COBIT where these have been adopted
- Reducing failed changes and therefore service disruption, defects and re-work
- Reducing the number of unauthorized changes, leading to reduced service disruption and reduced time to resolve change-related incidents
- Delivering change promptly to meet business timescales
- Tracking changes through the service lifecycle and to the assets of its customers
- Contributing to better estimates of the quality, time and cost of change
- Assessing the risks associated with the transition of services (introduction or disposal)
- Improving productivity of staff by minimizing disruptions caused by high levels of unplanned or 'emergency' change and hence maximizing service availability
- Reducing the mean time to restore service (MTRS), via quicker and more successful implementations of corrective changes
- Liaising with the business change process to identify opportunities for business improvement.

Example of IT service-initiated business change

In the retail industry, bar-coding of goods coupled with bar-code readers at the checkout was initially introduced to deliver savings by removing the need to label every item, automating stock control, speeding customer throughput and reducing checkout staff. Suggestions from IT to the business resulted in making use of this facility to power innovative concepts such as 'buy one get one free' and capturing data on each individual's purchasing habits.

The reliance on IT services and underlying information technology is now so complex that considerable time can be spent on:

- Assessing the impact of business change on IT
- Analysing the impact of a service or IT change on the business

- Notifying affected parties (of what is proposed, planned and implemented)
- Recording and maintaining accurate change, configuration, and release and deployment records
- Managing and resolving incidents caused by change
- Identifying the problems that continually arise which require more change
- Introducing new ideas and technology that cause even more change.

There are therefore considerable cost savings and efficiencies to be gained from well-structured and planned changes and releases.

As there is so much focus today on enterprise risk management, change management is a key process that comes under the scrutiny of auditors.

4.2.4 Policies, principles and basic concepts

This section sets out basic concepts within change management that support its effective execution.

4.2.4.1 Policies

Increasing the success rate of changes and releases requires executive support for implementing a culture that sets stakeholder expectations about changes and releases and reduces unplanned work.

Pressure will be applied to reduce timescales and meet deadlines; to cut budgets and operating costs; and to compromise testing. This must not be done without due diligence to governance and risk. The service transition management team will be called on from time to time to make a 'no go' decision and not implement a required change. There must be policies and standards defined which make it clear to the internal and external providers what must be done and what the consequences of non-adherence to policy will be.

Policies that support change management include:

- Creating a culture of change management across the organization where there is zero tolerance for unauthorized change
- Aligning the change management process with business, project and stakeholder change management processes
- Ensuring that changes create business value and that the benefits for the business created by each change are measured and reported

■ Prioritization of change, e.g. innovation versus preventive versus detective versus corrective change

■ Establishing accountability and responsibilities for changes through the service lifecycle

■ Segregation of duty controls

■ Establishing a single focal point for changes in order to minimize the likelihood of conflicting changes and potential disruption to supported environments

■ Preventing people who are not authorized to make a change from having access to supported environments

■ Integration with other service management processes to establish traceability of change, detect unauthorized change and identify change-related incidents

■ Change windows – enforcement and authorization for exceptions

■ Performance and risk evaluation of all changes that impact service capability

■ Performance measures for the process, e.g. efficiency and effectiveness.

4.2.4.2 Design and planning considerations

The change management process should be planned in conjunction with release and deployment management and service asset and configuration management. This helps the service provider to evaluate the impact of the change on the current and planned services and releases.

The requirements and design for the change management processes include:

■ Requirements, e.g. to comply with relevant legislation, industry codes of practice, standards and organizational practices

■ Approach to eliminating unauthorized change

■ Identification and classification:
  ● Change document identifiers
  ● Change document types, change documentation templates and expected content
  ● Impact, urgency, priorities

■ Organization, roles and responsibilities:
  ● Accountabilities and responsibilities of all stakeholders
  ● Approach to independent testing and formal evaluation of change

  ● Change authorization – levels of authorization and rules that govern decision-making and actions, e.g. escalation
  ● Composition of advisory boards, e.g. the change advisory board (CAB) and the emergency CAB (ECAB)

■ Stakeholders:
  ● Planning of changes and releases to enable stakeholders to make their own preparations and plan their activities
  ● Communicating changes, change schedule and release plans

■ Grouping and relating changes:
  ● Into a planned change window
  ● Into a release, build or baseline
  ● By linking several RFCs to a change proposal
  ● By linking several child RFCs to a master RFC

■ Procedures:
  ● Change authorization policies, rules and procedures
  ● Methods of raising an RFC
  ● Tracking and management of change requests, i.e. change records
  ● Prompt impact assessment and evaluation of change requests
  ● Identification of dependencies and incompatibilities between changes
  ● Verification of the implementation of a change
  ● Oversight and evaluation of deliverables from change and release implementation
  ● Measurement and reporting of change success and business value created
  ● Regular review of changes to identify trends and improvements, e.g. in the success or failure of changes and releases

■ Interfaces to other service management processes, for example service level management, IT service continuity management, information security management, availability management and capacity management for impact assessment and review

■ Approach to interfacing change, release and deployment, and service asset and configuration management with problem and incident management processes to measure and reduce change-related incidents

■ Service asset and configuration management interfaces:

- Providing quality information for impact assessment and reporting, e.g. comparison of current configuration to planned configuration
- Identifying high-risk, high-impact CIs
- Capturing CIs, configuration baselines and releases
- Capturing related deliverables, e.g. acceptance criteria, test and evaluation reports.

4.2.4.3 Types of change request

A change request is a formal communication seeking an alteration to one or more configuration items. This could take several forms, e.g. a 'request for change' document, service desk call or project initiation document. Different types of change may require different types of change request. For example, a major change may require a change proposal, which is usually created by the service portfolio management process. An organization needs to ensure that appropriate procedures and forms are available to cover the anticipated requests. Avoiding a bureaucratic approach to documenting a minor change removes some of the cultural barriers to adopting the change management process.

There are three different types of service change:

- **Standard change** A pre-authorized change that is low risk, relatively common and follows a procedure or work instruction.
- **Emergency change** A change that must be implemented as soon as possible, for example to resolve a major incident or implement a security patch.
- **Normal change** Any service change that is not a standard change or an emergency change.

Changes are often categorized as major, significant or minor, depending on the level of cost and risk involved, and on the scope and relationship to other changes. This categorization may be used to identify an appropriate change authority. See section 4.2.5.5 for more information about change authorities.

Management of standard changes is described in section 4.2.4.7. Management of normal changes is described in sections 4.2.5.1 to 4.2.5.10, and differences for managing emergency changes are described in section 4.2.5.11.

As much use as possible should be made of devolved authorization, both through the standard change procedure and through the authorization of minor changes by change management staff.

During the planning of different types of change requests, each must be defined with a unique naming convention (see section 4.3.5.3). Table 4.3 provides examples of different types of change request across the service lifecycle.

For different change types there are often specific procedures, e.g. for impact assessment and change authorization.

4.2.4.4 Changes, RFCs and change records

The terms 'change', 'change record' and 'RFC' are often used inconsistently, leading to confusion. The usage in this publication is as follows:

- **Change** The addition, modification or removal of anything that could have an effect on IT services. The scope should include changes to all architectures, processes, tools, metrics and documentation, as well as changes to IT services and other configuration items.
- **RFC** A request for change – a formal proposal for a change to be made. It includes details of the proposed change, and may be recorded on paper or electronically. The term RFC is often misused to mean a change record, or the change itself.
- **Change record** A record containing the details of a change. Each change record documents the lifecycle of a single change. A change record is created for every request for change that is received, even those that are subsequently rejected. Change records should reference the configuration items that are affected by the change. Change records may be stored in the configuration management system or elsewhere in the service knowledge management system.

RFCs are only used to submit requests; they are not used to communicate the decisions of change management or to document the details of the change. A change record contains all the required information about a change, including information from the RFC, and is used to manage the lifecycle of that change.

Table 4.3 Example of types of request by service lifecycle stage

Type of change with examples	Documented work procedures	Service strategy	Service design	Service transition	Service operation	Continual service improvement
Request for change to service portfolios	Service change management					
New portfolio line item		✓				
To predicted scope, business case, baseline						
Service pipeline						
Request for change to service or service definition	Service change management					
To existing or planned service attributes		✓	✓	✓	✓	✓
Project change that impacts service design, e.g. forecasted warranties						
Service improvement						
Project change proposal	Project change management procedure					
Business change			✓	✓		✓
No impact on service or design baseline						
User access request	User access procedure				✓	
User service request	Request fulfilment process					
Standard change					✓	
Operational activity	Local procedure (often pre-authorized – see section 4.2.4.7)					
Tuning (within specification/constraints)						
Restart application on failure if no impact on other services					✓	
Planned maintenance						
Operational repair	Service change management					
Emergency change					✓	

4.2.4.5 Change models and workflows

Organizations will find it helpful to predefine change models – and apply them to appropriate changes when they occur. A change model is a way of predefining the steps that should be taken to handle a particular type of change in an agreed way. Support tools can then be used to manage the required process. This will ensure that such changes are handled in a predefined path and to predefined timescales.

Changes that require specialized handling could be treated in this way, such as:

- Emergency changes that may have different authorization and may be documented retrospectively
- Changes to mainframe software that may require specific sequences of testing and implementation

■ Implementation of security patches for desktop operating systems that require specific testing and guaranteed deployment to large numbers of targets, some of which may not be online

■ Service requests that may be authorized and implemented with no further involvement from change management.

The change model includes:

■ Steps that should be taken to handle the change, including handling issues and unexpected events

■ The chronological order in which these steps should be taken, with any dependences or co-processing defined

■ Responsibilities – who should do what (including identification of those change authorities who will authorize the change and who will decide whether formal change evaluation is needed)

■ Timescales and thresholds for completion of the actions

■ Escalation procedures – who should be contacted and when.

These models are usually input to the change management support tools; the tools then automate the handling, management, reporting and escalation of the process.

4.2.4.6 Change proposals

Major changes that involve significant cost, risk or organizational impact will usually be initiated through the service portfolio management process. Before the new or changed service is chartered it is important that the change is reviewed for its potential impact on other services, on shared resources, and on the change schedule.

Change proposals are submitted to change management before chartering new or changed services in order to ensure that potential conflicts for resources or other issues are identified. Authorization of the change proposal does not authorize implementation of the change but simply allows the service to be chartered so that service design activity can commence.

A change proposal is used to communicate a high-level description of the change. This change proposal is normally created by the service portfolio management process and is passed to change management for authorization. In some

organizations, change proposals may be created by a programme management office or by individual projects. The change proposal should include:

■ A high-level description of the new, changed or retired service, including business outcomes to be supported, and utility and warranty to be provided

■ A full business case including risks, issues and alternatives, as well as budget and financial expectations

■ An outline schedule for design and implementation of the change.

Change management reviews the change proposal and the current change schedule, identifies any potential conflicts or issues and responds to the change proposal by either authorizing it or documenting the issues that need to be resolved. When the change proposal is authorized, the change schedule is updated to include outline implementation dates for the proposed change.

After the new or changed service is chartered, RFCs will be used in the normal way to request authorization for specific changes. These RFCs will be associated with the change proposal so that change management has a view of the overall strategic intent and can prioritize and review these RFCs appropriately.

More detail about the content of a change proposal can be found in section 4.2.5.2.

4.2.4.7 Standard changes (pre-authorized)

A standard change is a change to a service or other configuration item for which the approach is pre-authorized by change management, and this approach follows an accepted and established procedure to provide a specific change requirement. Every standard change should have a change model that defines the steps to follow, including how the change should be logged and managed as well as how it should be implemented.

Examples might include an upgrade of a PC in order to make use of specific standard and prebudgeted software, provision of standard equipment and services to a new employee, or a desktop move for a single user. Other examples include low-impact, routine application change to handle seasonal variation.

Authorization of each occurrence of a standard change will be granted by the delegated authority for that standard change (e.g. by the budget-holding customer for installation of software from an approved list on a PC registered to their organizational unit, or by the third-party engineer for replacement of a faulty desktop printer).

The crucial elements of a standard change are as follows:

■ There is a defined trigger to initiate the change, for example a service request or an exception generated by event management.
■ The tasks are well known, documented and proven.
■ Authority is effectively given in advance.
■ Budgetary approval will typically be preordained or within the control of the change requester.
■ The risk is usually low and always well understood.

Once the approach to manage standard changes has been agreed, standard change processes and associated change workflows should be developed and communicated. A change model would normally be associated with each standard change to ensure consistency of approach.

Standard changes should be identified early on when building the change management process to promote efficiency. Otherwise, a change management implementation can create unnecessarily high levels of administration and resistance to the change management process.

All changes, including standard changes, will have details of the change recorded. For some standard changes this may be different in nature from normal change records.

Some standard changes to configuration items may be tracked on the asset or configuration item lifecycle, particularly where there is a comprehensive CMS that provides reports of changes, their current status, the related configuration items and the status of the related CI versions. In these cases the change management and service asset and configuration management reporting is integrated, and change management can have 'oversight' of all changes to service CIs and release CIs.

Some standard changes will be triggered by the request fulfilment process and be directly recorded and passed for action by the service desk.

4.2.4.8 Remediation planning

Definition: remediation

Actions taken to recover after a failed change or release. Remediation may include back-out, invocation of service continuity plans, or other actions designed to enable the business process to continue.

No change should be authorized without having explicitly addressed the question of what to do if it is not successful. Ideally, there will be a back-out plan, which will restore the organization to its initial state, often through the reloading of a baselined set of CIs, especially software and data. However, not all changes are reversible, in which case an alternative approach to remediation is required. This remediation may require a revisiting of the change itself in the event of failure, or may be so severe that it requires invoking the organization's business continuity plan. Only by considering what remediation options are available before instigating a change, and by establishing that the remediation is viable (e.g. it is successful when tested), can the risk of the proposed change be determined and appropriate decisions taken.

Change implementation plans should include milestones and other triggers for implementation of remediation in order to ensure that there is sufficient time in the agreed change window for back-out or other remediation when necessary.

4.2.5 Process activities, methods and techniques

This section provides approaches to managing service changes effectively by addressing the tasks carried out to achieve and deliver controlled change.

Overall change management activities include:

■ Planning and controlling changes
■ Change and release scheduling (working with release and deployment management when appropriate)
■ Communications
■ Change decision-making and change authorization

- Ensuring that remediation plans are in place
- Measurement and control
- Management reporting
- Understanding the impact of change
- Continual improvement.

Typical activities in managing individual changes are:

- Create and record the RFC
- Review the RFC
  - Filter changes (e.g. incomplete or wrongly routed changes)
- Assess and evaluate the change
  - Establish the appropriate level of change authority
  - Establish relevant areas of interest (i.e. who should be involved in the CAB)
  - Evaluate the business justification, impact, cost, benefits, risks and predicted performance of the change
  - Submit a request for evaluation to initiate activity from the change evaluation process (see section 4.2.5.4)
- Authorize the change
  - Obtain authorization/rejection
  - Communicate the decision with all stakeholders, in particular the initiator of the request for change
- Plan updates
- Coordinate change implementation
- Review and close change
  - Collate the change documentation, e.g. baselines and evaluation reports
  - Review the change(s) and change documentation
  - Ensure that details of lessons learned have been entered into the service knowledge management system
  - Close the change document when all actions are completed.

Throughout all the process activities listed above and described within this section, information is gathered, stored in the SKMS, recorded in the CMS and reported.

Figure 4.2 shows an example of a change to the service provider's services, applications or infrastructure. Examples of the status of the change are shown in italics. Change and configuration information is updated all the

way through the activities. This example shows authorization for change build and test and for change deployment. In practice there may be additional authorization steps, for example to authorize change design or change development. Further information about the need for multiple evaluation and authorization steps can be found in section 4.2.5.4.

Figures 4.3 and 4.4 show the equivalent process flow for some examples of standard change process flows.

After a change has been built and tested, and the deployment procedure has been used successfully one or more times, then it may be appropriate to use a 'standard deployment request' change model for future deployments of the same change. This is much simpler than the full change management process flow. Figure 4.3 shows an example of a process flow for this kind of standard change.

Some very low-risk changes may be delegated to service operation staff as a change authority. The change model for this kind of standard change may be very simple, as depicted in Figure 4.4.

4.2.5.1 Normal change procedure

The following sections describe the management of a normal change. The general principles set out apply to all changes, but where normal change procedure can be modified for emergency changes, this is described in section 4.2.5.11.

4.2.5.2 Create and record request for change

The change is raised by a request from the initiator – the individual or organizational group that requires the change. For example, this may be a business unit that requires additional facilities or problem management staff instigating an error resolution.

Is a major change required?

For a major change with significant organizational and/or financial implications, a change proposal may be required. More information about change proposals can be found in section 4.2.4.6.

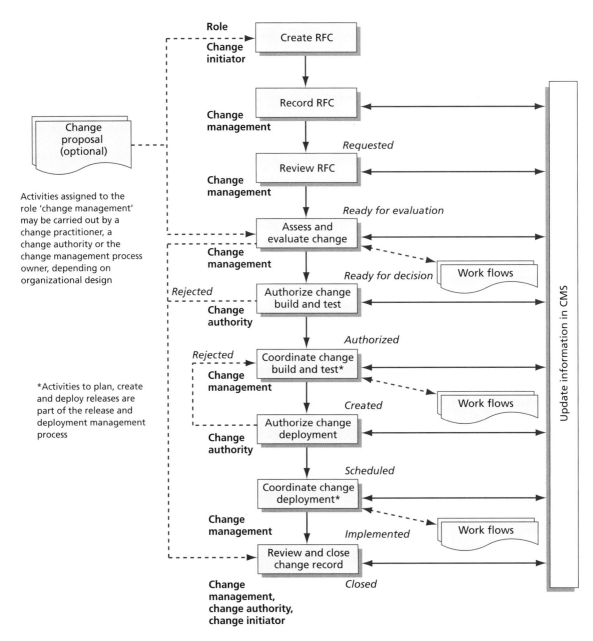

Figure 4.2 Example of a process flow for a normal change

Table 4.4 shows an example of the information recorded for a change; the level of detail depends on the size and impact of the change. Some information is recorded when the document is initiated and some information may be updated as the change document progresses through its lifecycle. Some information is recorded directly on the request for change form, and details of the change and actions may be recorded in other documents and referenced from the RFC, e.g. the business case or impact assessment report.

The change record holds the full history of the change, incorporating information from the RFC and subsequently recording agreed parameters such as priority and authorization, implementation and review information. There may be many different types of change records used to record different types of change. The documentation should be defined during the process design and planning stage.

Different types of change document will have different sets of attributes to be updated through the lifecycle. This may depend on various factors

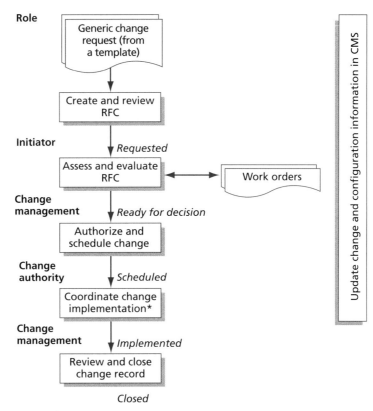

Standard deployment request (where the deployment process is tried and tested)

*Includes build and test the change

Figure 4.3 Example of a process flow for standard deployment request

such as the change model and change category, but it is recommended that the attributes are standardized wherever possible to aid reporting.

Some systems use work orders to progress the change, as this enables complete traceability of the change. For example, work orders may be issued to individuals or teams to do an impact assessment or to complete work required for a change that is scheduled for a specific time or where the work is to be done quickly.

As a change proceeds through its lifecycle, the change document, related records (such as work orders) and related configuration items are updated in the CMS, so that there is visibility of its status and compliance to the process. Estimates and actual resources, costs and outcome (success or failure) are recorded to enable management reporting.

Change logging

The procedures for logging and documenting RFCs should be decided. RFCs could be submitted on paper forms, through email or using a web-based interface, for example. Where a computer-based support tool is used, it is possible that the tool might restrict the format.

All RFCs received should be logged and allocated an identification number (in chronological sequence). Where change requests are submitted in response to a trigger such as a resolution to a problem record (PR), it is important that the

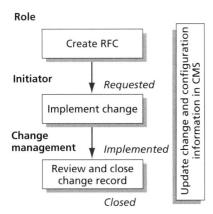

Figure 4.4 Example of a process flow for a standard operational change request

Table 4.4 Example of contents of change documentation

Attribute on the change record	RFC/change record	Change proposal (if appropriate)	Related assets/CIs
Unique number	✓		
Trigger (e.g. to purchase order, problem report number, error records, business need, legislation)	✓		
Description	Detailed description	Description at a business level	
Identity of item(s) to be changed – description of the desired change	Detailed description	High-level description	Service (for enhancement) or CI with errors (corrective changes)
Reason for change, e.g. business case	Full justification, except if a change proposal exists	Full business case	
Effect of not implementing the change (business, technical, financial etc.)	✓	Full business case	
Configuration items and baseline versions to be changed	✓	Affected baseline/release	Details of CIs in baseline/release
Contact and details of person proposing the change	✓	✓	
Date and time that the change was proposed	✓		
Change category, e.g. minor, significant, major	Proposed category	Used for major changes only	
Predicted timeframe, resources, costs and quality of service	Full	Full business case and summary of expected implementation dates	
Change priority	Proposed priority		
Risk assessment and risk management plan	Full	High-level risk assessment for the overall proposal	
Back-out or remediation plan	Full	High-level plan for the overall proposal	
Impact assessment and evaluation – resources and capacity, cost, benefits	Provisional	Full business case	✓
Would the change require consequential amendment of IT service continuity management (ITSCM) plan, capacity plan, security plan, test plan?	✓	✓	Plans affected
Change decision body	✓	✓	
Decision and recommendations accompanying the decision	✓	✓	
Authorization signature (could be electronic)	✓	✓	
Authorization date and time	✓	✓	
Target baseline or release to incorporate change into	✓		
Template change plan(s) to be used	✓		
Scheduled implementation time (change window, release window or date and time)	✓	Summary of expected implementation dates	
Location/reference to release/implementation plan	✓		
Details of change implementer	✓		

Table 4.4 *continued*

Attribute on the change record	RFC/change record	Change proposal (if appropriate)	Related assets/CIs
Test results	Summary and pointer to details		
Change implementation details (success/fail/remediation)	✓		✓
Actual implementation date and time	✓		
Evaluation report	Summary and pointer to details		
Review date(s)	✓		
Review results (including cross-reference to new RFC where necessary)	Summary		
Closure	Summary		

reference number of the triggering document is retained to provide traceability.

It is recommended that the logging of RFCs is done by means of an integrated service management tool, capable of storing data on all assets and CIs and also, importantly, the relationships between them. This will greatly assist when assessing the likely impact of a change to one component of the system on all other components. All actions should be recorded, as they are carried out, within the change management log. If this is not possible for any reason, then they should be manually recorded for inclusion at the next possible opportunity.

Procedures will specify the levels of access and who has access to the logging system. While any authorized personnel may create a change, or add reports of progress to it (though the support tool should keep change management aware of such actions) only change management staff will have permission to close a change.

4.2.5.3 Review RFC

As changes are logged, change management should ensure that all required information has been provided and filter out any requests that seem to be:

■ Totally impractical

■ Repeats of earlier RFCs, accepted, rejected or still under consideration

■ Incomplete submissions, e.g. those that contain inadequate descriptions or that do not have necessary budgetary approval.

These should be returned to the initiator, together with brief details of the reason for the rejection, and the log should record this fact. A right of appeal against rejection should exist, via normal management channels, and should be incorporated within the procedures.

4.2.5.4 Assess and evaluate the change

Changes that are considered to be significant should be subject to the formal change evaluation process, as described in section 4.6. There should be well-defined criteria to determine whether this formal change evaluation is needed, and this will normally be documented in the relevant change model. A formal request for evaluation should be submitted when required to trigger the change evaluation process. If formal change evaluation is not required, then the change will be evaluated by the appropriate change authority as described in this section.

The potential impact on the services of failed changes and their impact on service assets and configurations need to be considered. Generic questions (e.g. the 'seven Rs') provide a good starting point.

The seven Rs of change management

The following questions must be answered for all changes. Without this information, the impact assessment cannot be completed, and the balance of risk and benefit to the live service will not be understood. This could result in the change not delivering all the possible or expected business benefits or even in it having a detrimental, unexpected effect on the live service. The questions are:

- Who **raised** the change?
- What is the **reason** for the change?
- What is the **return** required from the change?
- What are the **risks** involved in the change?
- What **resources** are required to deliver the change?
- Who is **responsible** for the build, test and implementation of the change?
- What is the **relationship** between this change and other changes?

Many organizations develop specific impact assessment forms to prompt the impact assessors about specific types of change. This can help with the learning process, particularly for new services or when implementing a formal impact assessment step for the first time.

Responsibility for assessing each category of change should be assigned to a clearly identified change authority. It is not a best-practice issue because organizations are so diverse in size, structure and complexity that there is not a universal solution appropriate to all organizations. It is, however, recommended that major change is discussed at the outset with all stakeholders in order to arrive at sensible boundaries of responsibility and to improve communications.

Change management is responsible for ensuring that changes are evaluated and, if authorized, subsequently developed, tested, implemented and reviewed. Final responsibility for the IT service – including changes to it – will rest with the service owner. They control the funding available and will have been involved in the change process through direct or delegated membership of a CAB or other change authority.

When conducting the impact and resource assessment for RFCs, change management, the CAB, ECAB or any other change authority should consider relevant items, including:

- The impact that the change will make on the customer's business operation
- Any associated change proposal
- The effect on the infrastructure and customer service (as defined in the service requirements baselines, service model, SLA) and on the capacity and performance, reliability and resilience, contingency plans and security
- The effect of the change on the organization's green IT or sustainability plans
- The impact on other services that run on the same infrastructure (or on projects)
- The impact on non-IT infrastructures within the organization – for example, security, office services, transport, customer help desks
- The effect of not implementing the change
- The IT, business and other resources required to implement the change, covering the likely costs, the number and availability of people required, the elapsed time, and any new infrastructure elements required
- The current change schedule and projected service outage (PSO)
- Additional ongoing resources required if the change is implemented
- Impact on the continuity plan, capacity plan, security plan, regression test scripts and data and test environment, service operation practices.

No change is without risk

Simple changes may seem innocuous but can cause damage out of all apparent proportion to their complexity. There have been several examples in recent years of high-profile and expensive business impacts caused by the inclusion, exclusion or misplacing of a single dot in software code.

It is best practice to use a risk-based assessment during the evaluation of a change or set of changes, for example the risk for:

- An individual change
- A set of changes implemented in the same change window

- Impacting the timescales of authorized changes on change and release schedules.

The focus should be on identifying the factors that may disrupt the business, impede the delivery of service warranties or impact corporate objectives and policies. The same disciplines used for corporate risk management or in project management can be adopted and adapted.

Appendix B describes a number of different approaches that can be taken to assess and manage risks. Each organization should have its own approach to risk management, but this will often be based on one or more of these best-practice approaches.

Many organizations use a simple matrix like the one shown in Table 4.5 to categorize risk for changes, and from this the level of change assessment and authorization required.

Example of change in a high-risk industry

In one volatile and competitive business environment, the mobile telephone supply business, customers asked IT if they were now able to implement a much-needed change to the business software. The reply was that it could not go forward to the next change window because there was still a 30% risk of failure. Business reaction was to insist on implementation because, in their eyes, a 70% chance of success, and the concomitant business advantage, was without any hesitation the right and smart move. Very few of their business initiatives had such a high chance of success.

The point is that the risk and gamble of the business environment (selling mobile telephones) had not been understood within IT, and inappropriate (IT) rules had been applied.

The dominant risk is the business one and that should have been sought, established, understood and applied by the service provider. Sensibly, of course, this might well be accompanied by documentation of the risk-based decision, but nonetheless it is necessary to understand the business perspective and act accordingly.

Table 4.5 Example of a change impact and risk categorization matrix

Change impact	High impact Low probability Risk category: 2	High impact High probability Risk category: 1
	Low impact Low probability Risk category: 4	Low impact High probability Risk category: 3
	Probability	

The risk that should be considered is the risk to the business service. Changes require thorough assessment, widespread communication and appropriate authorization by the person or persons accountable for that business service. Assessing risk from the business perspective can produce a correct course of action very different from that which would have been chosen from an IT perspective, especially within high-risk industries.

Change evaluation

Based on the impact and risk assessments, the output of any formal evaluation, and the potential benefits of the change, each of the assessors should indicate whether they support authorization of the change. All members of the change authority should assess the change based on impact, urgency, risk, benefits and costs. Each will indicate whether they support authorization and be prepared to argue their case for any alterations that they see as necessary.

It is likely that each change or release will require authorization from change management at multiple points in its lifecycle, for example:

- Before service design activity takes place
- After service design is complete to authorize check-in of the service design package and start of release planning
- After release planning, to authorize release build and test
- After release build and test to authorize check-in of the release package to the DML
- Before each deployment, to authorize the deployment
- After deployment to authorize activating the release in the target environment
- Before closure of the change to accept the final configuration.

Not every change will require all of these authorizations. Each change model should include information about when authorization is required.

Before each authorization the change should be evaluated to ensure that risks have been managed and that predicted and actual performance match the business requirements. Some organizations require a separate RFC for each of these steps; others use a documented workflow to manage all of these stages with a single change request.

Section 4.6 describes a formal change evaluation process which may be used for evaluation of changes that have a significant impact, such as the introduction of a new service.

Allocation of priorities

Prioritization is used to establish the order in which changes that have been put forward should be considered.

Every RFC will include the originator's assessment of the impact and urgency of the change.

The priority of a change is derived from the agreed impact and urgency. Initial impact and urgency will be suggested by the change initiator but may well be modified in the change authorization process. Risk assessment is of crucial importance at this stage. The change authority will need information on business consequences in order to assess effectively the risk of implementing or rejecting the change.

Impact is based on the beneficial change to the business that will follow from a successful implementation of the change, or on the degree of damage and cost to the business resulting from the error that the change will correct. The impact may not be expressed in absolute terms but may depend on the probability of an event or circumstance; for example, a service may be acceptable at normal throughput levels but may deteriorate at high usage, which may be triggered by unpredictable external items.

The urgency of the change is based on how long the implementation can afford to be delayed.

Table 4.6 gives examples of change priorities for corrective changes (fixing identified errors that are hurting the business) and for enhancements (which will deliver additional benefits). Other types of change exist, e.g. to enable continuation of existing benefits, but these two are used to illustrate the concept here.

Change planning and scheduling

Careful planning of changes will ensure that there is no ambiguity about what tasks are included in the change management process, what tasks are included in other processes and how processes interface to any suppliers or projects that are providing a change or release.

Many changes may be grouped into one release and these may be designed, built, tested and deployed together if the number of changes involved can be handled by the business, the

Table 4.6 Change priority examples

Priority	Corrective change	Enhancement change
Immediate Treat as emergency change (see section 4.2.5.11)	Putting life at risk Causing significant loss of revenue or the inability to deliver important public services Immediate action required	Not appropriate for enhancement changes
High To be given highest priority for change building, testing and implementation resources	Severely affecting some key users, or impacting on a large number of users	Meets legislative requirements Responds to short-term market opportunities or public requirements Supports new business initiatives that will increase company market position
Medium	No severe impact, but rectification cannot be deferred until the next scheduled release or upgrade	Maintains business viability Supports planned business initiatives
Low	A change is justified and necessary but can wait until the next scheduled release or upgrade	Improvements in usability of a service Adds new facilities

service provider and its customers. However, if many independent changes are grouped into a release, then this may create unnecessary dependencies that are difficult to manage. If insufficient changes are grouped into a release then the overhead of managing more releases can be time-consuming and waste resources (see section 4.4 on release and deployment management).

It is strongly recommended that the change management schedule should be prioritized based on business rather than IT needs, avoiding critical business periods, but ensuring that required changes can be implemented in a timely manner.

Pre-agreed and established change and release windows help an organization to improve the planning and throughput of changes and releases. For example, a release window in a maintenance period of one hour each week may be sufficient to install minor releases only. Major releases may need to be scheduled with the business and stakeholders at a predetermined time. This approach is particularly relevant in high-change environments where a release is a bottleneck or in high-availability services where access to the live systems to implement releases is restricted. In many cases, the change or release may need to be adjusted 'on the fly', and efficient use of change windows will require:

- A list of possible substitutes to make use of the unexpectedly vacant slot
- Empowerment to make and implement release decisions
- Internal metrics that monitor (and reflect and encourage best use of) change and release windows
- A clear understanding of any sequential dependencies and impact on users.

Whenever possible, changes should be designed, built, tested and deployed in releases.

Change management is accountable for producing and distributing a change schedule and projected service outage (PSO). The change schedule contains details of all the changes authorized for implementation and their proposed implementation dates. It also contains estimated dates of longer-term major changes that have been authorized as change proposals. The PSO contains details of changes to agreed SLAs and service availability because of the currently planned

change schedule, in addition to planned downtime from other causes such as planned maintenance and data backup. These documents are agreed with the relevant customers within the business, with service level management, with the service desk and with availability management. The PSO may be produced jointly with other processes, including:

- Service level management, which is responsible for negotiating and agreeing availability targets and planned outages
- Business relationship management, which manages communication with senior management of the customer
- Availability management, which is responsible for ensuring that the planned and unplanned downtime are within agreed targets
- IT service continuity management, which may require planned downtime for testing and may contribute to alternative arrangements for avoiding planned downtime.

Inputs to the PSO should include:

- The change schedule
- Release schedules
- Planned and preventive maintenance schedules
- Limits for planned downtime from availability management
- Availability testing schedules
- ITSCM and business continuity management testing schedules
- Information from the business relationship management and the service level management processes about the customer's ability to accept planned downtime.

Once agreed, the service provider should communicate any planned additional downtime to the user community at large, using the most effective methods available.

The latest versions of these documents will be available to stakeholders within the organization, preferably contained within a commonly available internet or intranet server as part of an SKMS. This can usefully be reinforced with a proactive awareness programme where specific impact can be detected.

ASSESSING REMEDIATION

It is important to develop a remediation plan to address a failing change or release long before implementation. Very often, remediation is the last thing to be considered; risks may be assessed, mitigation plans cast in stone. How to get back to the original start point is often ignored – or considered only when regression is the last remaining option.

4.2.5.5 Authorize change build and test

Formal authorization is obtained for each change from a change authority that may be a role, person or a group of people. The levels of authorization for a particular type of change should be judged by the type, size, risk and potential business impact of the change, e.g. changes in a large enterprise that affect several distributed sites may need to be authorized by a higher-level change authority such as a global CAB or the board of directors.

The culture of the organization dictates, to a large extent, the manner in which changes are authorized. Hierarchical structures may well impose many levels of change authorization, while flatter structures could allow a more streamlined approach.

A degree of delegated authority may exist within an authorization level, e.g. delegating authority to a change manager according to preset parameters relating to:

■ Anticipated business risk
■ Financial implications
■ Scope of the change (e.g. internal effects only, within the finance service, specific outsourced services).

An example of a change authorization hierarchy is shown in Figure 4.5. Each organization should formally document its own change authorization hierarchy, which may be very different to the example shown here. All change authorities should be documented in the CMS.

If change assessment at level 2, 3 or 4 detects higher levels of risk, the authorization request is escalated to the appropriate higher level for the assessed level of risk. The use of delegated authority from higher levels to local levels must be accompanied by trust in the judgement, access to the appropriate information and supported by management. The level at which change is authorized should rest where accountability for accepting risk and remediation exist.

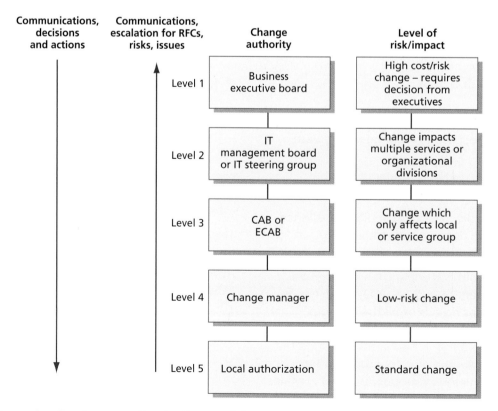

Figure 4.5 Example of a change authorization model

Should disputes arise over change authorization or rejection, there should be a right of appeal to the higher level. Changes that have been rejected should be formally reviewed and closed.

4.2.5.6   Coordinate change build and test

If this change is part of a release, then the work of packaging the change into a release and building and testing this release is coordinated by the release and deployment management process. For simple changes that are not part of a release, the change management process will coordinate this work.

Authorized changes should be passed to the relevant technical groups for building the changes. It is best practice to do this in a formal way that can be tracked, e.g. using work orders.

Change management has an oversight role to ensure that all changes that can be are thoroughly tested. In all cases involving changes that have not been fully tested, special care needs to be taken during implementation.

Testing may continue in parallel with early live usage of a service – looking at unusual, unexpected or future situations so that further corrective action can be taken before any detected errors become apparent in live operation.

4.2.5.7 Authorize change deployment

The design, build and testing of the change should be evaluated to ensure that risks have been managed and that predicted and actual performance match the business requirements. For significant changes, an interim evaluation report will be received from the change evaluation process; for smaller changes the change management process will carry out suitable checks. The result of this evaluation should be passed to the change authority for formal authorization to deploy the change.

If authorization is not given at this stage, the change authority may request changes to the design or to the deployment schedule. This can lead to an iterative approach where the change build and test and the authorization steps are carried out multiple times until the change authority is satisfied.

4.2.5.8 Coordinate change deployment

The work of deploying a release is part of the release and deployment management process. For simple changes that are not part of a release, the change management process will coordinate this activity.

Change management has responsibility for ensuring that changes are deployed as scheduled. This is largely a coordination role as the actual deployment will be the responsibility of others (e.g. people from the technical management function will implement hardware changes). This role is shared with release and deployment management; every service provider will identify the people and processes responsible for each activity based on the size and nature of the change.

Remediation procedures should be prepared and documented in advance for each authorized change so that if errors occur during or after implementation, these procedures can be quickly activated with minimum impact on service quality. Authority and responsibility for invoking remediation should be specifically mentioned in change documentation.

The deployment of changes should be scheduled when the least impact on live services is likely. Support staff should be on hand to deal quickly with any incidents that might arise.

Some changes, especially those that are subject to release and deployment management, may have multiple deployment stages. Each deployment must be authorized by an appropriate change authority. This may require multiple RFCs to be submitted, but some organizations use a single RFC with multiple authorization stages. Either of these is an acceptable approach, so long as every deployment is authorized following a repeatable documented process.

4.2.5.9 Review and close change record

Before the change is closed, an evaluation must be carried out to ensure that actual performance is acceptable and that there are no unacceptable risks. For significant changes an evaluation report will be received from the change evaluation process; for smaller changes the change management process will carry out suitable checks. If the assessment suggests that actual performance is creating unacceptable risks, the change authority will be advised that further action is needed.

If the evaluation shows that the change is acceptable, then it should be presented as a completed change for stakeholder agreement (including the closing of incidents, problems or known errors that the change has resolved). Clearly, for major changes there will be more customer and stakeholder input throughout the entire process.

The evaluation should also include any incidents arising as a result of the change (if they are known at this stage). If the change is part of a service managed by an external provider, details of any contractual service targets will be required (e.g. 'There will be no priority 1 incidents during first week after implementation.')

A change review, e.g. post-implementation review (PIR), should be carried out to confirm that the change has met its objectives, that the initiator and stakeholders are happy with the results and that there have been no unexpected side-effects. Lessons learned should be fed back into future changes. Small organizations may opt to use spot checking of changes rather than large-scale PIR; in larger organizations, sampling will have a value when there are many similar changes taking place.

There is a significantly different approach and profile between:

■ The review of a service change – immediately visible to the customer and scheduled for discussion at the next service level management review meeting
■ An infrastructure change – concerned with **how** IT delivers rather than **what** IT delivers, which will be (almost) invisible to the customer.

Change management must review new or changed services after a predefined period has elapsed. This process will involve CAB members, since change reviews are a standard CAB agenda item. If a formal change evaluation has taken place, the evaluation report will be a major input to this review. The purpose of such reviews is to establish whether:

■ The change has had the desired effect and met its objectives
■ Users, customers and other stakeholders are content with the results (or whether shortcomings have been identified)

■ There are unexpected or undesirable side-effects to functionality, service levels, warranties, e.g. availability, capacity, security, performance and costs
■ The resources used to implement the change were as planned
■ The deployment plan worked correctly (so include comments from the implementers)
■ The change was implemented on time and to cost
■ The remediation plan functioned correctly, if needed.

Any problems and discrepancies should be fed back to CAB members (where they have been consulted or where a committee was convened), other change authorities (if the change authority was not a CAB), impact assessors, product authorities and release authorities, so as to improve the processes for the future.

Where a change has not achieved its objectives, change management (or the change authority) should decide what follow-up action is required, which could involve raising a revised RFC. If the review is satisfactory or the original change is abandoned (e.g. the circumstances that required the change are no longer current and the requirement disappears), the change should be formally closed in the logging system.

4.2.5.10 Change advisory board

A change advisory board (CAB) is a body that exists to support the authorization of changes and to assist change management in the assessment, prioritization and scheduling of changes. A CAB is often the change authority for one or more change categories, but in some organizations the CAB just plays an advisory role. In a large organization there may be many different CABs with a global CAB that is responsible for the most significant changes and other CABs supporting different business units, geographies or technologies. It is important that each CAB has full visibility of all changes that could have an impact on the services and configuration items within its control. For each CAB meeting, members should be chosen who are capable of ensuring that all changes within the scope of the CAB are adequately assessed from both a business and a technical viewpoint.

A CAB may be asked to consider and recommend the adoption or rejection of changes appropriate for higher-level authorization, and then recommendations will be submitted to the appropriate change authority.

To achieve this, the CAB needs to include people with a clear understanding across the whole range of stakeholder needs. Some of these may be permanent members of the CAB, others will be invited to participate when they are needed because of the particular changes that are being discussed. The change manager will normally chair the CAB, and potential members include:

■ Customer(s)
■ User manager(s)
■ User group representative(s)
■ Business relationship managers
■ Service owners
■ Applications developers/maintainers
■ Specialists and/or technical consultants
■ Services and operations staff, e.g. service desk, test management, IT service continuity management, information security management, capacity management
■ Facilities/office services staff (where changes may affect moves/accommodation and vice versa)
■ Contractors' or third parties' representatives, e.g. in outsourcing situations
■ Other parties as applicable to specific circumstances (e.g. police if traffic disruptions are likely, marketing if public products could be affected).

It is important to emphasize that a CAB:

■ Will be composed of different stakeholders depending on the changes being considered
■ May vary considerably in makeup, even across the range of a single meeting
■ Should involve suppliers when that would be useful, for example:
  ● The external service provider if a significant part of the service is outsourced
  ● The hardware service provider when considering major firmware upgrades
■ Should reflect both users' and customers' views
■ Is likely to include the problem manager and service level manager and customer relations staff for at least part of the time.

When the need for emergency change arises, i.e. there may not be time to convene the full CAB, it is necessary to identify a smaller organization with authority to make emergency decisions. This body is an emergency change advisory board (ECAB) – see section 4.2.5.11. Change procedures should specify how the composition of the CAB and ECAB will be determined in each instance, based on the criteria listed above and any other criteria that may be appropriate to the business. This is intended to ensure that the composition of the CAB will be flexible in order to represent business interests properly when major changes are proposed. It will also ensure that the composition of the ECAB will provide the ability, both from a business perspective and from a technical standpoint, to make appropriate decisions in any conceivable eventuality.

A practical tip worth bearing in mind is that a CAB should have stated and agreed evaluation criteria. This will assist in the change assessment activities, acting as a template or framework by which members can assess each change.

CAB meetings
Many organizations run CABs electronically without frequent face-to-face meetings. There are benefits and challenges from such an approach. Much of the assessment and referral activities can be handled electronically via support tools or email. In complex, high-risk or high-impact cases, formal CAB meetings may be necessary.

Electronic communications are more convenient time-wise for CAB members but also highly inefficient when questions or concerns are raised such that many discussions go back and forth. A face-to-face meeting is generally more efficient but poses scheduling and time conflicts among CAB members and may also result in significant travel and staff costs for widely dispersed organizations.

Practical experience shows that regular meetings combined with electronic automation is a viable approach for many organizations, enabling the face-to-face CAB meetings to focus on understanding and evaluating difficult decisions. It can be beneficial to schedule regular face-to-face CAB meetings, especially when major projects are due to deliver releases. The meetings can then be used to provide a formal review and sign-off of authorized changes, a review of outstanding changes, and, of course, to discuss any impending major changes. Where meetings are appropriate, they should have a standard agenda.

A standard CAB agenda should include:

- Change proposals that have been received from service portfolio management
- RFCs to be assessed by CAB members – in structured and priority order
- RFCs that have been assessed by CAB members
- Change reviews
- Outstanding changes and changes in progress
- Evaluation reports and interim evaluation reports received from the change evaluation process
- Scheduling of changes and update of change schedule and PSO
- Review of unauthorized changes detected through service asset and configuration management, to understand underlying issues and take corrective action
- Failed changes, unauthorized, backed-out changes, or changes applied without reference to the CAB from incident management, problem management or change management
- Change management wins/accomplishments for the period under discussion, i.e. a review of the business benefits accrued by way of the change management process
- The change management process, including any amendments made to it during the period under discussion, as well as proposed changes
- Advance notice of RFCs expected for review at the next CAB.

CAB meetings represent a potentially large overhead on the time of members. Therefore, all change proposals and RFCs, together with evaluation reports, the change schedule and PSO, should be circulated in advance and flexibility allowed to CAB members on whether to attend in person, to send a deputy or to send any comments. Relevant papers should be circulated in advance to allow CAB members (and others who are required by change management or CAB members) to conduct impact and resource assessments.

In some circumstances it will be desirable to discuss RFCs at one CAB meeting for more detailed explanation or clarification (before CAB members take the papers away for consideration) in time for

a later meeting. A 'walkthrough' of major changes may be included at a CAB meeting before formal submission of the RFC.

CAB members should come to meetings prepared and empowered to express views and make decisions on behalf of the area they represent in respect of the submitted RFCs, based on prior assessment of the RFCs.

The CAB should be informed of any emergency changes or changes that have been implemented as a workaround to incidents and should be given the opportunity to recommend follow-up action.

Note that a CAB may be an advisory body only, depending on how the organization has assigned change authority. If the CAB cannot agree to a recommendation, the final decision on whether to authorize changes, and commit to the expense involved, is the responsibility of management (normally the director of IT or the services director, service owner or change manager as their delegated representative).

4.2.5.11 Emergency changes

Emergency changes are sometimes required and should be designed carefully and tested as much as possible before use, or the impact of the emergency change may be greater than the original incident. Details of emergency changes may be documented retrospectively.

The number of emergency changes proposed should be kept to an absolute minimum, because they are generally more disruptive and prone to failure. All changes likely to be required should, in general, be foreseen and planned, bearing in mind the availability of resources to build and test the changes. Nevertheless, occasions will occur when emergency changes are essential and so procedures should be devised to deal with them quickly, without sacrificing normal management controls.

The emergency change procedure is reserved for changes intended to repair an error in an IT service that is negatively impacting the business to a high degree. Changes intended to introduce immediately required business improvements are handled as normal changes, assessed as having the highest urgency. If a change is needed urgently (because of poor planning or sudden changes in business requirements) this should be treated as a normal change but given the highest priority.

Emergency change authorization

Defined authorization levels will exist for an emergency change, and the levels of delegated authority must be clearly documented and understood. In an emergency situation it may not be possible to convene a full CAB meeting. Where CAB authorization is required, this will be provided by the emergency CAB (ECAB).

Not all emergency changes will require the ECAB involvement; many may be predictable both in occurrence and resolution and well-understood changes available with authority delegated, e.g. to service operation functions who will action, document and report on the emergency change. For example, repair or replacement of server hardware may require a small change in the server revision or configuration that can be authorized by operational staff.

It is important that any decision to authorize an emergency change is documented to ensure that formal agreement from appropriate management has been received, and to provide proper records for audits of the process.

Emergency change building, testing and implementation

Authorized changes are allocated to the relevant technical group for building. Where timescales demand it, change management, in collaboration with the appropriate technical manager, ensures that sufficient staff and resources (e.g. machine time) are available to do this work. Procedures and agreements – approved and supported by management – must be in place to allow for this. Remediation must also be addressed.

The emergency change should be tested as fully as possible. Completely untested changes should not be implemented if this is at all avoidable. If a change goes wrong, the cost is usually greater than that of adequate testing. Consideration should be given to how much it would cost to test all changes fully against the cost of the change failing, factored by the anticipated likelihood of its failure.

This means that the less a change is considered likely to fail, the more reasonable it may be to reduce the degree of testing in an emergency. (Remember that there is still merit in testing even after a change has gone live.) When only limited testing is possible – and presuming that parallel

development of more robust versions continues alongside the emergency change – then testing should be targeted towards:

- Aspects of the service that will be used immediately (e.g. daily entry features, not end-of-month routines)
- Elements that would cause most short-term inconvenience.

The business should be made aware of associated risks and be responsible for ultimately accepting or rejecting the change based on the information presented.

Change management will give as much advance warning as possible to the service desk and other stakeholders, and arrange for adequate technical presence to be available, to support service operation.

If a change, once implemented, fails to rectify the urgent outstanding error, there may need to be iterative attempts at fixes. Change management should take responsibility at this point to ensure that business needs remain the primary concern and that each iteration is controlled in the manner described in this section. Change management should ensure that ineffective changes are swiftly backed out.

If too many attempts at an emergency change are ineffective, the following questions should be asked:

- Has the error been correctly identified, analysed and diagnosed?
- Has the proposed resolution been adequately tested?
- Has the solution been correctly implemented?

In such circumstances, it may be better to provide a partial service – with some user facilities withdrawn – in order to allow the change to be thoroughly tested, or perhaps to suspend the service temporarily and then implement the change.

Emergency change documentation

It may not be possible to update all change records at the time that urgent actions are being completed (e.g. during overnight or weekend working). It is, however, essential that temporary records are made during such periods, and that all records are completed retrospectively, at the earliest possible opportunity. An agreed time for completion of these updates should be documented when the change is authorized.

IT operations management, technical management and application management staff may have delegated authority to circumvent certain types of incident (e.g. hardware failure) without prior authorization by change management. Such circumventions should be limited to actions that do not change the specification of service assets and that do not attempt to correct software errors. The preferred methods for circumventing incidents caused by software errors should be to revert to the previous trusted state or version, as relevant, rather than attempting an unplanned and potentially dangerous change. Change authorization is still a prerequisite.

Effectively, the emergency change procedure will follow the normal change procedure except that:

- Authorization will be given by the ECAB rather than waiting for a CAB meeting
- Testing may be reduced, or in extreme cases forgone completely, if this is considered a necessary risk to deliver the change immediately
- Documentation, e.g. updating the change record and configuration data, may be deferred, typically until normal working hours.

4.2.6 Triggers, inputs, outputs and interfaces

4.2.6.1 Triggers

Requests for change can be triggered throughout the service lifecycle and at the interfaces with other organizations, e.g. customers and suppliers. There will also be other stakeholders such as partners who may be involved with the change management processes.

Typical examples of types of change that trigger the change management process are described below.

Strategic changes

Service strategies require changes to be implemented to achieve specific objectives while minimizing costs and risks. There are no cost-free and risk-free strategic plans or initiatives. There are always costs and risks associated with decisions such as introducing new services, entering

new market spaces and serving new customers. The following are examples of programmes and initiatives that implement strategic changes:

- Legal/regulatory change
- Organizational change
- Policy and standards change
- Change after analysing business, customer and user activity patterns
- Addition of new service to the market space
- Updates to the service portfolio, customer portfolio or customer agreement portfolio
- Change of sourcing model
- Technology innovation.

Change to one or more services

Changes to the planned services (in the service portfolio) and changes to the services in the service catalogue will trigger the change management process. These include changes to:

- Service catalogue
- Service package
- Service definition and characteristics
- Release package
- Capacity and resource requirements
- Service level requirements
- Warranties
- Utilities
- Cost of utilization
- Service assets
- Acceptance criteria
- Predicted quality of service
- Predicted performance
- Predicted value
- Organizational design
- Stakeholder and communications plans
- Physical change in the environment, e.g. building
- Measurement system
- Plans, e.g. capacity, ITSCM, change, transition, test, and release and deployment plans
- Decommission/retire services
- Procedures, manuals, service desk scripts.

Operational change

It is important to know the distinction between different types of requests that will be initiated by users. These types of request will depend on the nature of the organization and services and may include requests such as password reset, access request or request to move an IT asset. These types of change will often be managed as standard changes by the request fulfilment process.

Service operation functions will also implement corrective and preventative changes via the normal change procedure and the standard change procedure. These should be managed through change management, for example restarting an application, which may impact a shared service.

Changes to deliver continual improvement

When CSI determines that an improvement to a service is warranted, an RFC should be submitted to change management. Changes such as changes to processes can have an effect on service provision and may also affect other CSI initiatives.

Some strategy and service changes will be initiated by CSI.

4.2.6.2 Inputs
Changes may be submitted as an RFC, often with an associated change proposal that provides inputs from the service strategy stage of the service lifecycle. The inputs include:

- Policy and strategy for change and release
- Request for change
- Change proposal
- Plans – change, transition, release, test, evaluation and remediation
- Current change schedule and PSO
- Evaluation reports and interim evaluation reports
- Current assets or configuration items, e.g. baseline, service package, release package
- As-planned configuration baseline
- Test results, test report and evaluation report.

4.2.6.3 Outputs
Outputs from the process will be:

- Rejected and cancelled RFCs
- Authorized changes
- Authorized change proposals
- Change to the services, service or infrastructure resulting from authorized changes
- New, changed or disposed configuration items, e.g. baseline, service package, release package
- Revised change schedule
- Revised PSO

- Authorized change plans
- Change decisions and actions
- Change documents and records
- Change management reports.

4.2.6.4 Interfaces
Change management must work with transition planning and support to ensure that there is a coordinated overall approach to managing service transitions.

In order to be able to define clear boundaries, dependencies and rules, change management and release and deployment management should be integrated with processes used for organizational programmes or projects, with supplier management and also with suppliers' processes and procedures. There will be occasions when a proposed change will potentially have a wider impact on other parts of the organization (e.g. facilities or business operations), or vice versa, and the change management process must interface appropriately with other processes involved.

The change management process must be tightly integrated with change evaluation. There should be clear agreement on which types of change will be subject to formal change evaluation, and the time required for this evaluation must be included in the overall planning for the change. Change management provides the trigger for change evaluation, and the evaluation report must be delivered to change management in time for the CAB (or other change authority) to use it to assist in their decision-making.

Integration with business change processes

Where appropriate, change management should be involved with business programme and business project management teams to ensure that change issues, aims, impacts and developments are exchanged and cascaded throughout the organization where applicable. This means that changes to any business or project deliverables that do not impact services or service components may be subject to business or project change management procedures rather than the IT change management procedures. However, care must be taken to ensure that changes to service configuration baselines and releases do follow the change management process. The change management team will, however, be expected to liaise closely with projects to ensure smooth implementation and consistency within the changing management environments.

The service portfolio management process will submit change proposals to change management before chartering new or changed services, in order to ensure that potential conflicts for resources or other issues are identified.

Programme and project management

Programme and project management (usually based on PRINCE2 or PMBOK) must work in partnership to align all the processes and people involved in service change initiatives. Close alignment between change management and programme and project management is essential to ensure that the change schedule is effective and that all changes are well managed. Change management representatives may attend relevant project or programme meetings, especially at the initiation stages of projects or programmes, to identify potential risks to IT services and other configuration items.

For outsourced services, a key component is how deeply change processes and tools are embedded into the supplier organization (or vice versa) and where the release veto takes place. If the supplier has responsibility for the availability of the operational service, conflicts can arise.

Organizational and stakeholder change management

Organizational and stakeholder change management is discussed in Chapter 5.

In some organizations there is a separate function that manages organizational changes; in others this aspect of change management may be carried out within the IT organization. It is, however, always essential that organizational aspects of change management are properly considered and that the change management process has appropriate interfaces with the people carrying out this work.

Sourcing and partnering

Sourcing and partnering relationships cover internal and external vendors and suppliers who are providing a new or existing service to the organization. Effective change management practices and principles must be put into place to manage these relationships effectively to ensure

smooth delivery of service. Effort also should be put into finding out how well the partners themselves manage change, and care must be taken to choose partner and sourcing relationships accordingly.

Sourcing and partnering arrangements should clearly define the level of autonomy a partner may have in effecting change within their service domain without reference to the overall service provider.

It is important to ensure that service providers (whether outsourced or insourced) provide the change management personnel and processes that match the needs of the business and customers. Some organizations in outsourcing situations refer RFCs to their suppliers for estimates prior to authorization of changes. For further information, refer to guidance in *ITIL Service Design* on supplier management.

4.2.6.5 Interfaces within service management

All service management processes may require change management, for example to implement process improvements. Many service management processes will also be involved in the impact assessment and implementation of service changes, as discussed below.

Service asset and configuration management

The configuration management system provides reliable, quick and easy access to accurate configuration information to enable stakeholders and staff to assess the impact of proposed changes and to track change work flow. This information enables the correct CI versions to be released to the appropriate party or into the correct environment. As changes are implemented, the configuration management information is updated.

The CMS may also identify related CIs that will be affected by the change, but not included in the original request, or similar CIs that would benefit from similar changes.

An overview of how the change management and service asset and configuration management processes work together for an individual change is shown in Figure 4.6.

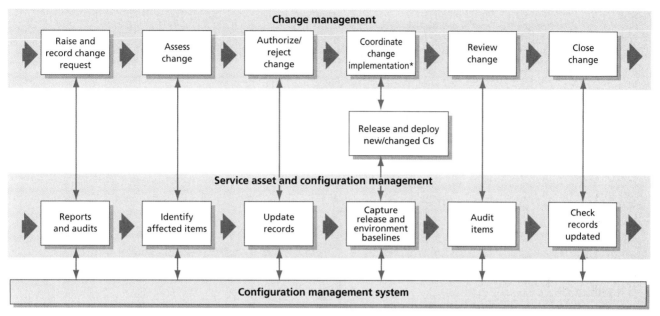

* Includes build and test where applicable

Figure 4.6 Interfaces between change management and service asset and configuration management

Problem management

Problem management is another key process, as changes are often required to implement workarounds and to fix known errors. Problem management is one of the major sources of RFCs and is also often a major contributor to CAB discussion.

IT service continuity management

IT service continuity management has many procedures and plans, which should be updated via change management to ensure that they are accurate and up to date, and that stakeholders are aware of changes.

Every change should be assessed for its impact on IT service continuity arrangements. For a standard change this will be done at the time the change model is authorized; for normal and emergency changes the assessment will be done as part of change assessment.

Information security management

Information security management interfaces with change management, since changes required by security will be implemented through the change management process and security will be a key contributor to CAB discussion on many services. Every significant change will be assessed for its potential impact on information security management.

Capacity management and demand management

Capacity management and demand management are critical aspects of change management. Poorly managed demand is a source of cost and risk for service providers because there is always a level of uncertainty associated with the demand for services. Capacity management has an important role in assessing proposed changes – not only the individual changes but the total impact of changes on service capacity. Changes arising from capacity management, including those set out in the capacity plan, will be initiated as RFCs through the change process.

Service portfolio management

The service portfolio management process prioritizes and charters strategic changes, and submits change proposals for these. Change proposals will be a significant input to long-term planning for the change schedule, and will also be a key input to help change management review and authorize related RFCs.

Some change requests will require analysis by the service portfolio management process, potentially adding to the service pipeline. Each organization should define criteria for deciding whether these requests are managed as part of the change management process or are passed to service portfolio management.

4.2.7 Information management

All change requests must be associated with services and other CIs. This means that either they must be included within the CMS or a mechanism must be provided to enable cross referencing and searching changes related to CIs. It is very common for a single tool to be used for managing incidents, problems and changes, as well as the CMS, and this kind of tool can help to improve the efficiency of the processes.

It is very important to be able to correlate changes with incidents and to review the history of changes to any CI as part of incident or problem management. This requires access to historical change information, which should be made available for searches.

Change management must have access to the CMS and to information and documents within the SKMS in order to plan and manage changes, to identify stakeholders in any change, and to predict the potential impact of changes.

4.2.8 Critical success factors and key performance indicators

All KPIs should be SMART – Specific, Measurable, Achievable, Relevant and Time-bound. While it is relatively easy to count the number of incidents that eventually generate changes, it is infinitely more valuable to look at the underlying cause of such changes and to identify trends. It is better still to be able to measure the impact of changes and to demonstrate reduced disruption over time because of the introduction of change management, and to measure the speed and effectiveness with which the service provider responds to identified business needs.

Measures taken should be linked to business goals wherever practical – and to cost, service availability and reliability. Any predictions should be compared with actual measurements.

The following list includes some sample CSFs for change management. Each organization should identify appropriate CSFs based on its objectives for the process. Each sample CSF is followed by a small number of typical KPIs that support the CSF. These KPIs should not be adopted without careful consideration. Each organization should develop KPIs that are appropriate for its level of maturity, its CSFs and its particular circumstances. Achievement against KPIs should be monitored and

used to identify opportunities for improvement, which should be logged in the CSI register for evaluation and possible implementation.

- ■ **CSF** Responding to business and IT requests for change that will align the services with the business needs while maximizing value
  - ● **KPI** Increase in the percentage of changes that meet the customer's agreed requirements, e.g. quality/cost/time
  - ● **KPI** The benefits of change (expressed as 'value of improvements made' + 'negative impacts prevented or terminated') exceed the costs of change
  - ● **KPI** Reduction in the backlog of change requests
  - ● **KPI** Average time to implement meets SLA targets, based on urgency/priority/change type
  - ● **KPI** Increase in accuracy of predictions for time, quality, cost, risk, resource and commercial impact
  - ● **KPI** Increase in scores in survey of stakeholder satisfaction for the change management process
- ■ **CSF** Optimizing overall business risk
  - ● **KPI** Reduction in the number of disruptions to services, defects and re-work caused by inaccurate specification, poor or incomplete impact assessment
  - ● **KPI** Reduction in the percentage of changes that are categorized as emergency changes
  - ● **KPI** Increase in change success rate (percentage of changes deemed successful at review/number of changes authorized)
  - ● **KPI** Reduction in the number of changes where remediation is invoked
  - ● **KPI** Reduction in the number of failed changes
  - ● **KPI** Reduction in the number of unauthorized changes identified
  - ● **KPI** Reduction in the number of incidents attributed to changes
- ■ **CSF** Ensuring that all changes to configuration items are well managed and recorded in the configuration management system
  - ● **KPI** Reduction in the number and percentage of changes with incomplete change specifications

- **KPI** Reduction in the number and percentage of changes with incomplete impact assessments
- **KPI** Reduction in number of audit compliance issues for the change management process
- **KPI** Reduction in number and percentage of discrepancies found by service asset and configuration management verification and audit.

4.2.9 Challenges and risks

4.2.9.1 Challenges

The major challenge for change management is ensuring that every change is recorded and managed. Regular communication of the scope and value of change management will help to ensure that IT staff understand the scope and value of change management and do not try to circumvent the process. One very important way to help manage this challenge is to ensure that there is active and visible sponsorship for change management from executives and senior management.

To gain support from customers, users and IT staff, the change management process must be seen to facilitate change, rather than to introduce delays. A change management process that is regarded as bureaucratic and time-wasting will not be valued. The challenge for change management is to make sure that it is seen to add value by helping changes happen faster and with higher success rates.

In some organizations change management has been implemented as an operational change authorization process. It can be a challenge to migrate to a true change management process that becomes involved early enough in the service lifecycle, includes assessment of benefits and costs, and helps to plan and manage changes.

In large organizations there can be a significant challenge to agree and document the many levels of change authority that are needed to manage change effectively and to communicate effectively between these change authorities.

4.2.9.2 Risks

Risks to change management include:

- Lack of commitment to the change management process by the business, and lack of business sponsorship
- Lack of commitment to the change management process by IT management, and lack of IT management sponsorship
- Lack of commitment to the change management process by IT staff
- Implementation of changes without the use of change management
- Change assessment being reduced to box ticking, without real consideration of the risks, costs and benefits
- Introduction of delays to change implementation without adding sufficient value
- Insufficient time being allowed for proper assessment of changes, and pressure from projects or the business to expedite decisions
- Insufficient time allowed for implementation of changes, and attempts to fit too many changes into a change window
- Insufficient resources for assessment, planning and implementation of the number of changes required by the business
- Lack of clarity on how change management should interact with other service management processes, such as release and deployment management or service asset and configuration management
- Lack of clarity on how change management should interact with project management or service design activities
- Excessively bureaucratic change management processes that introduce excessive delay to required changes.

4.3 SERVICE ASSET AND CONFIGURATION MANAGEMENT

This section addresses the process of service asset and configuration management (SACM) within IT service management. No organization can be fully efficient or effective unless it manages its assets well, particularly those assets that are vital to the running of the customer's or organization's business.

4.3.1 Purpose and objectives

The purpose of the SACM process is to ensure that the assets required to deliver services are properly controlled, and that accurate and reliable information about those assets is available when and where it is needed. This information includes details of how the assets have been configured and the relationships between assets.

The objectives of SACM are to:

- Ensure that assets under the control of the IT organization are identified, controlled and properly cared for throughout their lifecycle.
- Identify, control, record, report, audit and verify services and other configuration items (CIs), including versions, baselines, constituent components, their attributes and relationships.
- Account for, manage and protect the integrity of CIs through the service lifecycle by working with change management to ensure that only authorized components are used and only authorized changes are made.
- Ensure the integrity of CIs and configurations required to control the services by establishing and maintaining an accurate and complete configuration management system (CMS).
- Maintain accurate configuration information on the historical, planned and current state of services and other CIs.
- Support efficient and effective service management processes by providing accurate configuration information to enable people to make decisions at the right time – for example, to authorize changes and releases, or to resolve incidents and problems.

4.3.2 Scope

Service assets that need to be managed in order to deliver services are known as configuration items (CIs). Other service assets may be required to deliver the service, but if they cannot be individually managed then they are not configuration items. Every CI is a service asset, but many service assets are not CIs. For example, a server will be both a CI and an asset; the knowledge used by an experienced service desk person to manage incidents is an important asset but is not a CI. Also, information that is stored on the server but is not under the control of change management may be a very valuable asset, but it is not a configuration item. It is important to note that many virtual assets, such as a virtual servers or networks, may be CIs and require the same management control as physical assets.

The scope of SACM includes management of the complete lifecycle of every CI.

Service asset and configuration management ensures that CIs are identified, baselined and maintained and that changes to them are controlled. It also ensures that releases into controlled environments and operational use are done on the basis of formal authorization. It provides a configuration model of the services and service assets by recording the relationships between configuration items. SACM may cover non-IT assets, work products used to develop the services and CIs required to support the service that would not be classified as assets by other parts of the business.

The scope includes interfaces to internal and external service providers where there are assets and configuration items that need to be controlled, e.g. shared assets.

Most organizations have a process that tracks and reports the value and ownership of fixed assets throughout their lifecycle. This process is usually called *fixed asset management* or *financial asset management*. Fixed asset management maintains an asset register, which records financial information about all of the organization's fixed assets. Fixed asset management is not usually under the control of the same business unit as the IT services, but the SACM process must provide proper care for the fixed assets under the control of IT, and there must be well-defined interfaces between SACM and fixed asset management. Data from the asset register may be integrated with the configuration management system to provide a more complete view of the CIs. See section 4.3.4.4 for more information about asset management.

4.3.3 Value to business

Optimizing the performance of service assets and configurations improves the overall service performance and optimizes the costs and risks caused by poorly managed assets, e.g. service outages, fines, correct licence fees and failed audits.

SACM provides visibility of accurate representations of a service, release or environment that enables:

- IT staff to understand the configuration and relationships of services and the configuration items that provide them
- Better forecasting and planning of changes

- Successful assessment, planning and delivery of changes and releases
- Resolution of incidents and problems within the service level targets
- Delivery of service levels and warranties
- Better adherence to standards, legal and regulatory obligations (fewer non-conformances)
- More business opportunities as the service provider is able to demonstrate control of assets and services
- Traceability of changes from requirements
- The ability to identify the costs of a service
- Reduced cost and time to discover configuration information when it is needed
- Proper stewardship of fixed assets that are under the control of the service provider.

4.3.4 Policies, principles and basic concepts

In distributed environments and shared services, individual service components exist within many different services and configuration structures. For example, a person may use a desktop computer that is on the network for a building but may be running a central financial system that is linked to a database on the other side of the world. A change to the network or the financial system may have an impact on this person and the business process they support. In web-based services, there may be data feeds and interfaces from and to services owned by other organizations. Changes to these interfaces need to be managed and it is important to identify interfaces such as data feeds and the owner/custodian of these. Changes to any interface items need to be managed through change management. Similarly, many services may run on different virtual servers that are all hosted on the same physical computer. Changes to the physical server could impact all of these services.

4.3.4.1 Service asset and configuration management policies

The first step is to develop and maintain the SACM policies that set the objectives, scope, principles and critical success factors (CSFs) for whatever is to be achieved by the process. These policies are often considered with the change management and release and deployment management policies because they are closely related. The policies will be based on the organization's business drivers, contractual and service management requirements and on compliance to applicable laws, regulations and standards.

Asset policies may be applicable for specific asset types or services, e.g. desktop systems.

There are significant cost and resource implications in implementing SACM, and therefore strategic decisions need to be made about the priorities to be addressed. Many IT service providers focus initially on the basic IT assets (hardware and software) and the services and assets that are business critical or covered by legal and regulatory compliance, e.g. Sarbanes-Oxley, software licensing.

Service asset and configuration management principles

The main policy sets out the framework and key principles against which assets and configurations are developed and maintained. Typical principles include:

- Ensuring that service asset and configuration management operations costs and resources are commensurate with the potential risks to the services.
- The need to deliver governance requirements, such as software asset management, Sarbanes-Oxley, ISO/IEC 20000, ISO/IEC 38500 or COBIT.
- The need to deliver the capability, resources and warranties as defined by the service level agreements and contracts.
- The requirement for available, reliable and cost-effective services.
- The requirement for clear economic and performance criteria for interventions that reduce costs or optimize service delivery. For example, specifying the age at which PCs should be replaced based on cost of maintenance of older models.
- The application of whole-life cost appraisal methods.
- The transformation from 'find and fix' reactive maintenance to 'predict and prevent' proactive management.
- The requirement to maintain adequate configuration information for internal and external stakeholders.
- The level of control and requirements for traceability and auditability.

- The application of continual improvement methods to optimize the service levels, assets and configurations.
- Provision of accurate configuration information for other business and service management processes.
- Integration of service asset and configuration management with other processes.
- Migration to a common CMS architecture.
- Level of automation to reduce errors and costs.

4.3.4.2 Basic concepts

Service assets, configuration items, configuration records, the CMS and the SKMS

It is important to distinguish between service assets, configuration items and configuration records, as these concepts are often confused:

- A **service asset** is any resource or capability that could contribute to the delivery of a service. Examples of service assets include a virtual server, a physical server, a software licence, a piece of information stored in a service management system, or some knowledge in the head of a senior manager.
- A **configuration item** (CI) is a service asset that needs to be managed in order to deliver an IT service. All CIs are service assets, but many service assets are not configuration items. Examples of configuration items are a server or a software licence. Every CI must be under the control of change management.
- A **configuration record** is a set of attributes and relationships about a CI. Configuration records are stored in a configuration management database (CMDB) and managed with a configuration management system (CMS). It is important to note that CIs are not stored in a CMDB; configuration records describe CIs that are stored in the CMDB.
- The **service knowledge management system** (SKMS) is a set of tools and databases that are used to manage knowledge, information and data. Many configuration items are available in the form of knowledge or information, and these are typically stored in the SKMS – for example, a service level agreement, a report template or a definitive media library. The SACM process is not responsible for managing the SKMS. Some items in the SKMS will be

owned and managed by the SACM process, but others will be owned and managed by other processes or people.

More information about the content and relationships between configuration records, CIs, the CMS and the SKMS may be found throughout this publication, especially in sections 4.3.4.3 and 4.7.

The configuration model

Service asset and configuration management delivers a model of the services, assets and the infrastructure by recording the relationships between configuration items as shown in Figure 4.7. This enables other processes to access valuable information, for example:

- To assess the impact and cause of incidents and problems
- To assess the impact of proposed changes
- To plan and design new or changed services
- To plan technology refresh and software upgrades
- To plan releases and migrate service assets to different locations and service centres
- To optimize asset utilization and costs, e.g. consolidate data centres, reduce variations and re-use assets.

The real power of service asset and configuration management's logical model of the services and infrastructure is that it is **the** model – a single common representation used by all parts of IT service management, and beyond, such as HR, finance, supplier and customers.

> **'Danish clock'**
>
> There is a traditional Danish proverb that runs 'When you have a clock in your house, you know the time – once you get two clocks you are no longer certain.' SACM delivers that one clock for all processes and so glues them together, delivers consistency and helps to achieve common purpose (from Hans Dithmar).

The configuration items and related configuration information can be at varying levels of detail, e.g. an overview of all the services or a detailed level to view the specification for a service component.

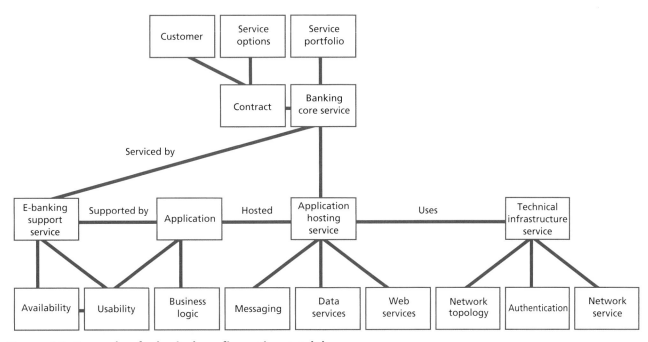

Figure 4.7 Example of a logical configuration model

Service asset and configuration management should be applied at a more detailed level where the service provider requires firm control, traceability and tight coupling of configuration information through the service lifecycle. A general rule for the level of detail required is that you should not include attributes or relationships unless these create more value than it costs to maintain them.

Configuration items

A configuration item (CI) is a service asset that needs to be managed in order to deliver an IT service. Configuration items may vary widely in complexity, size and type, ranging from an entire service or system including all hardware, software, documentation and support staff to a single software module or a minor hardware component. Configuration items may be grouped and managed together: e.g. a set of components may be grouped into a release. Configuration items should be selected using established selection criteria, grouped, classified and identified in such a way that they are manageable and traceable throughout the service lifecycle.

There will be a variety of CIs; the following categories may help to identify them. These are just examples – every organization will decide whether each of these is a configuration item or simply an attribute of a configuration item (or even something that they don't need to manage):

- **Service lifecycle CIs** such as the business case, service management plans, service lifecycle plans, service design package, release and change plans and test plans. They provide a picture of the service provider's services, how these services will be delivered, what benefits are expected, at what cost and when they will be realized.
- **Service CIs**:
  - Service capability assets: management, organization, processes, knowledge, people
  - Service resource assets: financial capital, systems, applications, information, data, infrastructure and facilities, financial capital, people
  - Service model
  - Service package
  - Release package
  - Service acceptance criteria.
- **Organization CIs** – some documentation will define the characteristics of a CI whereas other documentation will be a CI in its own right and need to be controlled, e.g. the organization's business strategy or other policies that are internal to the organization but independent of the service provider. Regulatory or statutory requirements also form external products that need to be tracked, as do products shared among more than one group.

- **Internal CIs** comprising those delivered by individual projects, including tangible (data centre) and intangible assets such as software that are required to deliver and maintain the service and infrastructure.
- **External CIs** such as external customer requirements and agreements, releases from suppliers or sub-contractors and external services.
- **Interface CIs** that are required to deliver the end-to-end service across a service provider interface (SPI), for example an escalation document that specifies how incidents will be transferred between two service providers.

4.3.4.3 Configuration management system

To manage large and complex IT services and infrastructures, service asset and configuration management requires the use of a supporting system known as the configuration management system (CMS). Discussion of tools for supporting a CMS can be found in Chapter 7.

The CMS holds all the information about CIs within the designated scope. Some of these items will have related specifications or files that contain the contents of the item (e.g. software, document or photograph), and these should be stored in the SKMS. For example, a service CI will include the details such as supplier, cost, purchase date and renewal date for licences and maintenance contracts; related documentation such as SLAs and underpinning contracts will be in the SKMS.

Figure 4.8 shows the relationship between configuration records, stored in the CMS, and the actual CIs, which may be stored in the SKMS or may be physical assets outside the SKMS.

Changes to every configuration item must be authorized by change management and all updates must include updates to the relevant configuration records. In some organizations, authority to modify CIs within the SKMS is assigned to configuration librarians, who are also responsible for modifying the configuration records in the CMS. In other organizations there is a separation of duties to ensure that no one person can update both the asset in the SKMS and the corresponding configuration record in the CMS.

The CMS is also used a for wide range of purposes: for example, asset data held in the CMS may be made available to external fixed asset management systems to perform financial reporting outside service asset and configuration management.

The CMS maintains the relationships between all service components and may also include records for related incidents, problems, known errors, changes and releases. The CMS may also link to corporate data about employees, suppliers, locations and business units, customers and users; alternatively, the CMS may hold copies of this information, depending on the capabilities of the tools in use.

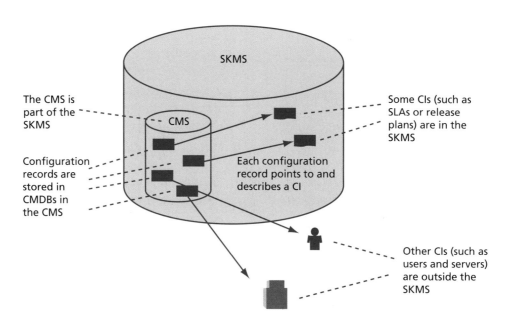

Figure 4.8 Example of relationships between the CMS and SKMS

At the data level, the CMS may include data from configuration records stored in several physical CMDBs, which come together at the information integration layer to form an integrated CMDB. The integrated CMDB may also incorporate information from external data sources such as an HR database or financial database. Since this data is normally owned by other business units, agreements will be needed about what data is to be made available and how this will be accessed and maintained. This arrangement should be formally documented in an OLA. The CMS will provide access to this external data wherever possible rather than duplicating data.

Records used to support service management processes, such as incident records, problem records, change records, release records and known error records, must be associated with the specific configuration items that they relate to. Many implementations include these records within the CMS; however, it is also acceptable practice for them to be included in the SKMS but outside the CMS. What is important is that there are appropriate links in place to enable all of these records to be located and searched as required to support the delivery of services.

Figure 4.9 shows the architectural layers of the CMS. These layers are described in more detail in section 4.7. The presentation layer of the CMS will contain views and dashboards that are required by people who need access to configuration information, for example:

- **Change and release view** Used by personnel responsible for change management and release and deployment management
- **Technical configuration view** Used to support the needs of personnel in technical and application management functions
- **Service desk view** For use by the service desk, for example when logging and managing incidents and service requests
- **Configuration lifecycle view** Used by service asset and configuration management personnel who are responsible for managing the lifecycle of configuration items.

Example of multiple configuration management databases

In the commonly encountered partially outsourced service provider, some elements of service management will be outsourced while others will remain in house, and different elements may be outsourced to different external suppliers. For example, the network and hardware support may be handled by supplier A, environment and facilities management by supplier B, and multiple applications suppliers and incident management handled internally. The service desk will access information to assist them from the CMS, but that system will derive its data input from discrete repositories – each one a CMDB – owned and maintained by the three parties, but working together to supply a single consistent information set. Ideally, the service desk will have access to a single federated CMDB.

Configuration information evolves as the service is developed through the service lifecycle. Often there are separate mechanisms for managing different service lifecycle stages as well as different means of managing different applications and platforms.

The CMS typically contains configuration data and information that combines into an integrated set of views for different stakeholders through the service lifecycle. It therefore needs to be based on appropriate web, reporting and database technologies that provide flexible and powerful visualization and mapping tools, interrogation and reporting facilities. The CMS is part of an SKMS that includes data, information integration, knowledge processing and presentation layers, as shown in Figure 4.9. In practice the service provider may use different tools for different purposes, and the CMS tool will often provide information integration, knowledge processing and presentation independently of other tools used for the SKMS.

Many organizations are already using some elements of SACM, often maintaining records in documents, spreadsheets or local databases, and some of these may be used in the overall CMS.

Automated processes to load and update the CMDBs should be developed where possible so

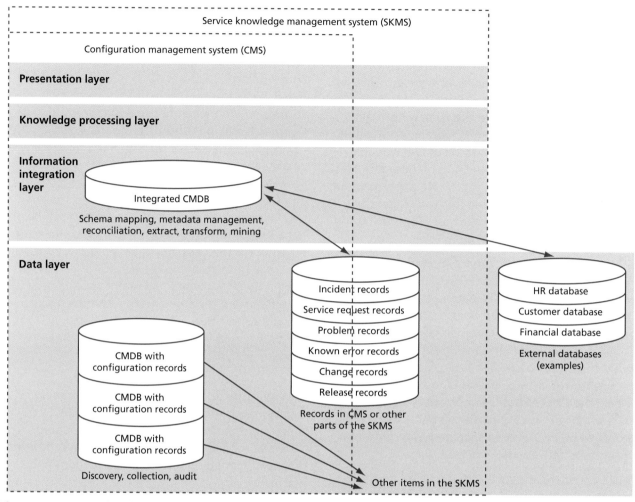

Figure 4.9 Example of the application of the architectural layers of the CMS

as to reduce errors and optimize costs. Discovery tools, inventory and audit tools, enterprise systems and network management tools can be interfaced to the CMS. These tools can be used initially to populate a CMDB, and subsequently to compare the actual 'live' configuration with the information and records stored in the CMS.

Configuration baseline

A configuration baseline is the configuration of a service, product or infrastructure that has been formally reviewed and agreed, which thereafter serves as the basis for further activities and can be changed only through formal change procedures. It captures the structure, contents and details of a configuration and represents a set of configuration items that are related to each other.

Establishing a baseline provides the ability to:

■ Mark a milestone in the development of a service, e.g. service design baseline

■ Build a service component from a defined set of inputs

■ Change or rebuild a specific version at a later date

■ Assemble all relevant components in readiness for a change or release

■ Provide the basis for a configuration audit and back-out, e.g. after a change.

Snapshot

A snapshot is the current state of a configuration item or an environment, e.g. from a discovery tool. This snapshot is recorded in the CMS and remains as a fixed historical record. Sometimes this is referred to as a *footprint*. A snapshot is not necessarily formally reviewed and agreed on – it is just a documentation of a state, which may contain faults and unauthorized CIs. One example is where a snapshot is established after an installation, perhaps using a discovery tool, and later compared to the original configuration baseline.

The snapshot:

- Enables problem management to analyse evidence about a situation pertaining at the time incidents actually occurred
- Facilitates system restore
- Supports security scanning software.

4.3.4.4 Asset management

Fixed assets of an organization are assets which have a financial value, can be used by the organization to help create products or services and have a long-term useful life. For an IT service provider these may include data centres, power distribution and air-handling components, servers, software licences, network components, PCs, data, information etc. Most organizations have a process that manages these assets. This process is usually called fixed asset management or financial asset management. It carries out activities such as:

- Identifying each asset, including unique naming and labels
- Identifying and recording asset owners
- Maintaining an asset register that includes details of all fixed assets
- Understanding the purchase cost, depreciation and net book value of each asset
- Helping to protect the assets from damage, theft etc.
- Carrying out regular audits to ensure the integrity of fixed assets.

Many configuration items that are managed by the service provider are fixed assets of the organization (or of their customer), and the service provider is responsible for protecting these assets in line with overall organizational policies. The service provider may carry out some or all of the following activities, depending on organizational policy and what has been agreed:

- Tracking and reporting CI lifecycle changes, for example when a CI has been received from a supplier or when it has been decommissioned. The service provider should also use this tracking as an opportunity to review maintenance contracts, to ensure that these are aligned with the assets that are in use.
- Providing unique names for assets and applying suitable labels to enable identification and audit.

- Protecting assets to ensure their integrity. For example by providing physical and logical security controls.
- Carrying out regular audits of the fixed assets under their control.

In some organizations the service provider may also carry out some of these activities for assets that are not service assets on behalf of the parent organization. For example while they are labelling or auditing desktop PCs, they may also label or audit other fixed assets such as phones, or office furniture.

Software asset management

Software assets are complex to manage because of the complexity of their lifecycle and because of a number of risks that do not apply to other types of asset, including the risk of:

- Software being used without licences being purchased
- Loss of proof of licences which have been purchased
- Terms and conditions being breached unknowingly
- Purchasing more licences than are needed and not being aware that these are under-utilized.

Software asset management (SAM) is responsible for the management of software, software licences and codes for activating software – whether these are installed on computer systems or held as copies that could be installed. SAM includes management, control and protection of software assets and the risks arising from their use.

The IT service provider must implement appropriate and auditable procedures for SAM. Ideally, these will be compliant with the international standard for SAM, ISO/IEC 19770.

Effective SAM is dependent on use of appropriate tools, including a CMS and a definitive media library (DML).

Secure libraries and secure stores

A secure library is a collection of software, electronic or document CIs of known type and status. Access to items in a secure library is restricted. Libraries are used for controlling and releasing components throughout the service lifecycle, e.g. in design, building, testing, deployment and operation.

A secure store is a location that warehouses IT assets. It is identified within SACM – e.g. secure stores used for desktop deployment. Secure stores play an important role in the provision of security and continuity, maintaining reliable access to equipment of known quality.

The contents of secure stores and secure libraries should be recorded in the CMS, and change management approval is needed to move things into or out of them.

Definitive spares

An area should be set aside for the secure storage of definitive hardware spares. These are spare components and assemblies that are maintained at the same revision level as the systems within the controlled test or live environment. Details of these components, their locations and their respective builds and contents should be comprehensively recorded in the CMS. These can then be used in a controlled manner when needed for additional systems or in the recovery from incidents. Once their (temporary) use has ended, they are returned to the spares store or replacements are obtained.

Definitive spares should be managed in the same way as other fixed assets, including adherence to policy and procedures for procurement, lifecycle management and disposal.

The definitive media library

The definitive media library (DML) is the secure library in which the definitive authorized versions of all media CIs are stored and protected. It stores master copies of versions that have passed quality assurance checks. This library may in reality consist of one or more software libraries or file-storage areas, separate from development, test or live file store areas. It contains the master copies of all controlled software in an organization. The DML should include definitive copies of purchased software (along with licence documents or information), as well as software developed on site. Master copies of controlled documentation for a system are also stored in the DML in electronic form.

The DML will also include a physical store to hold master copies, e.g. a fireproof safe. Only authorized media should be accepted into the DML, strictly controlled by SACM.

The DML is a foundation for release and deployment management (see section 4.4 on the release and deployment management process).

The exact configuration of the DML is defined during the planning activities. The definition includes:

■ Medium, physical location, hardware and software to be used, if kept online – some service asset and configuration management support tools incorporate document or software libraries, which can be regarded as a logical part of a DML
■ Naming conventions for file-store areas and physical media
■ Environments supported, e.g. test and live environments
■ Security arrangements for submitting changes and issuing documentation and software, plus backup and recovery procedures
■ The scope of the DML, e.g. source code, object code from controlled builds and associated documentation
■ Archive and retention periods
■ Capacity plans for the DML and procedures for monitoring growth in size
■ Audit procedures
■ Procedures to ensure that the DML is protected from erroneous or unauthorized change (e.g. entry and exit criteria for items)
■ Procedures to ensure that the DML is backed up and that the contents are available for use in service continuity plans as appropriate.

Electronic assets in the DML are held within the SKMS, and every item in the DML is a CI. Figure 4.10 shows the relationship between the DML and a CMDB in the CMS.

Decommissioning assets

Assets may be decommissioned for a number of reasons, for example:

■ When a service is retired the assets used to deliver that service will no longer be needed
■ A technology refresh may release old assets that have been replaced
■ Hardware failure may result in components, or even entire servers, being replaced and the old hardware being decommissioned
■ Changes in service demand may result in excess capacity and a need to remove components.

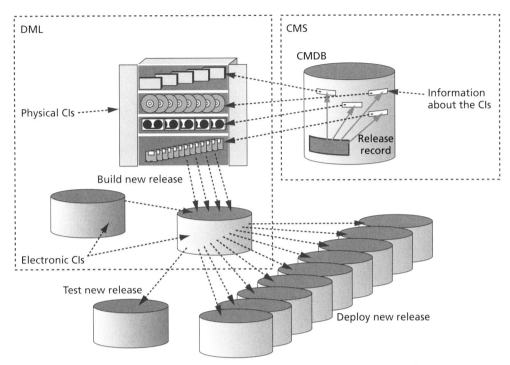

Figure 4.10 The relationship between the definitive media library and the configuration management system

Detail of the steps to be taken when decommissioning assets should be documented in a service design package, in the same way as for any other service transition.

Whatever the reason for the decommissioning, it is important that assets are decommissioned properly, this should include:

- Redeploying, re-using or selling the assets where appropriate, to maximize the value that the organization gets from them and to minimize waste and environmental impact – but note that this must only be done in accordance with any policy or regulatory requirements with a full understanding of the implications for information security.
- Ensuring that assets are disposed of in a way that meets the environmental standards of the organization and any regulatory or legal requirements.
- Ensuring that data stored on decommissioned assets is managed in a way that meets the requirements of the information security policy. This may require data to be deleted or erased, or even destruction of physical assets such as disk drives, depending on the sensitivity and classification of the data.
- Returning leased equipment if appropriate.

- Updating or cancelling maintenance contracts.
- Updating the configuration management system to show the new status of the asset.
- Communicating the new status to the fixed asset management process, to ensure that the asset register is updated if appropriate.

The value of proper decommissioning

A multinational organization had a long-term plan to consolidate more than a hundred in-country data centres to form three regional data centres.

One person was appointed full-time to recover any remaining value from data centres that were no longer in use, by selling air-handling units, leasing the buildings etc. One part of this person's role was to identify every software licence that had been in use in each data centre and was at risk of being lost, and to make these licences available for re-use within the organization. The value of these software licences was much more than the fully loaded cost of the employee.

4.3.5 Process activities, methods and techniques

4.3.5.1 Service asset and configuration management activities

High-level activities for service asset and configuration management are shown in an example of an activity model in Figure 4.11.

The activity model illustrated in Figure 4.11 is often used where there are many parties or suppliers, and activities need to be established to obtain the configuration information and data from third parties.

4.3.5.2 Management and planning

There is no standard template for determining the optimum approach for SACM. The management team should decide what level of service asset and configuration management is required for the selected service or project that is delivering changes and how this level will be achieved. This is documented in a SACM plan. Often there will be a SACM plan for a project, service or groups of services, e.g. network services. These plans define the specific service asset and configuration management activities within the context of the overarching SACM strategy.

Example of service asset and configuration management plan contents

Context and purpose

Scope:

- Applicable services
- Environments and infrastructure
- Geographical locations.

Requirements:

- Link to policy, strategy
- Link to business, service management and contractual requirements
- Summarize requirements for accountability, traceability, auditability
- Link to requirements for the configuration management system (CMS).

Applicable policies and standards

- Policies
- Industry standards, e.g. ISO/IEC 20000, ISO/IEC 19770-1

- Internal standards relevant to SACM, e.g. hardware standards, desktop standards.

Organization for SACM

- Roles and responsibilities
- Change advisory board
- Authorization – for establishing baseline, changes and releases.

SACM system and tools

Selection and application of processes and procedures to implement SACM activities, for example:

- Configuration identification
- Version management
- Interface management
- Supplier management
- Change management
- Release and deployment management
- Build management
- Establishment and maintenance of configuration baselines
- Maintenance of the CMS
- Procurement and retirement of CIs
- Review of the integrity of configurations and the CMS (verification and audit).
- Reference implementation plan, e.g. data migration and loading, training and knowledge transfer plan.

Relationships and interfaces with other processes and groups, for example:

- With fixed asset management
- With projects
- With development and testing
- With customers
- With service provider interfaces (SPI)
- With service operation functions including the service desk.
- Relationship management and control of suppliers and sub-contractors.

4.3.5.3 Configuration identification

When planning configuration identification it is important to:

- Define how the classes and types of assets and configuration items are to be selected, grouped, classified and defined by appropriate

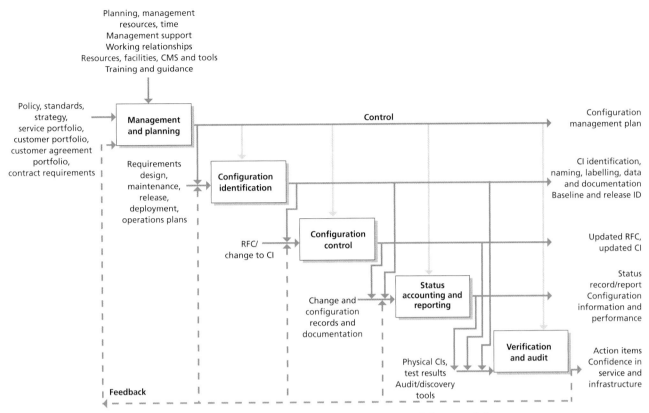

Figure 4.11 Typical service asset and configuration management activity model

characteristics (e.g. warranties for a service), to ensure that they are manageable and traceable throughout their lifecycle.

■ Define the approach to identification, uniquely naming and labelling all the assets or service components of interest across the service lifecycle and the relationships between them.

■ Define the roles and responsibilities of the owner or custodian for a configuration item type at each stage of its lifecycle, e.g. the service owner for a service or release at each stage of the service lifecycle.

The configuration identification process activities should:

■ Define and document criteria for selecting configuration items and the components that compose them.

■ Select the configuration items and their components according to documented criteria.

■ Assign unique identifiers to configuration items.

■ Specify the relevant attributes of each configuration item.

■ Specify when each configuration item is placed under control of service asset and configuration management.

■ Identify the owner responsible for each configuration item.

Configuration structures and the selection of configuration items

The configuration model should describe the relationship and position of configuration items (CIs) in each structure. There should be service configuration structures that identify all the components in a particular service (e.g. the retail service). An important part of SACM is deciding the level at which control is to be exercised, with top-level CIs broken down into components, which are themselves CIs, and so on.

CIs should be selected by applying a top-down approach, considering whether it is sensible to break down a CI into component CIs. A CI can exist as part of any number of different CIs or CI groups at the same time (for instance, a database product may be used by many applications). Relationship links to re-usable and common components of the service should be defined (for instance, a configuration structure for a retail service will use infrastructure CIs such as servers, network and software CIs). The ability to have multiple views through different configuration structures improves accessibility, impact analysis and reporting.

Service asset and configuration management of work products and service components from the service lifecycle may be performed at several levels of granularity. The items placed under SACM will typically include services, service components, release packages and products that are delivered to the customer, designated internal work products, acquired services, products, tools, systems and other items that are used in creating and describing the configurations required to design, transition and operate the service.

Figures 4.12 and 4.13 give examples in schematic representation of how a CI structure for an end-user computing service and a managed virtual system might be broken down.

If configuration information is collected at too low a level, or in too much detail, then the cost of collecting and maintaining this information may be greater than the value it provides. Choosing the right CI level is a matter of achieving a balance between information availability, the right level of control, and the resources and effort needed to support it. Information at a low CI level may not be valuable – for example, although a keyboard is usually exchanged independently, the organization sees it as a consumable so does not store data about it. CI information is valuable only if it facilitates the management of change, the

Factors that influence the recording level of configuration items

The factors that affect choice of the lowest CI level are not just financial. As mentioned above, most organizations do not store data on keyboards, because they consider them consumables to be thrown away when not working, as one would a broken pen. However, some organizations find it worth retaining data on keyboards – for example, in the United Nations, which supports many different languages within its office building, recording the specific language keyboard used is an important factor in speedy incident resolution when keyboards fail, i.e. it is important to know which kind of replacement keyboard to send to any given user.

control of incidents and problems, or the control of assets that can be independently moved, copied or changed.

The organization should plan to review the CI level regularly – to confirm (or otherwise) that information down to a low level is still valuable and useful, and that the handling of changes and problems and the management of assets is not deficient because the CMDB does not go down to a sufficient depth.

Each CI needs to be uniquely identified, whether it is generated inside or outside the organization. The identification should also differentiate between successive versions and should enable the items under control to be unambiguously traceable to their specifications or to equivalent, documented descriptions. Configuration descriptions and data should conform, where possible, to service, product or technology standards. Configuration data should permit forward and backward traceability to other baselined configuration states, where required.

Naming configuration items

Naming conventions should be established and applied to the identification of CIs, configuration documents and changes, as well as to baselines, builds, releases and assemblies.

Individual CIs should be uniquely identifiable by means of the identifier and version. The version identifies an updated instance of what can be regarded as the same CI. More than one version of a CI can coexist at any given time. The naming conventions should be unique and take into account the existing corporate or supplier naming/numbering structures. The naming conventions or information management information should include the management of:

■ Hierarchical relationships between CIs within a configuration structure
■ Hierarchical or subordinate relationships in each CI
■ Relationships between CIs and their associated documents
■ Relationships between CIs and changes
■ Relationships between CIs, incidents, problems and known errors.

SACM should arrange for a naming convention to be established for all documents, e.g. RFCs. Use of document templates is a good method

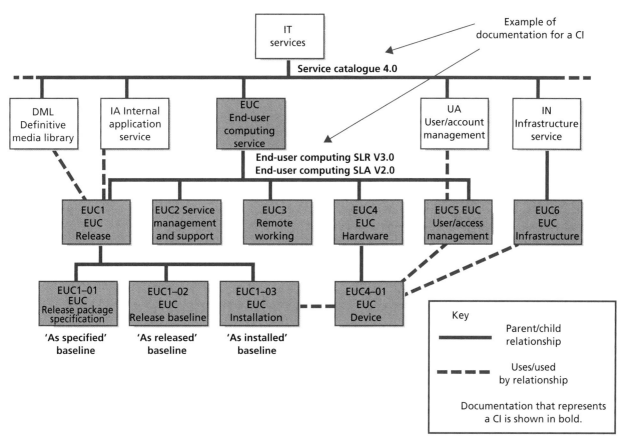

Figure 4.12 Example of a configuration breakdown for an end-user computing service

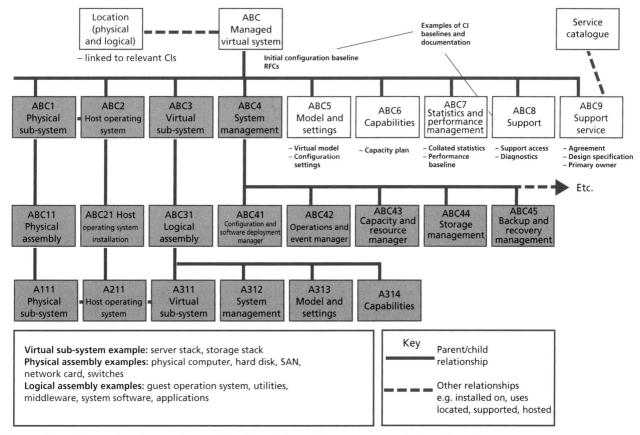

Figure 4.13 Example of a configuration breakdown for a managed virtual system

of standardizing configuration documentation. Without templates there are often far too many documents generated with overlapping content, which can make executing changes extremely difficult.

Each type of template and form should be uniquely identifiable with a version number. A typical method of identification is <Form type>_*nnnn* where *nnnn* is a sequentially assigned number for each new instance of the form.

When the naming convention is being planned, it is very important that sufficient account is taken of possible future growth. Identifiers should be relatively short, but meaningful, and should follow existing conventions wherever possible. For hardware, if the CI naming conventions are not based on suppliers' device names and models, a mechanism should be set up to relate SACM and suppliers' identifiers to one another, for example, for the convenience of procurement staff and hardware engineers. Standard terminology and abbreviations should be used throughout the organization as far as possible (e.g. NYC rather than sometimes NY or N York). Failure to do this will result in an inability to match common incidents, problems etc. Attributes that might change should never be used as a part of CI naming.

Labelling configuration items

All physical device CIs should be labelled with the configuration identifier so that they can be easily identified. Plans should be made to label CIs and to maintain the accuracy of their labels.

Items need to be distinguished by unique, durable identification, e.g. labels or markings that follow relevant standards where appropriate. Physical non-removable asset tags (labels) should be attached to all hardware CIs; cables/lines should be clearly labelled at each end and at any inspection points. It is advisable to use a standard format and colour for all such labels because this makes it easier for users to identify and quote from them (for instance when telephoning the service desk to report a fault). Bar-code-readable labels improve the efficiency of physical audits. There should be documented standards specifying how each type of CI will be labelled; for example if all hardware is labelled in the bottom left-hand corner of the left side it is much quicker and easier to explain to the user where they will find the required information.

It can be cost-effective to combine this activity with labelling of other assets that is carried out as part of the organization's fixed asset management process, for example asset labelling of office furniture or other non-IT assets.

Attributes for configuration items

Attributes describe the characteristics of a CI that are valuable to record and which will support SACM and the ITSM processes it supports.

Relationships show how CIs relate to each other and provide structure to the configuration management system. (For more information, see the section on relationships below.)

The SACM plan references the configuration information and data architecture. This includes the attributes and relationships to be recorded for each type of CI. Every CI must include the following attributes:

- Unique identifier
- CI type.

Other attributes depend on the CI type. Typical attributes include:

- Name/description
- Version (e.g. file, build, baseline, release)
- Supply date
- Licence details, e.g. expiry date
- Power utilization, carbon footprint or other information needed to support the organization's green, IT or sustainability plans
- Status
- Historical data, e.g. audit trail.

These attributes will define specific functional and physical characteristics of each type of CI, e.g. size or capacity, together with any documentation or specifications. In any particular CMS some of these attributes may actually be relationships, depending on implementation details.

Typical relationships include:

- Location
- Owner/custodian
- Supplier/source
- Service(s) supported
- Related document masters
- Related software masters
- Applicable SLA.

In any particular CMS some of these relationships may actually be attributes, depending on implementation details.

Defining configuration documentation

The characteristics of a CI are often contained in documents. For example, the service definition, requirements specification and service level agreement for a service describe the characteristics of a service CI. Many organizations specify mandatory and optional documents that describe a CI and use document templates to ensure that consistent information is entered. Table 4.7 is a RACI (Responsible, Accountable, Consulted, Informed) chart, which illustrates the types of documentation of service assets or configuration items that are the responsibility of different service lifecycle stages and typical documentation. See section 6.5 for more information on RACI charts.

Collecting CI attribute data can facilitate use/re-use/reference to existing documents, data, files, records, spreadsheets etc. This will help users implementing this to determine a good approach to collecting data.

Relationships

Relationships describe how the configuration items work together to deliver the services. These relationships are held in the CMS – this is the major difference between what is recorded in a CMS and what is held in an asset register.

A good starting point to help understand the relationships between CIs is the service model. This is part of the service design package for a new or changed service and shows how service assets interact with customer assets to create value.

The relationships between CIs are maintained so as to provide dependency information. For example:

■ A CI is a part of another CI – e.g. a software module is part of a program; a server is part of a site infrastructure – this is a 'parent–child' relationship.
■ A CI is connected to another CI – e.g. a desktop computer is connected to a LAN.
■ A CI uses another CI – e.g. a program uses a module from another program; a customer-facing service uses an infrastructure server.
■ A CI is installed on another – e.g. MS Project is installed on a desktop PC.

Although a 'child' CI should be 'owned' by one 'parent' CI, it can be 'used by' any number of other CIs. If a standard desktop build is supplied and installed on all PCs within a division or location, then that build, including all the software CIs, will be a CI that is linked by a relationship to the PCs. The software included will be 'part of' the build. This can considerably reduce the number of relationships that are needed compared with when individual software CI relationships are used.

Relationships are also the mechanism for associating change records, incident records, problem records, known errors and release records with the services and IT infrastructure CIs to which they refer. RFCs and change and release records will identify the CIs affected. If one or more of these record types is stored separately from the CMS, then the records must contain the unique name or ID of the associated CI to enable effective location and search of records.

Some of these relationships are shown in Figure 4.12. For example, EUC is the parent CI of EUC1 to EUC5, and EUC1 is in turn the parent of three CIs, EUC1–01 to EUC1–03, shown as the next level in the hierarchy. EUC1 uses the DML and internal application (IA) service.

Wherever possible, information about relationships between CIs should be identified automatically; this reduces the effort needed to maintain the data, as well as increasing the accuracy. It is important that automatically collected data is compared to the desired configuration, rather than simply being recorded and accepted as correct.

Relationships may be one-to-one, one-to-many and many-to-one. Managing portfolios within the CMS provides a good example. The combination of service portfolios and customer portfolios generates the customer agreement portfolio. In other words, every customer agreement is mapped to at least one service and at least one customer.

Types of configuration item

Components should be classified into CI types because this helps to identify and document what is in use, the status of the items and where they are located. Typical CI types include service, hardware, software, documentation and staff.

Table 4.7 Configuration documentation for assets and responsibilities through the service lifecycle

Service lifecycle stage	Examples of service lifecycle assets and CIs impacted	Service strategy	Service design	Service transition	Service operation	Continual service improvement
Service strategy	Portfolios – service contract, customer Service strategy requirements Service lifecycle model	A	C	C	R	C
Service design	Service design package, e.g. service model, contract, supplier's service management plan, process interface definition, customer engagement plan SLA Release policy Release package definition	I	A	C	R	C
Service transition	Service transition model Test plan Controlled environments Build/installation plan Build specification Release plan Deployment plan CMS SKMS Release package Release baseline Release documentation Evaluation report Test report	I	C	A	R	C
Service operation	Service operation model Service support model Service desk User assets User documentation Operations documentation Support documentation	I	C	C	A/R	R
Continual service improvement	CSI register Service improvement plan Service reporting activities	R or C	R or C	R or C	R or C	A

R=Responsible, A=Accountable, C=Consulted, I= Informed

Identification of media libraries

Physical and electronic media libraries should be uniquely identified and recorded in the CMS with the following information:

- Content, location and medium of each library
- Conditions for entering an item, including the minimum status compatible with the contents of the library

- How to protect the libraries from malicious and accidental harm and deterioration, together with effective recovery procedures
- Conditions and access controls for groups or types of person registering, reading, updating, copying, removing and deleting CIs
- Scope of applicability, e.g. applicable from environment 'system test' through to 'operation'.

Identification of configuration baselines

Configuration baselines should be established by formal agreement at specific points in time and used as departure points for the formal control of a configuration. Configuration baselines plus authorized changes to those baselines together constitute the currently approved configuration. Specific examples of baselines that may be identified include:

■ A particular 'standard' CI needed when buying many items of the same type (e.g. desktop computer) over a protracted period; if some are to include additional components (e.g. a DVD writer), this could correspond to 'baseline plus'; if all future desktop computers are to have features then a new baseline is created.
■ An application release and its associated documentation.

Several baselines corresponding to different stages in the life of a 'baselined item' can exist at any given time – for example, the baseline for an application release that is currently live, the one that was last live and has now been archived, the one that will next be installed (subject to change under SACM control) and one or more under test. Furthermore, if (for instance) new software is being introduced gradually regionally, more than one version of a baseline could be 'live' at the same time. It is therefore best to refer to each by a unique version number, rather than 'live', 'next' or 'old'.

By consolidating the evolving configuration states of configuration items to form documented baselines at designated points or times, SACM will be more effective and efficient. Each baseline is a mutually consistent set of CIs that can be declared at key milestones. An example of a baseline is an approved description of a service that includes internally consistent versions of requirements, requirement traceability matrices, design, specific service components and user documentation.

Each baseline forms a frame of reference for the service lifecycle as a whole. Baselines provide the basis for assessing progress and undertaking further work that is internally self-consistent and stable. For example, the service portfolio and the business case for a service should present a consistent and clear definition of what the service is intending to deliver. This may form the 'scope baseline' for the service(s) and give internal and

external parties a clear basis for subsequent analysis and development. An example of the baseline points is shown in Figure 4.14.

Baselines are added to the CMS as they are developed. Changes to baselines and the release of work products built from the CMS are systematically controlled and monitored via the change management process and the configuration control and configuration auditing functions of SACM. In configuration identification, the rationale for each baseline and associated authorizations required to approve the configuration baseline data is defined and recorded.

As a service progresses through the service lifecycle, each baseline provides progressively greater levels of detail regarding the eventual outputs to be delivered. Furthermore, this hierarchy of baselines enables the final outputs to be traced back to the original requirements.

It needs to be kept in mind that earlier baselines may not be totally up to date with changes that have been made later: e.g. 'course corrections' to requirements documentation may be reflected in the release documentation.

Identification of release unit

'Release unit' describes the portion of the service or infrastructure that is normally released as a single entity in accordance with an organization's release policy. The unit may vary, depending on the type(s) or item(s) of software and hardware.

Figure 4.15 gives a simplified example showing an IT infrastructure made up of systems, which are in turn made up of suites, comprising programs, which are made up of modules.

Release information is recorded within the CMS, supporting the release and deployment management process. Releases are uniquely identified according to a scheme defined in the release policy (see section 4.1.4.2). The release identification includes a reference to the CI that it represents and a version number that will often have two or three parts. Examples of release names are:

■ Major releases: Payroll_System v.1, v.2, v.3 etc.
■ Minor releases: Payroll_System v.1.1, v.1.2, v.1.3 etc.
■ Emergency fix releases: Payroll_System v.1.1.1, v.1.1.2, v.1.1.3 etc.

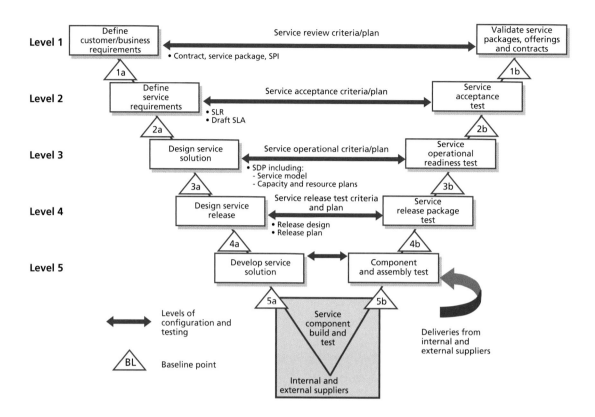

Figure 4.14 Example of service lifecycle configuration levels and baseline points

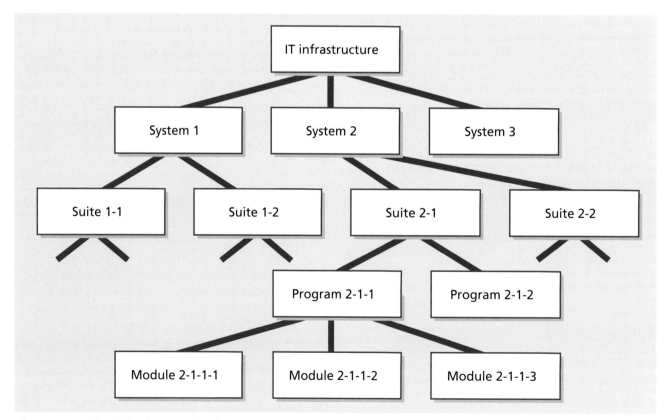

Figure 4.15 Simplified example of an IT infrastructure

4.3.5.4 Configuration control

Configuration control ensures that there are adequate control mechanisms over CIs while maintaining a record of changes to CIs, versions, location and custodianship/ownership. Without control of the physical or electronic assets and components, the configuration data and information there will be a mismatch with the physical world.

No CI should be added, modified, replaced or removed without an appropriate controlling documentation or procedure being followed. Policies and procedures should be in place to cover the following features:

- Licence control, to ensure that the correct number of people are using licences, that there is no unlicensed use and that unused licences are kept to a minimum
- Change management
- Version control of service asset, software and hardware versions, images/builds and releases
- Access control, e.g. to facilities, storage areas and CMS
- Build control, including the use of build specification from the CMS to perform a build
- Promotion, migration of electronic data and information
- Taking a configuration baseline of assets or CIs before performing a release (into system, acceptance test and live) in a manner that can be used for subsequent checking against actual deployment
- Deployment control including distribution
- Installation
- Maintaining the integrity of the DML.

There are many procedures that can change a CI; these should be reviewed and aligned with the CI types where possible as standardization prevents errors. During the planning stage it is important to design an effective configuration control model and implement this in a way that allows staff to easily locate and use the associated training products and procedures.

If many SACM tools are used, there is often a control plan for each tool that is aligned with the overall configuration control model. If configuration data is updated manually, then it

is important that the update uses a documented procedure, supported by checklists where appropriate.

Control should be passed from the project or supplier to the service provider at the scheduled time with accurate configuration information, documentation and records. A comprehensive checklist covering the service provider information requirements, supplier information and organizational information required can be made and signed off. Provisions for conducting SACM need to be established in supplier agreements. Methods to ensure that the configuration data is complete and consistent should be established and maintained. Such a method may include baseline on transition, defined audit policies and audit intervals. It is important that the need for this information and control method is established as early as possible during the development lifecycle and incorporated as a deliverable of the new or changed service.

4.3.5.5 Status accounting and reporting

Each CI will have one or more discrete states through which it can progress. The significance of each state should be defined in terms of what use can be made of the CI in that state. There will typically be a range of states relevant to the individual CIs.

A simple example of a lifecycle is:

- **Development or draft** Denoting that the CI is under development and that no particular reliance should be placed on it
- **Approved** Meaning that the CI may be used as a basis for further work
- **Withdrawn** Meaning that the CI has been withdrawn from use, either because it is no longer fit for purpose or because there is no further use for it.

The method by which CIs move from one state to another should be defined: e.g. an application release may be registered, accepted, installed or withdrawn. An example of a lifecycle for a package application release is shown in Figure 4.16. This will include defining the type of review and authorization required and the authority level necessary to give that authorization. In Figure 4.16 the process that can promote the CI from *accepted* to *installed* is 'release and deployment management'. At each lifecycle status change the

Application release

Figure 4.16 Example of a configuration item lifecycle

CMS should be updated with the reason, date-time stamp and person who made the status change. The planning activities should also establish any attributes that should be updated at each state.

Configuration status accounting and reporting is concerned with ensuring that all configuration data and documentation is recorded as each CI progresses through its lifecycle. It provides the status of the configuration of a service and its environment as the configuration evolves through the service lifecycle.

Status reporting provides the current and historical data concerned with each CI, which in turn enables tracking of changes to CIs and their records (i.e. tracking the status as a CI changes from one state to another, e.g. 'development', 'test', 'live' or 'withdrawn').

The organization should perform configuration status accounting and reporting activities throughout the lifecycle of the service in order to support and enable an efficient SACM process. Typical activities include:

- Maintaining configuration records through the service lifecycle and archiving them according to agreements, relevant legislation, best industry practice or standards such as ISO 9001
- Managing the recording, retrieval and consolidation of the current configuration status and the status of all preceding configurations to confirm information correctness, timeliness, integrity and security
- Making the status of items under SACM available throughout the lifecycle, e.g. to ensure that appropriate access, change, build and release controls (such as build specifications) are followed
- Recording changes to CIs from receipt to disposal
- Ensuring that changes to configuration baselines are properly documented. This can be achieved by consolidating the evolving configuration states of configuration items to form documented baselines at designated times or under defined circumstances.

Records

During the configuration identification and control activities, configuration records will be created. These records allow for visibility and traceability and for the efficient management of the evolving configuration. They typically include details of:

- Service configuration information (such as identification number, title, effective dates, version, status, change history and its inclusion in any baseline)
- The service or product configuration (such as design or build status)
- The status of new configuration information
- Changes implemented and in progress
- Capturing the results from quality assurance tests to update the configuration records.

The evolving service configuration information should be recorded in a manner that identifies the cross-references and interrelationships necessary to provide the required reports.

Service asset and configuration reports

Reports of varying types will be needed for service asset and configuration management purposes. Such reports may cover individual configuration items, a complete service or the full service portfolio. Typical reports include:

- A list of product configuration information included in a specific configuration baseline
- A list of configuration items and their configuration baselines
- Details of the current revision status and change history
- Status reports on changes, waivers and deviations, including unauthorized changes
- Details of the status of delivered and maintained products concerning part and traceability numbers
- Report on unauthorized usage of hardware, software or other CIs

- Unauthorized CIs detected and CIs that have been removed without authorization
- Variations from CMS to physical audit reports.

Status reports of assets for a business unit or software licence holdings are often required by financial management for budgeting, accounting and charging.

4.3.5.6 Verification and audit

The activities include a series of reviews or audits to:

- Ensure that there is conformity between the documented baselines (e.g. agreements, interface control documents) and the actual business environment to which they refer
- Verify the physical existence of CIs in the organization or in the DML and spares stores, the functional and operational characteristics of CIs and to check that the records in the CMS match the physical infrastructure
- Check that release and configuration documentation is present before making a release.

Before a major release or change, an audit of a specific configuration may be required to ensure that the customer's environment matches the CMS. Before acceptance into the live environment, new releases, builds, equipment and standards should be verified against the contracted or specified requirements. There should be a test certificate (or some other relevant document – e.g. change record), which proves that the functional requirements of a new or updated CI have been verified.

Plans should be made for regular configuration audits to check that the CMDB and related configuration information is consistent with the physical state of all CIs, and vice versa. Physical configuration audits should be carried out to verify that the 'as-built' configuration of a CI conforms to its 'as-planned' configuration and its associated documents. Interrogation facilities are required to check that the CMDB and the physical state of CIs are consistent. The audit should follow a documented procedure and be supported by checklists where appropriate.

These audits should verify that correct and authorized versions of CIs exist (and that only such CIs exist) and are in use in the supported

environment. The audits are equally applicable to CIs such as virtual servers, which are not physical assets but must be checked to ensure that they are included in the CMS and that the configuration data is accurate.

From the outset, any ad hoc tools, test equipment, personal computers and other unregistered items should either be removed or registered through formal service asset and configuration management. Registration or removal will be via the change management process and has to prevent the authorization of non-acceptable CIs or the removal of CIs that may be supporting business processes. Unregistered and unauthorized items that are discovered during configuration audits should be investigated and corrective action taken to address possible issues with procedures and the behaviour of personnel. All exceptions are logged and reported, and records of the audit should be created to support future compliance checking.

Configuration audits should check in addition that change and release records have been properly authorized by change management and that implemented changes are as authorized. Configuration audits should be considered at the following times:

- Shortly after changes to the CMS
- Before and after changes to the IT services or infrastructure
- Before a release or installation to ensure that the environment is as expected
- Following recovery from disasters and after a 'return to normal' (this audit should be included in contingency plans)
- At planned intervals
- At random intervals
- In response to the detection of any unauthorized CIs.

Automated audit tools enable regular checks to be made at regular intervals, e.g. weekly. For example, desktop audit tools compare the build of an individual's desktop to the master build that was installed. If exceptions are found, some organizations return the build to its original state.

A rolling programme of configuration audits can encourage more effective use of resources. The service desk and support groups will check that CIs brought to their attention, e.g. the software that a caller is using, are as recorded in the CMS. Any deviations are reported to service asset and configuration management for investigation.

If there is a high incidence of unauthorized CIs detected, the frequency or scope of configuration audits should be increased, certainly for those parts of the services or IT infrastructure affected by this problem. Note that unauthorized installations are discouraged when the SACM team is seen to be in control and to carry out regular and frequent audits. If an epidemic of unauthorized CIs is detected, selective or general configuration audits should be initiated to determine the scale of the problem, to put matters right and to discourage a proliferation of unauthorized CIs. Publicity will help to reduce further occurrences. Service design and service operation staff need to be notified and involved in the investigation of unauthorized CIs.

4.3.6 Triggers, inputs, outputs and interfaces

4.3.6.1 Triggers

Updates to service asset and configuration management could be triggered by:

- Updates from change management (see Figure 4.6)
- Updates from release and deployment management
- Purchase orders
- Acquisitions
- Service requests.

4.3.6.2 Inputs

Inputs to service asset and configuration management include:

- Designs, plans and configurations from service design packages
- Requests for change and work orders from change management
- Actual configuration information collected by tools and audits
- Information in the organization's fixed asset register.

4.3.6.3 Outputs

Outputs from service asset and configuration management include:

- New and updated configuration records
- Updated asset information for use in updating the fixed asset register
- Information about attributes and relationships of configuration items, for use by all other service management processes. This information should be presented in appropriate views for each audience
- Configuration snapshots and baselines
- Status reports and other consolidated configuration information
- Audit reports.

4.3.6.4 Interfaces

By its very nature – as the single virtual repository of configuration data and information for IT service management – SACM supports and interfaces with every other service management process and activity to some degree. Some of the more noteworthy interfaces are:

- Change management – identifying the impact of proposed changes
- Financial management for IT services – capturing key financial information such as cost, depreciation methods, owner and user (for budgeting and cost allocation), maintenance and repair costs
- ITSCM – awareness of the assets on which the business services depend, control of key spares and software
- Incident/problem/error – providing and maintaining key diagnostic information; maintenance and provision of data to the service desk
- Availability management in detection of points of failure.

The relationship with change and release and deployment management is synergistic, with these processes benefiting greatly from a single coordinated planning approach. Configuration control is synonymous with change control – understanding and capturing updates to the infrastructure and services.

SACM also has close relationships with some business processes, especially fixed asset management and procurement.

4.3.7 Information management

Backup copies of the CMS should be taken regularly and stored securely. It is advisable for one copy to be kept at a remote location for use in the event of a disaster. The frequency of copying and the retention policy will depend on the size and volatility of the IT infrastructure and the CMS. Certain tools may allow selective copying of CI records that are new or have been changed.

The CMS contains information on backup copies of CIs. It will also contain historical records of CIs and CI versions that are archived, and possibly also of deleted CIs or CI versions. The amount of historical information to be retained depends on its usefulness to the organization. The retention policy on historical CI records should be regularly reviewed and changed if necessary. If the cost to the organization of retaining CI information is greater than the current or potential value, do not retain it – bearing in mind relevant regulatory and statutory requirements in relation to retention of records.

Typically, the CMS should contain records only for items that are physically available or could be easily created using procedures known to, and under the control of, service asset and configuration management. When SACM has been operating for a period of time, regular housekeeping should be carried out to ensure that redundant CI records are systematically archived.

The CMS includes pointers to knowledge and information assets that are stored in the SKMS, and it is important to maintain these links and to verify their validity as part of regular audits. SACM is responsible for the maintenance of many knowledge and information assets within the SKMS, and these must be maintained with the same level of control as the CMS. Many organizations enforce separation of duties to ensure that anyone who can update the CMS cannot update the actual assets in the SKMS, to provide a higher level of assurance about the integrity of their assets.

4.3.8 Critical success factors and key performance indicators

As with all processes the performance of SACM should be monitored, reported on and action taken to improve it.

SACM is the central support process facilitating the exchange of information with other processes, and as such it has few customer-facing measures. However, as an underlying engine to other processes in the lifecycle, SACM must be measured for its contribution to these parts of the lifecycle and the overall KPIs that directly affect the customer.

The following list includes some sample CSFs for service asset and configuration management. Each organization should identify appropriate CSFs based on its objectives for the process. Each sample CSF is followed by a small number of typical KPIs that support the CSF. These KPIs should not be adopted without careful consideration. Each organization should develop KPIs that are appropriate for its level of maturity, its CSFs and its particular circumstances. Achievement against KPIs should be monitored and used to identify opportunities for improvement, which should be logged in the CSI register for evaluation and possible implementation.

- **CSF** Accounting for, managing and protecting the integrity of CIs throughout the service lifecycle
  - **KPI** Improved accuracy in budgets and charges for the assets utilized by each customer or business unit
  - **KPI** Increase in re-use and redistribution of under-utilized resources and assets
  - **KPI** Reduction in the use of unauthorized hardware and software, non-standard and variant builds that increase complexity, support costs and risk to the business services
  - **KPI** Reduced number of exceptions reported during configuration audits
- **CSF** Supporting efficient and effective service management processes by providing accurate configuration information at the right time
  - **KPI** Percentage improvement in maintenance scheduling over the life of an asset (not too much, not too late)
  - **KPI** Improved speed for incident management to identify faulty CIs and restore service
  - **KPI** Reduction in the average time and cost of diagnosing and resolving incidents and problems (by type)
  - **KPI** Improved ratio of used licences against paid-for licences

- **KPI** Improvement in time to identify poor-performing and poor-quality assets
- **KPI** Reduction in risks due to early identification of unauthorized change
- **KPI** Reduced percentage of changes not completed successfully or causing errors because of poor impact assessment, incorrect data in the CMS, or poor version control
- **CSF** Establishing and maintaining an accurate and complete configuration management system (CMS)
  - **KPI** Reduction in business impact of outages and incidents caused by poor service asset and configuration management
  - **KPI** Increased quality and accuracy of configuration information
  - **KPI** Improved audit compliance
  - **KPI** Shorter audits as quality configuration information is easily accessible
  - **KPI** Fewer errors caused by people working with out-of-date information.

4.3.9 Challenges and risks

4.3.9.1 Challenges

Challenges to SACM include:

- Persuading technical support staff to adopt a checking in/out policy – this can be perceived as being a hindrance to a fast and responsive support service; if the positives of such a system are not conveyed adequately, staff may be inclined to try and circumvent it. Even then, resistance can still occur – placing this as an objective in annual appraisal is one way to help enforce the policy.
- Attracting and justifying funding for SACM, since it is typically out of sight to the customer units empowered with funding control; in practice it is typically funded as an 'invisible' element of change management and other ITSM processes with more business visibility.
- An attitude of 'just collecting data because it is possible to do'; this leads SACM into a data overload, which is impossible, or at least disproportionately expensive, to maintain.
- Lack of commitment and support from management who do not understand the key role it must play in supporting other processes.

4.3.9.2 Risks

Risks to successful SACM include:

- The temptation to consider it technically focused (rather than service and business-focused), since technical competence is essential to its successful delivery.
- Degradation of the accuracy of configuration information over time, which can cause errors and be difficult and costly to correct.
- Setting the scope too wide, causing excessive cost and effort for insufficient benefit.
- Setting the scope too narrow, so that the process has too little benefit.
- The CMS becomes out of date due to the movement of hardware assets by non-authorized staff; regular physical audits should be conducted with discrepancies highlighted and investigated; managers should be informed of inconsistencies in their areas. The frequency of these audits could range from 10% of assets audited very two months to a full audit four times a year, depending on the size of the organization, the number and value of the assets, and the historical rate of audit issues.

4.4 RELEASE AND DEPLOYMENT MANAGEMENT

4.4.1 Purpose and objectives

The purpose of the release and deployment management process is to plan, schedule and control the build, test and deployment of releases, and to deliver new functionality required by the business while protecting the integrity of existing services.

The objectives of release and deployment management are to:

- Define and agree release and deployment management plans with customers and stakeholders
- Create and test release packages that consist of related configuration items that are compatible with each other
- Ensure that the integrity of a release package and its constituent components is maintained throughout the transition activities, and that all release packages are stored in a DML and recorded accurately in the CMS

- Deploy release packages from the DML to the live environment following an agreed plan and schedule
- Ensure that all release packages can be tracked, installed, tested, verified and/or uninstalled or backed out if appropriate
- Ensure that organization and stakeholder change is managed during release and deployment activities (see Chapter 5)
- Ensure that a new or changed service and its enabling systems, technology and organization are capable of delivering the agreed utility and warranty
- Record and manage deviations, risks and issues related to the new or changed service and take necessary corrective action
- Ensure that there is knowledge transfer to enable the customers and users to optimize their use of the service to support their business activities
- Ensure that skills and knowledge are transferred to service operation functions to enable them to effectively and efficiently deliver, support and maintain the service according to required warranties and service levels.

4.4.2 Scope

The scope of release and deployment management includes the processes, systems and functions to package, build, test and deploy a release into live use, establish the service specified in the service design package, and formally hand the service over to the service operation functions. The scope includes all configuration items required to implement a release, for example:

- Physical assets such as a server or network
- Virtual assets such as a virtual server or virtual storage
- Applications and software
- Training for users and IT staff
- Services, including all related contracts and agreements.

Although release and deployment management is responsible for ensuring that appropriate testing takes place, the actual testing is carried out as part of the service validation and testing process.

Release and deployment management is not responsible for authoring changes, and requires authorization from change management at various stages in the lifecycle of a release.

4.4.3 Value to business

Effective release and deployment management enables the service provider to add value to the business by:

- Delivering change, faster and at optimum cost and minimized risk
- Assuring that customers and users can use the new or changed service in a way that supports the business goals
- Improving consistency in implementation approach across the business change, service teams, suppliers and customers
- Contributing to meeting auditable requirements for traceability through service transition.

Well-planned and implemented release and deployment management will make a significant difference to an organization's service costs. A poorly designed release or deployment will, at best, force IT personnel to spend significant amounts of time troubleshooting problems and managing complexity. At worst, it can cripple the environment and degrade live services.

4.4.4 Policies, principles and basic concepts

4.4.4.1 Release and deployment management policies

Release and deployment management policies should be in place to help the organization achieve the correct balance between cost, service stability and agility.

For some services it is really important to maximize the stability of the service, even if this increases the amount of time required to design and test changes. For other services it may be more important to implement releases needed to support a rapidly changing business, and resources may be provided to ensure that this can be achieved.

Release and deployment management policies should help release and deployment management personnel to make decisions that support the overall objectives of the business. These policies can be set at an overall service provider level, for example 'All changes and releases must be fully tested under a realistic load before they are deployed' or for an individual service, for example 'All changes to the service will be packaged into annual releases and the only permitted changes between these releases will be to resolve problems that have a major impact on the business.'

4.4.4.2 Release unit and release package

A 'release unit' describes the portion of a service or IT infrastructure that is normally released as a single entity according to the organization's release policy. The unit may vary, depending on the type(s) or item(s) of service asset or service component such as software and hardware. Figure 4.17 gives a simplified example showing an IT service made up of systems and service assets, which are in turn made up of service components. The actual components to be released on a specific occasion may include one or more release units, or exceptionally may include only part of a release unit. These components are grouped together into a release package for that specific release.

In Figure 4.17 the assets and components might be:

■ **A1** Server
■ **A2** Application
■ **A2.1** Main application, developed within the IT organization
■ **A2.1.1** Commercial off-the-shelf reporting software used by the application
■ **A2.2** Second application, developed within the IT organization
■ **A3** Client software, developed within the IT organization
■ **A3.1** Commercial off-the-shelf library providing supporting routines for the client application.

The general aim is to decide the most appropriate release-unit level for each service asset or component. An organization may, for example, decide that the release unit for business-critical applications is the complete application in order to ensure that testing is comprehensive. The same organization may decide that a more appropriate release unit for a website is at the page level.

A 'release package' is a set of configuration items that will be built, tested and deployed together as a single release. Each release will take the documented release units into account when designing the contents of the release package. It may sometimes be necessary to create a release package that contains only part of one or more release units, but this would only happen in exceptional circumstances.

The following factors should be taken into account when deciding the appropriate level for release units:

■ The ease and amount of change necessary to release a release unit
■ The amount of resources and time needed to build, test, distribute and implement a release unit
■ The complexity of interfaces between the proposed unit and the rest of the services and IT infrastructure
■ The storage available in the build, test, distribution and live environments.

Releases should be uniquely identified according to a scheme defined in the release policy as discussed in section 4.1.4.2. The release identification should include a reference to the CIs that it represents and

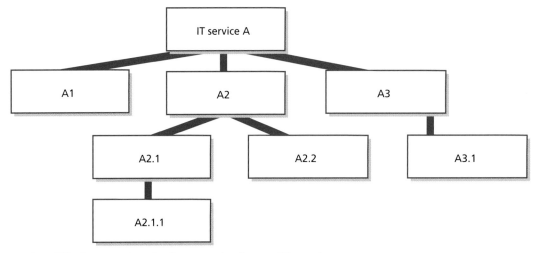

Figure 4.17 Simplified example of release units for an IT service

a version number that will often have two or three parts, e.g. emergency fix releases: Payroll_System v.1.1.1, v.1.1.2, v.1.1.3.

Designing releases and release packages

Figure 4.18 provides an example of how the architectural elements of a service may be changed from the current baseline to the new baseline with releases at each level. The architecture will be different in some organizations but is provided in this section to give a context for release activities. The release teams need to understand the relevant architecture in order to be able to plan, package, build and test a release to support the new or changed service. This helps to prioritize the release activities and manage dependencies: e.g. the technology infrastructure needs to be ready – with service operation functions prepared to support it with new or changed procedures – before an application is installed.

Figure 4.18 also shows how the service architectural elements depend on the service portfolio that defines the service offerings and service packages. Dependent services will need to be built and tested in service transition. For example, an IT financial service may be dependent on several internal support services and an external service. For more details about the structure of services, see *ITIL Service Strategy* and *ITIL Service Design*.

There are normally dependencies between particular versions of service components required for the service to operate. For example, a new

version of an application may need an upgrade to the operating system and one or other of these could require a hardware change, e.g. a faster processor or more memory. In some cases, the release package may include documentation and procedures. These could be deployed via a manual update or through an automatic publishing mechanism, e.g. to the SKMS/website.

A release package may be a single release unit or a structured set of release units such as the one shown in Figure 4.19. A release package may contain only part of one or more release units. This would only happen in exceptional circumstances, for example when creating an emergency release.

The example in Figure 4.19 shows an application with its user documentation and a release unit for each technology platform. On the right there is the customer service asset that is supported by two supporting services – SSA for the infrastructure service and SSB for the application service. These release units will contain information about the service, its utilities and warranties and release documentation. Often there will be different ways of designing a release package, and consideration should be given to establishing the most appropriate method for the identifiable circumstances, stakeholders and possibilities.

Where possible, release packages should be designed so that some release units can be removed if they cause issues in testing.

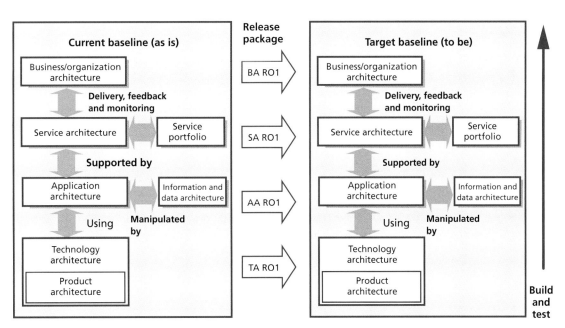

Figure 4.18 Architecture elements to be built and tested

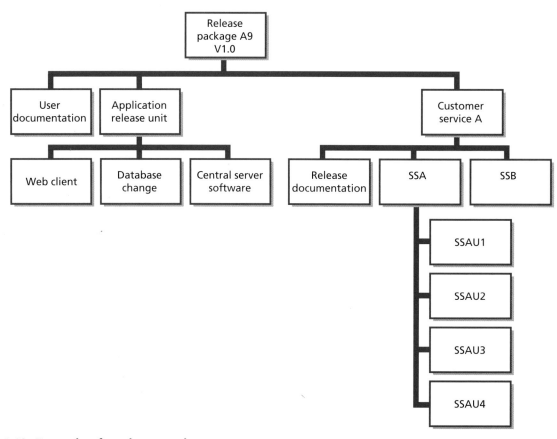

Figure 4.19 Example of a release package

Valuable release windows

A UK government department is especially well placed to make full use of all available release windows. The staff work in a secure financial, low-risk environment, with carefully planned changes scheduled well in advance and allocated to pre-arranged release windows, which are scheduled several months apart. Because of their careful and longer-term planning, when a change proves unsuitable for release (i.e. tests are failed), alternative, quality-assured changes are usually available – prepared and tested but lower in business priority and so targeted at later releases. These can be accelerated to make use of the unexpected vacancy created by the test failure. The test and build process also allows elements of later scheduled releases to be slotted in for release, or successful components of the failed release to be implemented, even though the full product is not ready. This allows the subsequent fuller release to be a 'smaller' product, which means that further additional changes can be scheduled alongside it in later release windows.

Any significant new or changed service or service offering will require the deployment stage to consider the full range of elements comprising that service – infrastructure, hardware, software, applications, documentation, knowledge etc. Effectively, this means that the deployment will contain sub-deployments for elements comprising the service as illustrated in Figure 4.20. The combination, relationship and interdependencies of these components will require careful and considered planning. Significant deployments will be complex projects in their own right.

To understand the deployment options, a high-level assessment of the deployment units, locations and environments may be required, for example:

- Assessment baseline – this is a snapshot of the relevant environment, services and infrastructure, including 'softer' elements such as skills level and attitudes where applicable, and should be taken as a first step.
- Identify the components – this may include deciding on the best way to break down a major deployment into components. Often there will be different ways of achieving this

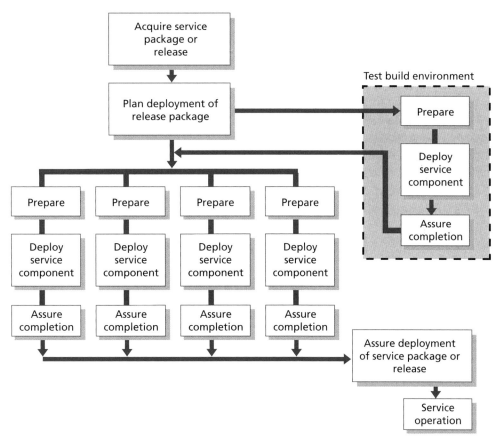

Figure 4.20 Coordinating the deployment of service components

breakdown, and consideration needs to be given to establishing the most appropriate method for all the identifiable circumstances, stakeholders and possibilities.

■ Determine the appropriate deployment approach for each.

4.4.4.3 Deployment options and considerations

Service design will define the approach to transitioning from the current service to the new or changed service or service offering. The SDP defines the service and solution design components to be transitioned to deliver the required service.

Common options for release and deployment that are considered in service design are discussed below. The selected option will have a significant impact on the release and deployment management resources as well as the business outcomes. It is important to understand the patterns of business activity (PBA) and user profiles when planning and designing the releases.

'Big bang' versus phased deployment

Options for deploying new releases to multiple locations are illustrated in Figure 4.21 and described below:

■ **'Big bang' option** The new or changed service is deployed to all user areas in one operation. This will often be used when introducing an application change and consistency of service across the organization is considered important. This option is sometimes called 'parallel deployment'.

■ **Phased approach** The service is deployed to a part of the user base initially, and then this operation is repeated for subsequent parts of the user base via a scheduled deployment plan. This will be the case in many scenarios such as in retail organizations for new services being introduced into the stores' environment in manageable phases.

Figure 4.21 also illustrates a possible sequence of events over time as follows:

■ There is an initial launch of 'Release 1' of the system to three workstations (1–3).

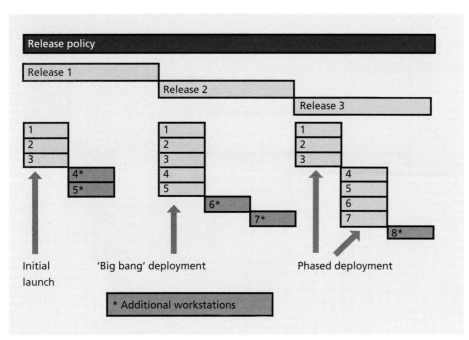

Figure 4.21 Options for 'big bang' and phased deployment

- Two further workstations (4+5) are then added at the same time.
- 'Release 2' of the system is then rolled out in a 'big bang' approach to all workstations (1–5) at once.
- Two further workstations (6+7) are then added, in another step.
- There is a phased implementation of the upgrade to 'Release 3' of the system, initially upgrading only three workstations (1–3) and then the remaining four (4–7).
- A further workstation (8) is then added to the system.

Variations of the phased approach include:

- Portions of the service are delivered to the live environment in phases, but all end users are affected simultaneously (e.g. incremental changes to a shared application).
- Each release is deployed gradually across the total population of end users (e.g. one geographical location at a time).
- Different types of service element are deployed in separate phases, e.g. hardware changes are first, followed by user training and then by the new or changed software.
- A combination of all of these approaches is usually adopted, and the plans may deliberately allow for variations in the light of actual deployment experience.

In the type of phased implementation illustrated above, it is only possible to employ this approach if the service has been designed to allow new and old versions to coexist. If this is not possible then the only alternative is to upgrade all affected parts together in a 'big bang' implementation. For elements such as documentation, this is rarely a problem for skilled staff – for many instances of hardware and software it is quite possible. However, for other transitions such as those involving major network changes, it can be virtually impossible to achieve.

Figure 4.22 illustrates phased deployment to a number of different geographical locations. It assumes that new versions will work alongside the previous one. The example used assumes that new functionality is implemented first in the head office of the organization, then in a single branch and finally in the remaining branches. If there are a very large number of locations to deal with, it may still take a long time to implement the initial system or upgrades in all branches, thus increasing the likelihood of needing to support even more versions of the system concurrently in the live environment.

Push and pull approaches

A push approach is used where the service component is deployed from the centre and pushed out to the target locations. In terms of service deployment, delivering updated service

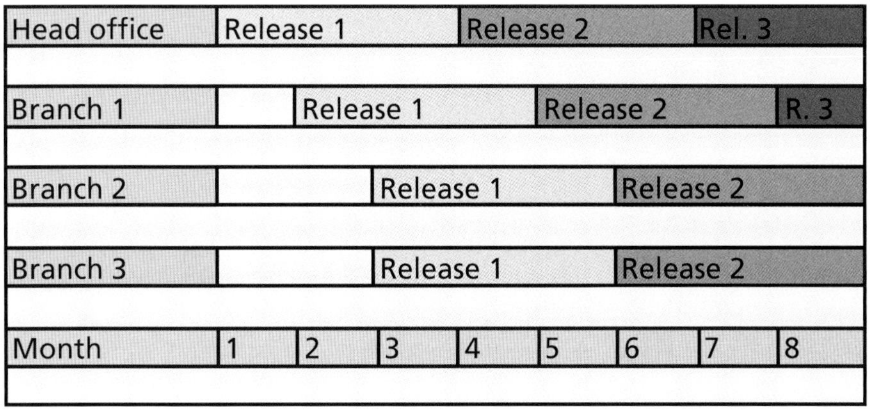

Head office	Release 1		Release 2		Rel. 3	
Branch 1		Release 1		Release 2		R. 3
Branch 2			Release 1		Release 2	
Branch 3			Release 1		Release 2	
Month	1	2	3	4	5	6	7	8

Figure 4.22 Phased deployment across geographical locations

components to all users – either in big bang or phased form – constitutes 'push', since the new or changed service is delivered into the users' environment at a time not of their choosing.

A pull approach is used for software releases where the software is made available in a central location, but users are free to pull the software down to their own location at a time of their choosing or when a user workstation restarts. The use of 'pull' updating a release over the internet has made this concept significantly more pervasive. A good example is virus signature updates, which are typically pulled down to update PCs and servers when it best suits the customer; however, at times of extreme virus risk this may be overridden by a release that is pushed to all known users.

In order to deploy via a 'push' approach, the data on all user locations must be available. Pull approaches do not rely so heavily on accurate configuration data and they can trigger an update to user records. This may be through new users appearing and requesting downloads or expected users not doing so, triggering investigation into their continued existence. As some users will never 'pull' a release it may be appropriate to allow a 'pull' within a specified time limit and if this is exceeded a push will be forced, e.g. for an antivirus update.

Automation versus manual methods

Whether by automation or other means, the mechanisms to deploy the correctly configured service components should be established in the release design stage and tested in the build and test stages.

Automation will help to ensure repeatability and consistency. The time required to provide a well-designed and efficient automated mechanism may not always be available or viable. If a manual mechanism is used, it is important to monitor and measure the impact of many repeated manual activities, as they are likely to be inefficient and error-prone. Too many manual activities will slow down the release team and create resource or capacity issues that affect the service levels.

Many release and deployment activities are capable of a degree of automation. For example:

■ Discovery tools aid release planning.
■ Discovery and installation software can check whether the required prerequisites and corequisites are in place before installation of new or changed software components.
■ Automated builds can significantly reduce build and recovery times, which in turn can resolve scheduling conflicts and delays.
■ Automated configuration baseline procedures save time and reduce errors in capturing the status of configurations and releases during release build, test and release deployment.
■ Automatic comparisons of the actual 'live' configuration with the expected configuration or CMS help to identify issues at the earliest opportunity that could cause incidents and delays during deployment.
■ Automated processes to load and update data to the CMS help to ensure that the records are accurate and complete.
■ Installation procedures automatically update user and licence information in the CMS.

4.4.4.4 Release and deployment models

A service may be deployed into the live environment in a number of ways. Service design will select the most suitable release and deployment models that include the approach, mechanisms, processes, procedures and resources required to build, test and deploy the release on time and within budget.

The release methods used during the early build and test stages may differ significantly from live operations, so plan ahead to ensure that appropriate release methods are adopted at the right time.

Common situations where release and deployment models might be useful include:

- Release of a new version of an existing desktop application
- Deployment of a new virtual server with a standard configuration
- Upgrade of the server operating system software to a new version
- Implementation of a security patch for network appliances.

Release and deployment models define:

- Release structure – the overall structure for building a release package and the target environments
- The exit and entry criteria, including mandatory and optional deliverables and documentation for each stage
- Controlled environments required to build and test the release for each release level; there will be multiple logical and physical environments through the service transition stage mapped to different physical environments available to the transition team
- The roles and responsibilities for each configuration item at each release level
- The release promotion and configuration baseline model
- Template release and deployment schedules
- Supporting systems, tools and procedures for documenting and tracking all release and deployment management activities
- The handover activities and responsibilities for executing the handover and acceptance for each stage of release and deployment management.

Considerations in designing the release and deployment model include activities to:

- Verify that a release complies with the SDP, architecture and related standards
- Ensure the integrity of hardware and software is protected during installation, handling, packaging and delivery
- Use standard release and deployment procedures and tools
- Automate the delivery, distribution, installation, build and configuration audit procedures where appropriate to reduce costly manual steps
- Manage and deploy/re-deploy/remove/retire software licences
- Package and build the release package so that it can be backed out or remediated if required
- Use SACM procedures, the CMS and DML to manage and control components during release and deployment management activities, e.g. to verify the prerequisites, corequisites and post-installation activities
- Document the release and deployment management steps
- Document the deployment group or target environment that will receive the release
- Issue service notifications
- Implement controls and checklists to ensure that all required activities take place and that records are maintained to support future audits of the process.

4.4.5 Process activities, methods and techniques

There are four phases to release and deployment management (see Figure 4.23):

- **Release and deployment planning** Plans for creating and deploying the release are created. This phase starts with change management authorization to plan a release and ends with change management authorization to create the release.
- **Release build and test** The release package is built, tested and checked into the DML. This phase starts with change management authorization to build the release and ends with change management authorization for the baselined release package to be checked into the DML by service asset and configuration management. This phase only happens once for each release.

- **Deployment** The release package in the DML is deployed to the live environment. This phase starts with change management authorization to deploy the release package to one or more target environments and ends with handover to the service operation functions and early life support. There may be many separate deployment phases for each release, depending on the planned deployment options.
- **Review and close** Experience and feedback are captured, performance targets and achievements are reviewed and lessons are learned.

Figure 4.23 shows multiple points where an authorized change triggers release and deployment management activity. This does not require a separate RFC at each stage. Some organizations manage a whole release with a single change request and separate authorization at each stage for activities to continue, while other organizations require a separate RFC for each stage. Both of these approaches are acceptable; what is important is that change management authorization is received before commencing each stage.

Figure 8.2 gives an example of the more complex interactions involved in managing relationships between all of the service transition processes.

4.4.5.1 Release and deployment planning

Most of the planning described here is carried out during the service design stage of the service lifecycle. These activities are carried out as part of the release and deployment management process, and the service design coordination process will ensure that the plans are documented as part of the service design package.

These plans form part of overall service transition plans, and should be coordinated with plans for other activities such as project plans, change management plans etc.

Plans for release and deployment should be based on service models (which show how the service assets should interact with customer assets to create value) and on the documented utility and warranty requirements for the service, as well as on technical data about the components that will make up the new, changed or retired service.

Release and deployment plans

Plans for release and deployment will be linked into the overall service transition plan and adopt the selected release and deployment model. The approach is to derive a sound set of guidelines for the release and deployment plans that can be scaled from small organizations to large multinationals. Although smaller organizations will have less complex environments, the disciplines detailed here are still relevant. Even within a single organization, the release and deployment plans need to be scalable since the extent of their scale

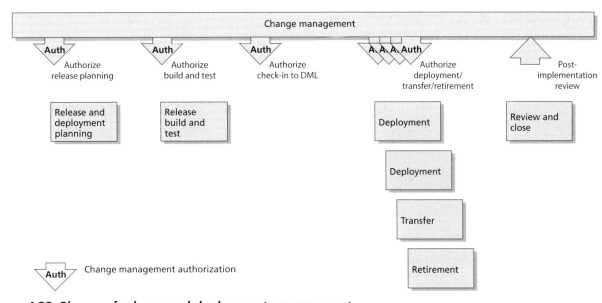

Figure 4.23 Phases of release and deployment management

of impact on the organization will vary, perhaps from impacting only one small specialist team in one location through to multinational impact on all users when introducing new desktop equipment and services or transferring services to different suppliers.

Release and deployment plans should be authorized through change management and should contain the following information:

- Scope and content of the release
- Risk assessment and risk profile for the release
- Organizations and stakeholders affected by the release
- Stakeholders that may authorize the change request for each stage of the release
- Team responsible for the release
- Deployment schedule for the release
- Approach to working with stakeholders and deployment groups to determine:
  - Delivery and deployment strategy
  - Resources for the release build, test and deployment, and for early life support
  - Amount of change that can be absorbed.

Pass/fail criteria

Service transition is responsible for planning the pass/fail situations. At a minimum these should be defined for each authorization point through release and deployment management. It is important to publish these criteria to relevant stakeholders well in advance to set expectations correctly. An example of a pass situation before build and test is:

- All tests are completed successfully; the evaluation report shows no unacceptable risks and change management authorizes check-in to the DML.

Examples of fail situations include:

- Insufficient resources to pass to the next stage. For example, an automated build is not possible and so the resource requirement becomes error-prone, too onerous and expensive; testing identifies that there will not be enough money to deliver the proposed design in the operation stage of the service lifecycle.
- Service operation does not have capabilities to offer particular service attributes.

- Service design does not conform to the service operation standards for technologies, protocols, regulations etc.
- The service cannot be delivered within the boundaries of the design constraints.
- Service acceptance criteria are not met.
- Mandatory documents are not signed off.
- SKMS and CMS are not updated, perhaps due to a process that is manually intensive.
- The incidents, problems and risks are higher than predicted, e.g. by over 5%.

Build and test planning

Build and test planning establishes the approach to building, testing and maintaining the controlled environments prior to live use. Build and test planning must work with service validation and testing to ensure that test plans can be carried out.

The activities include:

- Developing build plans from the SDP, design specifications and environment configuration requirements
- Establishing the logistics, lead times and build times to set up the environments
- Defining a configuration baseline for the build environment, to ensure that each build is carried out in a known environment
- Testing the build and related procedures
- Scheduling the build and test activities
- Assigning resources, roles and responsibilities to perform key activities, for example:
  - Security procedures and checks
  - Technical support
  - Preparing build and test environments
  - Managing test databases and test data
  - Software asset and licence management
  - Service asset and configuration management – configuration audit, build and baseline management
- Defining and agreeing the build exit and entry criteria.

Figure 4.14 provides an example of a model that can be used to represent the different configuration levels to be built and tested to deliver a service capability. The left-hand side represents the specification of the service requirements down to the detailed service design. The right-hand side focuses on the validation and test activities that are performed against the specifications defined on the left-hand side. At each stage on the left-hand side, there is direct involvement by the equivalent party on the right-hand side. It shows that service validation and acceptance test planning should start with the definition of the service requirements. For example, customers who sign off the agreed service requirements will also sign off the service acceptance criteria and test plan.

The V-model approach is traditionally associated with the waterfall lifecycle but is, in fact, just as applicable to other lifecycles, including iterative lifecycles such as prototyping and RAD approaches. Within each cycle of the iterative development, the V-model concepts of establishing acceptance criteria against the requirements and design can

apply, with each iterative design being considered for the degree of integrity and competence that would justify release to the customer for trial and assessment.

Further details on validation, testing and change evaluation are provided in sections 4.5 and 4.6. The test strategy defines the overall approach to service validation and testing. It includes the organization of service validation and testing activities and resources and can apply to the whole organization, a set of services or an individual service.

Typical levels of configuration for build and testing are shown in Table 4.8.

Table 4.8 Levels of configuration for build and testing

Level	Requirements and design	Build/deliverable	Validation and testing
Level 1 Customer/business needs	Structured definition of contract requirements	Customer contract (based on service portfolio, service options)	**Service test and evaluation** Determines whether a service can enable the users and customers to use the service to support their business needs (is fit for purpose and fit for use)
Level 2 Service requirements	Service requirement specifications and SAC, traceable back to the contract requirements	Service capability and resources to deliver against the SLA and service requirements	**Service test** Tests that the service acceptance criteria are met. Includes validation of service performance against the service level requirements and SLA in pilots, deployment and early life support
Level 3 Service solution	SDP, service model, service environments	Solution/system required to deliver the service capability; includes the service management and service operation systems and capabilities	**Service operational readiness test** Evaluates the integration and operation of the service capability and resources. It verifies that the target deployment organization and people are prepared to deploy and operate the new or changed service in the live environment, e.g. deployment team, service operation functions, customers, users and other stakeholders. Tests include scenario-based testing such as simulation and service rehearsal
Level 4 Service release		Release package	**Service release test** Tests that the service components can be integrated correctly and that the release can be installed, built and tested in the target environments. Service release testing includes non-functional testing that can be performed at this level
Level 5 Component and assemblies	Component and assembly test specification	Component or assembly of components	**Component and assembly test** Tests that a service component or assembly of components matches its detailed specification. Components or assemblies are tested in isolation, with a view to their delivering as specified, in terms of inputs generating expected outputs. Evidence of component quality or testing earlier in the chain may be obtained for test evidence, from both internal and external suppliers

Various controlled environments will need to be built or made available for the different types and levels of testing as well as to support other transition activities such as training. Existing deployment processes and procedures can be used to build the controlled test environments. The environments will need to be secure to ensure that there is no unauthorized access and that any segregation of duty requirements are met. The types of environments, both logical and physical, required during release and deployment management may include:

- **Build environments** Used to compile or assemble the release package or service assets
- **Unit test environment** Used for verifying the functionality, performance, recovery and usability characteristics of an individual service component, e.g. online procedure
- **Assembly test environment** Used for verifying the functionality, performance, recovery and usability characteristics of an assembly of service components
- **Integration environment** For building and integrating service components
- **System test environment** Used for testing all aspects of the integrated service architecture, including the application and technical infrastructure; substantial user acceptance testing is executed in this environment
- **Service release test environment** Used to install, build and test a release package in a controlled environment; this is often combined with the system test environment
- **Service operation readiness test environment** Used for testing the service and service unit capabilities before promotion into live; may include the service management acceptance test, some operational acceptance tests and user acceptance tests of the end-to-end service
- **Business simulation environments** To enable testing of the service in the context of the business process it supports
- **Performance/load /stress test environment** To enable testing of performance and throughput
- **Service management simulation environments** To enable testing of service management activities such as logging and managing incidents, service requests and changes
- **Training environments** Sometimes this may include an established test database that can be used as a safe and realistic training environment

- **Pilot environments** Including conference room pilots
- **Backup and recovery environments** For example disaster recovery.

Planning release packaging and build

Planning the release packaging and build activities includes developing mechanisms, plans or procedures for the following:

- Managing stakeholder change and communications by:
  - Obtaining and maintaining the list of contacts and their details
  - Communicating the proposed changes, the expected benefits and how the change affects the organization and staff
- Training people and transferring knowledge
- Establishing that the services and service assets (e.g. agreements and contracts) are in place
- Agreeing on schedules:
  - Agreeing the delivery schedules and handling any changes/delays
  - Finalizing the logistics and delivery procedures and checklists
  - Scheduling and allocating controlled transition environments, facilities and tools for: (i) acquisition of service assets and components, and (ii) release packaging, building and testing
- Developing procedures and mechanisms using available SACM, release, content/electronic publishing and other tools to:
  - Build, copy, promote, distribute, audit, install and activate a release
  - Manage software licences, digital rights and intellectual property rights (IPR)
- Converting systems and users from the current applications and technology to the new or changed service, e.g. migrate or reformat application data and information
- Developing the service management capability and resources for:
  - Conducting site surveys
  - Updating service information, e.g. service catalogue, release documentation
  - Building and preparing the management systems and other operational systems, e.g. systems and event management, measurement systems

- Operating and handling the predicted capacity required for support
- Operating the controlled environments including procedures to scale up capacity if required
- Documenting and providing the information to be created and/or updated during transition, e.g. remediation plans to be issued and published
- Installing the new or changed service ready for activation
- Transferring/transitioning a service or service team or organization
- Decommissioning and/or disposing of service assets and components
- Retiring services
■ Assessing the readiness of a target deployment group (customers, users and service operation functions) to take a release
■ Defining and agreeing the packaging entry and exit criteria.

Preparation for release build and test

Before authorizing the release build and test stage, the service design and the release design must be validated against the requirement for the new or changed service offering. This should result in constructive feedback on the service design. Record, track and measure any risks and issues against the services, service assets and CIs within the service package, SDP or release package. Prioritize the issues and actions to ensure they can be resolved in a timely manner. Finally, produce a validation report and associated results ready for change evaluation.

A formal evaluation of the service and release design uses the validation report and results (see section 4.6). This change evaluation checks that the change to the services or service offering will deliver the predicted outcomes, i.e. the service expected by the user or customer. Any issues are documented in an interim evaluation report. This report lists the deviations from the SDP, a risk profile and recommendations for change management. If there are deviations in the service level requirements, the service charter or SAC may be changed (via change management) and action should be taken to modify the proposed service release and related changes. Successful completion

of the evaluation of the service design baseline ensures that service release build and test starts with a stable, baselined and approved design.

For some releases the service transition manager may need to assign individuals or establish a team of competent people to execute the plans. If individuals are not dedicated there is risk that they may be diverted to work on other projects. Such risks need to be mitigated, as they are often the cause of delays.

On most occasions, the introduction of a technology-enabled service requires training for the release and deployment management teams. The training needs for different roles will vary. Recognition of the different skill sets, capabilities and competencies within the various groups is a useful prerequisite in identifying the necessary training. In specifying the training programme, the number of people who require training needs to be determined, and the way the knowledge can be provided needs to be considered. While the need for training differs from release to release, the impact of training can be significant. For example, if support staff are spread around many locations, specific training, automated mechanisms, such as e-learning or computer-based training (CBT) solutions over the internet or intranet may become an attractive proposition.

Examples of training needs include:

■ Interpreting the service design documentation and plans
■ Use of support tools, e.g. for central release staff
■ Changes in health and safety requirements
■ Changes in security policies and procedures
■ Technical training
■ Service management and process training, e.g. new build procedure for new configuration item type
■ Understanding the business context for the release, to enable IT staff to offer appropriate support to users.

Deployment planning

There are many planning considerations that need to be considered. Planners should be able to answer the questions included in Table 4.9.

Table 4.9 Questions to be answered when planning deployment

Deployment question	Examples
What needs to be deployed?	Do you have a good understanding of the service and release that is being deployed? What are the components that make up the release package? What are the business drivers for the deployment? Is it required to meet a critical business need?
Who are the users?	Which users are affected by the deployment? What language do they use? Do they need any special training?
Are there location dependencies?	Are there any holidays, shut-downs or other interruptions to normal business at this location? What level of detail needs to be recorded, e.g. building, floor, room?
Where are the users?	Are all the users and systems local to the deployment, or are some remote, and how will this affect the logistics?
Who else needs to be prepared well in advance?	Do the service desk and support staff need training? Are there any access issues to be solved – security or physical?
When does the deployment need to be completed?	Does the deployment need to be completed by a certain date and time or can it be completed by following a flexible schedule?
Why is the deployment happening?	Is the deployment needed to fix a problem or is it required for some new functionality that has been requested, and do the users understand what is coming?
What are the critical success factors and exit criteria?	How will you know that the deployment has been successful? Who will authorize the deployment? How will you know when the deployment is finished?
What is the current capability of the service provider?	What are the current services, processes and service management capability – capacity, financial aspects, current systems and infrastructure?

Logistics and delivery planning

Once the overall deployment approach is understood, develop the logistics and delivery plans. These plans deal with aspects such as:

- How and when release units and service components will be delivered
- What the typical lead times are; what happens if there is a delay
- How to track progress of the delivery and obtain confirmation of delivery
- Availability of secure storage where required
- Management of customs and other implications of international distribution.

As well as the delivery aspects, there are typically consequential logistics to be dealt with, e.g. decommissioning and disposing of redundant items, including software and licences, hardware, skills, computer and staff accommodation, support contracts (utility supply, maintenance, cleaners etc.). There may also be a need for temporary equipment (sometimes known as swing equipment) or temporary software that is required for the transition.

If the transition plans call for any parallel running of services or equipment, this is particularly taxing from a logistics perspective, since double facilities are likely to be required (ideally for a short time).

Once the logistics and delivery plans have been determined, they need to be communicated to all stakeholders, including formal notification to those consulted in devising the plan.

Delivery is not sufficient; successful logistics requires that the components arrive and perform as required. Therefore, deployment planning for all despatched items – hardware, software, documentation, and training – will address how components are tracked and documented on delivery. This should include:

- Checking against a definitive list of required service assets and components' unique IDs and versions
- A delivery note detailing the components to be delivered, including unique IDs, versions and quantities
- What there should be (contents list to check against)

- What needs to be there to meet the delivery in terms of equipment, prerequisites and corequisites
- How to ensure the components are correct/working – what tools, parameters, feedback mechanisms, acceptance criteria need to be applied?
- Metrics for monitoring and determining success of the deployment effort.

Planning of pilots

Pilots are useful for testing the service with a small part of the user base before rolling it out to the whole service community. It is important to determine the appropriate scope of a pilot (how much of the service is to be included in the pilot, size of department or user base). This is a key step in establishing the pilot effort. If the scope is too small, insufficient functionality and implementation variations will be tested, and the likelihood of significant errors not being discovered until full deployment is higher. If the scope is too large, it will not deliver sufficient speed and flexibility to provide the expected benefits but will effectively be a first deployment.

A pilot can be used to establish the viability of most, if not all, aspects of the service. But this will only happen if all stakeholders are actively involved in the pilot and use the service as if it were part of a full deployment.

The pilot should include steps to collect feedback on the effectiveness of the release and of the deployment plan. This can include:

- Surveying views and satisfaction from:
  - End users
  - Customers
  - Suppliers
  - Service desk and other support staff
- Service operation functions
- Data and knowledge management – statistics on use and effectiveness
- Analysing statistics from service desk calls, suppliers, capacity and availability.

Commitment to support the pilot is required from all involved parties. Obtaining that commitment can be a challenge since pilots typically will represent additional work for those users involved over and above their day jobs. Collaboration from suppliers and support staff (who may have

to support two versions of a service in parallel or deliver a small separate unit dedicated to supporting the pilot) must also be obtained.

Planning should accommodate rolling back a pilot. This will be required if there are significant failures during the pilot and may be needed to ensure that pilot users have the correct baseline before the full deployment of an authorized new service. In addition, users who were part of the pilot should be working with the same components of a service as other users after the full deployment, rather than the setup put in place for the pilot. If a decision is made not to roll back the pilot, it is essential to verify that pilot users have exactly the same final configuration as other users. This simplifies day-to-day operations in IT service management.

Although a pilot is often thought of as one trial in the live environment before rolling a service out across the full customer and user environment, there may be justification for a range of pilots, e.g. one for deployment to each geographical region. Many considerations are relevant, with the best solution for a given circumstance being a balance between benefit and cost. Factors include:

- **Speed and cost** A single pilot will be cheaper and faster than multiple trials, and will be the obvious choice for a homogeneous organization where a single pilot will encounter (almost) all eventualities and so provide a high degree of confidence that a successful pilot would be followed by a successful deployment across the wider organization.
- **Diverse organization** In an organization with a range of circumstances across the user base, or with multiple operating environments, a matching range of pilots may be sensible, with a trial in each of the areas. These can be managed in parallel, with simultaneous trialling in each environment, which reduces elapsed time but increases management overheads and complexity. Alternatively, by running the pilots serially, lessons learned in one environment may be usefully applied to the subsequent pilots, since even in a diverse organization there is likely to be significant common ground, e.g. within the actual service components. Examples of significant diversity include:
  - Different training methods needed for different groups

- Technology
- Language or culture
- Network capability.

■ **Pilot options** Where alternative solutions are possible for a major deployment, it may be worth trying each of the options in a separate pilot (preferably in closely matched areas to make comparisons meaningful). Armed with the results from each pilot, a decision as to the approach for the main deployment can be taken based on solid empirical evidence.

■ **Political considerations** Internal or external political issues may mean that a specific group or groups must be involved – or not involved – in a pilot for a new or changed service.

Example of the need for multiple piloting

A government organization delivers desktop IT services to all its staff – in corporate headquarters (HQ) and in locations throughout the world. When new or significant changes are to be deployed, typically three parallel pilots are carried out to test the three levels of communication and support technology that have been identified:

■ Those in HQ on direct network connection and with local dedicated support staff
■ Those in larger locations with reliable high-speed connection and semi-specialized local IT administrators
■ Those in smaller locations with unreliable communications and no trained local support.

Experience has shown that the three groups have different implementation and support issues and that the pilots with all three types of customer are worth the extra costs and complications.

Financial/commercial planning

Financial and commercial aspects will need to be specifically checked before the deployment, and activities should be added to the deployment plans where necessary. For example:

■ **Working capital** Are sufficient funds available to deliver the customer expectations, e.g. to fund initial changes to gain emotional acceptance during the deployment?

■ **Contracts and licences** Have all necessary contract and licence transfers been arranged?

■ **Funding** Is funding available for the supporting systems to manage the service, e.g. CMS and related licences?

■ **Intellectual property** Has the full range of IP, its ongoing ownership and usage been addressed, including:
- Software developed by one of the parties
- Documentation such as user manuals?

4.4.5.2 Release build and test

During the release build and test stage, the common services and infrastructure need to be managed carefully, since they can significantly affect the build and test of a technology-enabled service and its underlying technology infrastructure. Key aspects that need to be managed during the activities to build and test a service or service offering are:

■ Usage of the build and test environments
■ Standardization and integration aspects
■ Management of the configurations:
- During the build and test activities, e.g. version control, baseline management, control of inputs and outputs from a build or test stage
- Recording the complete record of the build so that it can be rebuilt if required
- Maintaining evidence of testing, e.g. test results and test report
- Controlling access rights to physical and technology components, e.g. setting parameters
- Checking that security requirements are met
- Verification activities, e.g. checking that prerequisites are met before a build or test begins
- Managing environmental issues, e.g. space, cooling, power, fire precautions, accessibility and safety measures
- Preparing and controlling the service release ready for promotion to the next environment
- Promoting or handing over the service release to the next stage or team.

Configuration baselines of the controlled environments and the release package before and after an installation, build or deployment are recorded in the CMS to provide a restore point. The configuration information also needs to be updated to reflect the receipt and implementation of a release unit or the complete release package to a deployment group or target environment. The definitive version of the release package (authorized by change management) must be placed in the DML even where the release package consists only of documentation for a hardware upgrade. The release package must always be taken from the DML to deploy to the service operation readiness, service acceptance and live environments.

Release and build documentation

Procedures, templates and guidance should be used to enable the release team to take service assets and products from internal and external suppliers and build an integrated release package efficiently and effectively.

Procedures and documents for purchasing, distributing, installing, moving and controlling assets and components that are relevant to acquiring, building and testing a release include:

- Contracts and agreements (e.g. for ordering new equipment or software)
- Purchase requests and ordering
- Request fulfilment
- Goods inwards and delivery
- Health and safety guidelines
- Security policies and procedures
- Leasing agreements
- Intellectual property rights/digital rights
- Support agreements
- Procedures for:
  - Managing service and infrastructure configurations
  - Distributing and installing software
  - Distributing, translating and converting data and information
  - Delivering, installing and moving equipment
  - Cleansing data and media
  - Disposing of documentation, media and equipment
  - Building, commissioning and decommissioning test environments, infrastructures and facilities
  - Publishing knowledge, information and data
  - Service validation and testing
  - Change management
- Service asset and configuration management
- Acceptance and authorization

- Documenting licence agreements and licence headings together with 'proof of licence'.

'Proof of licence' is what a court will accept as proof of a legal entity having a licence. Each software manufacturer in general states the requirements for their proof of licence, so no hard-and-fast rules can be given here. As a general principle, proof of licence requires some form of evidence directly from the software manufacturer. There is a spectrum of types of evidence for having a proof of licence. Typical examples include:

- Printed licence confirmation documents from software manufacturers (with security features)
- Electronic licence confirmation documents from software manufacturers held on controlled-access websites
- Certificates of authenticity (COAs), which are typically engraved or have other security features. These may be loose pieces of paper, pieces of paper pasted onto manual covers, labels glued onto equipment, labels printed or glued on retail boxes.

The proposed solution should be documented to enable knowledge gathered during the build and test stage to be handed over to the service operation functions and continual service improvement to be retained for future releases. It is important that the information is ordered and maintained in a systematic manner, as during the build and test activities, updates to the documentation will be required. The documentation includes:

- Roles and responsibilities
- Process descriptions and procedures
- Support and operations manuals, service desk scripts etc.
- Communications, training and knowledge transfer deliverables
- User manuals with work instructions
- Service information
- Business context and marketing information
- Service catalogue, SLA and supporting documentation:
  - Hardware and software information
  - Logical and physical architectural overview
  - Detailed technical descriptions and references
- Technical information
- Service management and operations plans

- IT service continuity planning details
- Index of documentation for the service and release – baselined.

Acquire and test input configuration items and components

Configuration items and components (e.g. services, service assets) are acquired from projects, suppliers, partners and development groups. To prevent the acquisition of unknown and potentially risky components for a build it is essential to use CIs that have achieved a certain quality level or components from a catalogue of standard components that have been previously assessed, tested and authorized for use in specific conditions. Otherwise, a request for change should be submitted to assess the component and either incorporate it into the standards catalogue or accept it as a one-off exception for this release.

The acquisition activities include:

- Interfacing with procurement processes to acquire the components (or with internal departments if supplied in-house)
- Capturing and recording:
  - New or updated service assets and CIs through SACM
  - Receipt of components
  - Delivery, change and release documentation from the supplier
- Checking, monitoring and reporting the quality of incoming CIs and service components
- Ensuring that proof of licence can be demonstrated where required
- Initiating action if quality is different from expectation, and assessing the likely impact of this on the transition
- Updating status of configuration items through SACM, e.g. to indicate that they are either ready to be released into the next stage or rejected.

Verification activities to check the components destined for a release package or build include:

- Establishing that all items are correct and have genuinely been ordered or commissioned
- Checking that standard labelling and naming conventions have been applied as specified in the design specifications for the CIs and service components

- Recording externally acquired items and checking these against their delivery and release documentation
- Checking that:
  - Developed products and service components have successfully passed appropriate documented quality reviews
  - All software is as expected and no malicious additions are included (e.g. software items that could contain viruses)
  - All amendments to previous versions or configuration baselines have been authorized by change management and no other amendments have been included – this may require a configuration audit and comparison facilities to check against the desired configuration
  - All definitive items have been added to the DML and correctly recorded in the CMS
  - Rejection/return of components is adequately controlled and documented.

Issues, non-conformance, known errors and deviations reports about the quality of service components and any risks should be passed to the relevant stakeholders, e.g. quality assurance, CSI or service design.

Release packaging

Build management procedures, methodologies, tools and checklists should be applied to ensure that the release package is built in a standard, controlled and reproducible way in line with the solution design defined in the service design package. As a release package progresses towards live use, it may need to be rebuilt (for example, if a newer version of a CI or component needs to be incorporated quickly to fix errors or if the documentation needs to be updated).

The key activities to build a release package are:

- Assemble and integrate the release components in a controlled manner to ensure a reproducible process
- Create the build and release documentation including:
  - Build, installation and test plans, procedures and scripts
  - Details of how to monitor and check the quality of the release and how to recognize and react to issues

- The automated or manual processes and procedures required to distribute, deploy and install the release into the target environment (or remove it as necessary)
- Procedures to back out release units or remediate a change should a release fail
- Procedures for tracking and managing software licences and digital rights

■ Install and verify the release package
■ Baseline the contents of the release package
■ Send a service notification to inform relevant parties that the release package is available for installation and use.

If testing of a release package is successful, then the release and the contents of the release package are baselined, verified against the release design and release package definition, and updated in the configuration management system. All changes to the release package are managed through change management, even minor changes to fix errors in testing. If at any step the testing of a release package does not complete successfully, reassessment and rescheduling of the release is managed through change management.

Build and manage the test environments

Effective build and test environment management is essential to ensure that the builds and tests are executed in a repeatable and manageable manner. Inadequate control of these environments can result in unplanned changes compromising the testing activities and/or causing significant re-work. Dedicated build environments should be established for assembling and building the components for controlled test and deployment environments.

Preparation of the test environments includes building, changing or enhancing the test environments ready to receive the release.

An IT service is, on most occasions, built from a number of technology resources or management assets. In the build phase, these different blocks, often from different suppliers, are installed and configured together to create the solution as designed. Standardization facilitates the integration of the different building blocks to provide a working solution and service.

Automating the installation of systems and application software onto servers and workstations reduces dependency on people and streamlines

the procedures. Depending on the release and deployment plans, the installation may be performed in advance (for example, if equipment is being replaced) or it may have to take place in the live environment.

The physical infrastructure elements, together with the environment in which they will operate, need to be tested appropriately. This may include testing the replication of the infrastructure solution from one environment to another. This gives a better guarantee that the deployment to the live environment will be successful.

Test environments must be actively maintained and protected using service management best practices. For any significant change to a service, the following question should be asked (as it is for the continued relevance of continuity and capacity plans): 'If this change goes ahead, will there need to be a consequential change to the test data?' During the build and test activities, operations and support teams need to be kept fully informed and involved as the solution is built to facilitate a structured transfer from the project to the operations team.

Service testing and pilots

The testing activities are coordinated through test management, which plans and controls the testing execution as described in section 4.5. Testing aims to build confidence in the service capability prior to final acceptance during pilot or early life support. It will be based on the test strategy and model for the service being changed.

The test criteria reflect the anticipated conditions in which the service is expected to operate and deliver benefit. However, these surrounding circumstances may change, and in many modern situations such change is almost inevitable and often unpredictable. These changes and their impact on service testing and acceptance must be observed, understood and documented. Their consequences need to be expressed in terms of changed acceptance criteria and updates to the service charter. This will need the collaboration and input of the business, customers and other affected stakeholders, which may well include suppliers and operations. The service designer will be involved in making any amendments since this knowledge may assist in building in additional and relevant flexibility to designs of future new or changed services.

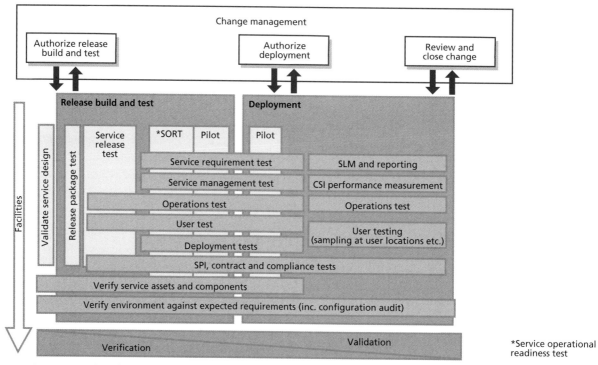

Figure 4.24 Example of service testing through service transition

An example of tests that can be executed during release and deployment management is shown in Figure 4.24. Further details of these tests are described in section 4.5 on service validation and testing. In practice, the test types overlap the different levels of testing to provide a full range of testing across the service lifecycle.

A service release test checks that the service components can be integrated correctly and that the release can be installed, built and tested in the target environment.

Service operation readiness testing ensures that a service and its underlying application and technology infrastructure can be transferred into the live environment in a controlled manner. It provides a level of confidence that the new or changed service will provide the level of service specified in the service requirements and service level requirements. However, it is too early to finalize the SLA at this point. The SLA is finalized in the pilot or more usually in early life support before the service transition is closed. The service operational readiness test aims to:

■ Determine whether a service and its underlying service assets can be released into the live environment, for the first time and for subsequent deployments

■ Ensure that the business processes, customers, users and service provider interfaces (SPIs) are capable of using the service properly

■ Ensure that the service teams are capable of operating the service and using the service management systems properly.

Tests that are conducted as part of service operational readiness test include:

■ **Deployment readiness test** To ensure that the deployment processes, procedures and systems can deploy, install, commission and decommission the release package and resultant new or changed service in the target environment

■ **Service management test** To ensure that the service performance can be measured, monitored and reported in live use

■ **Service operation test** To ensure that the service teams will be able to operate the service in live use

■ **Service level test** To ensure that the new or changed service will deliver the service level requirements

■ **User test** To ensure that users can access and use the new or changed service, e.g. they have access to the updated service catalogue and contact details for the service desk

- **Service provider interface test** To ensure that interfaces to the service are working
- **Deployment verification test** To ensure that the service capability has been correctly deployed for each target deployment group or environment.

Service rehearsals

A service rehearsal (sometimes referred to as 'model office') is a simulation of as much of the service as possible in an extensive and widely participatory practice session. It is the ultimate stage of internal testing – the last stage before any public live running. This is like a 'dress rehearsal' of a play, setting out all the elements – costume, lighting etc. – in a last private run-through of the performance. It can deliver significant benefits by identifying errors and unworkable procedures before they impact the business in live operation. However, service rehearsals are complex, time-consuming and relatively expensive to prepare, deliver and document. A careful and deliberate balance is therefore required between the anticipated costs and the issues that they could prevent.

A service rehearsal takes place just before deployment of the service. If it is held too early there is a significant chance that the environment, technology, people and legislation into which the service is being released will change and invalidate the results; if it occurs too close to the declared release date, any issues found will not be addressed before the service goes live.

The objectives of the service rehearsal include:

- Confirmation that all stakeholders have been identified and are committed to operating or using the service – if not this will be evidenced through lack of players for roles within the service rehearsal
- Verification that all stakeholders have processes and procedures in place and are ready to receive process and resolve incidents, problems and changes relating to the new or changed service
- Testing the effectiveness of 'mistake proofing' included within the service procedures. (Mistake proofing, often referred to by the Japanese term 'Poka Yoke', is about introducing advance warnings of user mistakes or bad practice and where possible introducing steps in the procedures to prevent these mistakes – for example electrical switch interlocks, and check-

sum digits in data entry.) While testing can check how a service reacts for predicted user error, the service rehearsal will encourage unforeseen behaviour and establish how that behaviour affects the service's ability to deliver the required benefits.

The service rehearsal requires adequate representation from all stakeholders, with commitment to providing staff for – typically – a full-day rehearsal for a new or significantly changed service. It is often beneficial to involve 'ordinary' representatives of the stakeholder community, rather than those with previous experience or knowledge of the service. Typical mistakes will be more likely to come from typical users – those who have been involved in design and development will find it impossible to 'unlearn' and will be coloured by their expectations of service behaviour.

The focus of a service rehearsal is typically on one day of actual rehearsal, but successful delivery of a service rehearsal involves more stages, including preparation and analysis, mirroring the Plan–Do–Check–Act cycle. Typical stages for a service rehearsal would include the following activities.

PLAN – PREPARE FOR THE DAY

A request is generated for a service rehearsal – the project or service implementation teams consider that a service rehearsal would be appropriate and trigger the process with a request.

Tasks include the following:

- Appoint a rehearsal manager who gathers all relevant information
- Identify key and secondary processes
- Identify all stakeholders and their contact information
- Produce the initial rehearsal guide – the script to be followed
- Establish and document typical examples of incidents, service requests, capacity and availability issues and other events that will need to be handled when the service is live
- Produce documentation to allow the simulation, processing, tracking and analysis of the expected scenarios
- Identify all stakeholders, supplier and service provider personnel who need to be involved and ensure their commitment, through direct funding, internal commitment etc.

- Create detailed scripts – in collaboration with the customer or business relationship manager
- Invite all stakeholders to planning and preparation meetings and briefings (this could be by documentation, email, webinars etc. if physical briefings are not practicable.)

DO – DELIVER THE REHEARSAL

Meetings are held to:

- Introduce the objectives, documents, involvement, recording etc.
- Walk through the scenarios and scripts to establish authenticity of the approach at a detailed level
- Carry out the rehearsal, i.e. let the players deliver the script and observe the processing of key events and elements, e.g. follow an incident through from occurrence to logging, diagnosis, resolution, recovery and closure.

CHECK – DOCUMENT THE DAY

Tasks include:

- Analysing and evaluating the results of the rehearsal and determining the implications
- Producing a written test report on the rehearsal, with recommendations, e.g. re-work the service before deployment
- Recording identified errors, issues and risks.

ACT – TAKE ACTION FOLLOWING THE REHEARSAL

Considering the results from the rehearsal, the options will be:

- Declare service to have passed without serious concern.
- Consider that the service is not suitable for progressing at this stage and refer back to service design and/or service transition for re-work and rescheduling. (It may occasionally be that service rehearsal shows that the actual environment in which the service is expected to function is sufficiently different from expectation to prevent acceptable behaviour from the service in reality – this might require rethink and revision at the service strategy and/or business process level.)
- Review and close the service rehearsal, providing improvement ideas to the CSI register, service design and service transition lifecycle stages as appropriate.

Pilots

Pursuing the theatrical analogy seen in service rehearsal, if the service rehearsal is the 'dress rehearsal' – the last practice before being seen by the public – then the pilot is the 'off Broadway' run of a play. It is done for real and in public, but for a small audience only and with the expectation of further (hopefully minor) polishing of the performance, script, scenery and effects. Conducting a pilot is easier to control as it is deployed to a smaller environment/user base.

A pilot sets out to detect if any elements of the service do not deliver as required and to identify gaps/issues in service management that put the service and/or the customer's business and assets at risk. It does not need to cover all service and system functionality, but will focus on the areas of risk and perform enough of the service to determine if it will work sufficiently well in deployment. It aims to ensure that the service capability supports delivery of the service requirements and service level requirements. As far as possible it should check that the utilities are fit for purpose and the warranties are fit for use.

Establish clear objectives for the pilot implementation such as:

- To establish metrics and provide confidence that the predicted performance and service levels will be met
- To evaluate the actual benefits and costs achieved during the pilot against the business case
- To create acceptance of new processes and ways of working within the user base, service provider and suppliers
- To identify, assess and mitigate some of the risks associated with a full deployment.

As there are likely to be design changes and improvements that need to be built into the release before full deployment, it is important to agree how these will be funded up front. It is also important to ensure that there is common understanding about how the pilot implementation will be signed off.

During the pilot, the release and deployment management team should:

- Be ready to invoke contingency/recovery procedures

- Involve key people that will be involved in the full deployment
- Ensure that people involved in the pilot are trained and that they understand their new/changed roles and responsibilities
- Document necessary operational and support procedures, information and training materials that cannot be adequately simulated in a test environment
- Establish the viability of training and support documentation and modify where necessary
- Establish customer, user and stakeholder interaction with the service in real-time situations, e.g. with real business decisions being made
- Capture appropriate metrics to compare with the service performance model
- Establish additional criteria that may need to be met before full deployment starts
- Determine the likely level of service support and service management resources that will be required and resolve any issues
- Discover and fix issues and errors early and fix many of them before final deployment. This includes the less critical minor irritations and eccentricities of a service that would not necessarily cause non-acceptance but do significantly reduce the emotional acceptance of the service among the user community
- Document improvements and where appropriate incorporate them into plans for full deployment or add them to the CSI register.

When the release has been in use for a sufficient period during a pilot it is important to check that the service is capable of delivering the requirements of the customer, users and the service design as well as the predicted outcomes (although not all of these will be realized at this point).

If the pilot is of sufficient length, it may be appropriate to conduct a formal change evaluation to compare the actual versus predicted service capability and performance (specified in the service design) on behalf of the stakeholders, users and customers. This change evaluation includes a risk assessment on whether the service will continue to deliver the service requirements, e.g. service levels and warranties.

The outputs from a successfully delivered service pilot will include:

- New or changed service and capabilities that have been tested and evaluated
- Pilot test report and results
- Report generated by the change evaluation process, which is passed to change management and which comprises an updated risk profile, deviations report and recommendation
- Key stakeholder agreement that the release is ready for a full deployment
- Demonstrated benefits of the service (within agreed tolerance levels)
- Confirmation that the deployment team has tested the deployment process and accepts the cost model, deployment model and metrics to be used for monitoring during deployment and early life support
- Target deployment groups in different geographical locations accepting the service release and committing to the deployment plans, particularly groups with different cultures and languages.

4.4.5.3 Deployment

Plan and prepare for deployment

The planning and preparation activities prepare the group for deployment. This is an opportunity to prepare the organization and people for organizational change; see section 5.2. The overall approach to planning the deployment is described in release and deployment planning (see section 4.4.5.1). During the actual deployment stage the detailed implementation plan is developed. This includes assigning individuals to specific activities. For example, a specific individual may be assigned to deliver training for a training activity on the deployment plan.

The entry criteria for planning and preparing a target deployment group or environment include:

- Deployment stakeholders are sufficiently confident in the service release to deploy the release, own their aspects of deployment and are committed to the deployment (see section 5.2).
- Senior management, customers, the business and service provider teams accept the deployment costs, management, organization and people implications of the release as well as any organization, function and process changes.

An example of the deployment activities that apply to the deployment for a target group is shown in Figure 4.25.

Preparing for deployment includes assessing each deployment group's readiness to receive and implement a release package, identifying gaps that need to be filled and planning the activities required to deploy, transfer or decommission/retire services or service assets. It may also include transferring a service or a service unit within an organization or between organizations, as well as moving and disposal activities.

ASSESS READINESS OF TARGET GROUP

Although the deployment assessment should be conducted early, it should be revisited periodically. The results of this assessment are fed into detailed implementation planning for the target deployment group.

The readiness assessment for a deployment group identifies:

■ Issues and risks in delivering the current services that may affect the deployment. The kinds of risk include:
  ● Lack of dedicated internal resources and external supplier resources
  ● Lack of training, skills and awareness
  ● Unplanned or late change in requirements
■ Anticipated impacts, e.g. on the organizational structure, environment for the new or changed services, direct customers and users, partners or suppliers
■ Gaps that need to be filled.

The aspects to assess include:

■ Financial aspects and assets:
  ● Current and required working capital
  ● Establishment of new or changed contracts, licences, IPR and digital rights
■ Issues and risks in delivering the current services that may affect the deployment

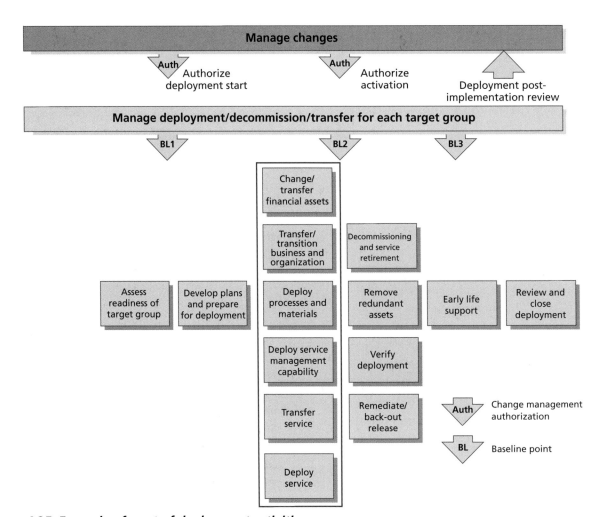

Figure 4.25 Example of a set of deployment activities

- Applicable health, safety, security and environmental regulations, supplier and procurement aspects
- Current capability of the business customers and users to use and gain value from the new or changed service
- Current service, service capability and resources used including:
  - Service structure
  - Service dynamics
  - Service metrics and reports, including warranties and service levels achieved
- Current service management capability and resources including:
  - Differences from the prerequisites for deployment, e.g. inadequate licensing arrangements, network bandwidth
  - Current operations and support resources, e.g. tools, people
  - Support resources and workloads as there may be a significant increase in the number of incidents per user, which can stretch the resources for managing incidents, problems and fixes
  - Performance reports and improvement plans
  - Ability to predict and track the actual incident and problem volumes during deployment; this may require updating asset or user records with the date and time of installation or deployment to enable trend analysis
- Identifying requirements to tailor the new or changed service or underlying solution, e.g. processes, procedures, work instructions
- Organizational readiness:
  - Role, resource and skills gap analysis
  - Training needs analysis
  - Ability to assign competent individuals to the required roles
  - Motivation and empowerment – do the current organization and culture encourage the application of the required skills? Is there the right leadership and commitment?
  - Assess the readiness of customers, users, service provider staff and other stakeholders such as suppliers and partners
- Aspects relating to applications, information and data:
  - Access to application, information and data
  - Access to secret, restricted or confidential documents and data
  - Knowledge and experience in using the application – users and support staff
- Infrastructure and facilities:
  - Difficult access, e.g. located high up in a building without appropriate lifting equipment (elevator or crane etc.); city centre with restricted parking; remote locations
  - Intermediate and final storage and stores for definitive hardware and media
  - IT equipment space and capacity requirements such as size and equipment footprints; power requirements and circuit-breaker ratings; uninterruptible power supply (UPS) and generator loadings; temperature and humidity requirements; heat outputs and air-conditioning requirements; door clearance and engineering access requirements; cabling requirements
  - Electromagnetic interference (EMI) and radio frequency interference (RFI) requirements
  - Air quality requirements
  - Weight and floor loadings
  - Network considerations
  - Equipment health, safety, security and environmental requirements.

DEVELOP PLANS

Planning for a specific deployment includes assigning specific resources to perform deployment and early life support activities. While developing these plans, identify and assess risks specific to this deployment group by using the service model to identify business and service-critical assets that have the highest risk of causing disruption. The activities include:

- Risk mitigation plans
- Developing transfer/transition, upgrade, conversion, disposal, retirement plans
- Logistics and delivery planning:
  - Service assets and components for deployment, establishing how and when they will be delivered, and confirmation that delivery has been successfully achieved and recorded

- Site preparation in accordance with applicable health, safety, security and environmental regulations and requirements
- Tailoring processes, procedures and knowledge, e.g. language translation, time frame adjustments
- Knowledge transfer and training stakeholders in how to use, benefit, manage, support and operate the new or changed service:
  - Identify essential and potential recipients of training (such as customer, users, ITSM, service desk, support, operations, deployment teams, projects)
  - Update service desk with knowledge of the target deployment group and their environment
- Communicating to the people involved:
  - About the changes and the expected benefits
  - How the change affects the organization and staff
- Making any changes in emergency or continuity plans and procedures
- Mobilizing the service operation functions and support organization
- Mobilizing users to be ready to use the service
- Additional activities identified from the assessment.

The next step is to verify the detailed deployment plans, perform any deployment readiness tests and obtain authorization for release deployment from the change management process. The service is then ready for deployment.

Perform transfer, deployment and retirement

The following activities provide an example of the different aspects that will be performed in the order specified on the deployment plan.

CHANGE/TRANSFER FINANCIAL ASSETS

Changes and transfers of financial assets need to be completed as part of deployment. This will include but is not constrained by the following:

- Any changes in supplier financial agreements and charges
- Purchase or transfer of annual support and maintenance costs including systems to manage the service, e.g. CMS
- New licence costs and renewals
- Annual disaster recovery contracts with third parties

- Provision or transfer of working capital
- Transfer of intellectual property.

TRANSFER/TRANSITION BUSINESS AND ORGANIZATION

Transfer of a business unit, service or service unit will involve change to the organization itself. The subject of organizational and stakeholder change is addressed in Chapter 5. Activities that need to be performed include:

- Finalize organization structure, roles and responsibilities
- Communicate change in organization design, roles and responsibilities
- Ensure that people adapt to and adopt new practices. This requires good communication of the consequences and requirements of the deployed service, e.g. best use of resources to deliver the message; understanding personal and group concerns; and ensuring that messages to diverse and related groups are consistent and appropriate
- Engender, at the very least, acceptance and preferably active support of the changes imposed on people
- Ensure that people understand the continuity plans and procedures.

When the change includes a transfer of service provider – e.g. new outsourcing, insourcing or change of outsourced provider – some specific organizational elements need to be considered, e.g. organizational change, quick wins to avoid confusion and higher staff turnaround.

Competent people with the right skills are required to perform the deployment, operate and manage the new or changed service in the business, customer and service provider organization. The related activities include:

- Recruit staff with appropriate skills. Rather than developing new skills for existing staff, it may be more efficient to recruit new staff who already have the required skills. This may be in addition to existing staff, or may require the replacement of some staff who have inappropriate skills with more relevant staff for the revised circumstances of the new service.
- Identify existing people (e.g. staff, suppliers, users) with appropriate skills, moving or re-allocating people as necessary. For the skills

required to actually deploy the new or changed service, temporary secondment, or even overtime, may be the most efficient approach.

■ Consider using outsource/contract resources to provide the required skills. This is similar to seconding internal staff, but in this case buying the temporarily required skills from external providers where they already exist. If skills are needed for the longer term, a requirement to pass those skills on to permanent (or longer-term) staff can be useful.

■ Provide training. Manage the training logistics, coordination, setup, communications, registration, delivery and evaluation activities including users and service operation functions.

■ Execute the knowledge transfer plan and track progress to completion.

■ Evaluate competence of new and changed staff and other people.

DEPLOY PROCESSES AND MATERIALS

Deploy or publish the processes and materials ready for people involved in the business and service organization change, e.g. users and service operation functions that need to execute the new or changed processes. The materials may include policies, processes, procedures, manuals, overviews, training products, organizational change products etc.

Training people to use new processes and procedures can take time, particularly for a global deployment to thousands of people.

DEPLOY SERVICE MANAGEMENT CAPABILITY

Deploy new or changed processes, systems and tools to the service provider teams responsible for service management activities. Check that everyone is competent and confident to operate, maintain and manage the service in accordance with the service model and processes. Remove or archive redundant services and assets, e.g. processes, procedures and tools.

During deployment monitor the service against the service model and performance standards as far as possible.

TRANSFER SERVICE

Transferring a service will also involve organizational change described earlier in this section. The issues around transferring a service and the activities that need to be performed include:

■ Reviewing the service performance, issues and risks, by performing some service tests and a change evaluation prior to the transfer

■ Configuration auditing of service assets and configurations

■ Finalizing service catalogue (add or remove the service) and related information

■ Sending a service notification to communicate the change to relevant stakeholders.

When the change includes a transfer of service provider, e.g. new outsourcing, insourcing or change of outsourced provider, some specific service elements need to be considered that include:

■ Managing contract changes

■ Managing changes to existing agreements

■ Updating contract details and information in the supplier and contract management information system (SCMIS)

■ Transferring ownership of service assets and configuration items, remembering to update the CMS.

DEPLOY SERVICE

Deploy the service release and carry out the activities to distribute and install the service, supporting services, applications, data, information, infrastructure and facilities. These will include:

■ Distributing and delivering the service and service components at the correct location and time

■ Building, installing and configuring the services and service components with any converted or new data and information

■ Testing the system and services according to the installation and acceptance tests and producing the installation and test reports

■ Recording any incidents, unexpected events, issues or deviations from the plans

■ Correcting any deviations that are outside the design limitations and constraints.

DECOMMISSIONING AND SERVICE RETIREMENT

Some specific aspects need to be considered for decommissioning and retiring services and service assets. For example, the procedures for retiring, transferring (e.g. to another budget holder) or redeploying service assets should take into account any security, confidentiality, licensing, environmental or other contractual requirements. This includes:

■ Removing deployed copies of software and data from retired hardware; failure to do this may result in licence contravention or in staff using unsupported software

■ Identifying licences and other assets which can be redeployed; software being retired from use in one area may well remain in active use elsewhere

■ Disposing of equipment according to environmental policies and procedures

■ Updating or archiving processes, procedures, standards, documentation and any other data or information in the SKMS that were used to support the retired service

■ Updating records in the CMS

■ Moving assets that can be redeployed to secure storage areas if required. If the assets being retired are remaining in use elsewhere, especially for hardware, the released assets may serve a useful role as spare equipment to be retained in asset stores for speedy redeployment in the event of failures.

It is very important to plan for how the data and information from a retired service will be made available to the business if it is needed in the future. This may require archival to suitable long-term storage, or migration to a new service. This can be particularly difficult if there are third parties involved in managing parts of the service.

Records of retirement, transfer and disposal should be maintained and used to update other information such as licence information.

REMOVE REDUNDANT ASSETS

A comprehensive understanding of the assets used by a retired service needs to be gained and managed. With a full understanding any redundant assets can be identified and removed, thereby potentially saving licence fees, liberating

capacity and preventing accidental use. Failure to develop and properly perform these activities can result in:

■ Wasted disk space and licences

■ Overpayment of licence and maintenance fees

■ Removal of assets associated with the redundant service but also used by other services, causing incidents within those services, e.g. common software components and network elements.

As part of the clean-up activities it is important to delete or archive redundant data, information and records related to the previous service or products. The full scope and scale of a service or service asset needs to be considered, and this should extend to the following areas:

■ Support contracts with third-party suppliers, as changes in likely usage may require renegotiation of contracts

■ In-house second/third-level support staff with specialist knowledge may no longer require that knowledge. This may require re-assessment of their role, level of payment, retention etc. and opportunities for redeployment may be identified

■ Service desk workload may be affected

■ Any sensitive information or data must be securely erased before assets are released

■ Records within the knowledge base relating to the decommissioned components may need to be archived and deleted.

Further discussion of issues relating to decommissioning assets can be found in section 4.3.4.4.

Verify deployment

When the deployment activities are complete, it is important to verify that users, service operation functions, other staff and stakeholders are capable of using or operating the service. The tests should specifically verify that:

■ The service, service assets and service capability/resources are in place, e.g. by performing an audit such as a configuration audit of the deployed baseline against the as-planned baseline.

- Updates to documentation and information are completed, e.g. service catalogue, contracts, agreements, contact details in the supplier and contract management information system (SCMIS).
- Communications, orientation and learning materials are ready to distribute to stakeholders, service operation functions and users.
- All roles are assigned to individuals/organizations.
- People and other resources are prepared to operate and use the new or changed service or service capability in normal, emergency and disaster situations.
- People have access to the information necessary to use, operate or support the service.
- Measurement and reporting systems are established to assess performance of the service and underlying resources.

This is a good point to gather feedback on the deployment process to feed into future improvements, e.g. using satisfaction surveys.

Report any issues and incidents and take corrective actions as necessary.

Successful confirmation of the deployment verification triggers the initiation and launch of early life support for the deployment group.

REMEDIATE/BACK OUT RELEASE

A decision may be made to remediate the release because:

- A documented milestone is not met during the deployment
- A deployment step fails, or behaves in an unexpected manner
- Verification shows that the deployment has not succeeded.

The most common form of remediation is to back out the release, restoring all hardware, software and data to the previous baseline. Alternative forms of remediation include implementing normal changes or emergency changes to resolve problems, or invoking IT service continuity plans to provide the service.

Early life support

Early life support (ELS) provides the opportunity to transition the new or changed service to service operation in a controlled manner and establish the new service capability and resources. Formal handover of the new or changed service to the service operation functions happens in two stages. At the beginning of early life support there should be a formal notification that the service is now in live use. At the end of early life support there should be a formal notification that all SLAs are now being enforced and the service is fully operational.

An example of the ELS activities is shown in Figure 4.26.

In service design, the stakeholders will have agreed the entry and exit criteria from early life support, but it may be necessary to renegotiate performance targets and exit criteria in this stage. This can help people to understand the deployment verification process and set customer and stakeholder expectations about the handover of the service to service operation.

ELS provides appropriate resources to resolve operational and support issues quickly, centrally and locally, to ensure that the users can use the service to support their business activities without unwarranted disruption. The deployment teams should analyse where users and support resources might experience problems, perhaps based on previous experience; for example it might be helpful to clarify the following:

- Role assignments, roles and responsibilities
- Financial and funding arrangements
- Procurement and request fulfilment
- Security policies and procedures
- Raising incidents and change requests
- Escalation procedures
- Complaints procedure
- Use of diagnostics tools and aids
- Software licensing rules.

During ELS, the deployment team implements improvements and resolves problems that help to stabilize the service. *ITIL Continual Service Improvement* provides relevant information on measurement and service improvements. The deployment resources will gradually back out from providing the additional support as the users and service operation functions become familiar with the changes and the incidents and risks reduce.

Metrics for the target deployment group or environment measure service performance, performance of the service management and operations processes and teams and the number of

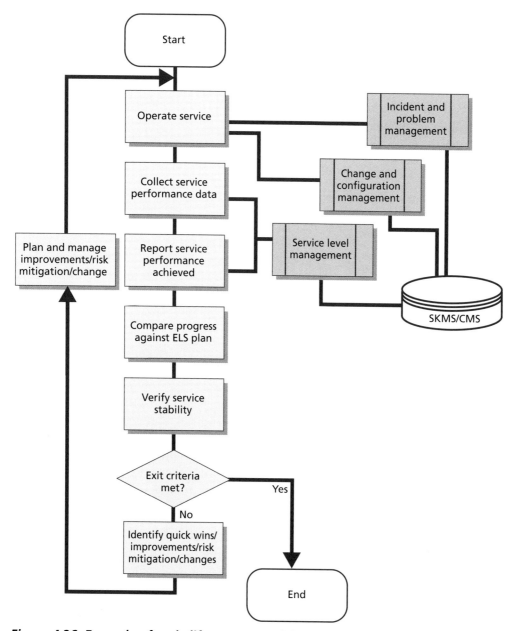

Figure 4.26 Example of early life support activities

incidents and problems by type. The deployment team's aim is to stabilize the service for the target deployment group or environment as quickly and effectively as possible. An example of a deployment performance graph is shown in Figure 4.27.

Variation in performance between different deployment groups and service units should be analysed and lessons learned from one deployment used to improve subsequent deployments.

The example shown in Figure 4.27 shows the number of incidents for two branches of a retail organization that have the same number of users and the same deployment schedule. In deployment

A the incident levels have reduced faster. On further investigation the service transition manager discovered that the team responsible for deployment A was more competent at training users and transferring knowledge to the service desk so that they could help users to be more effective more quickly.

During ELS, the deployment team should ensure that the documentation and knowledge base are updated with additional diagnostics, known errors, workarounds and frequently asked questions. The team should also resolve any knowledge transfer or training gaps.

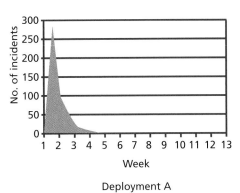

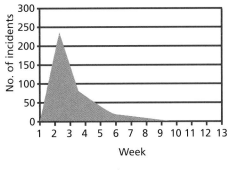

Figure 4.27 Illustration of the benefits of targeted early life support

At agreed milestones in early life support, it is important to assess the issues and risks, particularly those that impact the handover schedule and costs. Service transition monitors the performance of the new or changed service in early life support until the exit criteria are achieved. This is achieved when:

- Users can use the service effectively and efficiently for their business activities.
- Service owners and process owners are committed to manage and operate the service in accordance with the service model, performance standards and processes.
- Service delivery is managed and controlled across any service provider interface.
- Consistent progress is being made towards delivering the expected benefits and value at each milestone in early life support.
- Service levels and service performance standards are being consistently achieved without unexpected variation.
- SLAs and any other agreements are finalized and signed off by senior management and customers.
- Unexpected variations in the performance of the service and customer assets such as changes in residual risks are monitored, reported and managed appropriately.
- Checks establish that training and knowledge transfer activities are completed by obtaining positive confirmation from the target audience. These may be in the form of competency tests.
- The service release and any contractual deliverables are signed off.

4.4.5.4 Review and close

Review and close a deployment

When reviewing a deployment the following activities should be included:

- Capture experiences and feedback on customer, user and service provider satisfaction with the deployment, e.g. through feedback surveys.
- Highlight quality criteria that were not met.
- Check that any actions, necessary fixes and changes are complete.
- Review open changes and ensure that funding and responsibility for open changes are agreed before handover.
- Review performance targets and achievements, including resource use and capacity such as user accesses, transactions and data volumes.
- Make sure there are no capability, resource, capacity or performance issues at the end of the deployment.
- Check that any problems, known errors and workarounds are documented and accepted by the customers/business and/or suppliers.
- Review the risk register and identify items that impact service operation and support. Address risks or agree action such as moving the risks to the service transition risk register.
- Check that redundant assets have been removed.
- Check that the service is ready for transition from early life support into service operation.

Each deployment should consider whether any relevant issues have been detected that should be passed through to CSI, such as:

- Feedback on the deployment model and plan
- Errors in procedures detected

- 'Near misses' where things could have gone wrong in foreseeable circumstances or where intervention was required
- Incorrect data or information in relevant records
- Incident and problems caused by deployment
- Difficulties with updating records.

Deployment is completed with a handover of the support for the deployment group or target environment to the service operation functions.

A post-implementation review of each deployment is conducted through change management (note that a single transition may involve many separate deployments).

Review and close a service transition

In order to finalize that a service transition is completed, there should be a formal review carried out that is appropriate to the scale and magnitude of the change. A review of the service transition should include:

- Checking that all transition activities completed, e.g. documentation and information, are captured, updated, secured and archived
- Checking that accurate metrics were captured.

Formal evaluation of the service release uses the outputs from deployment. This change evaluation checks the actual performance and outcomes of the new or changed service against the predicted performance and outcomes, i.e. the service expected by the user or customer. An evaluation report (see section 4.6.5) is prepared that lists the deviations from the service charter/SDP, a risk profile and recommendations for change management. If there are deviations in the service level requirements then the service charter or SAC may need to change (via change management, in agreement with the customer representative and other stakeholders). Successful completion of the change evaluation ensures that the service can be formally closed and handed over to the service operation functions and CSI.

A transition report should be produced that summarizes the outcomes. As part of producing such a report a post-transition workshop could be held involving all parties as a 'lessons learned' exercise. Lessons learned and improvements are fed into change management for a post-implementation review and into continual service improvement for future transitions.

4.4.6 Triggers, inputs, outputs and interfaces

4.4.6.1 Triggers

Release and deployment management starts with receipt of an authorized change to plan, build and test a production-ready release package. Deployment starts with receipt of an authorized change to deploy a release package to a target deployment group or environment, e.g. business unit, customer group and/or service unit.

4.4.6.2 Inputs

The inputs to release and deployment management are:

- Authorized change
- Service design package (SDP) including:
  - A service charter that defines the requirements from the business/customer for the service, including a description of the expected utility and warranty, as well as outline budgets and timescales
  - Service models that describe the structure and dynamics of how the service is operated and managed
  - Service acceptance criteria
- IT service continuity plan and related business continuity plan
- Service management and operations plans and standards
- Technology and procurement standards and catalogues
- Acquired service assets and components and their documentation
- Build models and plans
- Environment requirements and specifications for build, test, release, training, disaster recovery, pilot and deployment
- Release policy and release design from service design
- Release and deployment models including template plans
- Exit and entry criteria for each stage of release and deployment management.

4.4.6.3 Outputs

The outputs from release and deployment management are:

- New, changed or retired services
- Release and deployment plan
- Updates to change management for the release and deployment activities
- Service notification
- Notification to service catalogue management to update the service catalogue with the relevant information about the new or changed service
- New tested service capability and environment including SLA, other agreements and contracts, changed organization, competent and motivated people, established business and service management processes, installed applications, converted databases, technology infrastructure, products and facilities
- New or changed service management documentation
- SLA, underpinning OLAs and contracts
- New or changed service reports
- Tested continuity plans
- Complete and accurate configuration item list with an audit trail for the CIs in the release package and also the new or changed service and infrastructure configurations
- Updated service capacity plan aligned to the relevant business plans
- Baselined release package – checked in to DML and ready for future deployments
- Service transition report.

4.4.6.4 Interfaces

Service design coordination

The service design coordination process creates the service design package that defines the new service, including all aspects of how it should be created. The SDP is a major input to release and deployment management.

Release and deployment management also has a significant role to play in production of the SDP. Plans and packages should be developed and documented during the service design stage of the service lifecycle, and service design coordination will ensure that these are documented in the SDP.

Transition planning and support

Each transition will include a requirement for release and deployment. Transition planning and support provides the framework for release and

deployment management to operate in, and transition plans provide the context for release and deployment plans.

Change management

Release and deployment management must be tightly integrated with change management. Change management provides the authorization for the work that is carried out by release and deployment management, and release and deployment management provides the actual execution of many changes.

Release and deployment plans are a significant part of the change schedule, and these must be managed together. Every deployment must be reviewed and closed when it is complete, and this will commonly be combined with the review and closure of the change.

Service asset and configuration management

Release and deployment management depends on data and information in the CMS, and provides many updates to the CMS. It is important that these updates are coordinated and managed properly as otherwise the data will not be kept up to date.

Service validation and testing

Release and deployment management must coordinate with service validation and testing, to ensure that testing is carried out when necessary, and that builds are available when required by service validation and testing.

4.4.7 Information management

Throughout the release and deployment management process, appropriate records will be created and maintained. As configuration items are successfully deployed, the CMS will be updated with information such as:

- New, changed or removed configuration items
- Relationships between requirements and test cases
- New, changed or removed locations and users
- Status updates (e.g. from allocated to live)
- Change in ownership of assets
- Licence holding.

Other data and information will also be captured and recorded within the broader service knowledge management system. This could include:

- Release packages in the DML
- Installation/build plans
- Logistics and delivery plans
- Validation and test plans, evidence and reports
- Deployment information, history of the deployment itself, who was involved, timings etc.
- Training records, typically held by HR in many organizations, but for ITSM staff the responsibility for their update will logically rest with ITSM also
- Access rules and levels
- Known errors. Typically, a new or changed service will be introduced with identified errors, which while not according to the original service design specification are nonetheless minor enough in nature to be acceptable in live operation. These may well be under active investigation and resolution by the service builders or may be considered acceptable. In either case the errors will be deployed into the live error database as an element of the deployment of the live service. This information will be made available through the SKMS to the service desk who will then be able to link incidents reported against these known errors. Known error records may be part of the CMS or maintained in some other part of the SKMS. In either case they must be linked to CIs so that they can be referenced when needed.

As part of the deployment clean-up activities it is important to delete or archive redundant records related to the previous service or products.

4.4.8 Critical success factors and key performance indicators

The following list includes some sample CSFs for release and deployment management. Each organization should identify appropriate CSFs based on its objectives for the process. Each sample CSF is followed by a small number of typical KPIs that support the CSF. These KPIs should not be adopted without careful consideration. Each organization should develop KPIs that are appropriate for its level of maturity, its CSFs and its particular circumstances. Achievement against KPIs should be monitored and used to identify opportunities for improvement, which should be logged in the CSI register for evaluation and possible implementation.

- **CSF** Defining and agreeing release plans with customers and stakeholders
  - **KPI** Increased number and percentage of releases that make use of a common framework of standards, re-usable processes and supporting documentation
  - **KPI** Increased number and percentage of releases that meet customer expectations for cost, time and quality
- **CSF** Ensuring integrity of a release package and its constituent components throughout the transition activities
  - **KPI** Reduced number of CMS and DML audit failures related to releases
  - **KPI** Reduced number of deployments from sources other than the DML
  - **KPI** Reduced number of incidents due to incorrect components being deployed
- **CSF** Ensuring that the new or changed service is capable of delivering the agreed utility and warranty
  - **KPI** Reduced variance from service performance required by customers
  - **KPI** Number of incidents against the service (low and reducing)
  - **KPI** Increased customer and user satisfaction with the services delivered
  - **KPI** Decreased customer dissatisfaction – service issues resulting from poorly tested or untested services increase the negative perception on the service provider organization as a whole
  - **KPI** Reduced resources and costs to diagnose and fix incidents and problems in deployment and live use
- **CSF** Ensuring that there is appropriate knowledge transfer
  - **KPI** Reduced number of incidents categorized as 'user knowledge'
  - **KPI** Increased percentage of incidents solved by level 1 and level 2 support
  - **KPI** Increased score in surveys of customer, user and service operation function satisfaction with release and deployment management.

4.4.9 Challenges and risks

4.4.9.1 Challenges

Challenges for release and deployment management include:

- Developing standard performance measures and measurement methods across projects and suppliers
- Dealing with projects and suppliers where estimated delivery dates are inaccurate and there are delays in scheduling service transition activities
- Understanding the different stakeholder perspectives that underpin effective risk management for the change impact assessment and test activities
- Building a thorough understanding of risks that have impacted or may impact successful service transition of services and releases
- Encouraging a risk management culture where people share information and take a pragmatic and measured approach to risk.

4.4.9.2 Risks

Risks to successful release and deployment management include:

- Poorly defined scope and understanding of dependencies in earlier lifecycle stages leading to scope creep during release and deployment management
- Using staff who are not dedicated to release and deployment management activities, especially if the effort takes a significant amount of their time
- Failing to use the release and deployment management process to manage service retirement
- Finances:
  - Shortage of finances
  - Delays move deployment into a different financial year
  - Lack of clarity on funding for changes/fixes during transition
- Controls:
  - Inadequate corporate policies, e.g. security, software licensing

  - Lack of definition of the required controls leads to poorly evaluated and unauthorized changes, adversely affecting release and deployment plans
  - Difficulty tracking and managing software licences, e.g. due to complexity
  - Unexpected changes in regulatory controls or licensing requirements
- Management of organizational and stakeholder change:
  - Unclear expectations/objectives from customers, users, suppliers and other stakeholders
  - Cultural differences/misunderstandings
  - Human factors
  - Relationships with suppliers/partners
  - Poor communication
  - Organizational change affecting employee morale
  - Problems arising from infringement of personal data protection criteria
  - Personality clashes
  - Key personnel who have inadequate authority to fulfil their roles
  - Poor staff recruitment and selection procedures
  - Lack of clarity over roles and responsibilities
  - Vested interests creating conflict and compromising quality
  - Individual or group interests given unwarranted priority
- Poor commitment and decision-making
- Failure to obtain appropriate authorization at the right time
- Indecision or late decision-making
- Lack of operational support
- Inadequate or inaccurate information
- Health and safety compromised
- Time allowed for release and deployment management – will it make or break the project?
- Suppliers/sourcing/partnering relationships during transition:
  - Failure of suppliers to meet contractual obligations; this could be in terms of quality, quantity, timescales or their own exposure to risk
  - Delays in contract negotiation

- Organizational change having a major impact on employee morale, employee and supplier performance
- Data protection impacting on data sharing
- Shrinking resource pool from disaffected employees
- Senior management commitment missing in one or other of the organizations
- Immature or non-existent supplier management process
- Changes in work practices and procedures adversely affecting one or other of the organizations
- Inadequate 'back-out' or 'contingency' plan if sourcing/partnering fails
- Application/technical infrastructure risks:
  - Inadequate design
  - Professional negligence
  - Human error/incompetence
  - Infrastructure failure
  - Differences/dependencies in infrastructure/applications
  - Increased dismantling/decommissioning costs
  - Safety being compromised
  - Performance failure (people or equipment)
  - Breaches in physical security/information security
  - Unforeseen barriers or constraints due to infrastructure.

4.5 SERVICE VALIDATION AND TESTING

The underlying concept to which service validation and testing contributes is quality assurance – establishing that the service design and release will deliver a new or changed service or service offering that is fit for purpose and fit for use. Testing is a vital area within service management and has often been the unseen underlying cause of what was taken to be inefficient service management processes. If services are not tested sufficiently, their introduction into the live environment will bring a rise in:

- Incidents, since failures in service elements and mismatches between what was wanted and what was delivered impact on business support
- Service desk calls for clarification, since services that are not functioning as intended are inherently less intuitive, causing a higher support requirement

- Problems and errors that are harder to diagnose in the live environment
- Costs, since errors are more expensive to fix in the live environment than if found in testing
- Services that are not used effectively by the users to deliver the desired value.

4.5.1 Purpose and objectives

The purpose of the service validation and testing process is to ensure that a new or changed IT service matches its design specification and will meet the needs of the business.

The objectives of service validation and testing are to:

- Provide confidence that a release will create a new or changed service that delivers the expected outcomes and value for the customers within the projected costs, capacity and constraints
- Quality assure a release, its constituent service components, the resultant service and service capability delivered by a release
- Validate that a service is 'fit for purpose' – it will deliver the required utility
- Provide assurance that a service is 'fit for use' – it will deliver the agreed warranty
- Confirm that the customer and stakeholder requirements for the new or changed service are correctly defined and remedy any errors or variances early in the service lifecycle as this is considerably cheaper than fixing errors in the live environment
- Plan and implement a structured validation and testing process that provides objective evidence that the new or changed service will support the customer's business and stakeholder requirements, including the agreed service levels
- Identify, assess and address issues, errors and risks throughout service transition.

4.5.2 Scope

The service provider takes responsibility for delivering, operating and/or maintaining customer or service assets at specified levels of warranty, under a service agreement. Service validation and testing can be applied throughout the service lifecycle to quality assure any aspect of a service and the service providers' capability, resources and capacity to deliver a service and/or service release successfully. When validating and testing an end-to-end service, the interfaces to suppliers, customers and partners are important. Service provider interface definitions define the boundaries of the service to be tested, e.g. process interfaces and organizational interfaces.

Testing is equally applicable to in-house or developed services, hardware, software or knowledge-based services. It includes the testing of new or changed services or service components and examines the behaviour of these in the target business unit, service unit, deployment group or environment. This environment could have aspects outside the control of the service provider, e.g. public networks, user skill levels or customer assets.

Testing directly supports the release and deployment management process by ensuring that appropriate levels of testing are performed during release and deployment management activities. It evaluates the detailed service models to ensure that they are fit for purpose and fit for use before being authorized to enter service operation, through the service catalogue. The output from testing is used by the change evaluation process to provide information on whether the service is formally judged to be delivering the service performance with an acceptable risk profile.

4.5.3 Value to business

Service failures can harm the service provider's business and the customer's assets and result in outcomes such as loss of reputation, loss of money, loss of time, injury and death. Key values to the business and customers from service testing and validation are, firstly, confidence that a new or changed service will deliver the value and outcomes required of it and, secondly, an understanding of the risks.

Successful testing depends on all parties understanding that it cannot give, indeed should not give, any guarantees but provides a measured degree of confidence. The required degree of confidence varies depending on the customer's business requirements and pressures of an organization.

4.5.4 Policies, principles and basic concepts

4.5.4.1 Service validation and testing policies

Policies for the service validation and testing process will reflect the requirements from service strategy and service design and should help service validation and testing staff to meet the expectations of the business. Typical policy statements might include:

■ All tests must be designed and carried out by people who have not been involved in other design or development activities for the service.

■ Test pass/fail criteria must be documented in a service design package before the start of any testing. Every test environment must be restored to a known state before testing is started.

■ Test library and re-use policy. The nature of IT service management is repetitive and benefits greatly from re-use. Service validation and testing should create, catalogue and maintain a library of test models, test cases, test scripts and test data that can be re-used. Projects and service teams need to be motivated and incentivized to create re-usable test assets and re-use test assets.

■ Integrate testing into the project and service lifecycle. This helps to detect and remove functional and non-functional defects as soon as possible and reduces the incidents in the live environment.

■ Adopt a risk-based testing approach aimed at reducing risk to the service and the customer's business.

■ Engage with customers, stakeholders, users and service teams throughout the project and service lifecycle to enhance their testing skills and capture feedback on the quality of services and service assets.

■ Establish test measurements and monitoring systems to improve the efficiency and effectiveness of service validation and testing.

■ Automate using automated testing tools and systems, particularly where:
  ● Complex systems and services are involved, such as geographically distributed services, large-scale infrastructures and business-critical applications.

- Time to change is critical, e.g. if there are tight deadlines and a tendency to squeeze testing windows.

Service validation and testing is also affected by policies from many other areas of service management. Policies that drive and support service validation and testing include service quality policy, risk policy, service transition policy, release policy and change management policy.

Service quality policy

Senior leadership will define the meaning of service quality, based on input from customers and other stakeholders. Service strategy discusses the quality perspectives that a service provider needs to consider. In addition to service level metrics, service quality takes into account the positive impact of the service (utility) and the certainty of impact (warranty). *ITIL Service Strategy* outlines four quality perspectives:

- Level of excellence
- Value for money
- Conformance to specifications
- Meeting or exceeding expectations.

One or more, if not all four, of these perspectives is usually required to guide the measurement and control of service management processes. The dominant perspective will influence how services are measured and controlled, which in turn will influence how services are designed and operated. Understanding the quality perspective will influence the service design and the approach to service validation and testing.

Risk policy

Different customer segments, organizations, business units and service units have different attitudes to risk. Where an organization is an enthusiastic taker of business risk, testing will be looking to establish a lower degree of confidence than a safety-critical or regulated organization might seek. The risk policy will influence control required through service transition including the degree and level of validation and testing of service level requirements, utility and warranty, i.e. availability risks, security risks, continuity risks and capacity risks.

Appendix B has more information about approaches to risk assessment and management.

Service transition policy

See Chapter 3.

Release policy

The type and frequency of releases will influence the testing approach. Frequent releases, such as those produced once a day, drive requirements for re-usable test models and automated testing.

Change management policy

The use of change windows can influence the testing that needs to be considered. For example, if there is a policy of 'substituting' a release package late in the change schedule or if the scheduled release package is delayed then additional testing may be required to assess this combination if there are dependencies.

4.5.4.2 Inputs from service design

A service is defined by a service design package (SDP), which is produced under the control of the service design coordination process. The SDP includes the service charter, which documents the agreed utility and warranty for the service from the perspective of outcomes, assets and patterns of business activity. The service charter is therefore a key input to test planning and design.

The design of a service is related to the context in which a service will be used (the categories of customer asset). The attributes of a service characterize the form and function of the service from a utilization perspective. These attributes should be traceable to the predicted business outcomes that provide the utility from the service. Some attributes are more important than others for different sets of users and customers, e.g. basic, performance and excitement attributes. A well-designed service provides a combination of these to deliver an appropriate level of utility for the customer.

The SDP defines the agreed requirements of the service, expressed in terms of the service model and service operation plan that provide key input to test planning and design. Service models are described further in *ITIL Service Strategy*.

The service model describes the structure and dynamics of a service that will be delivered by service operation, through the service operation plan. Service transition evaluates these during the validation and test stages.

Structure is defined in terms of particular customer-facing and supporting services and the service assets needed and the patterns in which they are configured. As the new or changed service is designed, developed and built, the service assets are tested and verified against the requirements and design specifications to assess whether the service asset is built correctly.

For example, the design for managed storage services must have input on how customer assets such as business applications utilize the storage, the way in which storage adds value to the applications, and what costs and risks the customer would like to avoid. The information on risks is of particular importance to service testing, as this will influence the test coverage and prioritization.

Service models also describe the dynamics of creating value. Activities, flow of resources, coordination and interactions describe the dynamics (see Figure 4.28). This includes the cooperation and communication between service users and service agents such as service provider staff, processes or systems that the user interacts with, e.g. a self-service menu. The dynamics of a service include patterns of business activity, demand patterns, exceptions and variations.

Service design uses process maps, workflow diagrams, queuing models and activity patterns to define the service models. As service transition

evaluates the detailed service models to ensure that they are fit for purpose and fit for use it is important to have access to these models to develop the test models and plans.

The SDP defines a set of design constraints (Figure 4.29) against which the service release and new or changed service will be developed and built. Service validation and testing should test the service at the boundaries to check that the design constraints are correctly defined, particularly if there is a design improvement to add or remove a constraint.

4.5.4.3 Service quality and assurance

Service assurance is delivered though verification and validation, which in turn are delivered through testing (trying something out in conditions that represent the final live situation – a test environment) and by observation or review against a standard or specification.

Validation confirms, through the provision of objective evidence, that the requirements for a specific intended use or application have been fulfilled. Validation in a lifecycle context is the set of activities ensuring and gaining confidence that a system or service is able to accomplish its intended use, goals and objectives.

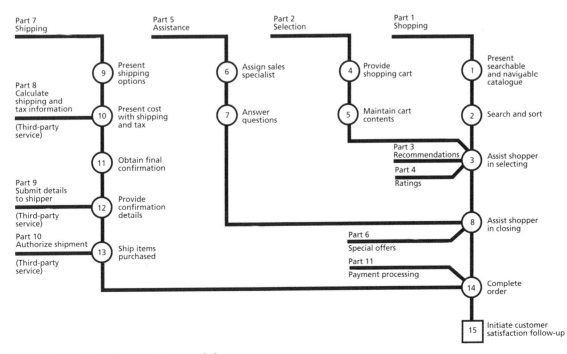

Figure 4.28 Dynamics of a service model

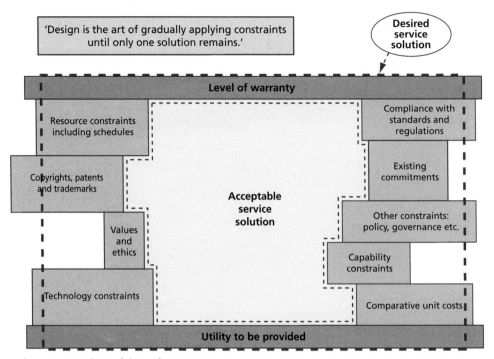

Figure 4.29 Design constraints driven by strategy

The validation of the service requirements and the related service acceptance criteria begins from the time that the service requirements are defined. There will be increasing levels of service validation and testing performed as a service release progresses through the service lifecycle. See section 4.4.5.1 for information about the service V-model and how this can be used to help identify required levels of testing.

Verification is confirmation, through the provision of objective evidence, that specified requirements have been fulfilled, e.g. a service asset meets its specification.

Early in the service lifecycle, validation confirms that the customer needs and service attributes, which are specified in the service charter, are translated correctly into the service design as service level requirements and constraints, e.g. capacity and demand limitations. Later in the service lifecycle, tests are performed to assess whether the actual service delivers the required levels of service, utilities and warranties. The warranty is an assurance that a product or service will be provided or will meet certain specifications. Value is created for customers if the utilities are fit for purpose and the warranties are fit for use (see Figure 2.2). This is the focus of service validation.

4.5.4.4 Test strategy

A test strategy defines the overall approach to organizing testing and allocating testing resources. It can apply to the whole organization, to a set of services or to an individual service. Any test strategy needs to be developed with appropriate stakeholders to ensure that there is sufficient buy-in to the approach.

Early in the lifecycle the service validation and test process needs to work with the service design coordination, release and deployment management and change evaluation processes to plan and design the test approach. This planning should use information from the SDP (including the service charter) and the interim evaluation report. The activities will include:

■ Translating the service requirements and service design into test requirements and test models, e.g. understanding combinations of service assets required to deliver a service as well as the constraints that define the context, approach and boundaries to be tested.

■ Establishing the best approach to optimize the test coverage, given the risk profile and change impact and resource assessment.

■ Translating the service acceptance criteria into entry and exit criteria at each level of testing to define the acceptable level of margin for errors at each level.

- Translating risks and issues from the impact, resource and risk assessment on the related RFC for the SDP/service release into test requirements.

It is also vital to work with project managers to ensure that:

- Appropriate test activities and resources are included in project plans. Test resource plans should include all required resources, for example test environments, test data, personnel (including management, testers and users) and test scripts.
- Specialist testing resources (people, tools, licences) are allocated if required.
- Project personnel understand the mandatory and optional testing deliverables.
- The testing activities are managed, monitored and controlled.

The aspects to consider and document in developing the test strategy and related plans are shown below. Some of the information may also be specified in the service transition plan or other test plans, and it is important to structure the plans so that there is minimal duplication.

Test strategy and plan contents

- Policies, processes and practices applicable to testing
- Purpose and objectives of testing
- Context, for example organizational boundaries, regulatory concerns
- Applicable standards, legal and regulatory requirements
- Applicable contracts and agreements:
  - Service management policies, processes and standards
- Scope and organizations:
  - Service provider teams
  - Test organization
  - Third parties, strategic partners, suppliers
  - Business units/locations
  - Customers and users
- Test process:
  - Test management and control – recording, progress monitoring and reporting
  - Test planning and estimation, including cost estimates for service planning, resources, scheduling
  - Test preparation, e.g. site/environment preparation, installation prerequisites

- Test activities – planning, performing and documenting test cases and results
- Test metrics and improvement
- Identification of items to be tested:
  - Service charter
  - SDP – service model (structure and dynamics), solution architecture design
- Service operation test plan
- Service management test plan:
  - Critical elements on which business priorities and risk assessment suggest testing should concentrate
  - Business units, service units, locations where the tests will be performed
- Service provider interfaces
- Approach:
  - Selecting the test model
  - Test levels, for example there may be a hierarchy of tests with different things being tested at each level
  - Types of test, e.g. regression testing, modelling, simulation
  - Degree of independence for performing, analysing and evaluating tests
  - Re-use – experience, expertise, knowledge and historical data
  - Timing, e.g. focus on testing individual service assets early versus testing later when the whole service is built
  - Developing and re-using test designs, tools, scripts and data
  - Error and change handling and control
  - Measurement system
- Criteria:
  - Pass/fail criteria
  - Entry and exit criteria for each test stage
  - For stopping or re-starting testing activities
- People requirements:
  - Roles and responsibilities including authorization/rejection (these may be at different levels, e.g. rejecting an expensive and long-running project typically requires higher authority than accepting it as planned)
  - Assigning and scheduling training and knowledge transfer
  - Stakeholders – service provider, suppliers, customer, user involvement

- Environment requirements:
  - Test environments to be used, locations, organizational, technical
  - Requirements for each test environment
  - Planning and commissioning of test environment
- Deliverables:
  - Mandatory and optional documentation
  - Test plans
  - Test specifications – test design, test case, test procedure
  - Test results and reports
  - Validation and qualification report
  - Test summary reports.

4.5.4.5 Test models

A test model includes a test plan, what is to be tested and the test scripts that define how each element will be tested. A test model ensures that testing is executed consistently in a repeatable way that is effective and efficient. The test scripts define the release test conditions, associated expected results and test cycles.

To ensure that the process is repeatable, test models need to be well structured in a way that:

- Provides traceability back to the requirement or design criteria
- Enables auditability through test execution, evaluation and reporting
- Ensures the test elements can be maintained and changed.

Examples of test models are illustrated in Table 4.10.

As the service design stage progresses, the tester can use the emerging service design and release plan to determine the specific requirements, validation and test conditions, cases and mechanisms to be tested. An example is shown in Table 4.11.

4.5.4.6 Service validation and testing perspectives

Effective validation and testing focuses on whether the service will deliver as required. This is based on the perspective of those who will use, deliver, deploy, manage and operate the service. The test entry and exit criteria are developed as the service design package is developed. These will cover all aspects of the service provision from different perspectives including:

- Service design – functional, management and operational
- Technology design
- Process design
- Measurement design
- Documentation
- Skills and knowledge.

Service acceptance testing starts with the verification of the service requirements. For example, customers, customer representatives and other stakeholders who sign off the agreed service requirements will also sign off the service acceptance criteria and service acceptance test plan. The stakeholders include:

- Business customers/customer representatives
- Users of the service within the customer's business who will use the new or changed service to assist them in delivering their work objectives and in delivering service and/or product to their customers
- Suppliers
- Service provider/service unit.

Business users and customer perspective

The business involvement in acceptance testing is central to its success and is included in the service design package, enabling adequate resource planning.

From the business's perspective this is important in order to:

- Have a defined and agreed means for measuring the acceptability of the service, including interfaces with the service provider, e.g. how errors or queries are communicated via a single point of contact, monitoring progress and closure of change requests and incidents
- Understand and make available the appropriate level and capability of resource to undertake service acceptance.

From the service provider's perspective the business involvement is important to:

- Keep the business involved during build and testing of the service to avoid any surprises when service acceptance takes place
- Ensure that the overall quality of the service delivered into acceptance is robust, since this starts to set business perceptions about the quality, reliability and usability of the system, even before it goes live

Table 4.10 Examples of service test models

Test model	Objective/target deliverable	Test conditions based on
Service contract test model	To validate that the customer can use the service to deliver a value proposition	Contract requirements. Fit for purpose, fit for use criteria
Service requirements test model	To validate that the service provider can deliver/has delivered the service required and expected by the customer	Service requirements and service acceptance criteria
Service level test model	To ensure that the service provider can deliver the service level requirements, and that service level requirements can be met in the live environment, e.g. testing the response and fix time, availability, product delivery times, support services etc.	Service level requirements, SLA, OLA
Service test model	To ensure that the service provider is capable of delivering, operating and managing the new or changed service using the 'as-designed' service model that includes the resource model, cost model, integrated process model, capacity and performance model etc.	Service model
Operations test model	To ensure that the service operation functions can operate and support the new or changed service/service component including the service desk, IT operations, application management, technical management. It includes local IT support staff and business representatives responsible for IT service support and operations. There may be different models at different release/test levels, e.g. technology infrastructure, applications etc.	Service model, service operation standards, processes and plans
Release deployment test model	To verify that the deployment team, tools and procedures can deploy the release package into a target deployment group or environment within the estimated timeframe. To ensure that the release package contains all the service components required for deployment, e.g. by performing a configuration audit	Release and deployment design and plan
Deployment installation test model	To test that the deployment team, tools and procedures can install the release package into a target environment within the estimated timeframe	Release and deployment design and plan
Deployment verification test model	To test that a deployment has completed successfully and that all service assets and configurations are in place as planned and meet their quality criteria	Tests and audits of 'actual' service assets and configurations

■ Deliver and maintain solid and robust acceptance test facilities in line with business requirements
■ Understand where the acceptance test fits into any overall business service or product development-testing activity.

Even when in live operation, a service is not 'emotionally' accepted by the customer and users until they become familiar and content with it. The full benefit of a service will not be realized until that emotional acceptance has been achieved.

Emotional (non) acceptance

Southern US Steel Mill implemented a new order-manufacturing service. It was commissioned, designed and delivered by an outside vendor. The service delivered was innovative and fully met the agreed criteria.

The end result was that the company sued the vendor citing that the service was not usable because factory personnel (due to lack of training) did not know how to use the system and therefore emotionally did not accept it.

Table 4.11 Service requirements, 1: improve user accessibility and usability

Validation reference	Validation condition	Test levels	Test case*	Mechanism
1.1	20% improvement in user survey rating	1	M020	Survey
1.2	20% reduction in user complaints	1	M023	Process metrics
1.3	20% increase in use of self-service channel	2	M123	Usage statistics
1.4	Help function available on front page of self-service point application	3	T235	Functional test
1.5	Web pages comply with web accessibility standards	4 (Application)	T201	Usability test
1.6	10% increase in public self-service points	4/5 Technical infrastructure	T234	Installation statistics
1.7	Public self-service points comply with standard IS1223.	4/5 Technical infrastructure	T234	Compliance test

* Each test case defines the test conditions, test data, actions, scripts and expected results that will demonstrate that a requirement has been met.

Testing is a situation where 'use cases' can be a valuable aid to effective assessment of a service's usefulness to the business. Use cases define realistic scenarios that describe interactions between users and an IT service or other system.

User testing – application, system, service

Testing comprises tests to determine whether the service meets the functional and quality requirements of the end users (customers) by executing defined business processes in an environment that, as closely as possible, simulates the live operational environment. This will include changes to the system or business process. Full details of the scope and coverage will be defined in the user test and user acceptance test (UAT) plans. The end users will test the functional requirements, establishing to the customer's agreed degree of confidence that the service will deliver as they require. They will also perform tests of the service management activities that they are involved in, e.g. ability to contact and use the service desk, response to diagnostics scripts, incident management, request fulfilment, change management.

A key practice is to make sure that business users participating in testing have their expectations clearly set, that they realize that this is a test and expect that some things may not go well. There is a risk that they may form an opinion too early about the quality of the service being tested and word may spread that the quality of the service is poor and should not be used.

Service operations and continual service improvement perspective

Steps must be taken to ensure that IT staff requirements have been delivered before deployment of the service. Staff working in the service operation functions will use the service acceptance step to ensure that appropriate:

- Technological facilities are in place to deliver the new or changed service
- Staff skills, knowledge and resource are available to support the service after go-live
- Supporting processes and resources are in place, e.g. service desk, second/third-line support, including third-party contracts, capacity and availability monitoring and alerting
- Business and IT continuity has been considered
- Access is available to documentation and SKMS.

The continual service improvement team will also inherit the new or changed service into the scope of their improvement programme, and should satisfy themselves that they have sufficient understanding of its objectives and characteristics.

4.5.4.7 Levels of testing and test models

Testing is directly related to the building of service assets and products, so each one has an associated acceptance test and activity to ensure that it meets requirements. This involves testing individual service assets and components before they are used in the new or changed service.

Each service model and associated service deliverable is supported by its own re-usable test model that can be used for regression testing during the deployment of a specific release as well as for regression testing in future releases. Test models help with building quality early into the service lifecycle rather than waiting for results from tests on a release at the end.

Levels of build and testing are described in section 4.4.5.2. The levels of testing that are to be performed are defined by the selected test model.

Using a model such as the V-model (see Figure 4.14) builds in service validation and testing early in the service lifecycle. It provides a framework for organizing the levels of configuration items to be managed through the lifecycle and the associated validation and testing activities both within and across stages. Using the V-model ensures that testing covers business and service requirements, as well as technical ones, so that the delivered service will meet customer expectations for utility and warranty.

The level of test is derived from the way a system is designed and built up. This is known as a V-model, which maps the types of test to each stage of development. The V-model provides one example of how the service transition levels of testing can be matched to corresponding stages of service requirements and design.

The left-hand side represents the specification of the service requirements down to the detailed service design. The right-hand side focuses on the validation activities that are performed against the specifications defined on the left-hand side. At each stage on the left-hand side, there is direct involvement by the equivalent party on the right-hand side. It shows that service validation and acceptance test planning should start with the definition of the service requirements. For example, customers who sign off the agreed service requirements will also sign off the service acceptance criteria and test plan.

4.5.4.8 Testing approaches and techniques

There are many approaches that can be combined to conduct validation activities and tests, depending on the constraints. Different approaches can be combined to meet the

requirements of different types of service, service model, risk profile, skill levels, test objectives and levels of testing. Examples include:

- Document review
- Modelling and measuring – suitable for testing the service model and service operation plan
- Risk-based approach that focuses on areas of greatest risk, e.g. business critical services, risks identified in change impact analysis and/or change evaluation
- Standards compliance approach, e.g. international or national standards or industry-specific standards
- Experience-based approach, e.g. using subject matter experts in the business, service or technical arenas to provide guidance on test coverage
- Approach based on an organization's software development lifecycle methods, e.g. waterfall, agile
- Simulation
- Scenario testing
- Role playing
- Prototyping
- Laboratory testing
- Regression testing
- Joint walkthrough/workshops
- Dress/service rehearsal
- Conference room pilot
- Live pilot.

In order to optimize the testing resources, test activities must be allocated against service importance, anticipated business impact and risk. Business impact analyses carried out during design for business and IT service continuity management and availability purposes are often very relevant to establishing testing priorities and schedules and should be available, subject to confidentiality and security concerns.

4.5.4.9 Design considerations

Service test design aims to develop test models and test cases that measure the correct things in order to establish whether the service will meet its intended use within the specified constraints. It is important to avoid focusing too much on the lower-level components that are often easier to test and measure. Adopting a structured approach to scoping and designing the tests helps to ensure that priority is given to testing the right items. Test models must be well structured and repeatable to facilitate auditability and maintainability.

The service is designed in response to the agreed business and service requirements and testing aims to identify if these have been achieved. Service validation and test designs consider potential changes in circumstances and are flexible enough to be changed. They may need to be changed if failures in early service tests identify a change in the environment or circumstances and therefore a change on the testing approach.

Design considerations are applicable for service test models, test cases and test scripts and include:

- Business/organization:
  - Alignment with business services, processes and procedures
  - Business dependencies, priorities, criticality and impact
  - Business cycles and seasonal variations
  - Business transaction levels
  - The numbers and types of users and anticipated future growth
  - Possible requirements due to new facilities and functionality
  - Business scenarios to test the end-to-end service
  - Requirement for segregation of duties to protect business assets during testing
- Service architecture and performance:
  - Service portfolio/structure of the services, e.g. core service, supporting services and underpinning supplier services
  - Options for testing different types of service assets, utilities and warranty, e.g. availability, security, continuity (including resilience and failover testing)
  - Service level requirements and service level targets
  - Service transaction levels
  - Constraints
  - Performance and volume predictions
  - Monitoring, modelling and measurement system, e.g. is there a need for significant simulation to recreate peak business periods? Will the new or changed service interface with existing monitoring and management tools?
- Service release test environment requirements

- Service management:
  - Service management models, e.g. capacity, cost, performance models
  - Service operation model
  - Service support model
  - Changes in requirements for service management information
  - Changes in volumes of service users and transactions
- Application information and data:
  - Validating that the application works with the information/databases and technical infrastructure
  - Functionality testing to assess the behaviour of the infrastructure solution and verify that: (i) there are no conflicts in versions of software, hardware or network components; and (ii) common infrastructure services are used according to the design
  - Access rights are set correctly
- Technical infrastructure:
  - Physical assets – do they meet their specifications?
  - Technical resource capacity, e.g. storage, processing power, power, network bandwidth
  - Spares – are sufficient spares available or ordered and scheduled for delivery? Are hardware/software settings recorded and correct?

Aspects that generally need to be considered in designing service tests include:

- **Finance** Is the agreed budget adequate, has spending exceeded budget, have costs altered (e.g. software licence and maintenance charge increases)?
- **Documentation** Is all necessary documentation available or scheduled for live use, is it practicable (sufficiently intuitive for the intended audience, available in all required languages), in correct formats such as checklists, service desk scripts?
- **Supplier of the service, service asset, component** What are the internal or external interfaces?
- **Build** Can the service, service asset or component be built into a release package and test environments?
- **Testable** Is it testable with the resources, time and facilities available or obtainable?

- **Traceability** What traceability is there back to the requirements?
- **Where and when could testing take place**? Are there unusual conditions under which a service might need to run that should be tested?
- **Remediation** What plans are there to remediate or back out a release through the environments?

Awareness of current technological environments for different types of business, customer, staff and user is essential to maintaining a valid test environment. The design of the test environments must consider the current and anticipated live environment when the service is due for operational handover and for the period of its expected operation. In practice, for most organizations, looking more than six to nine months into the business or technological future is about the practical limit. In some sectors, however, much longer lead times require the need to predict further into the future, even to the extent of restricting technological innovation in the interests of thorough and expansive testing – examples are military systems, NASA and other safety-critical environments.

The design of management and maintenance of test data should address issues such as:

- Separation of test data from any live data, including steps to ensure that test data cannot be mistaken for live data when being used, and vice versa (there are many real-life examples of test data being copied and used as live data and being the basis for business decisions, e.g. desktop icons pointing at the wrong database)
- Data protection regulations – when live data is used to generate a test database; if information can be traced to individuals it may well be covered by data protection legislation, which for example may forbid its transportation between countries
- Backup of test data, and restoration to a known baseline to enable repeatable testing; this also applies to initiation conditions for hardware tests that should be baselined
- Volatility of test data and test environments, processes and procedures, which should be in place to quickly build and tear down the test environment for a variety of testing needs; care

must be taken to ensure that testing activities for one group do not compromise testing activities for another group
- Balancing cost and benefit – as test environments populated with relevant data are expensive to build and to maintain, so the benefits in terms of risk reduction to the customer-facing services must be balanced against the cost of provision. Also, how closely the test environment matches the live environment is a key consideration that needs to be weighed when balancing cost with risk.

4.5.4.10 Types of testing

The following types of test are used to verify that the service meets the user and customer requirements as well as the service provider's requirements for managing, operating and supporting the service. Care must be taken to establish the full range of likely users, and then to test all the aspects of the service, including support and reporting.

Functional testing will depend on the type of service and channel of delivery. Functional testing is covered in many testing standards and best practices (see References and Further Reading).

Service testing will include many non-functional tests. These tests can be conducted at several levels to help build up confidence in the service release. They include:

- Usability testing
- Accessibility testing
- Process and procedure testing
- Knowledge transfer and competence testing
- Performance, capacity and resilience testing
- Volume, stress, load and scalability testing
- Availability and failover testing
- Backup and recovery testing
- Compatibility testing
- Documentation testing
- Regulatory and compliance testing
- Security testing
- Logistics, deployability and migration testing
- Coexistence and compatibility testing
- Remediation, continuity and recovery testing
- Configuration, build and installability testing
- Testing service measurement and reporting
- Operability and maintainability testing.

There are several types of testing from different perspectives, which are described below.

Service requirements and structure testing – service provider, users and customers

Validation of the service attributes against the contract, service charter and service model includes evaluating the integration or 'fit' of the utilities across the customer-facing and supporting services and service assets to ensure that there is complete coverage and that there are no conflicts.

Figure 4.30 shows a matrix of utility to service reporting and the service assets that support each utility. Each row of the diagram shows the test cases that cover one specific utility requirement. Each column shows the test cases that cover one specific service asset or warranty requirement. This matrix can be used to design the service tests to ensure that the service structure and test design coverage is appropriate. Service test cases are designed to test the service requirements in terms of utility, capacity, resource utilization, finance and risks; for example, approaches to testing the risk of service failure include performance, stress, usability and security testing.

SERVICE LEVEL TESTING – SERVICE LEVEL MANAGERS, OPERATIONS MANAGERS AND CUSTOMERS

This validates that the service provider can deliver the service level requirements, e.g. testing the response and fix time, availability, product delivery times and support services.

The performance from a service asset should deliver the utility or service expected. This does not necessarily mean that the asset can deliver what it should be capable of in its own right. For example, a car's factory specification may assert that it is capable of 150 kph, but for most customers delivering 100 kph will fully meet the requirement.

WARRANTY AND ASSURANCE TESTS – FIT FOR USE TESTING

As discussed earlier in this section, customers see the service delivered in terms of warranties against the utilities that add value to their assets in order to deliver the expected business support. For any service, the warranties are expressed in measurable terms that enable tests to be designed to establish that the warranty can be delivered (within the agreed degree of confidence). The degree of detail may vary considerably, but will always reflect the agreement established during service design. In all cases the warranty will be described, and should be measurable, in terms of the customer's business and the potential effects on it of success or failure of the service to meet that warranty.

Asset 1	Asset 2	Asset 3	Asset 4	Utility	Warranty 1	Warranty 2	Warranty 3	Warranty 4
TC1				U1	TC1	TC1/ TC2	TC1	
	TC2	TC3/ TC4		U2		TC2		TC3/ TC4
TC3	TC2/ TC3			U3		TC2		
		TC5		U4		TC2/ TC5		
	TC3/ TC4			U5		TC2/ TC5		
			TC1	U6		TC1/ TC2		TC1

TCn = Test case identifier

Figure 4.30 Designing tests to cover a range of service assets, utilities and warranties

The following tests are used to provide confidence that the warranties can be delivered, i.e. that the service is fit for use:

- **Availability** is the most elementary aspect of assuring value to customers. It assures the customer that services will be available for use under agreed terms and conditions. Services are expected to be made available to designated users only within specified areas, locations and time schedules.

- **Capacity** assures the customer that a service will support a specified level of business activity or demand at a specified level of service quality. Customers can make changes to their utilization of services while being assured that their business processes and systems will be adequately supported by the service. Capacity management is a critical aspect of service management because it has a direct impact on the availability of services. The capacity available to support services also has an impact of the level of service continuity committed or delivered. Effective management of service capacity can therefore have first-order and second-order effects on warranty.

- **Continuity** is the level of assurance provided to customers that the service will continue to support the business through major failures or disruptive events. The service provider undertakes to maintain service assets that will provide a sufficient level of contingency and responsiveness. Specialized systems and processes will kick in to ensure that the service levels received by the customer's assets do not fall below a predefined level. Assurance is also provided that normal service levels will be restored within a predefined time limit to restrict the overall impact of a failure or event. The effectiveness of service continuity is measured in terms of disturbance to the productive state of customer assets.

- **Security** provides assurance that the utilization of services by customers will be secure. This means that customer assets within the scope of service delivery and support will not be exposed to certain security risks. Service providers undertake to implement general and service-level controls that will ensure that the value provided to customers is complete and not eroded by any avoidable costs and risks. Service security covers the following aspects of reducing risks:
  - Monitors authorized and accountable usage of services as specified by the customer
  - Protects customer assets from unauthorized or malicious access
  - Sets up security zones between customer assets and service assets
  - Plays a supporting role to the other three aspects of warranty
  - When effective, has a positive impact on those aspects.

- Service security inherits all the general properties of the security of physical and human assets, as well as intangibles such as data, information, coordination and communication.

USABILITY – USERS AND MAINTAINERS

Usability testing is likely to be of increasing importance as more services become widely used as a part of everyday life and ordinary business usage. Focusing on the intuitiveness of a service can significantly increase efficiency and reduce the unit costs of both using and supporting a service.

User accessibility testing considers the restricted abilities of actual or potential users of a new or changed service and is commonly used for testing web services. Care must be taken to establish the types of likely users, e.g. hearing-impaired users may be able to operate a PC-based service but would not be supported by a telephone-only-based service desk support system. This testing might focus on usability for:

- Disabled users, e.g. those who are visually or hearing impaired
- Sensory-restricted users, e.g. those who are colour blind
- Users working in second language or based in a different culture.

CONTRACT AND REGULATION TESTING

Audits and tests are conducted to check that the criteria in contracts have been agreed before acceptance of the end-to-end service. Service providers may have a contractual requirement to comply with the requirements of ISO/IEC 20000 or other standards and they would need to ensure that the relevant clauses of the standard are met during implementation of a new or changed service and release.

Regulatory acceptance testing is required in some industries such as defence, financial services and pharmaceuticals.

COMPLIANCE TESTING

Testing is conducted to check compliance against internal regulations and existing commitments of the organization, e.g. fraud checks.

SERVICE MANAGEMENT TESTING

The service models will dictate the approach that is chosen for testing the integrated service management processes. ISO/IEC 20000 covers the minimum requirements for each process to be compliant with the standard and maintenance of the process interrelationships.

Examples of service management manageability tests are shown in Table 4.12.

OPERATIONAL TESTS – SYSTEMS, SERVICES

There will be many operational tests depending on the type of service. Typical tests include:

- **Load and stress** These tests establish if the new or changed service will perform to the required levels on the capacity likely to be available. The capacity elements may include any anticipated bottlenecks within the infrastructure that might be expected to restrict performance, including:
  - Load and throughput
  - Behaviour at the upper limits of system capability
  - Network bandwidth
  - Data storage
  - Processing power or live memory
  - Service desk resources – people and technology such as telephone lines and logging
  - Available software licences/concurrent seats
  - Support staff – both numbers and skills
  - Training facilities, classrooms, trainers, CBT licences etc.
  - Overnight batch processing timings, including backup tasks.
- **Security** All services should be considered for their potential impact on relevant security concerns and subsequently tested for their actual likely impact on security. Any service that

has an anticipated security impact or exposes an anticipated security risk will have been assessed at design stage, and the requirement for security involvement built into the service charter. Organizations should make reference to and may wish to seek compliance with ISO 27000 where security is a significant concern to their services.

- **Recoverability** Every significant change will have been assessed for the question 'If this change is made, will the disaster recovery (DR) plan need to be changed accordingly?' Notwithstanding that consideration earlier in the lifecycle, it is appropriate to test that the new or changed service is catered for within the existing (or amended with the changed) DR plan. Typically, concerns identified during testing should be addressed to the service continuity team and considered as active elements for future DR tests.

REGRESSION TESTING

Regression testing means 'repeating a test already run successfully, and comparing the new results with the earlier valid results'. During each iteration of true regression testing, all existing validated tests are run and the new results are compared with the already achieved standards. Regression testing ensures that a new or changed service does not introduce errors into aspects of the services or IT infrastructure that previously worked without error. Simple examples of the type of error that can be detected are software contention issues, hardware and network incompatibility. Regression testing also applies to other elements such as service management process testing and measurement. In reality, it is the integrated concept of service testing – assessing whether the service will deliver the business benefit – that makes regression testing so very important in modern organizations (and will make it ever more important in the future).

4.5.5 Process activities, methods and techniques

The testing process is shown schematically in Figure 4.31. The test activities are not undertaken in a sequence. Several activities may be done in parallel, e.g. test execution can begin before all the test design is complete. The activities are described below.

Table 4.12 Examples of service management manageability tests

Service management process	Examples of service design manageability checks	Examples of build and test manageability checks	Examples of release deployment manageability checks	Examples of operating manageability checks	Examples of early life support and CSI manageability checks
Service asset and configuration management	Are the designers aware of the corporate standards used for SACM? How does the design meet organizational standards for acceptable configurations? Does the design support the concept of version control? Is the design created in a way that allows for the logical breakdown of the service into configuration items (CIs)?	Have the developers built the service, application and infrastructure to conform to the corporate standards that are used for SACM? Does the service use only standard supporting systems and tools that are considered acceptable? Does the service include support for version, build, baseline and release control and management? Have the developers built in the chosen CI structure to the service, application and infrastructure?	Does the service deployment trigger SACM to update the CMS at each stage of the deployment? Is the deployment team using an updated inventory to complete the plan and the deployment?	Can the operations team gain access to the CMS so that they can confirm that the service they are managing is the correct version and configured correctly? Are the operating instructions under version and build control similar to those used for the application builds?	As the service is reviewed within the optimize phase, is the CMS used to assist with the review? Are SACM personnel involved in the optimization process, including providing advice in the use of and updating the inventory?
Change management	Does the service design cope with change? Do the designers understand the change management process used by the organization?	Have the service assets and components been built and tested in accordance with the corporate change management process? Has the emergency change process been tested? Is the impact assessment procedure for the CI type clearly defined and has it been tested?	Are the corporate change management process and standards used during deployment?	Is the operations team involved in the change management process; is it part of the sign-off and verification process? Does a member of the operations team attend the change management meetings?	As modifications are identified, does the team use the change management system to coordinate the changes? Does the optimization team understand the change management process?

Table continued

Table 4.12 *continued*

Service management process	Examples of service design manageability checks	Examples of build and test manageability checks	Examples of release deployment manageability checks	Examples of operating manageability checks	Examples of early life support and CSI manageability checks
Release and deployment management	Do the service designers understand the standards and tools used for releasing and deploying services? How will the design ensure that the new or changed service can be deployed into the environment in a simple and efficient way?	Has the service, application and infrastructure been built and tested in ways that ensure it can be released into the environment in a simple and efficient way?	Is the service being deployed in a manner that minimizes risks, such as a phased deployment? Has a remediation/back-out option been included in the release package or process for the service and its constituent components?	Does the release and deployment process ensure that deployment information is available to the operations teams? Do the service operation functions have access to release and information even before the service or application is deployed into the live environment?	Do members of the CSI team understand the release and deployment management process, and are they using this for planning the deployment of improvements? Is release and deployment management involved in providing advice to the assessment process?
Information security management	How does the design ensure that the service is planned with security at the forefront?	Is the build process following security best practice for this activity?	Can the service be deployed in a manner that meets organizational security standards and requirements?	Does the service support the ongoing and periodic checks that information security management needs to complete while the service is in operational use?	
Incident management	Does the design facilitate simple creation of incidents when something goes wrong? Is the design compatible with the organizational incident management system? Does the design accommodate automatic logging and detection of incidents?	Is a simple creation-of-incidents process, for when something goes wrong, built into services and tested (e.g. with notification from applications)? Has the compatibility with the organizational incident management system been tested?	Does the deployment use the incident management system for reporting issues and problems? Do members of the deployment team have access to the incident management system so that they can record incidents and also view incidents that relate to the deployment?	Does the operations team have access to the incident management system and can it update information within this system? Does the operations team understand its responsibilities in dealing with incidents? Is the operations team provided with reports on how well it deals with incidents, and does it act on these?	Do members of the CSI team have access to the incident management system so that they can record incidents and also view incidents that may be addressed in optimization?

Table 4.12 *continued*

Service management process	Examples of service design manageability checks	Examples of build and test manageability checks	Examples of release deployment manageability checks	Examples of operating manageability checks	Examples of early life support and CSI manageability checks
Problem management	How does the design facilitate the methods used for root cause analysis within the organization?	Has the method of providing information to facilitate root cause analysis and problem management been tested?	Has a problem manager been appointed for this deployment and does the deployment team know who this is?	Does the operations team contribute to the problem management process, ideally by assisting with and facilitating root cause analysis? Does the operations team meet problem management staff regularly? Does the operations team see the weekly/ monthly problem management report?	Is the optimization process being provided with information by problem management to incorporate into the assessment process?
Capacity management	Are the designers aware of the approach to capacity management used within the organization? How should operations and performance be measured? Is modelling being used to ensure that the design meets capacity needs?	Has the service been built and tested to ensure that it meets the capacity requirements? Has the capacity information provided by the service been tested and verified? Are stress and volume characteristics built into the services and constituent applications?	Is capacity management involved in the deployment process so that it can monitor the capacity of the resources involved in the deployment?	Is capacity information being monitored and reported on as the service is used, and is this information provided to capacity management?	Is capacity management feeding information into the optimization process?

Table continued

Table 4.12 *continued*

Service management process	Examples of service design manageability checks	Examples of build and test manageability checks	Examples of release deployment manageability checks	Examples of operating manageability checks	Examples of early life support and CSI manageability checks
Availability management	Does the design address the availability requirements of the service? Has the service been planned to fit in with backup and recovery capabilities of the organization?	How has the service been built to address the availability requirements, and how has this been tested? What testing has been done to ensure that the service meets the backup and recovery capabilities of the organization? What happens when the service and underlying applications are under stress?	Is availability management monitoring the availability of the service, the applications being deployed and the rest of the technology infrastructure to ensure that the deployment is not affecting availability? How is the ability to back up and recover the service during deployment being dealt with?	How is the service's availability being measured, and is this information being fed back to the availability management function within the IT organization?	Does the assessment use the availability information to complete the proposal of modifications that are needed for the service? Do procedures for backup and recovery of the service need to be improved?
IT service continuity management	How does the design meet the service continuity requirements of the organization? Will the design meet the needs of the business recovery process following a disaster?	Has the service been built to support the business recovery process following a disaster, and how has this been tested?	Will any changes be required to the business recovery process following a disaster if one should occur during or after the deployment of this service?	Is the business recovery process for the service tested regularly by operations?	What optimization is required in the business recovery process to meet the business needs?
Service level management	How does the design meet the SLA requirements of the organization?	Does the service meet the SLA and performance requirements, and has this been tested?	Is service level management aware of the deployment of this service? Does this service have an initial SLA for the deployment phase? Does the service affect the SLA requirements during deployment?	Is the SLA visible and understood by the operations team so that it appreciates how its running of the service affects the delivery of the SLA? Does the operations team see the weekly/ monthly service level report?	Is service level management information available for inclusion in the optimization process?

Table 4.12 *continued*

Service management process	Examples of service design manageability checks	Examples of build and test manageability checks	Examples of release deployment manageability checks	Examples of operating manageability checks	Examples of early life support and CSI manageability checks
Financial management for IT services	Does the design meet the financial requirements for this service? How does the design ensure that the final new or changed service will meet return of investment expectations?	Has the service been built to deliver financial information, and how is this being tested?	Is management accounting being done during the deployment so that the total cost of deployment can be included within the cost of ownership?	Does the operations team provide input into the financial information about the service? For example, if a service requires an operator to perform additional tasks at night, is this recorded?	Is financial information available for inclusion in the assessment process?

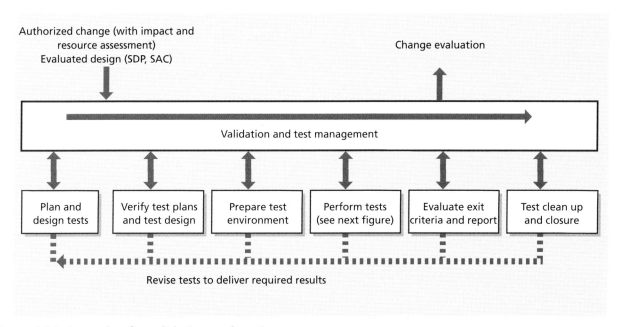

Figure 4.31 Example of a validation and testing process

4.5.5.1 Validation and test management

Test management includes the planning, control and reporting of activities through the test stages of service transition. These activities include:

- Planning the test resources
- Prioritizing and scheduling what is to be tested and when
- Checking that incoming known errors and their documentation are processed
- Monitoring progress and collating feedback from validation and test activities

- Management of incidents, problems, errors, non-conformances, risks and issues discovered during transition. Note that incidents and problems that are not directly related to the components under test will be managed using the normal incident management and problem management processes
- Consequential changes, to reduce errors going into live use
- Capturing configuration baseline
- Test metrics collection, analysis, reporting and management.

Test management includes managing issues, mitigating risks and implementing changes identified from the testing activities, as these can impose delays and create dependencies that need to be proactively managed.

Test metrics are used to measure the test process and manage and control the testing activities. They enable the test manager to determine the progress of testing, the earned value and the outstanding testing, and this helps the test manager to estimate when testing will be completed. Good metrics provide information for management decisions on prioritization, scheduling and risk management. They also provide useful information for estimating and scheduling of future releases.

4.5.5.2 Plan and design tests

Test planning and design activities start early in the service lifecycle and include:

- Resourcing
- Hardware, networking, staff numbers and skills capacity
- Business/customer resources required, e.g. components or raw materials for production control services, cash for ATM services
- Supporting services including access, security, catering, communications
- Schedule of milestones, handover and delivery dates
- Agreed time for consideration of reports and other deliverables
- Point and time of delivery and acceptance
- Financial requirements – budgets and funding.

4.5.5.3 Verify test plans and test design

Verify the test plans and test design to ensure that:

- The test model delivers adequate and appropriate test coverage for the risk profile of the service
- The test model covers the key integration aspects and interfaces, e.g. at the SPIs
- The test scripts are accurate and complete.

4.5.5.4 Prepare test environment

Prepare the test environment by using the services of the build and test environment resource, and also use the release and deployment management processes to prepare the test environment where possible; see section 4.4.5.2. Capture a configuration baseline of the initial test environment.

4.5.5.5 Perform tests

Carry out the tests using manual or automated techniques and procedures. Testers must record their findings during the tests. If a test fails, the reasons for failure must be fully documented. Testing should continue according to the test plans and scripts, if at all possible. When part of a test fails, the incident or issues should be resolved or documented (e.g. as a known error) and the appropriate re-tests should be performed by the same tester.

An example of the test execution activities is shown in Figure 4.32. The deliverables from testing are:

- Actual results showing proof of testing with cross-references to the test model, test cycles and conditions
- Problems, errors, issues, non-conformances and risks remaining to be resolved
- Resolved problems/known errors and related changes
- Sign-off.

4.5.5.6 Evaluate exit criteria and report

The actual results are compared to the expected results. The results may be interpreted in terms of pass/fail; risk to the business/service provider; or if there is a change in a projected value, e.g. higher cost to deliver intended benefits.

To produce the report, gather the test metrics and summarize the results of the tests. Examples of exit criteria are:

- The service, with its underlying applications and technology infrastructure, enables the business users to perform all aspects of function as defined.
- The service meets the quality requirements.
- Configuration baselines are captured into the CMS.

4.5.5.7 Test clean up and closure

Ensure that the test environments are cleaned up or initialized. Review the testing approach and identify improvements to input to design/build, buy/build decision parameters and future testing policy/procedures.

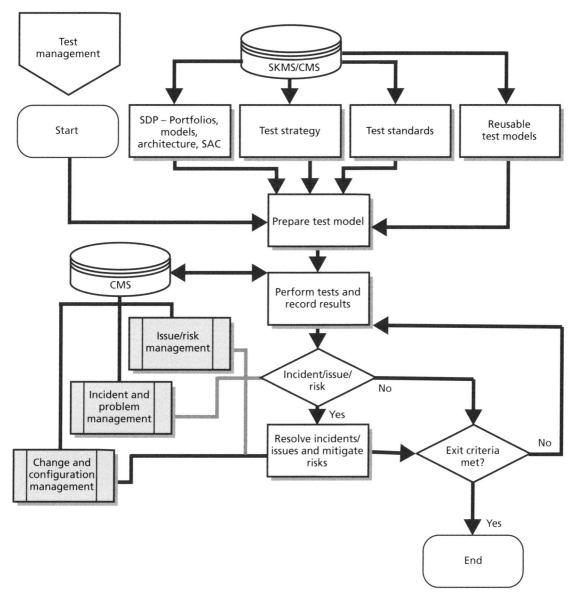

Figure 4.32 Performing test activities – an example

4.5.6 Triggers, inputs, outputs and interfaces

4.5.6.1 Trigger

The trigger for testing is a scheduled activity on a release plan, test plan or quality assurance plan.

4.5.6.2 Inputs

The key inputs to the process are:

■ **The service design package** This defines the agreed requirements of the service, expressed in terms of the service model and service operation plan. It includes:

- The service charter, which defines the requirements from the business/customer for the service, including a description of the expected utility and warranty from the perspective of outcomes, assets and patterns of business activity of customers (PBA)
- Service provider interface definitions, which define the interfaces to be tested at the boundaries of the service being delivered, e.g. process interfaces, organizational interfaces
- Operation models (including support resources, escalation procedures and critical situation handling procedures)

- Capacity/resource model and plans – combined with performance and availability aspects
- Financial/economic/cost models (with TCO, TCU)
- Service management model (e.g. integrated process model as in ISO/IEC 20000)
- Test conditions and expected results
- Design and interface specifications
- Release and deployment plans, which define all stages of the build, test and deployment of a release
- Acceptance criteria – these exist at all levels at which testing and acceptance are foreseen
- **RFCs** These instigate required changes to the environment within which the service functions or will function.

4.5.6.3 Outputs

The direct output from testing is the report delivered to change evaluation (see section 4.6). This sets out:

- Configuration baseline of the testing environment
- Testing carried out (including options chosen and constraints encountered)
- Results from those tests
- Analysis of the results, e.g. comparison of actual results with expected results, risks identified during testing activities.

After the service has been in use for a reasonable time, there should be sufficient data to perform an evaluation of the actual versus predicted service capability and performance. If the change evaluation is successful, an evaluation report is sent to change management with a recommendation to promote the service release out of early life support and into normal operation.

Other outputs include:

- Updated data, information and knowledge to be added to the service knowledge management system, e.g. errors and workarounds, testing techniques, analysis methods
- Test incidents, problems and error records
- Entries in the CSI register to address potential improvements in any area that impacts on testing:

- To the testing process itself
- To the nature and documentation of the service design outputs
- Third-party relationships, suppliers of equipment or services, partners (co-suppliers to end customers), users and customers or other stakeholders.

4.5.6.4 Interfaces

Testing supports all of the release and deployment management steps within service transition. Release and deployment management is responsible for ensuring that appropriate testing takes place, but the actual testing is carried out as part of the service validation and testing process.

The output of service validation and testing is a key input to change evaluation, and must be provided at an appropriate time and in a suitable format to enable changes to be evaluated in time for change management decision-making.

Although this section focuses on the application of testing within the service transition stage of the service lifecycle, the test strategy will ensure that the testing process works with all stages of the lifecycle:

- Working with service design coordination to ensure that designs are inherently testable and providing positive support in achieving this; examples range from including self-monitoring within hardware and software, the re-use of previously tested and known service elements through to ensuring rights of access to third-party suppliers so that they can easily carry out inspection and observation on delivered service elements.
- Working closely with CSI to feed failure information and improvement ideas resulting from testing exercises.
- Service operation will use maintenance tests to ensure the continued efficacy of services; these tests will require maintenance to cope with innovation and change in environmental circumstances.
- Service strategy should accommodate testing in terms of adequate funding, resource, profile etc.

4.5.7 Information management

The nature of IT service management is repetitive, and this ability to benefit from re-use is recognized in the suggested use of transition models. Testing benefits greatly from re-use and to this end it is sensible to create and maintain a library of relevant tests and an updated and maintained data set for applying and performing tests. The test management group within an organization should take responsibility for creating, cataloguing and maintaining test scripts, test cases and test data that can be re-used.

Similarly, the use of automated testing tools (computer-aided software testing – CAST) is becoming ever more central to effective testing in complex software environments. Equivalently standard and automated hardware testing approaches are fast and effective.

4.5.7.1 Test data

However well a test has been designed, it relies on the relevance of the data used to run it. This clearly applies to software testing, but equivalent concerns relate to the environments within which hardware, documentation etc. is tested. Testing electrical equipment in a protected environment – with smoothed power supply, and dust, temperature and humidity control – will not be a valuable test if the equipment will be used in a normal office.

4.5.7.2 Test environments

Test environments must be actively maintained and protected. For any significant change to a service, the question should be asked (as for continued relevance of the continuity and capacity plans, should the change be accepted and implemented): 'If this change goes ahead, will there need to be a consequential impact to the test data?' If so, it may involve updating test data as part of the change, and the dependency of a service, or service element, on test data or test environment will be evident from the SKMS, via records and relationships held within the CMS. Outcomes from this question include:

- Consequential updating of the test data
- A new separate set of data or a new test environment, since the original is still required for other services
- Redundancy of the test data or environment – since the change will allow testing within another existing test environment, with or without modification to that data/environment (this may in fact be the justification behind a perfective change to reduce testing costs)

- Acceptance that a lower level of testing will be accepted since the test data/environment cannot be updated to deliver equivalent test coverage for the changed service.

Maintenance of test data should be an active exercise and should address relevant issues including:

- Separation from any live data, and steps to ensure that it cannot be mistaken for live data when being used, and vice versa (there are many real-life examples of test data being copied and used as live data and being the basis for business decisions)
- Data protection regulations – when live data is used to generate a test database, if information can be traced to individuals it may well be covered by data protection legislation that, for example, may forbid its transportation between countries
- Backup of test data, and restoration to a known baseline for enabling repeatable testing; this also applies to initiation conditions for hardware tests that should be baselined.

An established test database can also be used as a safe and realistic training environment for a service.

4.5.8 Critical success factors and key performance indicators

The following list includes some sample CSFs for service validation and testing. Each organization should identify appropriate CSFs based on its objectives for the process. Each sample CSF is followed by a small number of typical KPIs that support the CSF. These KPIs should not be adopted without careful consideration. Each organization should develop KPIs that are appropriate for its level of maturity, its CSFs and its particular circumstances. Achievement against KPIs should be monitored and used to identify opportunities for improvement, which should be logged in the CSI register for evaluation and possible implementation.

- **CSF** Understanding the different stakeholder perspectives that underpin effective risk management for the change impact assessment and test activities
  - **KPI** Roles and responsibilities for impact assessment and test activities have been agreed and documented

- **KPI** Increase in the number of new or changed services for which all roles and responsibilities for customers, users and service provider personnel have been agreed and documented
- **KPI** Increase in the percentage of impact assessments and test activities where the documented roles have been correctly involved
- **KPI** Increase in satisfaction ratings in stakeholder survey of the service validation and testing process

- **CSF** Building a thorough understanding of risks that have impacted or may impact successful service transition of services and releases
  - **KPI** Reduction in the impact of incidents and errors for newly transitioned services
  - **KPI** Increased number of risks identified in service design or early in service transition compared to those detected during or after testing
  - **KPI** Increased ratio of errors detected in service design compared to service transition, and of errors detected in service transition compared to service operation

- **CSF** Encouraging a risk management culture where people share information and take a pragmatic and measured approach to risk
  - **KPI** Increase in the number of people who identify risks for new or changed services
  - **KPI** Increase in the number of documented risks for each new or changed service
  - **KPI** Increase in the percentage of risks on the risk register which have been managed

- **CSF** Providing evidence that the service assets and configurations have been built and implemented correctly in addition to the service delivering what the customer needs
  - **KPI** Increased percentage of service acceptance criteria that have been tested for new and changed services
  - **KPI** Increased percentage of services for which build and implementation have been tested, separately to any tests of utility or warranty

- **CSF** Developing re-usable test models
  - **KPI** Increased number of tests in a repository for re-usable tests
  - **KPI** Increased number of times that tests are re-used

- **CSF** Achieving a balance between cost of testing and effectiveness of testing
  - **KPI** Reduced variance between test budget and test expenditure
  - **KPI** Reduced cost of fixing errors, due to earlier detection
  - **KPI** Reduction in business impact due to delays in testing
  - **KPI** Reduced variance between planned and actual cost of customer and user time to support testing.

4.5.9 Challenges and risks

4.5.9.1 Challenges

Still the most frequent challenges to effective testing are based on lack of respect and understanding for the role of testing. Traditionally, testing has been starved of funding, and this results in:

- Inability to maintain a test environment and test data that matches the live environment
- Insufficient staff, skills and testing tools to deliver adequate testing coverage
- Projects overrunning and allocated testing time frames being squeezed to restore project go-live dates but at the cost of quality
- Development of standard performance measures and measurement methods across projects and suppliers
- Projects and suppliers estimating delivery dates inaccurately and causing delays in scheduling service transition activities.

4.5.9.2 Risks

Risks to successful service validation and testing include:

- Unclear expectations/objectives
- Lack of understanding of the risks resulting in testing that is not targeted at critical elements which need to be well controlled and therefore tested
- Resource shortages (e.g. users, support staff), which introduce delays and have an impact on other service transitions.

4.6 CHANGE EVALUATION

4.6.1 Purpose and objectives

The purpose of the change evaluation process is to provide a consistent and standardized means of determining the performance of a service change in the context of likely impacts on business outcomes, and on existing and proposed services and IT infrastructure. The actual performance of a change is assessed against its predicted performance. Risks and issues related to the change are identified and managed.

The objectives of change evaluation are to:

- Set stakeholder expectations correctly and provide effective and accurate information to change management to make sure that changes which adversely affect service capability and introduce risk are not transitioned unchecked
- Evaluate the intended effects of a service change and as much of the unintended effects as is reasonably practical given capacity, resource and organizational constraints
- Provide good-quality outputs so that change management can expedite an effective decision about whether or not a service change is to be authorized.

4.6.2 Scope

Every change must be authorized by a suitable change authority at various points in its lifecycle; for example before build and test, before it is checked in to the DML and before it is deployed to the live environment. Evaluation is required before each of these authorizations, to provide the change authority with advice and guidance.

This change evaluation process describes a formal evaluation that is suitable for use when significant changes are being evaluated. Each organization must decide which changes should use this formal change evaluation, and which can be evaluated as part of the change management process. This decision will normally be documented in change models used to manage each type of change.

4.6.3 Value to business

Change evaluation is, by its very nature, concerned with value. Specifically effective change evaluation will establish the use made of resources in terms of delivered benefit, and this information will allow a more accurate focus on value in future service

development and change management. There is a great deal of intelligence that continual service improvement can take from change evaluation to inform future improvements to the process of change and the predictions and measurement of service change performance.

4.6.4 Policies, principles and basic concepts

4.6.4.1 Policies

The following examples of policies apply to the change evaluation process:

- Service designs or service changes will be evaluated before being transitioned.
- Every change must be evaluated, but only significant changes will use the formal change evaluation process, criteria must be defined to identify which changes are in scope of this process.
- Change evaluation will identify risks and issues related to the service that is being changed, and to any other services or shared infrastructure.
- Any deviation from predicted to actual performance will be managed by the customer or customer representative by (i) accepting the change even though actual performance is different from what was predicted, (ii) rejecting the change, or (iii) requiring a new change to be implemented with revised predicted performance agreed in advance. No other outcomes of change evaluation are allowed.

Note: The term 'performance' is used in change evaluation to mean the utilities and warranties for the service, which provide the ability of the service to contribute to the performance of the customer's assets.

4.6.4.2 Principles

The following principles shall guide the execution of the change evaluation process:

- As far as is reasonably practical, the unintended as well as the intended effects of a change need to be identified and their consequences understood and considered. This includes effects on other services or shared infrastructure as well as the effects on the service being changed.
- A service change will be fairly, consistently, openly and, wherever possible, objectively evaluated.

■ An evaluation report, or interim evaluation report, will be provided to change management to facilitate decision-making at each point at which authorization is required.

4.6.4.3 Basic concepts

The change evaluation process uses the Plan–Do–Check–Act (PDCA) model to ensure consistency across all evaluations. Each evaluation is planned and then carried out in multiple stages, the results of the evaluation are checked and actions are taken to resolve any issues found.

4.6.5 Process activities, methods and techniques

4.6.5.1 Change evaluation terms

The key terms shown in Table 4.13 are used by the change evaluation process. Some of the definitions may differ from those found in the glossary at the end of this publication.

4.6.5.2 Change evaluation process

Figure 4.33 shows the change evaluation process with key inputs and outputs.

4.6.5.3 Evaluation plan

Evaluation of a change should be carried out from a number of different perspectives to ensure that unintended effects of the change are understood, as well as intended effects.

Generally speaking we would expect the intended effects of a change to be beneficial. The unintended effects are harder to predict, often not seen even after the service change is implemented and frequently ignored. Additionally, unintended effects will not always be beneficial, for example in terms of impact on other services, impact on customers and users of the service, and network overloading.

Intended effects of a change should match the acceptance criteria. Unintended effects are often not seen until pilot stage or even once in live use; they are difficult to predict or measure.

4.6.5.4 Understanding the intended effect of a change

The details of the service change, customer requirements and service design package should be carefully analysed to understand fully the

Table 4.13 Key terms that apply to the change evaluation process

Term	Meaning
Actual performance	The performance achieved following a service change.
Countermeasure	The mitigation that is implemented to reduce risk.
Deviations report	A report of the difference between predicted and actual performance.
Evaluation report	A report generated by the change evaluation process, which is passed to change management and which comprises: ■ A risk profile ■ A deviations report ■ A recommendation ■ A qualification statement.
Performance	The utilities and warranties of a service.
Performance model	A representation of a service that is used to help predict performance.
Predicted performance	The expected performance of a service following a service change.
Residual risk	The remaining risk after countermeasures have been deployed.
Service capability	The ability of a service to perform as required.
Service change	A change to an existing service or the introduction of a new service.
Test plan and results	The test plan is a response to an impact assessment of the proposed service change. Typically the plan will specify how the change will be tested; what records will result from testing and where they will be stored; who will authorize the change; and how it will be ensured that the change and the service(s) it affects will remain stable over time. The test plan may include a qualification plan and a validation plan if the change affects a regulated environment. The results represent the actual performance following implementation of the change.

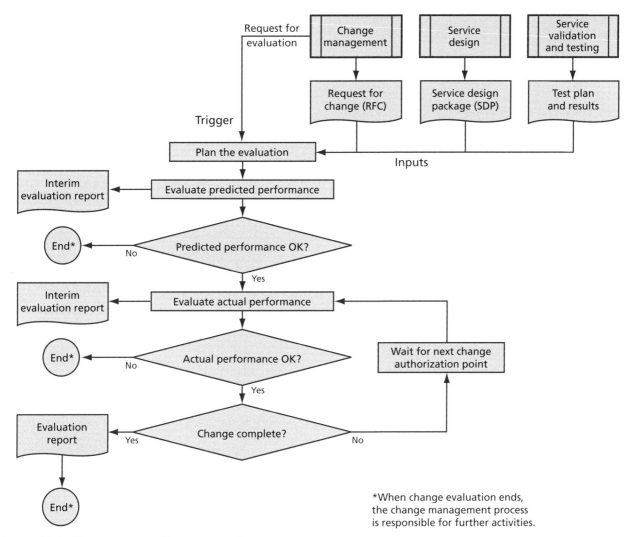

Figure 4.33 Change evaluation process flow

purpose of the change and the expected benefit from implementing it. Examples might include: reduce cost of running the service; increase service performance; reduce resources required to operate the service; or improve service capability. Change evaluation should ensure that these benefits are actually realized, and should provide evidence to demonstrate this.

The change documentation should make clear what the intended effect of the change will be and specific measures that should be used to determine effectiveness of that change. If they are in any way unclear or ambiguous, the evaluation should stop and a recommendation not to proceed should be forwarded to change management.

Even some deliberately designed changes may be detrimental to some elements of the service – for example, the introduction of Sarbanes-Oxley-

compliant procedures, which, while delivering the benefit of legal compliance, introduce extra work steps and costs.

4.6.5.5 Understanding the unintended effect of a change

In addition to the expected effects on the service and broader organization, there are likely to be additional effects which were not expected or planned for. These effects must also be identified and considered if the full impact of a service change is to be understood. One of the most effective ways of identifying such effects is by discussion with all stakeholders – not just customers, but also users of the service, those who maintain it, those who fund it etc. Care should be taken in presenting the details of the change to ensure that stakeholders fully understand the implications and can therefore provide accurate feedback.

4.6.5.6 Factors for considering the effect of a service change

Table 4.14 shows the factors to be included when considering the effect of a service change.

4.6.5.7 Evaluation of predicted performance

Using customer requirements (including acceptance criteria), the predicted performance and the performance model, a risk assessment is carried out, and an interim evaluation report is sent to change management.

The interim evaluation report includes the outcome of the risk assessment and/or the outcome of the predicted performance versus acceptance criteria, together with a recommendation to accept or reject the service change in its current form.

If change evaluation recommends that the change should not proceed then activities end at this point, pending a decision from change management. If the recommendation is to proceed with the change then evaluation activities pause to wait for the next change authorization point.

4.6.5.8 Evaluation of actual performance

Before change management make a decision on whether to authorize each step in a change, change evaluation will evaluate the actual performance. The extent to which actual performance can be evaluated depends on how far through the change lifecycle the evaluation is performed. The results of this evaluation are sent to change management in the form of an interim evaluation report. This interim evaluation report includes the outcome of the risk assessment and/or the outcome of the actual performance versus acceptance criteria, together with a recommendation on whether to authorize the next step.

If change evaluation recommends that the change should not proceed then activities end at this point, pending a decision from change management. If the recommendation is to proceed with the change, then evaluation activities pause to wait for the next change authorization point.

Once the service change has been implemented, a report on actual performance is received from operations. Using customer requirements (including acceptance criteria), the actual performance and the performance model, a risk assessment is carried out.

If the risk assessment suggests that the actual performance is creating unacceptable risks, an interim evaluation report is sent to change management. The interim evaluation report includes the outcome of the risk assessment and/or the outcome of the actual performance versus acceptance criteria, together with a recommendation to remediate the service change. Evaluation activities cease at this point pending a decision from change management.

Table 4.14 Factors to consider when assessing the effect of a service change

Factor	Evaluation of service design
S – Service provider capability	The ability of a service provider or service unit to perform as required.
T – Tolerance	The ability or capacity of a service to absorb the service change or release.
O – Organizational setting	The ability of an organization to accept the proposed change. For example, is appropriate access available for the implementation team? Have all existing services that would be affected by the change been updated to ensure smooth transition?
R – Resources	The availability of appropriately skilled and knowledgeable people, sufficient finances, infrastructure, applications and other resources necessary to run the service following transition.
M – Modelling and measurement	The extent to which the predictions of behaviour generated from the model match the actual behaviour of the new or changed service.
P – People	The people within a system and the effect of change on them.
U – Use	Will the service be fit for use? Will it be able to deliver the warranties? Is it continuously available? Is there enough capacity? Will it be secure enough?
P – Purpose	Will the new or changed service be fit for purpose? Can the required performance be supported? Will the constraints be removed as planned?

If, however, the risk assessment shows an acceptable level of risk then an evaluation report is sent to change management.

4.6.5.9 Risk management

Appendix B describes a number of different approaches that can be taken to assess and manage risks. Each organization should have its own approach to risk management, but this will often be based on one or more of these best-practice approaches.

Regardless of which risk management approach the organization has adopted, it is a clear requirement that a proposed service change must assess the existing risks within a service and the predicted risks following implementation of the change.

If the risk level has increased then the second stage of risk management is used to mitigate the risk. Mitigation may include steps to eliminate a threat or weakness and use disaster recovery and backup techniques to increase the resilience of a service on which the organization has become more dependent.

Following mitigation, the risk level is re-assessed and compared with the original. This second assessment and any subsequent assessments are in effect determining residual risk – the risk that remains after mitigation. Assessment of residual risk and associated mitigation continues to cycle until risk is managed down to an acceptable level.

The guiding principle here is that the level of risk should be appropriate for the expected benefits and the business appetite for risk. Ideally, every change will lead to reduced risk, but the business may choose to accept an increased level of risk in order to gain benefits. If the level of risk is not acceptable, then evaluation will recommend rejection of a proposed service change, or back-out of an implemented service change.

Deviations – predicted versus actual performance

Once the service change passes the evaluation of predicted performance and actual performance, essentially as standalone evaluations, a comparison of the two is carried out. To have reached this point it will have been determined that predicted performance and actual performance are acceptable and that there are no unacceptable risks. The output of this activity is a deviations report. For each factor in Table 4.14 the report states the extent of any deviation between predicted and actual performance.

Test plan and results

The service validation and testing process provides the means for determining the actual performance of the service following implementation of a service change. This provides the change evaluation process with the test plan and a report on the results of any testing. Test results are made available to change evaluation and are evaluated and used as described in section 4.6.5.8.

In some circumstances it is necessary to provide a statement of qualification and/or validation status following a change. This takes place in regulated environments such as pharmaceuticals and defence.

The context for these activities is shown in Figure 4.34.

The inputs to these activities are the qualification plan and results and/or validation plan and results. The evaluation process ensures that the results meet the requirements of the plans. A qualification and/or validation statement is provided as output.

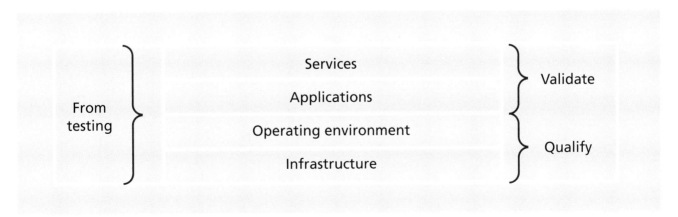

Figure 4.34 Context for qualification and validation activities

4.6.5.10 Evaluation report

The evaluation report contains the following sections:

- **Risk profile** A representation of the residual risk left after a change has been implemented and after countermeasures have been applied.
- **Deviations** The difference between predicted and actual performance following the implementation of a change.
- **A qualification statement (if appropriate)** Following review of qualification test results and the qualification plan, a statement of whether or not the change has left the service in a state whereby it could not be qualified. The qualification statement formally states that the IT infrastructure is appropriate and correctly configured to support the specific application or IT service.
- **A validation statement (if appropriate)** Following review of validation test results and the validation plan, a statement of whether or not the change has left the service in a state whereby it could not be validated. The validation statement formally states that the new or changed service or application meets a documented set of requirements.
- **A recommendation** Based on the other factors within the evaluation report, a recommendation to change management to accept or reject the change.

4.6.6 Triggers, inputs, outputs and interfaces

4.6.6.1 Trigger

The trigger for change evaluation is receipt of a request for evaluation from change management.

4.6.6.2 Inputs

Inputs to change evaluation include:

- SDP, including service charter and SAC
- Change proposal
- RFC, change record and detailed change documentation
- Discussions with stakeholders
- Test results and report.

4.6.6.3 Outputs

The outputs from change evaluation are:

- Interim evaluation report(s) for change management
- Evaluation report for change management.

4.6.6.4 Interfaces

Change evaluation is part of the overall process for managing significant service transitions, and should work with transition planning and control to ensure that appropriate resources are available when needed and that each service transition is well managed.

The change evaluation process must be tightly integrated with change management. There should be clear agreement on which types of change will be subject to formal evaluation, and the time required for this evaluation must be included in the overall planning for the change. Change management provides the trigger for change evaluation, and the evaluation report must be delivered to change management in time for the CAB (or other change authority) to use it to assist in their decision-making.

Change evaluation requires information about the service, which is supplied by service design coordination in the form of a service design package.

Change evaluation may need to work with service level management or business relationship management to ensure a full understanding of the impact of any issues identified, and to obtain use of user or customer resources if these are needed to help perform the evaluation.

Change evaluation requires information from the service validation and testing process, and must coordinate activities with this process to ensure that required inputs are available in sufficient time.

4.6.7 Information management

Much of the information required for change evaluation should be available from the SKMS. All evaluation reports should be checked in to the CMS and softcopy versions of the reports should be stored in the SKMS.

4.6.8 Critical success factors and key performance indicators

The following list includes some sample CSFs for change evaluation. Each organization should identify appropriate CSFs based on its objectives for the process. Each sample CSF is followed by a small number of typical KPIs that support the CSF. These KPIs should not be adopted without careful consideration. Each organization should develop KPIs that are appropriate for its level of maturity, its CSFs and its particular circumstances. Achievement against KPIs should be monitored and used to identify opportunities for improvement, which should be logged in the CSI register for evaluation and possible implementation.

- **CSF** Stakeholders have a good understanding of the expected performance of new and changed services
  - **KPI** Reduced number of incidents for new or changed services due to failure to deliver expected utility or warranty
  - **KPI** Increased stakeholder satisfaction with new or changed services as measured in customer surveys
- **CSF** Change management has good quality evaluations to help them make correct decisions
  - **KPI** Increased percentage of evaluations delivered by agreed times
  - **KPI** Reduced number of changes that have to be backed out due to unexpected errors or failures
  - **KPI** Reduced number of failed changes
  - **KPI** Increased change management personnel satisfaction with the change evaluation process as measured in regular surveys.

4.6.9 Challenges and risks

4.6.9.1 Challenges

Challenges to change evaluation include:

- Developing standard performance measures and measurement methods across projects and suppliers
- Understanding the different stakeholder perspectives that underpin effective risk management for the change evaluation activities
- Understanding, and being able to assess, the balance between managing risk and taking risks as this affects the overall strategy of the organization and service delivery
- Measuring and demonstrating less variation in predictions during and after transition

- Taking a pragmatic and measured approach to risk
- Communicating the organization's attitude to risk and approach to risk management effectively during risk evaluation
- Building a thorough understanding of risks that have impacted or may impact successful service transition of services and releases
- Encouraging a risk management culture where people share information.

4.6.9.2 Risks

Risks to change evaluation include:

- Lack of clear criteria for when change evaluation should be used
- Unrealistic expectations of the time required for change evaluation
- Change evaluation personnel with insufficient experience or organizational authority to be able to influence change authorities
- Projects and suppliers estimating delivery dates inaccurately and causing delays in scheduling change evaluation activities.

4.7 KNOWLEDGE MANAGEMENT

The ability to deliver a quality service or process rests to a significant extent on the ability of those involved to respond to circumstances – and that in turn rests heavily on their understanding of the situation, the options and the consequences and benefits, i.e. their knowledge of the situation in which they are currently, or in which they may find themselves. That knowledge within the service transition domain might include:

- Identity of stakeholders
- Acceptable risk levels and performance expectations
- Available resource and timescales.

The quality and relevance of the knowledge rests in turn on the accessibility, quality and continued relevance of the underpinning data and information available to service staff.

4.7.1 Purpose and objectives

The purpose of the knowledge management process is to share perspectives, ideas, experience and information; to ensure that these are available in the right place at the right time to enable informed decisions; and to improve efficiency by reducing the need to rediscover knowledge.

The objectives of knowledge management are to:

■ Improve the quality of management decision-making by ensuring that reliable and secure knowledge, information and data is available throughout the service lifecycle

■ Enable the service provider to be more efficient and improve quality of service, increase satisfaction and reduce the cost of service by reducing the need to rediscover knowledge

■ Ensure that staff have a clear and common understanding of the value that their services provide to customers and the ways in which benefits are realized from the use of those services

■ Maintain a service knowledge management system (SKMS) that provides controlled access to knowledge, information and data that is appropriate for each audience

■ Gather, analyse, store, share, use and maintain knowledge, information and data throughout the service provider organization.

4.7.2 Scope

Knowledge management is a whole lifecycle-wide process in that it is relevant to all lifecycle stages and hence is referenced throughout ITIL from the perspective of each publication. It is dealt with to some degree within other ITIL publications, but this section sets out the basic concept, from a service transition focus.

4.7.2.1 Inclusions

Knowledge management includes oversight of the management of knowledge, the information and data from which that knowledge derives.

4.7.2.2 Exclusions

Detailed attention to the capturing, maintenance and use of configuration data is set out in section 4.3.

4.7.3 Value to business

Successful management of data, information and knowledge will deliver:

■ Conformance with legal and other requirements, e.g. company policy, codes of professional conduct

■ Documented requirements for retention of each category of data, information and knowledge

■ Defined forms of data, knowledge and information in a fashion that is easily usable by the organization

■ Data, information and knowledge that is current, complete and valid

■ Data, information and knowledge to the people who need it when they need it

■ Disposal of data, information and knowledge as required.

Knowledge management provides value to all stages of the service lifecycle by providing secure and controlled access to the knowledge, information and data that is needed to manage and deliver services.

Knowledge management is especially significant within service transition since relevant and appropriate knowledge is one of the key service elements being transitioned. Examples where successful transition rests on appropriate knowledge management include:

■ User, service desk, support staff and supplier understanding of the new or changed service, including knowledge of errors signed off before deployment, to facilitate the roles within that service

■ Awareness of the use of the service, and the discontinuation of previous versions

■ Establishment of the acceptable risk and confidence levels associated with the transition, e.g. measuring, understanding and acting correctly on results of testing and other assurance results.

Effective knowledge management is a powerful asset for people in all roles across all stages of the service lifecycle. It is an excellent method for individuals and teams to share data, information and knowledge about all facets of an IT service. The creation of a single system for knowledge management is recommended.

Specific application to service transition domain can be illustrated through considering the following examples:

- Blurring of the concept of intellectual property and information when engaged in sourcing and partnering, therefore new approaches to controlling 'knowledge' must be addressed and managed during service transition
- Knowledge transfer often being a crucial factor in facilitating effective transition of new or changed services and essential to operational readiness
- Training of users, support staff, suppliers and other stakeholders in new or changed services
- Recording of errors, faults, workarounds etc. detected and documented during the service transition stage of the service lifecycle
- Capturing of implementation and testing information
- Re-using previously developed and quality-assured testing, training and documentation
- Compliance with legislative requirements, e.g. Sarbanes-Oxley, and conformance to standards such as ISO 9000 and ISO/IEC 20000
- Assisting decisions on whether to accept or proceed with items and services by delivering all available relevant information (and omitting unnecessary and confusing information) to key decision makers.

4.7.4 Policies, principles and basic concepts

4.7.4.1 Knowledge management policies

Knowledge management policies are required to guide all staff in the behaviours needed to make knowledge management effective. Policy statements will be very dependent on the culture of the organization, but typically might include the following:

- Knowledge and information needed to support the services will be stored in a way that allows them to be accessed by all staff when and where they are needed.
- All policies, plans and processes must be reviewed at least once per year.
- All knowledge and information should be created, reviewed, approved, maintained, controlled and disposed of following a formal documented process.

4.7.4.2 The Data-to-Information-to-Knowledge-to-Wisdom structure

Knowledge management is typically displayed within the Data-to-Information-to-Knowledge-to-Wisdom (DIKW) structure. The use of these terms is set out below.

Data is a set of discrete facts. Most organizations capture significant amounts of data in highly structured databases such as service management and service asset and configuration management tools/systems and databases.

The key knowledge management activities around data are the ability to:

- Capture accurate data
- Analyse, synthesize and then transform the data into information
- Identify relevant data and concentrate resources on its capture
- Maintain integrity of the data
- Archive and purge data to ensure optimal balance between availability of data and use of resources.

An example of data is the date and time at which an incident was logged.

Information comes from providing context to data. Information is typically stored in semi-structured content such as documents, email and multimedia.

The key knowledge management activity around information is managing the content in a way that makes it easy to capture, query, find, re-use and learn from experiences so that mistakes are not repeated and work is not duplicated.

An example of information is the average time to close priority 2 incidents. This information is created by combining data from the start time, end time and priority of many incidents.

Knowledge is composed of the tacit experiences, ideas, insights, values and judgements of individuals. People gain knowledge both from their own and from their peers' expertise, as well as from the analysis of information (and data). Through the synthesis of these elements, new knowledge is created.

Knowledge is dynamic and context-based. Knowledge puts information into an 'ease of use' form, which can facilitate decision-making. In service transition this knowledge is not solely based on the transition in progress, but is gathered from experience of previous transitions, awareness of recent and anticipated changes and other areas, which experienced staff will have been unconsciously collecting for some time.

An example of knowledge is that the average time to close priority 2 incidents has increased by about 10% since a new version of the service was released.

Wisdom makes use of knowledge to create value through correct and well-informed decisions. Wisdom involves having the application and contextual awareness to provide strong common-sense judgement.

An example of wisdom is recognizing that the increase in time to close priority 2 incidents is due to poor-quality documentation for the new version of the service. This is shown in Figure 4.35.

4.7.4.3 The service knowledge management system

Specifically within IT service management, knowledge management will be focused within the service knowledge management system (SKMS), which is concerned, as its name implies, with knowledge. Underpinning this knowledge will be a considerable quantity of data, which will also be held in the SKMS. One very important part of the SKMS is the configuration management system (CMS). The CMS describes the attributes

and relationships of configuration items, many of which are themselves knowledge, information or data assets stored in the SKMS. The relationship between the CMS and the SKMS is shown in Figure 4.8.

Figure 4.36 is a very simplified illustration of the relationship of the three levels, with configuration data being recorded within the CMDB, and feeding through the CMS into the SKMS. The SKMS supports delivery of the services and informed decision-making.

The SKMS will contain many different types of data, information and knowledge. Examples of items that should be stored in an SKMS include:

- The service portfolio
- The configuration management system (CMS)
- The definitive media library (DML)
- Service level agreements (SLAs), contracts and operation level agreements (OLAs)
- The information security policy
- The supplier and contract management information system (SCMIS), including suppliers' and partners' requirements, abilities and expectations
- Budgets
- Cost models
- Business plans
- CSI register
- Service improvement plans

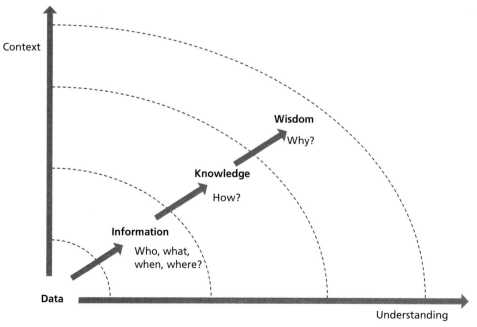

Figure 4.35 The flow from data to wisdom

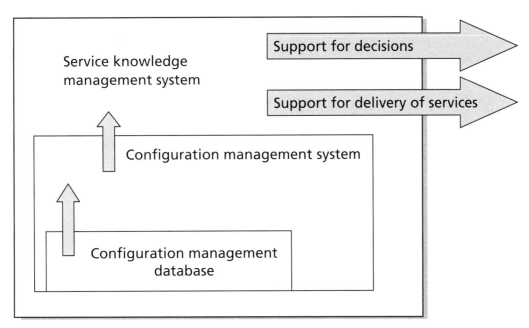

Figure 4.36 Relationship of the CMDB, the CMS and the SKMS

- The capacity plan and capacity management information system (CMIS)
- The availability plan and availability management information system (AMIS)
- Service continuity invocation procedure
- Service reports
- A discussion forum where practitioners can ask questions, answer each other's questions, and search for previous questions and answers
- An indexed and searchable repository of project plans from previous projects
- A known error database provided by a vendor which lists common issues in their product and how to resolve them
- Skills register, and typical and anticipated user skill levels
- Diagnostic scripts
- A managed set of web-based training courses
- Weather reports, needed to support business and IT decision-making (for example, an organization may need to know whether rain is likely at the time of an outdoor event)
- Customer/user personal information, for example to support a blind user who needs to have specific support from the service desk.

Many of these knowledge and information assets are configuration items. Changes to CIs must be under the control of the change management process, and details of their attributes and relationships will be documented in the CMS.

Figure 4.37 shows examples of information that should be in an SKMS. The meanings of all abbreviations in this figure can be found in the list of abbreviations at the end of this publication. The arrows represent the fact that all configuration items are described within the configuration management system.

4.7.5 Process activities, methods and techniques

4.7.5.1 Knowledge management strategy

An overall strategy for knowledge management is required. Where there is an organizational approach to knowledge management, initiatives within service transition, IT service management or other groupings should be designed to fit within the overall organizational approach.

In the absence of an organizational knowledge management approach, appropriate steps to establish knowledge management within service transition or within IT service management will be required. Even in this case it is important to manage knowledge with as wide a scope as practicable – covering direct IT staff, users, third-party support and others likely to contribute to, or make beneficial use of, the knowledge.

The strategy – either in place in the wider organization or being developed – will address:

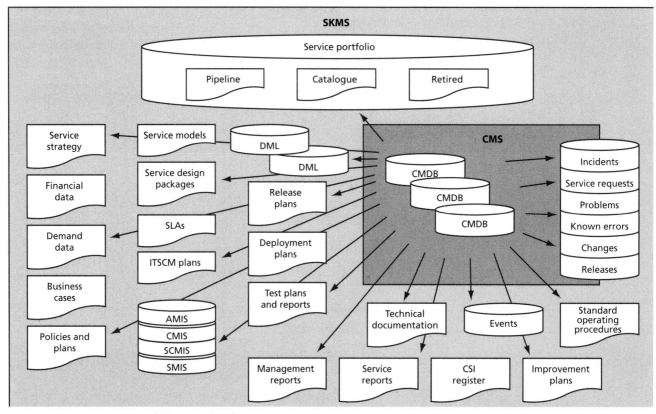

Figure 4.37 Examples of data and information in the service knowledge management system

■ The governance model, including the requirements of software asset management, Sarbanes-Oxley, ISO/IEC 20000, ISO/IEC 38500 and COBIT if these are applicable

■ Organizational changes under way and planned and consequential changes in roles and responsibilities

■ Establishment of roles and responsibilities and ongoing funding

■ Policies, processes, procedures and methods for knowledge management

■ Technology and other resource requirements

■ Performance measures.

Knowledge identification, capture and maintenance

Specifically, the strategy will identify and plan for the capture of relevant knowledge and the consequential information and data that will support it. The steps to delivering this include:

■ Assisting an organization to identify knowledge that will be useful

■ Creating a knowledge taxonomy and categorizing knowledge

■ Designing a systematic process for organizing, distilling, storing and presenting information in a way that improves people's comprehension in a relevant area

■ Accumulating knowledge through processes and workflow

■ Generating new knowledge

■ Accessing valuable knowledge from outside sources

■ Capturing external knowledge and adapting it – data, information and knowledge from diverse sources such as databases, websites, employees, suppliers and partners

■ Reviewing stored knowledge to ensure that it is still relevant and correct

■ Updating, purging and archiving knowledge.

4.7.5.2 Knowledge transfer

During the service lifecycle an organization needs to focus on retrieving, sharing and utilizing its knowledge through problem solving, dynamic learning, strategic planning and decision-making. To achieve this, knowledge needs to be transferred to other people and to other parts of the organization at specific points in the lifecycle. Many of the service management processes will link into this, for example allowing the service desk to have optimum knowledge and understanding at the point of any service transition into support. They will be reliant on information sourced from release and deployment management such as known errors going into live use but which are not show stoppers for the release schedule, or diagnostic scripts from any of the technical support teams. Links with HR, facilities and other supporting services need to be established, maintained and utilized. There must be an effective and efficient mechanism to allow people to search and retrieve relevant knowledge.

The challenge is often the practical problem of getting knowledge from one person or one part of the organization to another. It is more than just sending an email! Knowledge transfer is more complex; more accurately it is the activity through which one person or unit (e.g. a group, department or division) is able to learn from the experience, ideas or perspective of another. Its form must be applicable for those using it, and achieve a positive rating for 'ease of use'. The transfer of knowledge can be observed through changes in the knowledge or performance of recipients, at an individual or unit level.

An analysis of the knowledge gap (if any) within the organization should be undertaken. The gap will need to be researched and established by direct investigation of staff's understanding of the knowledge requirements for them to deliver their responsibilities compared with their actual observed knowledge. This can be a difficult task to deliver objectively and, rather than risk resentment or suspicion, it is often worth seeking skilled and experienced support to build this. The output from the knowledge gap exercise will form the basis for a communications improvement plan, which will enable planning and measurement of success in communication of knowledge.

Traditionally, knowledge transfer has been based on formal classroom training and documentation. In many cases the initial training is provided to a representative from a work group who is then required to cascade the knowledge to working colleagues. Other techniques are often appropriate and form useful tools in the service transition armoury. Techniques worth considering include the following.

Learning styles

Different people learn in different ways, and the best method of transferring and maintaining knowledge within the service management and user community will need to be established. Learning styles vary with age, culture, attitude and personality. IT staff can be usefully reminded that merely because a knowledge transfer mechanism works for them, it may not be appropriate for their current user base (especially where they are supporting users in a different working style, e.g. graphics design, performers, sales teams).

For many, some element of 'hands-on' experience is a positive support for learning, and simulation exercises or supervised experience and experimentation can be a useful consideration.

Knowledge visualization

This aims to improve the transfer of knowledge by using computer- and non-computer-based visuals such as diagrams, images, photographs and storyboards. It focuses on the transfer of knowledge between people and aims to transfer insights, experiences, attitudes, values, expectations, perspectives, opinions and predictions by using various complementary visualizations. Dynamic forms of visualization such as educational animation have the potential to enhance understanding of systems that change over time. For example, this can be particularly useful during a hardware refresh when the location of a component may change on an item, although the functionality does not alter.

Driving behaviour

Knowledge transfer aims to ensure that staff are able to decide on the correct actions to deliver their tasks in any foreseeable circumstance. For predictable and consistent tasks, the procedure can be incorporated within software tools that the staff use for those tasks. These procedures then drive behaviour in the accepted way. Change models (see Figure 4.2) and service desk scripts are excellent examples. This includes the ability to recognize when the laid-down practices are or might be inappropriate, e.g. in unexpected circumstances, when staff will either move away from the laid-down rules when they do not deliver as required or else will escalate the situation.

Seminars, webinars and documentation

Formally launching a new or changed service can create an 'event' that enhances the transfer of knowledge. Technology-based events such as webinars offer the ability to provide a high-profile knowledge delivery mechanism with the ability to retain it online and deliver it subsequently to other locations and new staff. Internet and intranet portals can convey equivalent messages in an ongoing fashion and allow discussion forums to question and develop knowledge. Product documentation should be designed in a way that facilitates knowledge transfer, and must be made available when and where it is needed.

Journals and newsletters

Regular communication channels, once established, are useful in allowing knowledge to be transferred in smaller units – incrementally rather than 'big bang' can be easier to absorb and retain. They also allow for progressive training and adaptation to circumstance and time periods. Crucially, these techniques can be made entertaining and targeted at specific groups.

Discussion forums and social media

There are many different tools that can provide informal channels to allow consumers of knowledge to also create, update and share knowledge based on their own experiences and perspectives. These channels require careful monitoring and management to ensure the accuracy and relevance of their content, but they can greatly increase the speed of knowledge creation and the relevance and accessibility of this knowledge.

It is important to train staff to understand the importance of not revealing confidential information or sharing valuable intellectual property outside the appropriate boundaries when they make use of these communication channels. There should be a clear distinction between resources on the public internet and private resources within the organization.

Aimed at the audience

A stock control system was introduced with staff in the warehouses directly inputting and working with the new system. Initially, all documentation was formal and written in semi-technical terms and the staff were taught how to use the system via traditional training and coaching. Once the system had settled in, a monthly newsletter was planned to keep staff aware of changes, improvements, hints, tips etc. The first versions were, again, formal and addressed the required information only.

It quickly became clear that the required knowledge was not in place among the staff. However, success followed when the updates evolved into a genuine newsletter – the required user knowledge was transferred much more successfully when it appeared among competitions, holiday snaps, humorous and even satirical articles. The lesson was that by targeting communications accurately at a known and understood audience, and making the experience pleasant, the required knowledge transferred along with the rest. And as a bonus, the staff contributed entertaining articles and their own hints and tips.

4.7.5.3 Managing data, information and knowledge

Knowledge rests on the management of the information and data that underpins it. To be efficient this process requires an understanding of some key process inputs, such as how the data, information and knowledge will be used. This includes an understanding of:

■ What knowledge is necessary, based on which decisions must be made and how services should be supported

■ Which conditions need to be monitored (changing external and internal circumstances, ranging from end-user demand, legal requirements through to weather forecasts)

■ What data is available (what could be captured), as well as rejecting possible data capture as infeasible; this input may trigger justification for expenditure or changes in working practices designed to facilitate the capture of relevant data that would otherwise not be available

- The cost of capturing and maintaining data, and the value that data is likely to bring, bearing in mind the negative impact of data overload on effective knowledge transfer
- Applicable policies, legislation, standards and other requirements
- Intellectual property rights and copyright issues.

Establishing data, information and knowledge requirements

The following activities should be planned and implemented in accordance with applicable organizational policies and procedures with respect to the data and information management process. These planning and design activities are carried out during the service strategy and service design stages of the service lifecycle.

Often, data and information is collected with no clear understanding of how it will be used, and this can be costly. Efficiency and effectiveness are delivered by establishing the requirements for information. Sensible considerations, within the constraints determined as described above, might include:

- Establishing the designated data, information and knowledge items, their content and form, together with the reason, e.g. technical, project, organizational, service management process, agreement, operations and information. Data is costly to collect and often even more expensive to maintain, and so should be collected only when needed
- Encouraging the use of common and uniform content and format requirements to facilitate better and faster understanding of the content and help with consistent management of the data, information and knowledge resources
- Establishing the requirements for data protection, privacy, security, ownership, agreement restrictions, rights of access, intellectual property and patents with the relevant stakeholder
- Defining who needs access to what data, information and knowledge as well as when they access it, including the relative importance of it at different times. For example, access to payroll information might be considered more important on the day before payroll is run than at other times of the month

- Considering any changes to the knowledge management process through change management.

Defining the information architecture

In order to make effective use of data, in terms of delivering the required knowledge, a relevant architecture matched to the organizational situation and the knowledge requirements is essential. This in turn rests on:

- Creating and regularly updating a service management information model that enables the creation, use and sharing of information that is flexible, timely and cost-effective
- Defining systems that optimize the use of the information while maintaining data and information integrity
- Adopting data classification schemes that are in use across the organization, and if necessary negotiating changes to enable them to deliver within the service management area. Where such organization-wide (or supply chain or industry sector) schemes do not exist, data classification schemes derived for use within service management should be designed with the intention of their being applicable across the organization to facilitate support for future organization-wide knowledge management.

An example of a knowledge, information and data architecture is shown in Figure 2.7. The four layers include examples of possible content at each layer. In practice it is likely that there will be multiple tools in use, each of which presents these four layers for a more limited purpose. For example, there may be a tool that provides all four layers for the CMS, or for support of incident and problem management.

The four layers in Figure 2.7 include the following example content:

- **The data layer** includes all of the tools needed to discover, collect, protect, share, audit and archive the data, as well as all of the data items themselves. Data items include all of the CMDBs and DMLs as well as many other data assets needed to manage the services.
- **The information integration layer** includes tools that enable data from multiple sources to be integrated, as well as the integrated information itself. Tools at this layer include:

- **Schema mapping** This facilitates integration of databases by defining which fields have similar data and how this can be transformed. For example, one database may have a field called 'CPU Type' which contains up to 10 characters. Another database might store the same information in a 20-character field called 'CPUTYPE'. Schema mapping would allow these to be consolidated in the integrated database.
- **Metadata management** This manages 'information about information', data dictionaries, field names, access rights etc.
- **Reconciliation** This deals with inconsistencies within and between multiple data sources – selecting preferred data when there are multiple sources, correcting data based on rules etc.
- **Extract** This deals with getting data out of multiple sources in order to re-use it.
- **Transform** This converts data from one format to another, often based on metadata from the schema mapping. For example, names might be stored as ASCII character set but need converting to a multinational character set for use within an integrated database.
- **Mining** This extracts patterns from data in order to transform it into information – for example identifying common types of incident from data in the free text fields in incident records.

- **The knowledge processing layer** is where the information is converted into useful knowledge. Tools in use at this layer may include:
  - **Query and analysis tools** For example to enable identification of configuration items that may require a particular security patch.
  - **Reporting tools** To assemble information into useful reports.
  - **Performance management** To analyse performance and capacity data and information.
  - **Modelling tools** To perform 'what if' analysis on data and information, identifying consequences and alternative options.
  - **Monitoring and alerting tools** To identify exceptions and issues relating to the data and information.

- **The presentation layer** provides tools to enable searching, browsing, retrieving, updating, publishing, subscribing and collaboration. At this layer there are different views of the lower three layers, which are suitable for different audiences. This may include a wide range of dashboards, scorecards, report formats, web pages, alerts etc. Each view should be protected to ensure that only authorized people can see or modify the underlying knowledge, information and data. In practice there are likely to be multiple tools, each providing this presentation for a different purpose. The example views shown in Figure 2.7 include:
  - **IT governance view** Including, for example, service portfolio reports, continual improvement information, risk and issue registers.
  - **Quality management view** With policies, processes, procedures, forms, templates and checklists.
  - **Services view** With service catalogue, utilities, warranties, packages and service reports.
  - **Asset and configuration view** Providing access to service assets, the CMS, status reports, CMDB data and other related information.
  - **Service desk and support view** This may include the service catalogue, users and stakeholders, configuration items, incidents, problems, changes, releases, configurations, performance etc.
  - **Self-service view** Service and product catalogues, contacts, FAQs, procurement, incident management, access management and request fulfilment.

Establishing data, information and knowledge management procedures

When the requirements and architecture have been set up, data and information management to support knowledge management can be established. The key steps involve setting up mechanisms to:

- Identify the service lifecycle data and information to be collected
- Define the procedure required to maintain the data and information, and make it available to those requiring it

- Define the activities and transformations that will be used to convert data into information and then to knowledge
- Store and retrieve
- Establish authority and responsibility for all required items
- Define and publicize rights, obligations and commitments regarding the retention of, transmission of and access to knowledge, information and data items (based on applicable requirements and protecting security, integrity and consistency)
- Establish adequate backup and recovery of data and information; this should address reinstating the ability to make constructive use of information, not just the re-establishment of a database
- Identify the requirements to review, in the light of changing technology, organizational requirements, evolving policy and legislation (and if necessary to adapt to) changes in:
  - Information system infrastructure in the light of evolving hardware and software technology
  - Security, service continuity, storage and capacity
- Deal with collection and retention requirements
- Review stored knowledge, information and data to ensure that it is still relevant and correct
- Update, purge and archive knowledge, information and data in accordance with documented policies.

When the procedures are designed, put into effect and accepted the organization can:

- Implement mechanisms to capture, store and retrieve the identified data from the relevant sources
- Manage the data, information and knowledge storage and movement, especially in line with appropriate legislation
- Archive designated information, in accordance with the data, information and knowledge management plan, including safely disposing of unwanted, invalid or unverifiable information according to the organization policy.

Evaluation and improvement

As with all processes, the capture and usage of data and information to support knowledge management and decision-making requires

attention to ongoing improvement, and the CSI register and service improvement plans will take as relevant input:

- Measurement of the use made of the data and information management–data transactions
- Evaluation of the usefulness of the data and information – identified by relevance of reports produced
- Identification of any data or information or registered users that no longer seem relevant to the organization's knowledge requirements.

4.7.5.4 Using the service knowledge management system

Providing services to customers across time zones, work cycles and geographies requires good knowledge-sharing across all locations and time periods of service operation. A service provider must first establish a service knowledge management system (SKMS) that can be shared, updated and used by its operating entities, partners and customers. Figure 2.7 shows an example of the architecture for such a system.

Implementation of a service knowledge management system helps to reduce the costs of maintaining and managing the services, both by increasing the efficiency of operational management procedures and by reducing the risks that arise from the lack of proper mechanisms.

Case study – Implementing an SKMS

Situation

An organization analysed that at least 75% of the cost of delivering support comes from resolving incidents. It was using point technologies such as a service desk workflow tool, search engines, scripting tools or simple knowledge bases. These systems generally focused on parts of the resolution process and they were not very effective. This contributed to dissatisfied customers, resulted in an ineffective service desk and caused integration issues for IT.

Solution

A comprehensive SKMS was implemented to help to address these obstacles by combining intelligent search and knowledge management with service management and business process support, authoring workflows and comprehensive self-service facilities.

The SKMS was supported by the problem management and change management processes.

The experience of end users who come to the website for help has been dramatically improved. Instead of an empty search box followed by no results or far too many, the application leads the user through a structured set of steps. Based on the specifics of the incident or request and the customer, web screens guide users to specific answers, follow-up questions, escalation options, opportunities to drill down or just highly relevant search results. The following improvements were achieved:

- Increased agent productivity
- Reduced aversion to web self-service
- Fewer escalations.

Over time the web workflows were tuned to deliver more and more optimized experiences. Good experiences helped to add value to the product and services and this resulted in greater loyalty that in turn increased profits.

Conclusion

A wealth of information exists in most organizations, which is not initially thought to contribute to the decision process, but when it is used to supplement traditional configuration data it can bring the lessons of history into sharp focus. Often this information is only available in an informal fashion. Marketing, sales, customer and staff information is a commonly overlooked source of valuable trend data that, along with traditional configuration, can paint a larger, more meaningful picture of the landscape and uncover the right 'course corrections' to bring a service transition or operational support for a service back on track and keep an organization travelling towards its objectives. Without this clear picture, the effectiveness diminishes and efficiency will decay. By recognizing this, organizations can more easily justify the resource costs of establishing and maintaining the data, processes, knowledge and skills needed to make it as effective as possible and maximize the benefits.

All training and knowledge material needs to be aligned to the business perspective. Materials that can be included are:

- The business language and terminology and how IT terminology is translated
- The business processes and where IT underpins them
- Any SLAs, and supporting agreements and contracts that would change as a result of the new service transition – this is especially important for the service desk analysts whose target at support transition will be to sustain service; if classifications are accurate this will facilitate the whole process.

For those in the service transition process a good way of consolidating understanding is to either spend time in the development areas, taking part in some of the testing processes, or to spend time in the business at the receiving end of the service transition to understand the process from the business perspective.

Useful materials include:

- Process maps to understand all the integrated activities
- Any known error logs and the workarounds – again particularly important for the service desk
- Business and other public calendars.

Technology for service desks and customer service needs to make it easier for customers, users and service desk agents. Some minimal progress has been made with generic knowledge management tools and there are significant developments in the service management industry to develop mature, process-oriented business applications supported by comprehensive knowledge bases. Examples of potential benefits are:

- **Agent efficiency** The largest component of return on investment (ROI) from knowledge management is reduced incident-handling time and increased agent productivity.
- **Self-service** A comprehensive SKMS provides the customer with knowledge directly on the support website. The cost of self-service is an order of magnitude lower than assisted service.

4.7.6 Triggers, inputs, outputs and interfaces

4.7.6.1 Triggers

Knowledge management has many triggers, relating to every requirement for storing, maintaining or using knowledge, information or data within the organization. For example:

- Business relationship management storing the minutes of a customer meeting
- Updates to the service catalogue or service portfolio
- Modification of a service design package
- Creation of a new or updated capacity plan
- Receipt of an updated user manual from a supplier
- Creation of a customer report
- Updates to the CSI register.

4.7.6.2 Inputs

Inputs to knowledge management include all knowledge, information and data used by the service provider, as well as relevant business data.

4.7.6.3 Outputs

The key output of knowledge management is the knowledge required to make decisions and to manage the IT services maintained within an SKMS.

Crucial to knowledge management is the need to ensure that the benefits of knowledge management are understood and enthusiastically embraced within the whole organization. Specifically, effective knowledge management depends on the committed support and delivery by most, if not all, of those working in and around IT service management.

Errors within the service detected during transition will be recorded and analysed and the knowledge about their existence, consequences and workarounds will be made available to staff working in the service operation functions in an easy-to-use format.

Service operation staff

- Front-line incident management staff, on the service desk and second-line support, are the point of capture for much of the everyday IT service management data. If these staff do not understand the importance of their roles then knowledge management will not be effective.

Traditionally, support analysts have been reluctant to record their actions fully, feeling that this can undermine their position within the organization – allowing issues to be resolved without them. Changing this to an attitude of appreciating the benefits (to individuals and the organization) of widely re-usable knowledge is the key to successful knowledge management.

- Problem-management staff will be key users of collected knowledge and typically responsible for the normalization of data capture by means of developing and maintaining scripts supporting data capture within incident management.

Transition staff

Service transition staff capture data of relevance through all lifecycle stages and so need to be aware of the importance of collecting it accurately and completely. Service transition staff capture data and information:

- Relevant to adaptability and accessibility of the service as designed, to be fed back via CSI to service design
- Make 'course corrections' and other adaptations to the design required during transition. Awareness and understanding of these will make subsequent transitions easier.

4.7.6.4 Interfaces

Knowledge management has interfaces to every other service management process in every stage of the lifecycle. The SKMS can only be truly effective if all processes and activities use it to store and manage their information and data, so that the maximum value can be extracted. Even processes that manage their data and information separately should still use knowledge management concepts and activities to manage these.

It is likely that knowledge management tool selection will have an impact on tool selection for all other service management processes, and this is an important consideration when first setting up knowledge management.

4.7.7 Information management

Creation of a service knowledge management system can involve a large investment in tools to store and manage data, information and knowledge. Every organization will start this work in a different place and have its own vision of where it wants to be, so there is no simple answer to the question 'What tools and systems are needed to support knowledge management?'

In practice, a service knowledge management system is likely to consist of a large number of tools and repositories, some running independently and others having links between them to allow for cross referencing and creation of added value.

The most important aspect of information management is understanding, and documenting, for each item of data, information or knowledge that the organization needs:

- How does it relate to other data, information and knowledge?
- Where and how is it stored?
- Who is responsible for collecting, updating and maintaining it?
- What legal, regulatory or governance considerations apply to it?
- How long is it needed for, and how will it be consolidated, archived or deleted when it is no longer needed?
- Who should be allowed to access it? Where from? When?
- Who should be allowed to change it?
- Does it need to be audited, if so how, who by and how often?

This understanding can then be used to help formulate an approach to creation of the SKMS, and decisions on what tools are needed to support this.

4.7.8 Critical success factors and key performance indicators

The following list includes some sample CSFs for knowledge management. Each organization should identify appropriate CSFs based on its objectives for the process. Each sample CSF is followed by a small number of typical KPIs that support the CSF. These KPIs should not be adopted without careful consideration. Each organization should develop KPIs that are appropriate for its level of maturity, its CSFs and its particular circumstances. Achievement against KPIs should be monitored and used to identify opportunities for improvement, which should be logged in the CSI register for evaluation and possible implementation.

- **CSF** Availability of knowledge and information that helps to support management decision-making
  - **KPI** Increased number of accesses to the SKMS by managers
  - **KPI** Increased percentage of SKMS searches by managers that receive a rating of 'good'
- **CSF** Reduced time and effort required to support and maintain services
  - **KPI** Increased number of times that material is re-used in documentation such as procedures, test design and service desk scripts
  - **KPI** Increased number of accesses to the SKMS by service operation teams
  - **KPI** Reduced transfer of issues to other people and more resolution at lower staff levels
  - **KPI** Increased percentage of incidents solved by use of known errors
  - **KPI** Increased results in knowledge management satisfaction survey of service operation teams
- **CSF** Successful implementation and early life operation of new and changed services with few knowledge-related errors
  - **KPI** Reduced number of incidents and problems categorized as 'knowledge-related'
  - **KPI** Increased percentage of successful service transitions
- **CSF** Improved accessibility and management of standards and policies
  - **KPI** Increased number of standards and policies stored in the SKMS
  - **KPI** Increased number of times that standards and policies in the SKMS have been accessed
  - **KPI** Increased percentage of standards and policies that have been reviewed by the agreed review date
- **CSF** Reduced dependency on personnel for knowledge.
  - **KPI** Increased number of times that the SKMS is accessed
  - **KPI** Increased percentage of SKMS searches that receive a rating of 'good' by the user
  - **KPI** Increased scores in regular customer satisfaction survey for knowledge management.

4.7.8.1 Measuring benefit from knowledge transfer

Although it is hard to measure the value of knowledge, it is nonetheless important to determine its value to the organization in order to ensure that the case for expenditure and support of knowledge management is maintainable. The costs associated with knowledge management can then be measured and compared against that value.

The value of improved knowledge transfer during service transition through improved knowledge management can be measured via the increased effectiveness of staff using and supporting the new or changed service. This (effectively the steepness of the learning curve) in turn can be measured through:

- Incidents and lost time categorized as 'lack of user knowledge'
- Average diagnosis and repair time for faults fixed in-house
- Incidents related to new or changed services fixed by reference to knowledge base.

Although not every element of the above can be directly attributable to knowledge management, the trends in these measures will be influenced by the quality of knowledge management, as shown by the example in Figure 4.38.

Clearly, the performance of the support groups post transition will be a determining factor of the quality of the knowledge transfer, typically delivered via training; however, it is more proactive to check understanding before arriving at this point. After each piece of training activity there should be a feedback mechanism to check understanding and quality of delivery. This could be in the form of a post-course questionnaire, or even a test to confirm understanding.

4.7.9 Challenges and risks

4.7.9.1 Challenges

Implementing knowledge management can be a difficult task. Most organizations already have stores of knowledge, information and data that meet many of their needs, and it can be challenging to justify the effort that would be needed to create a consistent architecture for managing these.

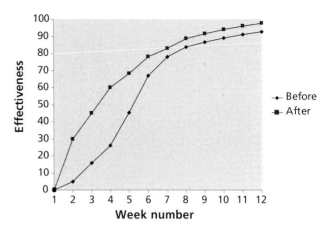

Figure 4.38 Contribution of knowledge to effectiveness of support staff

Each group or team within the service provider may own and manage information that they use, and may see knowledge management as interfering in their work. The challenge is to help all the stakeholders understand the added value that a more holistic approach to knowledge management can bring, and to continue to demonstrate this value as an SKMS is built.

4.7.9.2 Risks

Risks to knowledge management include:

- Focusing on the supporting tools, rather than on the creation of value
- Insufficient understanding of what knowledge, information and data are needed by the organization
- Lack of investment in the tools and people needed to support the SKMS
- Spending too much effort on knowledge capture with insufficient attention to knowledge transfer and re-use
- Storing and sharing knowledge and information that are not up to date and relevant
- Lack of support and commitment from stakeholders.

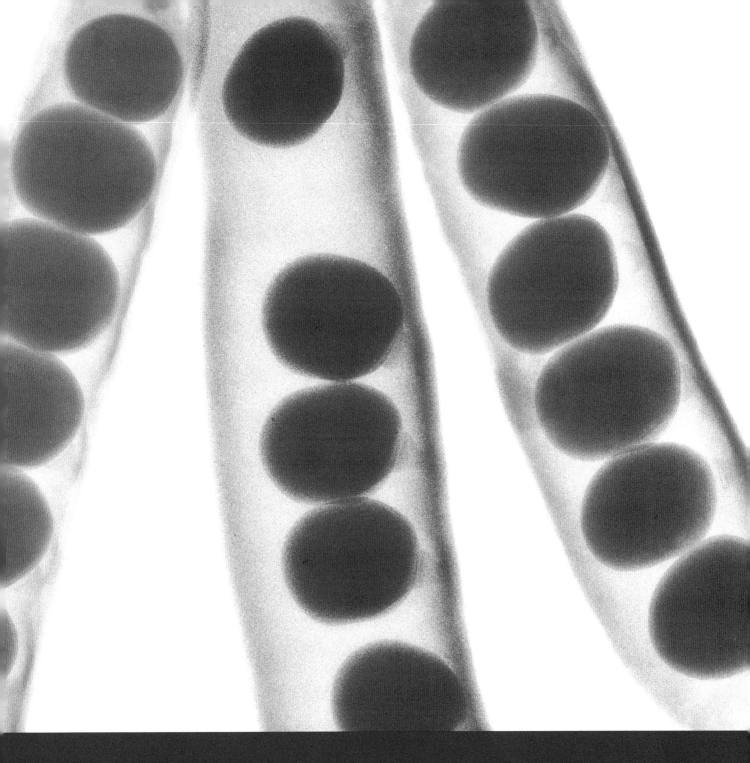

Managing people through service transitions

5

5 Managing people through service transitions

In addition to the processes discussed in Chapter 4, service transition supports and is supported by other activities. This chapter deals with those elements that are an essential part of, or a strong contributor towards, service transition.

Management of organizational change is an extensive field, and there are many sources of best practice in this area. This chapter describes a selection of these practices in order to address two specific activities that are important to service transition:

- **Communications** One of the major traditional weaknesses in service transition has been the inability to deliver sufficiently prompt understanding of the implications, benefits and usage of IT services.
- **Organizational and stakeholder change** Reflecting the holistic nature of change on which service transition must be based, organizations do not transform their IT service by only changing the IT services. Modern innovations mean that the organization itself will also inevitably change to make use of the new and changed services available.

5.1 MANAGING COMMUNICATIONS AND COMMITMENT

Communication is central to any service transition change process. The greater the change, the greater the need for clear communication about the reasons and rationale behind it, the benefits expected, the plans for its implementation and its proposed effects. Communications need to be timely, targeted at the right audience and clearly communicate the messages and benefits consistently. If some details of the transition cannot be shared, admit this and explain why it is not possible, e.g. for security reasons. Understanding people's commitment is important before planning the communications.

5.1.1 Communications during service transition

Typically, many people are affected by a service change and, consequently, sufficient stakeholder buy-in is required to carry the transition forward successfully. It is important to establish an individual's stage within the 'emotional cycle' to understand the method of approach. It is important to identify:

- Those who are already in support of the transition (and on whom it is not sensible to spend time right now since they do not need conversion); they will be picked up at the 'acceptance' stage.
- Those who are strongly opposed, and who would be unlikely to respond positively to persuasion. It is not constructive to spend time on these people since effort is most likely to be unrewarded at the moment.

The best use of time is to concentrate on those people who are between the two extremes, e.g. stakeholders capable of understanding and welcoming the transition. Although this seems obvious, it is common for people to spend too much time talking to those who are sympathetic to an idea, since this is easier and delivers the positive feedback that people tend to require to feed their confidence and job satisfaction. At this stage the service transition team needs to be attuned to its audience.

The service transition team will soon become familiar with the need to change attitudes and the operation of converting culture. For them it is a routine task, holding no threat. It can be hard to remember that, for those affected by the change, it is not a usual situation – they will be worried and a shared understanding will help greatly.

Example – emergency-room syndrome

A hospital doctor working in the emergency room will be used to seeing typical patients presenting typical symptoms. Thus, at 3 a.m., the doctor, possibly after a very long shift and while grabbing some well-deserved rest, is called to see a patient who is, in their mind, just another middle-aged man with severe chest pains. Although routine and unexciting to the doctor, nonetheless a good doctor will remember that it is the first time this particular man has nearly died from a heart attack.

Doctors in such a situation will not let their familiarity with the situation and lack of enthusiasm show. Instead, they will match their manner to that of the patient and treat the situation with the urgency and importance the customer expects.

It is important that the service transition team members are capable of understanding the impact of their work on others and tailoring their own approach to the stakeholder audience. Ultimately, the service transition team's goal is to build enthusiasm and commitment to the change, while ensuring that all stakeholders are clear about how the changes will impact on themselves and what will be expected of them in the coming months. Clear two-way communication channels will help employees to feel that their feedback and ideas are valued.

Stakeholder management can consume significant amounts of labour, with up to 50% of staff effort often consumed by this task during significant organizational change periods.

5.1.2 Communication planning

After establishing the strategies that will promote positive change enablers, and having understood the level of commitment within the organization, service transition must ensure that there is a detailed communications plan that will target information where it will be most effective.

When announcing information during a service transition change, the following considerations should be made for each statement you need to communicate:

■ What is the objective of the communication and what are the desired outcomes?

■ How formal and robust does the communication plan need to be? Some transitions will need a fully integrated and documented communication plan, but a more simple approach may be appropriate for smaller transitions.

■ How should the information be delivered – all at once or divided into segments and released over a period of time? If it is going to be released in segments, what are the components and what is the sequence of timing for the communication message delivery?

■ What should the tone of each message be (see section 4.7.5.2.)? What tone and style should be used to convey the message – upbeat, cautious, optimistic?

■ What actions could be taken before the communication that will increase the understanding and the acceptance of the information given?

■ How and when will groups be involved during the cascading of the communication information to other levels in the organization?

■ Are the communications successful in overcoming the particular communication barriers on this service transition (e.g. cultural differences, the added structure of large teams, the additional requirements associated with geographically dispersed personnel)?

■ Is there consideration to address the communication needs of other stakeholders in the project (e.g. decision makers, opinion leaders, system users, internal and external regulatory bodies and any other persons impacted by the implementation of the new service transition)?

■ How will success of the communication be measured?

Figure 5.1 shows an overview of the key elements for consideration when planning for effective communication.

To ensure that a communication strategy is effective, surveys and measures should be determined for regular monitoring. This will require feedback from people who have received the communication. It should also include how people are feeling on their 'change cycle' to establish that the target is right. The results of this feedback may identify individuals who should be

Communication strategy

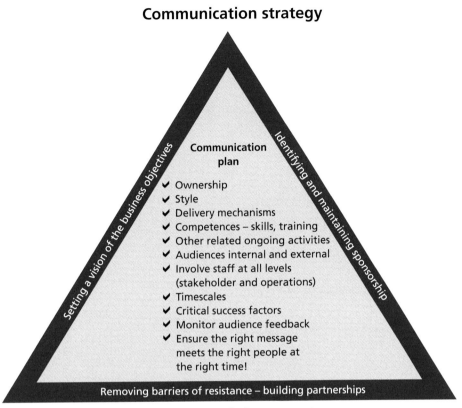

Communication plan

✔ Ownership
✔ Style
✔ Delivery mechanisms
✔ Competences – skills, training
✔ Other related ongoing activities
✔ Audiences internal and external
✔ Involve staff at all levels
  (stakeholder and operations)
✔ Timescales
✔ Critical success factors
✔ Monitor audience feedback
✔ Ensure the right message
  meets the right people at
  the right time!

Setting a vision of the business objectives

Identifying and maintaining sponsorship

Removing barriers of resistance – building partnerships

Figure 5.1 Example of a communication strategy and plan contents

receiving more personal contact from the service transition team in order for them to achieve an acceptable level of buy-in.

To obtain an appreciation of the sequence of events, a communication path diagram such as the one shown in Figure 5.2 helps with the planning of the communication process. This figure simply shows the typical communication activities that might occur in a sample project.

5.1.3 Methods of communication

Using multiple communication means will help understanding of the overall message. Common media types include:

■ **Workshops** deliver a clear and consistent message to the target audience on the overall service transition approach; this will generally be useful at the start of any communication strategy in order to build understanding, ownership and even excitement across the teams.

■ Organization, business unit or IT **newsletters** to reinforce any messages already delivered; however, care needs to be taken that this

approach is used as reinforcement rather than as the first time that employees may have seen the communication cascade.

■ **Training sessions** As part of the service transition, roles or processes will be likely to change; this requires targeted training, which should be planned giving sufficient time for employees to get to grips with any new ways of working.

■ **Team meetings** give support to team leaders from the service transition team, who will ensure at their own weekly meetings that they can reinforce any messages. Employees' questions may be better understood at these lower-level meetings – people are more comfortable because they are used to this method of communication with colleagues with whom they work daily.

■ **Meetings of the whole organization**, which may be face-to-face or use video or audio technology, depending on the size and type of organization.

■ **One-to-one meetings** where key stakeholders make time to visit staff in their work environment (floor walks), to set a positive

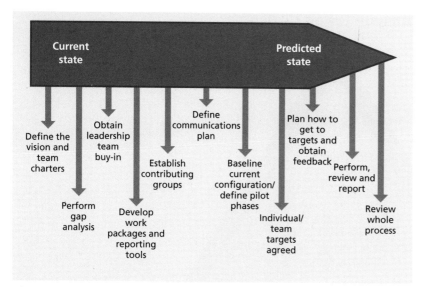

Figure 5.2 Example of a communication path

example of the support by senior management and allow employees to ask questions pertinent to themselves.

- **Q&A feedback** postings on boards or in mail boxes where employees can raise anonymous questions and receive feedback on any concerns they may have.
- Corporate **intranet**.
- **Simulation games** can be a practical and fun way of trying out a new way of working.
- Consistent **reinforcement memos** from the senior stakeholder, emphasizing key information or giving an update on the implementation activities, will keep the service transition alive for those people not perhaps actually involved at all stages.
- **Posters/roadmaps** – good-quality colourful communications on office walls showing implementation activities, progress or general updates are a positive way of keeping communications alive and delivering a consistent message.
- **Pay advice notes** – key communications attached to payslips can ensure a practical 100% communication update.
- **'Z-cards'/encapsulated reference cards** – small credit-card-sized documents holding key information and expected to be carried by staff in their wallets or purses.

Example – the service desk

It is important to understand the dynamics of the service desk operation. In some cases this group of staff will be doing shift work, with hours covering early mornings, evenings and weekends. They also tend to be one of the largest groups within the support operation, so it is particularly important that they get a consistent message during communication about the change. One of the communication methods that would be appropriate for this audience could be as follows:

- Taking selected key people from the service desk such as the shift leaders and team leaders to hear the main workshop brief. This will ensure that a large enough group have heard the full brief, and they will then be in a position to debrief their smaller teams.
- Members of the service transition team could then attend the individual team meetings to support the team leader as they conduct the debrief and answer any questions.
- Using reinforcement memos encourages service desk staff to feel that the senior stakeholder is communicating with them directly and avoids the risk of them feeling left out. This will also help at the point where they are about to take over any support from the service transition changes. This is also a cost-effective means of keeping a large group of people up to date and engaged in the process.

Models help to communicate expectations for each service or each type of change. Figure 5.3 is an example of a change model used to transition services from an organization to an external service provider (outsource). This is an example of a total organizational change, where there will be changes in management, processes and staffing, although many staff may transfer into the new service provider organization. Having access to a set of service, change and transition models in a form that is easy to communicate will help to set expectations during the service transition.

5.1.4 Motivation and the importance of communication

People need to be kept up to date with the progress of change, good or bad, if they are to be motivated to make it happen. Hackman and Oldham (1980) described the state of affairs when people try to do well because they find the work satisfying as 'internal motivation'. The concept is defined in Table 5.1.

People will be mobilized and engaged if they can see progress. Short-term wins should be communicated and progress celebrated.

Table 5.1 Job characteristics that motivate people

The essential characteristics of the job	Benefit for the employees	The result if all these characteristics are present
Feedback from the job	Knowledge of the actual results of work activities	High internal work motivation
Autonomy	Experienced responsibility for outcomes of work	
Skill variety Task identity Task significance	Experienced meaningfulness of the work	

5.2 MANAGING ORGANIZATION AND STAKEHOLDER CHANGE

Service transition's basic role is, on the basis of agreed design, to implement a new or changed service, effectively making the organization different from the way that it was previously. For a change of any significance, this is delivering an organizational change, ranging from moving a few staff to work from new premises through to major alterations in the nature of business working, e.g. from face-to-face retail to web-based trading.

Change is an inevitable and important part of organizational development and growth. Change can occur in incremental phases or suddenly,

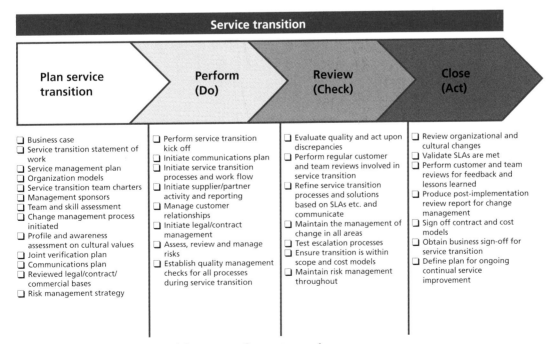

Figure 5.3 Example of service transition steps for outsourcing

affecting part or the whole of an organization, its people and its culture. Without change, progress does not happen. Organizational change is an essential part of continual improvement and must be built into all transitions to enable them to deliver value to the business.

Organizational change efforts fail or fall short of their goals because changes and transitions are not led, managed and monitored efficiently across the organization and throughout the change process. These gaps in key organizational activities often result in resistance, dissatisfaction and increased costs. Change is never easy; it usually takes longer than planned and creates barriers and resistance along the way. Effective leaders and managers understand the change process and plan and lead accordingly. Major negative impact can come from losing staff – disillusioned people leaving – which brings risks to the organization, e.g. loss of knowledge and lack of handover.

This section provides more detail about the involvement of service transition in managing organizational change. It includes assurance of the organization change products from service design, stakeholder management and communications, and offers various approaches for coping with change during transition.

5.2.1 The emotional cycle of change

What creates confusion and chaos in organizations more than change not managed well or not managed at all? Research shows that many change efforts fail, fall short of their goals or result in organizational dissatisfaction and inefficiency.

The research on change management strongly suggests that without the support of people, change will not happen. Business managers and change agents must understand the emotional impact that change has on people and how to manage it accordingly. Much research has been done on the emotional impact of change.

What this means is that failure to consider organizational change and how it affects people is a significant factor in the failure of transitions. In order to facilitate the acceptance of change, it is important to understand the 'emotional stages' that a person needs to get through before acceptance. This is illustrated in Figure 5.4.

For all significant changes, individuals will go through this process. At first they enter into a degree of shock, before going into avoidance. This will often manifest itself in increased efficiency while the situation is denied. This is usually a rapid stage, at which point performance drops as people choose to 'shoot the messenger' and blame the change initiators and service transition team, followed by self-blame as insecurity and the threat of the situation is felt. Performance is now at its lowest. It follows that the quicker the

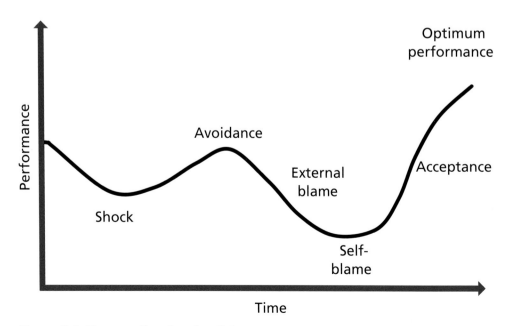

Figure 5.4 The emotional cycle of change

service transition team can get individuals through the cycle, the shorter the timescales before acceptance and optimum performance. One can use the experience of those within the affected area to understand concerns and the nature of resistance in order to communicate effectively at the appropriate stages. This may often take considerable personal time of the service transition team to listen to people's concerns, but ultimately will get individuals engaged and performing in as short a time as possible.

Appropriate communication through these stages of transition will drive the energy of individuals from low to high, obtaining involvement and generating a more positive attitude as the change takes place. As emphasized, this is a pattern followed by individuals, and different people will pass through these typical phases at different speeds, so understanding where individuals are on this curve and supporting and progressing them can be a significant resource commitment for service transition.

5.2.1.1 Effective management of change

There are five important ingredients of change: necessity, vision, plan, resources and competence. These are all discussed in this chapter. If there is no necessity established, there is lot of resistance from the people; if there is no vision, there is confusion among the employees; if there is no plan, there is chaos in the activities and transition; if there are no/fewer resources, there is a frustration among the employees; and if there is no competence, there is a fear of failure among the employees. Therefore, it is extremely important to pay adequate attention and establish management commitment to take adequate care of these requirements of the change.

5.2.2 Organization, roles and responsibilities

Managing change and transition is the responsibility of the managers and executives involved in that change. They must have an awareness that change has to be managed, that people have to be communicated with openly and honestly and that resistance has to be sought out, listened to and responded to appropriately. This is especially the case if a change is on a scale that is significant enough to affect the organization as a whole. The management board and executive must

ensure that there are adequate connections and controls throughout the organization to alert them to any barriers and to facilitate the transition to its goal.

A clear, strategic vision coming from the management board and/or executive is imperative to drive and maintain the change.

5.2.3 Service transition's role in organizational change

Organizational change is always a challenge. Factors that drive successful change initiatives at the organization level include:

- Leadership for the change
- Organization adoption
- Governance
- Organization capabilities
- Business and service performance measures
- A strong communication process with regular opportunity for staff feedback.

Although service transition is not accountable for the overall management of business and technical change, the service transition process owner or manager is a key stakeholder and needs to be proactive in reporting issues and risks to the change leaders, e.g. when the volume of changes may impact service operation's ability to keep the services running.

Organizational adoption is a subset of change management practice. It typically happens at two levels: individual and organizational. It is important to understand the culture of the organizations and the people involved. This will often be quite diverse across different cultures, business units, geographies and include:

- Business culture – this may be different depending on the industry, geography, etc.
- Culture of customer organization(s)
- Culture of service provider/IT organization
- Culture of supplier organization(s)
- Individual personalities, especially of senior managers and change champions.

Cultural and organizational assessment and change design are the responsibility of strategy and design. However, most significant service transitions will have an effect on working practices and so require a change in the behaviour and attitudes of many teams and stakeholder groups. Understanding the organizational change elements of a transition is therefore vital. The assessment of the likely risks and success is an important element of the transition as a whole. Service transition will be involved early in the lifecycle to ensure that these aspects are assessed and incorporated into the design and build of the organizational change.

Service transition must be actively involved in changing the mindsets of people across the lifecycle to ensure they are ready to play their role in service transition. These people will include:

- Service transition staff
- Customers
- Users
- Service operation functions
- Suppliers
- Key stakeholders.

Service transition will focus on simple messages at any one time to ensure that there is consistency in the implementation of the changes. For example, service transition would be interested in helping people to:

- Understand the need for knowledge and effective knowledge transfer
- Understand the importance of making decisions at the right speed/within the appropriate time frame
- Understand the need to complete and review configuration baselines in a timely manner
- Apply more effective risk assessment and management methods for service transition
- Follow the deadlines for submitting changes and releases.

Service design will perform the assessment of the capability and capacity of the IT organization to transition the new or changed services. Service transition has a quality assurance role to check that the organization and stakeholders are ready for the change, and it will raise any issues and risks related to organizational change that are identified, e.g. during testing, pilots, deployment and early life support.

Service transition is also responsible for ensuring that the organizational change happens according to the plans, that the change is still relevant in current circumstances and that the organizational change delivers the predicted organization, capabilities and resources. This will involve checking that changes are being adopted,

e.g. that a critical mass of customers, users and service operation staff accept the change and make a personal commitment to implementing it. Anecdotal evidence suggests that once a 'critical mass' of around 70% of affected people have accepted the change into their normal way of working, the change can safely be held as established behaviour. If the adoption rate is lower, then a significant chance exists that an organization might revert to the 'old ways'. The actual figure will be greatly influenced by the degree of staff involvement with a particular change, e.g. a few key staff can deliver a disproportionately major influence for acceptance or rejection.

Achieving successful service transition requires organized, competent and well-motivated people to build, test, deploy and operate the service. Successful service transitions rely on changing the organization and people, and it is important to focus on such aspects as competency assessment and development, recruiting, skills development, knowledge transfer, team building, process improvements and resource deployment. If there is a gap in capability, then service transition will provide input into the relevant party, e.g. project management, service design or continual service improvement.

5.2.3.1 Understanding the organizational culture

For successful service transition, an organization needs to determine the underlying values and drivers that enable effective management of change. Each organization and combination of organizations is different, so the service transition approach to change is determined, in part, by the culture and may vary across the organization.

Organizational culture is the whole of the ideas, corporate values, beliefs, practices and expectations about behaviour and daily customs that are shared by the employees in an organization. Culture can support an implementation or it can be the source of resistance.

When performing service transition activities it is important to gain an understanding of the type of culture currently existing in the organization and how this is likely to be affected by any proposed changes. Conversely, it is equally important to understand the effect that current culture may have as a 'barrier' to realizing change. Examples of key questions to be posed to help identify culture are shown in Table 5.2. These questions are useful when reviewing the service strategy and service design deliverables.

5.2.4 Strategy and design for managing organizational change

As discussed in *ITIL Service Strategy*, an organization's age and size affect its structure.

During a service transition, changes in roles, processes and relationships must be made or problems will arise. Understanding the different phases of development of the stakeholder organizations helps service transition to manage the stakeholders and users better.

Table 5.2 Understanding the culture of the parties involved

Cultural aspect	Question
Language	Is there a common language or shared language(s)? Does the language inhibit and reinforce boundaries or facilitate effective change and knowledge transfer? Is the organizational language style mostly formal or informal?
Change	Does the organization appear to resist change or is it constantly evolving?
Communication	What are the preferred modes of communication? What is the content and style of internal communications? Where does official and unofficial communication happen? Are communication channels open and democratic or closed and hierarchical? How is knowledge and experience shared? Are rumours/gossip prevalent?
Knowledge flow	How do people describe the way knowledge and information is transferred around the organization? How easy is it to find what you need to know, when you need it? How easy is it to find the right person with the right experience?
Communities	Are there identifiable 'communities' within the organization? Is there a community leader, e.g. problem management community leader? What is the structure and function of these communities?
Networks	Are an individual's networks well developed, on the whole? What kind of information is exchanged by these people?
Working environment	Does the working environment create the right conditions for knowledge transfer and integrated working, e.g. close proximity physically and/or electronic tools? How are desks configured? How are communal areas used?
History	How does the organization see its own history? Is it valued and used or quickly forgotten? How does the organization value past experiences, e.g. do people still refer back to their old company after a merger?
Meetings	Are meetings seen as productive? How are they managed? Are they effective? Does everyone feel safe to speak? How is opinion or criticism handled? How is output captured or taken forward?
Rewards and motivations	How are individuals/teams rewarded or recognized for sharing knowledge/information and experience? What motivates people in the organization? What else might be blocking engagement of an individual/team, e.g. other major change, major incident handling?
Time	What are individuals', teams' and the organizational attitudes to time, e.g. busy or relaxed; punctual, rigid and unchanging or flexible?

5.2.5 Planning and implementing organizational change

Frequently, plans and designs for managing change are not balanced and the organization and people side of change are omitted. Within IT organizations, project managers often focus on the technical activities rather than on the changes required for the organization or individuals. It is important that project plans are reviewed to ensure that the organizational change activities are included.

In order to manage organization change it is important that the stakeholders and teams understand what is required and can answer these questions:

- What are the business and organizational strategic drivers, personalities and policy changes?
- What issues does the proposed change solve?
- What will the new or changed service deliver?
- What does the new or changed service look like?
- How do current objectives need to be modified?
- What are the objectives of the change as defined by management, and how will success be judged throughout the levels of the organization?
- What are the processes, templates, decision points and systems to be used and what level of reporting data is required for the decisions to be made?
- Who will be involved and who will no longer be involved?
- Who will be affected within and outside the organization?
- What are the constraints – type, range and flexibility – time slots, equipment, staff and supplier availability?
- What is the planned timescale?
- Who or what can help in planning the implementation?
- What skills and measures should be considered?
- How will 'normal' life be affected?
- What will the consequential changes be, e.g. to business methods?

As part of quality assurance and implementation, the stakeholders and IT teams can be sampled to understand and clarify their expectations about these aspects.

5.2.6 Organizational change products

The change in the organization from the current state to a new state can require a combination of elements to be adjusted in order to fully realize the organization transformation. The required service is defined in the service design package. The following work products are typical outputs from service strategy and service design that assist with managing organizational change during service transition:

- Stakeholder map
- Current organization and capability assessment
- Current and required competency model and competency assessments
- Constraints (including organization, capability, resources)
- Service management process model
- Policies, processes and procedures
- Roles and responsibility definitions, e.g. a RACI (Responsible, Accountable, Consulted, Informed) matrix (see section 6.5 for more information on RACI charts)
- Relationship management
- Communication plan
- Supplier framework, especially where multiple suppliers are involved.

An example of a RACI matrix for managing change during the service lifecycle that supports service transition activities is shown in Table 5.3. In many instances on the chart the 'R' for responsibility appears in more than one column. This is indicative of the hierarchical nature of the responsibility, with strategic, tactical and operational responsibilities being required and thus spreading across more than a single column. In these instances the left-hand occurrences are more managerial, while the ones to the right focus on delivery.

Service transition will check that organizational change products and services are fit for purpose. For large-scale changes, such as mergers and acquisitions and outsourcing, this will include validation of the approach to:

- **Career development** Are succession plans being built? Do individuals have an understanding of their progression prospects?
- **Performance evaluation at organization, team and individual level** Are regular reviews conducted? Is the documentation formal, and is there demonstration of a consistent approach?

Table 5.3 Example of a RACI matrix for managing change

Role responsibility	Change sponsor, e.g. business and IT leader	Change enabler, e.g. process owner, service owner	Change agent, e.g. team leader instructing change	Change target, e.g. individual performing the change
Articulate a vision for the business and service change in the domain	AR	R	C	I
Recognize and handle resistance to change	R	A	R	C
Initiate change, understand the levers for change and the obstacles	R	AR	C	C
Manage change and input to change plan	C	AR	C	C
Input to design of target organization or structure, etc.	C	AR	C	I
Set up a system for communicating change	AR	R	C	I
Steer change	AR	R	R	C
Mobilize the organization	AR	C	C	C
Mobilize the department, unit, team	AR	R	R	I
Lead workshops and group analysis of the current processes	I	AR	R	I

■ **Rewards and compensation** Is there a net benefit to people affected by the change?
■ **Recruitment and selection** Where there is a shortfall in any roles required, is there a fair and consistent process for selection, including the process of internal movement as well as selection from the external market?
■ **Consideration of relevant laws and agreements** For example the European Union Acquired Rights Directive (ARD), the UK Transfer of Undertakings regulations (TUPE), or agreements with works councils and trade unions.

Typical work products from the build stage on which the service transition team depends are:

■ Organization model
  ● New or changed organizational structure
  ● Career development structure
  ● Reward and compensation structure
  ● Performance evaluation structure
  ● Performance measurement structure
■ Competency model detailed design
  ● Competency list
  ● Competency/activity matrix
  ● Target job, role, staffing and competence requirements matrix
  ● Job definition and design
  ● Role definitions and descriptions
  ● Staffing plan

■ Individual
  ● Individual assessment
  ● Competency assessment (including role and skill assessment)
  ● Performance assessment
  ● Performance enhancement needs assessment
  ● Learning needs assessment
■ Education and training
  ● Learning approach
  ● Learning test approach
  ● Performance enhancement design
  ● Learning definition and design
  ● Course definition
  ● Performance enhancement support design
  ● Performance enhancement support plan.

5.2.7 Assessing organizational readiness for change

The checklist presented in Table 5.4 can be used to assess the role and skill requirements during service transition.

5.2.8 Monitoring progress of organizational change

To enable a service transition programme to be effective and successful, regular checks/surveys should be performed throughout many different

Table 5.4 Organizational role and skills assessment checklist

Check	Evidence
Is there an assessment of the number of staff required and their current skill levels?	Plan
Is there a documented vision/strategy to address any risks in each area (e.g. resource shortfalls – start hiring actions, sub-contract or outsource the whole area)?	Vision/strategy
Have the generic roles and interactions throughout the service transition been reviewed?	Roles and responsibilities interaction matrix
Are the specific roles and measures defined?	Performance measures by role
Have the skills for each area, i.e. content, application, technical and business, been defined?	Skills requirements for each area
Is there an assessment of the organization's personnel against the requirements?	Assessment report
Have personnel from areas in the organization other than the areas covered by the service transition been considered?	Assessment report
Have the requirements for both development and maintenance that support the business needs been considered?	Requirements
Has the level of risk that relates to the support available for certain areas been documented? Also the areas that cannot be supported and the assumptions that apply to the analysis?	Risk assessment report

levels of the organization. Table 5.5 shows a feedback survey that could be used with individuals and teams involved.

The results of any survey should be useful in determining the progress made through service transition. This will include the status of employee commitment and any areas for improvement. This will also serve as a useful tool at various milestones within the transition journey. Employees will feel that their opinions count at a critical time as they go into the service transition programme. This is where positive engagement of the new processes can be increased by 'taking the majority with you'.

Monitoring is, of course, only the first part of a series of actions. The responses obtained must be analysed and understood. Where required, issues should be addressed and fixed as soon as possible. Respondents to the survey must be kept informed of changes that result from their feedback. Only in this way can staff have confidence that their feedback matters and achieves improvements.

Often, improvements will be identified in the post-implementation review of the service change and can feed into the CSI register.

5.2.9 Dealing with the organization and people in sourcing changes

A change in sourcing of IT services is one of the most significant, and often most traumatic, kinds of organizational change. Several different impacts and effects on staff will need to be considered, planned and prepared for.

5.2.9.1 Employee shock

One of the biggest changes that will be caused by sourcing is 'employee shock'. Many staff functions may evolve into more generic concerns such as project management and negotiation management. There will also be a morale issue caused by transition of staff replaced by the sourcing function. These perceptions need to be addressed early on, at the beginning of the initiative, so that the employees are completely aware of what is about to happen. Lack of communication and secretive behaviour only promotes suspicion and can lead to negative and disruptive attitudes. Sourcing is best done in an open atmosphere where all the options are clear and identified.

5.2.9.2 Business change

Another major change is the way business is conducted. Sharing 'everything' with an external service provider may lead to distrust if it is not presented in the correct terms. Care must be taken

Table 5.5 Example of a feedback survey

Aspect	Response
Service transition meetings are properly managed and run effectively.	
I have a clear idea of what is expected of me during this service transition.	
I am confident that I can successfully accomplish the assigned service transition work.	
My manager encourages me to exchange ideas about how to work better and/or improve the current processes.	
My manager is willing to listen to my concerns and ideas and pursue them on my behalf.	
The service transition communication methods, frequency and content meet my needs.	
The atmosphere during the service transition is friendly and helpful and open.	
There is sufficient effort being made to gather and evaluate the opinions and thinking of all members of the service transition team.	
I clearly understand the operational needs of this service transition.	
The work that I am responsible for will meet the service transition and operational needs of the business users.	
The job requirements allow me to balance my workload and personal life.	
I believe that real actions and service transition management consideration will result from my feedback captured from surveys.	

to ensure that information is passed to the service provider on a 'need-to-know' basis. This will keep the relationship professional.

5.2.9.3 Location change

The location of the sourcing can also present issues and risks during service transition. Typical sourcing locations are presented below, and each represents a difference from where the service was provided before:

- Local sourcing exists in the same geographical area
- Global (multi-shore) sourcing chooses the best solution non-dependent on geographical location
- Near-shore sourcing borders the client location offering same language, time zones and culture
- Offshore sourcing is located in one specific geographical location
- Combinations are becoming common with different functions, or aspects of functions, delivered in different fashions, e.g. a 9 to 5 service desk delivered locally but out-of-hours service supported from offshore.

The cultural and organizational issues relating to the change in location need to be addressed to guarantee a successful service transition.

5.2.9.4 Linking of sourcing activities throughout the organization

In planning a service transition to an external service provider, the sourcing strategy is mapped across the organization. This is where the budget is tied to the financial group, services are tied to the service delivery group, security considerations are tied to the security group etc.

Each group that is linked to the sourcing initiative must make provisions for interaction with the external service provider so that the sourcing operation will continue to run smoothly. It is important to obtain commitment from key people, and commitment-planning techniques can be used (see section 5.2.8). The links should be tested during each phase of the transition process to verify that the link is working and providing the correct transaction between the business and the external service provider.

For example, if the business wants to update the security software on the systems that the external service provider is using to run the business's financial information, the security group should have an established contact with the vendor to convey this need.

If the vendor needs to increase the business-specific skill level of a new employee, it should have an established contact to the training department of the business and/or specialist experts within the organization.

Every aspect of the sourcing operation as it pertains to the business it supports must be linked to the appropriate area/group within the business. These links need to be identified and established early on or the sourcing relationship will not be efficient and will have many bottlenecks that will affect productivity. Service transition will need to test these links as early as possible.

5.2.10 Methods, practices and techniques

5.2.10.1 Hints and tips on managing change

There is a tendency for senior executives to skip the need for organizational change by dictating what behaviours are appropriate or by transferring or terminating employees to get the message across. Typically it works in the short term, but then falls apart after the key executive leaves or moves on to something else.

Table 5.6 provides useful advice on the dos and don'ts of managing change.

5.2.10.2 J. P. Kotter's eight steps to transform your organization

J. P. Kotter's eight steps to transform your organization, shown in Table 5.7, is a well-proven approach to managing transformation. This is a useful method to use to identify gaps in plans for managing organizational change.

Further detail on J. P. Kotter's eight steps to transform your organization is described in *ITIL Continual Service Improvement*. These are iterative stages, and at each communication event, people's understanding needs to be checked.

5.2.10.3 Organizational change strategies

Service transition will be interested in the proposed strategies for managing organizational change. These can be used to assess the approach from service design and to manage change during service transition and identify issues and risks relating to organizational change.

Table 5.6 Tips for managing change

Do	Don't
Establish a baseline and vision.	Try to micro-manage everything.
Develop a communication strategy and check that communications are understood.	Put minor changes through bureaucratic processes.
Identify impact on other services, processes, systems and people not involved in service transition.	Forget the agreed degree of exposure to risk – in many circumstances the business is taking commercial risks as a deliberate policy, but IT and others stand to undermine the business justifications and policies by trying to remove risk from their component of a business change.
Identify impact on customers/users and other stakeholders.	
Get stakeholders to participate in the decision-making, prioritization, execution and benefit measurement.	Ignore input from stakeholders.
Be able to articulate and communicate why we are making this change.	Focus solely on the IT – all components of a service must be transitioned.
Identify new skills/knowledge required.	Forget the people.
Consider development requirements and how these requirements will be addressed – training, coaching, mentoring.	Over-complicate things – this makes them harder for people to understand.
Promote the right culture.	Ignore the after-effects of failed changes on people.
Promote organizational discipline.	Neglect the costs of transition.
Integrate HR support.	Succumb to inertia – instead re-assess validity and relevance of the service or change.
Put the right people in the right role/job.	Pretend that there will be no losers.
Help people to manage stress.	
Encourage people to think that the situation can be improved – it generally can be.	
Provide easy access to information about the change.	
Ensure new or changed documentation/instructions are concise and understandable for the target audience.	

Table 5.7 J. P. Kotter's 'eight steps to transform your organization'

Leading change: eight steps	Core challenge	Desired behaviour
1. Establish a sense of urgency.	Get people 'out of the bunker' and ready to move.	People start telling each other, 'Let's go, we need to change things!'
2. Create a guiding coalition.	Get the right people in place with the trust, emotional commitment and teamwork to guide the difficult change process.	A group powerful enough to guide large changes (and that works well together) influences others to accept change.
3. Develop a vision and strategy.	Get the guiding team to create the right vision and strategies to guide action in all of the remaining stages of change. This requires moving beyond number crunching to address the creative and emotional components of vision.	The guiding team develops the right vision and strategy for the change effort.
4. Communicate the change vision (and, communicate it over and over again).	Get as many people as possible acting to make the vision a reality.	People begin to buy in to the change and this shows in their behaviour.
5. Empower broad-based action.	Remove key obstacles that stop people from acting on the vision.	More people feel able to act, and do act, on the vision.
6. Create short-term wins.	Produce enough short-term (quick) wins fast enough to energize the change helpers, enlighten the pessimists, defuse the cynics and build momentum for the effort.	Momentum builds as people try to fulfil the vision, while fewer and fewer resist change.
7. Consolidate gains and produce more change.	Continue with wave after wave of change, not stopping until the vision is a reality – no matter how big the obstacles.	People remain energized and motivated to push change forward until the vision is fulfilled – fully realized.
8. Anchor new approaches in the culture.	Create a supporting structure that provides roots for the new ways of operating.	New and winning behaviour continues despite the pull of tradition, turnover of change leaders etc.

Kotter and Schlesinger (1979) suggested the following strategies that work well in practice:

- **Education and commitment** The sooner managers give people information about the change and the implications for them, the more successful the implementation of change is likely to be. Education and commitment begin in the early planning activities. The discussions generated around the pros and cons of the plan will help to dispel scepticism about the need for change and forge strong alliances that can be used as a change agent.

- **Participation and involvement** Allowing people to participate in the change normally overcomes resistance. On its own it is not enough; it must be used in conjunction with a policy of education and commitment (so that people understand the need for change) and effective monitoring and review for managers to be able to assess the impact of change on the service transition programme. It is not unusual for people to revert to familiar working practices, even though they support the changes. 'Change fatigue' is a well-recognized concept that can be expected at some stage and should be monitored.

- **Facilitation and support** Managers should be ready to respond positively when fears and anxieties about the change are expressed. Talking through the issues and performing a skills gap analysis may be sufficient, but at other times training in the new processes will be necessary, preferably prior to implementation. The manager should constantly promote the benefits of the change, reminding people of the objectives, and communicating a clear vision of what the organization will look like in the future and how employees' contribution is valuable in making that happen. Some expressed resistance can be positive because it shows that the employees are involved and can probably be moved through the cycle (see Figure 5.4) to a point of acceptance. Employees who show no visible emotion are the ones who need extra attention to identify the hidden issues and deal with them, otherwise secretive and subversive activities may result.

- **Negotiation and agreement** Change is easier to implement if you have agreement; gaining agreement suggests negotiation, so managers should be prepared to negotiate, formally if necessary. The relative cost of gaining agreement should be set against the importance of the change. Service transition has a major role in ensuring that such agreement is gained after each service lifecycle stage. Involvement with unions or works councils and HR will be needed, especially if negative impact on individuals is expected.

- **Manipulation and co-option** It is sometimes necessary to strike deals with those who oppose change, either by making them privy to restricted information or by 'buying them off', i.e. giving them extra rewards (financial or otherwise) to gain their participation. This approach should be used with the caveat that it is likely to cause problems later on. It is often used when the service provider changes and there is a risk to the operational services if key staff with irreplaceable knowledge and experience leave.

- **Explicit and implicit coercion** There are occasions when coercion is the appropriate tactic. It will come with associated costs, similar to the directive approach of 'act now explain later'. Coercion may well run counter to the values and beliefs of your organization and, by inference, to individuals working in it. Strong leadership is needed if using this strategy, together with a full knowledge of the situation and the possible problems that will be caused.

Other methods that managers commonly use are:

- Rewarding desirable behaviour, while at the same time ignoring or discouraging inappropriate behaviour that is detrimental to the service transition programme.

- Treating 'hurting' systems by identifying what it is that the people, whose commitment you need, dislike about the current system and putting it right. Managers can do this for individuals or encourage them to identify their own solutions.

- Exposing the issues in a sensitive manner. People are likely to take a stance against the change if they are made to feel that their worries are insignificant or they are being backed into a corner. Holding an informal, open meeting at which no minutes are taken, where all the issues are discussed, in order to gain a greater understanding of one another's viewpoint on the services to date and the transition plan, will help to avoid entrenched attitudes.

- Being a role model for the change. Managers should behave in ways that are congruent with the expected outcome, reinforcing the vision of the change. Their enthusiasm can be infectious, acting as a positive agent for change.

- Using peer-group pressure to persuade people that the change is good for the organization. Managers need to identify those individuals who command respect among their peers and gain their support. The Pareto principle of 80:20 is an effective measure – once 80% of the people will let change happen (or even make change happen) you can move on to the next phase; the other 20% will follow.

- Encouraging the sharing of positive changes and celebrating success; allowing others to see that it really does work will encourage them to embrace the change.

5.2.10.4 Techniques to overcome individuals' resistance to change

Rosabeth Moss Kanter identified ten reasons why people would resist change, and optional strategies that will promote positive change enablers. These can be helpful for service transition staff when they are involved in managing stakeholder change to overcome issues from individuals during transition. The ten reasons are:

- **Loss of control** When you move people from a process with which they are familiar to one they know little about, they will experience a feeling of losing control. This can be overcome by involving them in the decision-making, even allowing them to make decisions for themselves. It is essential to inform people of what choices they have – even if they are extremely limited. Managers should anticipate who is likely to oppose the changes and decide how to win them over. A detailed explanation of the business benefit and the return on investment (ROI) will strike a sense of urgency and awareness as to how the new service transition will support the business needs.

■ **Excessive personal uncertainty** The first question most people will ask is 'What is this going to mean for my job?' This can be answered effectively by explaining the need for, and implication of, the change at both a business and a personal level, including the often difficult issue of estimating how long the period of uncertainty will last. Honesty is the best policy.

■ **Avoid surprises** People like to be given the opportunity to think through the implications of change to/for them; springing new ideas on them will create scepticism.

■ **The difference effect** People build identities around many facets of their work – their role, the job, the building, the corporate name – it gives them a sense of tradition. Managers should only change what they must, keeping familiar symbols wherever possible.

■ **Loss of face** People dislike moving from a position of competence to one of incompetence, which can often happen when new processes, systems and ways of working are introduced. Managers can alleviate this problem by acknowledging the person's competence under the old regime and letting them participate in deciding the change process. This can also be done by allowing a joint responsibility for personal objective setting. This will generate early engagement as the change transitions.

■ **Fear about competence** Some people will believe that they cannot adopt the new ways of working – 'You can't teach an old dog new tricks!' The solution is to give them the training/ coaching they need before the new system is implemented, allowing them to have practice runs before the system goes live so that they prove their competence to themselves, thereby creating enhanced levels of confidence. This can have the added bonus of increasing their desire for change, and personal responsibility to their own career development.

■ **Ripples** The unexpected effect of an action taken in one area on another. Managers would be naïve to think that planned change is trouble free; sometimes it is impossible to predict accurately the effect that one change will have on another part of the organization. During the planning phase people should be encouraged to think widely and divergently, considering unlikely as well as likely possibilities when attempting to predict outcomes; this catastrophe planning can help to minimize the ripple effect.

■ **Increase in workload** Change frequently results in more work. If this is the reality, it should be acknowledged and rewarded if possible.

■ **Past resentments** If the proposed change is associated with an individual or organization about which the person has a grievance, they will resist the change. If people are allowed to air their resentments, managers will have the opportunity to remove or repair the grievances.

■ **Real threats** There are times when change is going to have a negative impact on the individual, and they are justified in resisting. Pretending it is going to be all right does not help; managers need to act first and act fast by talking with people as soon as possible, and involving them in the solution.

5.3 STAKEHOLDER MANAGEMENT

Stakeholder management is a crucial success factor in service transition. The new or changed service must support and deliver stakeholder requirements to be considered successful, and the active involvement of stakeholders will increase the likelihood of delivering as required. Failure to properly identify all stakeholder groups makes it almost inevitable that many of those affected will be unaware of proposed changes and unable to register their concerns and wishes; nor will they be able to be supportive if they are not included.

5.3.1 Stakeholder management strategy

The stakeholder management strategy from service design sets out:

■ Who the stakeholders are
■ What their interests and influences are likely to be
■ How the project or programme will engage with them
■ What information will be communicated
■ How feedback will be processed.

It is helpful for service transition if stakeholders are listed under categories such as 'users/beneficiaries' or 'providers'. Each category can then be broken down further if necessary. Categories should be recognizable groups rather than abstract ones; for example, 'employees based in one geographical location' are a readily identifiable group, whereas 'members of the public who support human rights' are not. Some categories may identify the same individuals, but it is often useful to differentiate between stakeholders 'wearing different hats', such as those shown in Figure 5.5.

5.3.2 Stakeholder map and analysis

Stakeholders inevitably have different interest areas in the overall change: for example, some will be concerned with how the change will affect their working environment; others will want to influence changes in the way customers are handled. A stakeholder map (see Figure 5.6) is a useful way of plotting the various stakeholders against their interests in the service transition, its activities and outcomes. Service transition should work with service design to ensure that there is an accurate and relevant stakeholder map or equivalent.

Examples of those who may be affected are:

- Sponsors of the service change, e.g. technology refresh
- Those affected by the service change or service transition
- Suppliers of goods or services
- Service management teams involved in the new or changed service
- Customers or consumers who will be affected by the service transition or the new or changed service
- Relationship management staff
- Internal and/or external audit
- Information security
- Fraud unit
- Risk management
- Shareholders, management and staff of the organization
- Labour groups/trade unions/works councils
- Political or regulatory bodies
- The wider community, such as the general public
- Project and programme management teams delivering the projects within the overall service lifecycle.

A stakeholder analysis helps to ensure that there is sufficient understanding of the stakeholder requirements and the stakeholders' interests in, and impacts on, the change. Stakeholders' positions (in terms of influence and impact) may be rational and justifiable or emotional and unfounded. However, they must all be taken into account since, by definition, stakeholders can affect the change process and hence the service transition.

Figure 5.5 Potential stakeholders

Stakeholders	Strategic direction	Financial	Operational changes	Interface with customers	Public safety	Competitive position
Business partner	●	●		●		●
Project teams			●			
Customers		●		●	●	
Press and media						●
Trade unions			●			
Staff	●		●			
Regulatory bodies		●			●	

Figure 5.6 Example of a stakeholder map

There is often a re-usable element of the stakeholder map and analysis. For example, where many projects are delivering into a shared service and infrastructure, the stakeholders may be the same: including the business sponsor, the service operation manager, the head of service management and permanent members of a change advisory board.

The stakeholder analysis helps to ensure that communication channels are targeted appropriately and that messages, media and levels of detail reflect the needs of the relevant stakeholders. The communications channels may need to accommodate stakeholders who cannot be engaged directly with the service transition. In many cases, working through partners, industry groups, regulatory bodies etc. may be required. Often, one larger communication approach, covering all areas, can help to deliver a more consistent and stronger message than by operating at functional level.

One technique for analysing stakeholders is to consider each stakeholder in terms of their importance to service transition and the potential impact of the change on them and 'plot' them on a matrix (see Figure 5.7). This will guide the activities that service transition should adopt. For example:

- A business sponsor will have a 'high' status of importance to the overall service change, and, depending on the scale and opportunities for any return on their investment, the impact of the new or changed service may be 'low', 'medium' or 'high'.

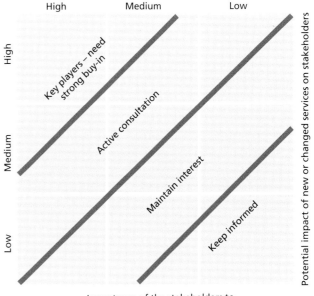

Figure 5.7 Power impact matrix

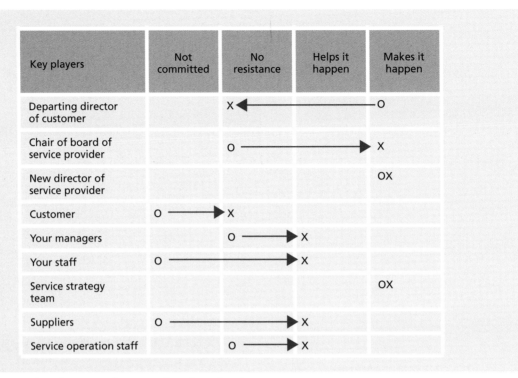

Key players	Not committed	No resistance	Helps it happen	Makes it happen
Departing director of customer		X ←		O
Chair of board of service provider		O →		X
New director of service provider				OX
Customer	O →	X		
Your managers		O →	X	
Your staff	O →		X	
Service strategy team				OX
Suppliers	O →		X	
Service operation staff		O →	X	

Figure 5.8 Example of a commitment planning chart

- Someone who works on the service desk, supporting a different service, will have a low importance to the overall service change and the service impact will have a low impact on them.

Stakeholders may move up or down the matrix as the service progresses through the lifecycle, so it is important to revisit the stakeholder analysis work, particularly during the detailed planning for service transition. Responsible stakeholders can and should enhance and even alter the course of the service transition.

5.3.2.1 Stakeholder changes

During the service lifecycle, stakeholders may come and go. Key stakeholders, such as the change sponsors, should (hopefully!) remain constant throughout. But sufficient records and documentation will be maintained to enable effective handover in the event that individuals are replaced: 'sufficient' is adjudged in accordance with business risk and cost.

Some stakeholders will be able to participate in advisory or assurance roles; some will be important in assessing the realization of the benefits; others will have an audit perspective.

5.3.3 Changes in stakeholder commitment

Figure 5.8 is a sample commitment plan. It shows the current commitment level of individuals and groups, and how that commitment must change if the transition is to be successful.

Each individual is rated with an 'O' to indicate their current position and an 'X' to indicate the degree of commitment needed from them. Sometimes they need to step back, e.g. the departing director of customer in this table would need to hand over the leadership role.

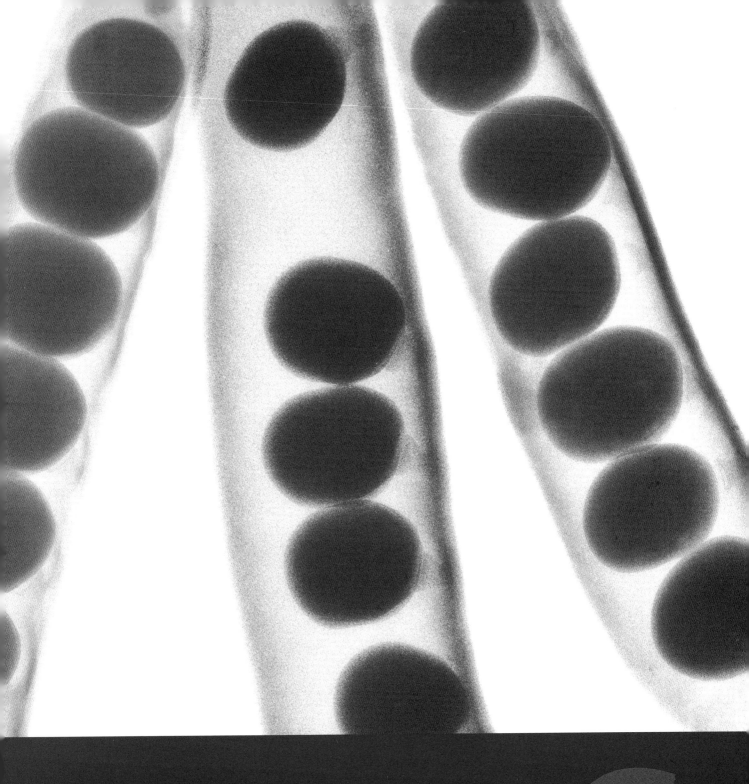

Organizing for service
transition

6

6 Organizing for service transition

This chapter describes the general concepts of organizing for service management in relation to service transition and the related practices. It includes generic roles, responsibilities and competencies that apply across the service lifecycle and specific aspects for the processes described in this publication.

Section 2.2.3 describes the basic concepts of organization, function, group, team, department, division and role that are used in this chapter.

6.1 ORGANIZATIONAL DEVELOPMENT

There is no single best way to organize, and best practices described in ITIL need to be tailored to suit individual organizations and situations. Any changes made will need to take into account resource constraints and the size, nature and needs of the business and customers. The starting point for organizational design is strategy. Organizational development for service management is described in more detail in Chapter 6 of *ITIL Service Strategy*.

6.2 FUNCTIONS

A function is a team or group of people and the tools or other resources that they use to carry out one or more processes or activities. In larger organizations, a function may be broken out and performed by several departments, teams and groups, or it may be embodied within a single organizational unit (e.g. the service desk). In smaller organizations, one person or group can perform multiple functions – e.g. a technical management department could also incorporate the service desk function.

For service transition to be successful, an organization will need to clearly define the roles and responsibilities required to undertake the processes and activities identified in Chapters 4 and 5. These roles will need to be assigned to individuals, and an appropriate organization structure of teams, groups or functions established and managed.

ITIL Service Transition does not define any specific functions of its own, but it does rely on the technical and application management functions described in *ITIL Service Operation*. Technical and application management provide the technical resources and expertise to manage the whole service lifecycle, and practitioner roles within service transition may be performed by members of these functions.

6.2.1 Examples of service transition organizational structures

The following sample organizational structures show how the various service transition roles might be combined and structured. Each organization should consider all of the roles that it requires and how these can be combined within its organizational constraints to create a structure that meets its needs.

6.2.1.1 Small organization

Figure 6.1 shows an example of service transition in a small organization. In this small organization there is a service transition manager who is the process owner, process manager and process practitioner for transition planning and support.

The change, configuration and release (CCR) manager is the process owner and the process manager for change management, service asset and configuration management (SACM), release and deployment management, and knowledge management. The CCR manager has a small team of practitioners who carry out specific activities for these processes.

The evaluation and test manager is the process owner and the process manager for change evaluation and for service validation and test. This manager also has a small team of practitioners.

6.2.1.2 Larger organization

Figure 6.2 shows an example of service transition in a larger organization. In this larger organization there is a central HQ organization which includes all process owners, as well as a change

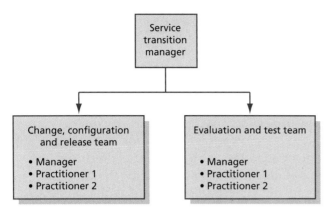

Figure 6.1 Example of service transition organizational structure for a small organization

management team, release managers for each category of business application and a validation and test team.

Each geographical area has its own process managers and practitioners for change management, SACM and deployment, and a knowledge manager.

6.3 ORGANIZATIONAL CONTEXT FOR TRANSITIONING A SERVICE

Other organizational units and third parties need to have clearly defined interface and handover points with service transition to ensure the delivery of the defined deliverables within the agreed schedule.

Programmes, projects, service design and suppliers are responsible for the delivery of service assets and components in accordance with the requirements of the service design, service level agreements (SLAs) and contracts, in addition to initiating any changes that affect a service release or deployment.

Service transition will acquire changes, service assets and components from these parties. An example of a service transition organization is illustrated in Figure 6.3 in addition to other teams within the IT services organization.

Interfaces to projects and business operations need to be clearly defined. It is essential that throughout the service lifecycle there is clear interaction and understanding of responsibility by all. It is critical

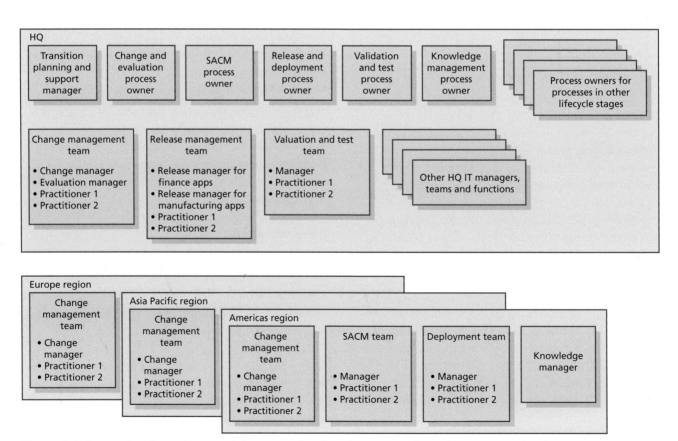

Figure 6.2 Example of service transition organizational structure for a larger organization

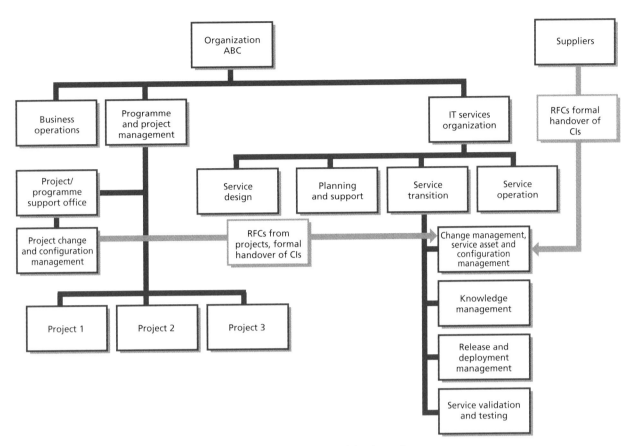

Figure 6.3 Example of service transition organization and its interfaces

that projects have a clear understanding of service design, transition and operations requirements and objective of delivery, and vice versa.

Often projects and programmes will work in isolation from service transition and operations, believing that they have no part to play in the ongoing service delivery. Similarly, transition and operations can ignore ongoing project activity; working on the basis that they will only be concerned about it once it is 'their turn' to deal with it. This is a very short-sighted approach and should be discouraged.

Cooperation, understanding and mutual respect are critical to ensuring that new, changed and ongoing delivery of services to the customer are optimized.

Figure 6.4 illustrates the required interaction between programmes, projects and service management elements. The figure assumes that the organization has a programme and project director responsible for overall management of programmes and projects and a service provider director responsible for all aspects of service management.

During the release and deployment there will be interactions with the business, customers and users, and these responsibilities are defined in this section.

6.4 ROLES

A number of roles need to be performed in support of service transition. Please note that this section provides guidelines and examples of role descriptions. These are not exhaustive or prescriptive, and in many cases roles will need to be combined or separated. Organizations should take care to apply this guidance in a way that suits their own structures and objectives.

A role is a set of responsibilities, activities and authorities granted to a person or team. A role is defined in a process or function. One person or team may have multiple roles; for example, the roles of configuration manager and change manager may be carried out by a single person.

Roles are often confused with job titles, but it is important to realize that they are not the same. Each organization will define appropriate job

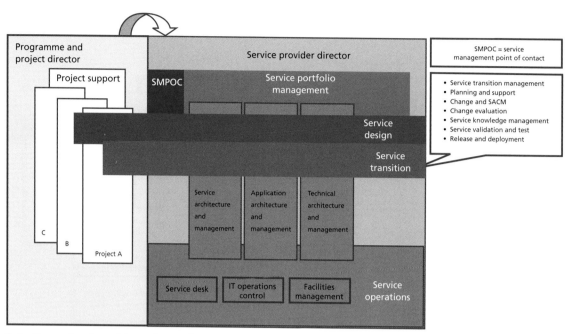

Figure 6.4 Organizational interfaces for a service transition

titles and job descriptions that suit its needs, and individuals holding these job titles can perform one or more of the required roles.

It should also be recognized that a person may, as part of their job assignment, perform a single task that represents participation in more than one process. For example, a technical analyst who submits a request for change (RFC) to add memory to a server to resolve a performance problem is participating in activities of the change management process at the same time as taking part in activities of the capacity management and problem management processes.

Roles fall into two main categories – generic roles such as process manager and process owner, and specific roles that are involved within a particular lifecycle stage or process such as a change administrator or knowledge management process owner. Roles can be combined in a number of different ways, depending on the organizational context. For example, in many organizations there will be someone with the job title of change manager who combines the roles of the change management process owner, change management process manager, change administrator and chair of a change advisory board (CAB). In a small organization the change manager role may be combined with roles from service asset and configuration management or release and deployment management. In larger organizations there may be many different people carrying out

each of these roles, split by geography, technology or other criteria. The exceptions to this are that there must be only one process owner for each process and one service owner for each service.

Roles are accountable or responsible for an activity. They may also be consulted or informed about something: for example a service owner may be consulted about a change during an impact assessment activity. The RACI model, described in section 6.5, provides a useful way of defining and communicating roles and responsibilities.

What is a service manager?

Service manager is a generic term for any manager within the service provider. The term is commonly used to refer to a business relationship manager, a process manager or a senior manager with responsibility for IT services overall. A service manager is often assigned several roles such as business relationship management, service level management and continual service improvement.

6.4.1 Generic service owner role

To ensure that a service is managed with a business focus, the definition of a single point of accountability is absolutely essential to provide the level of attention and focus required for its delivery.

The service owner is accountable for the delivery of a specific IT service. The service owner is responsible to the customer for the initiation, transition and ongoing maintenance and support of a particular service and accountable to the IT director or service management director for the delivery of the service. The service owner's accountability for a specific service within an organization is independent of where the underpinning technology components, processes or professional capabilities reside.

Service ownership is as critical to service management as establishing ownership for processes which cross multiple vertical silos or departments. It is possible that a single person may fulfil the service owner role for more than one service.

The service owner has the following responsibilities:

- Ensuring that the ongoing service delivery and support meet agreed customer requirements
- Working with business relationship management to understand and translate customer requirements into activities, measures or service components that will ensure that the service provider can meet those requirements
- Ensuring consistent and appropriate communication with customer(s) for service-related enquiries and issues
- Assisting in defining service models and in assessing the impact of new services or changes to existing services through the service portfolio management process
- Identifying opportunities for service improvements, discussing these with the customer and raising RFCs as appropriate
- Liaising with the appropriate process owners throughout the service lifecycle
- Soliciting required data, statistics and reports for analysis and to facilitate effective service monitoring and performance
- Providing input in service attributes such as performance, availability etc.
- Representing the service across the organization
- Understanding the service (components etc.)
- Serving as the point of escalation (notification) for major incidents relating to the service
- Representing the service in change advisory board (CAB) meetings

- Participating in internal service review meetings (within IT)
- Participating in external service review meetings (with the business)
- Ensuring that the service entry in the service catalogue is accurate and is maintained
- Participating in negotiating SLAs and operational level agreements (OLAs) relating to the service
- Identifying improvement opportunities for inclusion in the continual service improvement (CSI) register
- Working with the CSI manager to review and prioritize improvements in the CSI register
- Making improvements to the service.

The service owner is responsible for continual improvement and the management of change affecting the service under their care. The service owner is a primary stakeholder in all of the underlying IT processes which enable or support the service they own. For example:

- **Incident management** Is involved in (or perhaps chairs) the crisis management team for high-priority incidents impacting the service owned
- **Problem management** Plays a major role in establishing the root cause and proposed permanent fix for the service being evaluated
- **Release and deployment management** Is a key stakeholder in determining whether a new release affecting a service in production is ready for promotion
- **Change management** Participates in CAB decisions, authorizing changes to the services they own
- **Service asset and configuration management** Ensures that all groups which maintain the data and relationships for the service architecture they are responsible for have done so with the level of integrity required
- **Service level management** Acts as the single point of contact for a specific service and ensures that the service portfolio and service catalogue are accurate in relation to their service
- **Availability management and capacity management** Reviews technical monitoring data from a domain perspective to ensure that the needs of the overall service are being met

- **IT service continuity management** Understands and is responsible for ensuring that all elements required to restore their service are known and in place in the event of a crisis
- **Information security management** Ensures that the service conforms to information security management policies
- **Financial management for IT services** Assists in defining and tracking the cost models in relation to how their service is costed and recovered.

6.4.2 Generic process owner role

The process owner role is accountable for ensuring that a process is fit for purpose. This role is often assigned to the same person who carries out the process manager role, but the two roles may be separate in larger organizations. The process owner role is accountable for ensuring that their process is performed according to the agreed and documented standard and meets the aims of the process definition.

The process owner's accountabilities include:

- Sponsoring, designing and change managing the process and its metrics
- Defining the process strategy
- Assisting with process design
- Ensuring that appropriate process documentation is available and current
- Defining appropriate policies and standards to be employed throughout the process
- Periodically auditing the process to ensure compliance to policy and standards
- Periodically reviewing the process strategy to ensure that it is still appropriate and change as required
- Communicating process information or changes as appropriate to ensure awareness
- Providing process resources to support activities required throughout the service lifecycle
- Ensuring that process technicians have the required knowledge and the required technical and business understanding to deliver the process, and understand their role in the process
- Reviewing opportunities for process enhancements and for improving the efficiency and effectiveness of the process
- Addressing issues with the running of the process

- Identifying improvement opportunities for inclusion in the CSI register
- Working with the CSI manager and process manager to review and prioritize improvements in the CSI register
- Making improvements to the process.

Further detail on the role and responsibilities of the process owner can be found in *ITIL Service Strategy* and *ITIL Service Design*.

6.4.3 Generic process manager role

The process manager role is accountable for operational management of a process. There may be several process managers for one process, for example regional change managers or IT service continuity managers for each data centre. The process manager role is often assigned to the person who carries out the process owner role, but the two roles may be separate in larger organizations.

The process manager's accountabilities include:

- Working with the process owner to plan and coordinate all process activities
- Ensuring that all activities are carried out as required throughout the service lifecycle
- Appointing people to the required roles
- Managing resources assigned to the process
- Working with service owners and other process managers to ensure the smooth running of services
- Monitoring and reporting on process performance
- Identifying improvement opportunities for inclusion in the CSI register
- Working with the CSI manager and process owner to review and prioritize improvements in the CSI register
- Making improvements to the process implementation.

6.4.4 Generic process practitioner role

A process practitioner is responsible for carrying out one or more process activities.

In some organizations, and for some processes, the process practitioner role may be combined with the process manager role; in others there may be large numbers of practitioners carrying out different parts of the process.

The process practitioner's responsibilities typically include:

- Carrying out one or more activities of a process
- Understanding how their role contributes to the overall delivery of service and creation of value for the business
- Working with other stakeholders, such as their manager, co-workers, users and customers, to ensure that their contributions are effective
- Ensuring that inputs, outputs and interfaces for their activities are correct
- Creating or updating records to show that activities have been carried out correctly.

6.4.5 Transition planning and support roles

This section describes a number of roles that need to be performed in support of the transition planning and support process. These roles are not job titles, and each organization will have to define appropriate job titles and job descriptions for its needs.

6.4.5.1 Service transition manager

Many organizations will have a person with the job title 'service transition manager'. This job typically combines the roles of transition planning and support process owner and transition planning and support process manager.

6.4.5.2 Transition planning and support process owner

The transition planning and support process owner's responsibilities typically include:

- Carrying out the generic process owner role for the transition planning and support process (see section 6.4.2 for more detail)
- Setting the scope and policies for service transition
- Overseeing the overall design of all service transition processes to ensure that they will work together to meet the transition needs of the business.

6.4.5.3 Transition planning and support process manager

The transition planning and support process manager's responsibilities typically include:

- Carrying out the generic process manager role for the change management process (see section 6.4.3 for more detail)
- Managing and coordinating the functions that are involved in service transition
- Budgeting and accounting for service transition activities and resources
- Acting as the prime interface for senior management for service transition planning and reporting
- Managing and coordinating requests for resources
- Coordinating service transition activities across projects, suppliers and service teams (working with project managers and other personnel as required)
- Ensuring that the final delivery of each service transition meets the agreed customer and stakeholder requirements specified in the service design package.

6.4.5.4 Transition planning and support practitioner

The transition planning and support practitioner's responsibilities typically include:

- Maintaining and integrating plans for specific service transitions
- Maintaining and monitoring progress for service transition changes, issues, risks and deviations; including tracking progress on actions and mitigation of risks
- Maintaining records and providing management information on resource use, project/service transition progress, budgeted and actual spend
- Communicating with stakeholders.

6.4.6 Change management roles

This section describes a number of roles that need to be performed in support of the change management process. These roles are not job titles, and each organization will have to define appropriate job titles and job descriptions for its needs.

6.4.6.1 Change management process owner

The change management process owner's responsibilities typically include:

- Carrying out the generic process owner role for the change management process (see section 6.4.2 for more detail)
- Designing change authority hierarchy and criteria for allocating RFCs to change authorities
- Designing change models and workflows
- Working with other process owners to ensure that there is an integrated approach to the design and implementation of change management, service asset and configuration management, release and deployment management, and service validation and testing.

6.4.6.2 Change management process manager

The change management process manager's responsibilities typically include:

- Carrying out the generic process manager role for the change management process (see section 6.4.3 for more detail)
- Planning and managing support for change management tools and processes
- Maintaining the change schedule and projected service outage
- Coordinating interfaces between change management and other processes – especially service asset and configuration management and release and deployment management.

6.4.6.3 Change initiator

Many different people in the organization may carry out this role; it is not usually carried out by people who work in change management. Each change will only have a single change initiator.

The change initiator's responsibilities typically include:

- Identifying the requirement for a change
- Completing and submitting a change proposal if appropriate
- Completing and submitting an RFC
- Attending CAB meetings to provide further information about the RFC or change proposal if invited
- Reviewing change when requested by change management, and specifically before closure.

6.4.6.4 Change practitioner

The change practitioner's responsibilities typically include:

- Verifying that RFCs are correctly completed
- Allocating RFCs to appropriate change authorities based on defined criteria
- Submitting requests for evaluation to trigger the change evaluation process
- Formally communicating decisions of change authorities to affected parties
- Monitoring and reviewing activities of teams and functions that build and test changes to ensure that the work is carried out correctly. (This will be carried out as part of the release and deployment management process for a change that is part of a release.)
- Publishing the change schedule and projected service outage and ensuring that they are available when and where needed.

6.4.6.5 Change authority

There will normally be different change authorities for each category of change. See section 4.2.5.5 for more information about change authorities.

The change authority's responsibilities typically include:

- Reviewing specific categories of RFC
- Formally authorizing changes at agreed points in the change lifecycle
- Participating in the change review before changes are closed
- Attending CAB meetings to discuss and review changes when required.

6.4.6.6 CAB member

In many organizations, the CAB is the change authority for some categories of change. In other organizations the CAB is just an advisory body. Some CAB members may also be change authorities for other specific categories of change: for example, an operations manager may be a CAB member, and may also have the power to authorize reboot of a server outside of service hours to resolve an incident. See section 4.2.5.10 for more detail on the CAB.

The CAB member's responsibilities typically include:

- Participating in CAB meetings

- Authority to represent a particular group or function
- Preparing for CAB meetings by circulating RFCs within their own group and coordinating feedback
- Reviewing RFCs and recommending whether they should be authorized
- Reviewing successful and failed changes
- Reviewing unauthorized changes
- Reviewing the change schedule and providing information to help identify conflicts or resource issues
- Reviewing the projected service outage and providing feedback on the impact of planned outages.

6.4.6.7 CAB chair

If there is a single CAB then the CAB chair will almost always be the change manager. If there are multiple CABs then there may be multiple change managers, each chairing a different CAB.

The CAB chair's responsibilities typically include:

- Deciding who should attend CAB meetings
- Planning, scheduling, managing and chairing CAB meetings
- Selecting RFCs for review at CAB meetings, based on the change policy
- Circulating RFCs in advance of CAB meetings to allow prior consideration
- Convening emergency change advisory board (ECAB) meetings for consideration of emergency changes
- Selecting successful and failed changes for review at CAB meetings.

6.4.7 Service asset and configuration management roles

This section describes a number of roles that need to be performed in support of the service asset and configuration management process. These roles are not job titles, and each organization will have to define appropriate job titles and job descriptions for its needs.

6.4.7.1 SACM process owner

The SACM process owner's responsibilities typically include:

- Carrying out the generic process owner role for the SACM process (see section 6.4.2 for more detail)
- Agreeing and documenting the scope for SACM, including the policy for determining which service assets should be treated as configuration items
- Working with other process owners to ensure there is an integrated approach to the design and implementation of SACM, change management, release and deployment management, and knowledge management.

6.4.7.2 SACM process manager

The SACM process manager's responsibilities typically include:

- Carrying out the generic process manager role for the SACM process (see section 6.4.3 for more detail)
- Accountable to the organization for stewardship of fixed assets of the organization that are under the control of IT
- Defining and agreeing the service assets that will be treated as configuration items
- Ensuring that configuration data is available when and where it is needed to support other service management processes
- Planning and managing support for SACM tools and processes
- Coordinating interfaces between SACM and other processes, especially change management, release and deployment management, and knowledge management.

6.4.7.3 Configuration analyst

The configuration analyst role will often be combined with the role of the SACM process manager, or that of the configuration librarian, depending on the size, structure and culture of the organization.

The configuration analyst's responsibilities typically include:

- Proposing scope for service asset and configuration management
- Supporting the process owner and process manager in the creation of principles, processes and procedures

- Defining the structure of the configuration management system, including CI types, naming conventions, required and optional attributes and relationships
- Training staff in SACM principles, processes and procedures
- Performing configuration audits.

6.4.7.4 Configuration librarian

A configuration librarian is the custodian of service assets that are registered in the configuration management system.

The configuration librarian's responsibilities typically include:

- Controlling the receipt, identification, storage and withdrawal of all supported CIs
- Maintaining status information on CIs and providing this as appropriate
- Archiving superseded CIs
- Assisting in conducting configuration audits
- Identifying, recording, storing and distributing issues relating to service asset and configuration management.

6.4.8 Release and deployment management roles

This section describes a number of roles that need to be performed in support of the release and deployment management process. These roles are not job titles, and each organization will have to define appropriate job titles and job descriptions for its needs.

6.4.8.1 Release and deployment management process owner

The release and deployment management process owner's responsibilities typically include:

- Carrying out the generic process owner role for the release and deployment management process (see section 6.4.2 for more detail)
- Designing release models and workflows
- Working with other process owners to ensure there is an integrated approach to the design and implementation of change management, service asset and configuration management, release and deployment management, and service validation and testing.

6.4.8.2 Release and deployment management process manager

It is important that this role is assigned to a different person from whoever is responsible for service validation and testing, to avoid conflicts of interest.

The release and deployment management process manager's responsibilities typically include:

- Carrying out the generic process manager role for the release and deployment management process (see section 6.4.3 for more detail)
- Planning and coordinating all resources needed to build, test and deploy each release, including resources from other functions such as technical management or application management
- Planning and managing support for release and deployment management tools and processes
- Ensuring that change authorization is provided before any activity that requires this, for example before a release is checked in to the definitive media library (DML) and before it is deployed to a live environment
- Coordinating interfaces between release and deployment management and other processes, especially change management, SACM, and service validation and testing.

6.4.8.3 Release packaging and build practitioner

In smaller organizations, this role may be combined with the role of the release and deployment manager process manager. It may also be combined with the role of the deployment practitioner, and in some organizations it may be carried out by personnel working for the technical management or application management functions.

The release packaging and build practitioner's responsibilities typically include:

- Helping to design the release package, during the service design stage of the service lifecycle, in conjunction with personnel from other teams and functions
- Establishing the final release configuration, including knowledge, information, hardware, software and infrastructure
- Building the release
- Testing the release prior to independent testing
- Establishing and reporting outstanding known errors and workarounds

■ Providing input to support change authorization for check-in of the release to the DML.

6.4.8.4 Deployment practitioner

This role may be combined with the role of release packaging and build practitioner. It may also be carried out by personnel from the technical management or application management functions.

The deployment practitioner's responsibilities typically include:

■ Helping to plan the deployment, during the service design stage of the service lifecycle, in conjunction with personnel from other teams and functions

■ Ensuring that all deployment activity has been authorized by change management

■ Carrying out the final physical delivery of the deployment

■ Coordinating release documentation and communications, including training and customer, service management and technical release notes

■ Providing technical and application guidance and support throughout the release process, including known errors and workarounds

■ Providing feedback on the effectiveness of the release

■ Recording and reporting deployment metrics to ensure that these are within agreed SLAs.

6.4.8.5 Early life support practitioner

This role will often be carried out by personnel from the technical management or application management functions. It may also be combined with the roles of release packaging and build practitioner or deployment practitioner.

The early life support practitioner's responsibilities typically include:

■ Providing IT service and business functional support from deployment to final acceptance

■ Ensuring delivery of appropriate support documentation

■ Providing release acceptance for provision of initial support

■ Providing support to assist the service desk in responding to incidents and errors detected within a new or changed service

■ Adapting and perfecting elements that evolve with final usage, such as:
  ● User documentation
  ● Support documentation, including service desk scripts
  ● Data management, including archiving

■ Embedding activities for a new or changed service

■ Dealing with final transition of the service to service operation and continual service improvement

■ Monitoring incidents and problems and undertaking problem management during release and deployment, raising RFCs as required

■ Providing initial performance reporting and undertaking service risk assessment based on performance.

6.4.8.6 Build and test environment manager

This role will often be carried out by personnel from the technical management or application management functions. It may be combined with the deployment practitioner role.

Build and test environment manager responsibilities typically include:

■ Ensuring that service infrastructure and application are built to design specification

■ Planning the acquisition, build, implementation and maintenance of ICT infrastructure

■ Ensuring that all components are from controlled sources

■ Developing an integrated application software and infrastructure build

■ Delivering appropriate build, operations and support documentation for the build and test environments

■ Building, delivering and maintaining required test environments.

6.4.9 Service validation and testing roles

This section describes a number of roles that need to be performed in support of the service validation and testing process. These roles are not job titles, and each organization will have to define appropriate job titles and job descriptions for its needs.

6.4.9.1 Service validation and testing process owner

The service validation and testing process owner's responsibilities typically include:

- Carrying out the generic process owner role for the service validation and testing process (see section 6.4.2 for more detail)
- Defining the overall test strategy for the organization
- Working with other process owners to ensure that there is an integrated approach to the design and implementation of change management, change evaluation, release and deployment management, and service validation and testing.

6.4.9.2 Service validation and testing process manager

It is important that this role is assigned to a different person from whoever is responsible for release and deployment management, to avoid conflicts of interest.

The service validation and testing process manager's responsibilities typically include:

- Carrying out the generic process manager role for the service validation and testing process (see section 6.4.3 for more detail)
- Helping to design and plan testing conditions, test scripts and test data sets during the service design stage of the service lifecycle, to ensure appropriate and adequate coverage and control
- Allocating and overseeing test resources, ensuring that test policies are adhered to
- Verifying tests conducted by release and deployment management or other teams
- Managing test environment requirements
- Planning and managing support for service testing and validation tools and processes
- Providing management reporting on test progress, test outcomes, success rates, issues and risks.

6.4.9.3 Service validation and testing practitioner

The service validation and testing practitioner's responsibilities typically include:

- Conducting tests as defined in the test plans and designs, and documented in the service design package
- Recording, analysing, diagnosing, reporting and managing test events, incidents, problems and retest dependent on agreed criteria
- Administering test assets and components.

6.4.9.4 Contribution of other roles to service validation and testing

A number of other roles play a significant part in service validation and testing. These include:

- **Change management personnel** Ensure that tests are developed that are appropriate for the authorized changes, and that agreed testing strategy and policy are applied to all changes.
- **Developers/suppliers** Establish the root cause of test failures. For complex situations this may require collaboration between testing staff and development/build/supplier personnel.
- **Service design personnel** Design tests as an element of the overall design. For many services, standard tests will exist, possibly defined in a service transition model or a release and deployment model.
- **Customers and users** Perform acceptance testing. These roles should be able to cover the full range of user profiles and requirements and adequately sign off the conformance of a new or changed service. They will already have played a major role in helping to design the acceptance-testing approaches during the service design stage of the service lifecycle.

6.4.10 Change evaluation roles

This section describes a number of roles that need to be performed in support of the change evaluation process. These roles are not job titles, and each organization will have to define appropriate job titles and job descriptions for its needs.

6.4.10.1 Change evaluation process owner

The change evaluation process owner's responsibilities typically include:

- Carrying out the generic process owner role for the change evaluation process (see section 6.4.2 for more detail)

■ Working with other process owners to ensure that there is an integrated approach to the design and implementation of change management, change evaluation, release and deployment management, and service validation and testing.

6.4.10.2 Change evaluation process manager

The change evaluation process manager's responsibilities typically include:

■ Carrying out the generic process manager role for the change evaluation process (see section 6.4.3 for more detail)
■ Planning and coordinating all resources needed to evaluate changes
■ Ensuring that change evaluation delivers evaluation reports and interim evaluation reports in time to ensure that change authorities are able to use them to support their decision-making.

6.4.10.3 Change evaluation process practitioner

The change evaluation process practitioner's responsibilities typically include:

■ Using the service design and the release package to develop an evaluation plan as input to service validation and testing
■ Establishing risks and issues associated with all aspects of the service transition, e.g. through risk workshops.
■ Creating an evaluation report as input to change management.

6.4.11 Knowledge management roles

This section describes a number of roles that need to be performed in support of the knowledge management process. These roles are not job titles, and each organization will have to define appropriate job titles and job descriptions for its needs.

6.4.11.1 Knowledge management process owner

In many organizations this role will be combined with that of the knowledge management process manager, and in very small organizations these roles may be combined with roles from service asset and configuration management.

The knowledge management process owner's responsibilities typically include:

■ Carrying out the generic process owner role for the knowledge management process (see section 6.4.2 for more detail)
■ Creating overall architecture for identification, capture and maintenance of knowledge within the organization.

6.4.11.2 Knowledge management process manager

The knowledge management process manager's responsibilities typically include:

■ Carrying out the generic process manager role for the knowledge management process (see section 6.4.3 for more detail)
■ Ensuring that all knowledge items are made accessible to those who need them in an efficient and effective manner
■ Planning and managing support for knowledge management tools and processes
■ Encouraging people throughout the service provider to contribute knowledge to the service knowledge management system (SKMS)
■ Acting as an adviser to business and IT personnel on knowledge management matters, including policy decisions on storage, value, worth etc.

6.4.11.3 Knowledge management process practitioner

In many organizations the person carrying out this role is called a 'knowledge librarian'. The knowledge management process practitioner's responsibilities typically include:

■ Identifying, controlling and storing any information deemed to be pertinent to the services provided that is not available by other means
■ Maintaining controlled knowledge items to ensure that they are current, relevant and valid
■ Monitoring publicity regarding the knowledge information to ensure that information is not duplicated and is recognized as a central source of information etc.

6.4.11.4 Knowledge creator

This role may be carried out by many different people in the organization. Creation and sharing of knowledge is often written into the job descriptions of people in many different roles within IT and the business.

6.5 RESPONSIBILITY MODEL – RACI

Clear definitions of accountability and responsibility are essential for effective service management. To help with this task the RACI model or 'authority matrix' is often used within organizations to define the roles and responsibilities in relation to processes and activities. The RACI matrix provides a compact, concise, easy method of tracking who does what in each process and it enables decisions to be made with pace and confidence.

RACI is an acronym for the four main roles of being:

- **Responsible** The person or people responsible for correct execution – for getting the job done
- **Accountable** The person who has ownership of quality and the end result. Only one person can be accountable for each task
- **Consulted** The people who are consulted and whose opinions are sought. They have involvement through input of knowledge and information
- **Informed** The people who are kept up to date on progress. They receive information about process execution and quality.

When using RACI, there is only one person accountable for an activity for a defined scope of applicability. Several people may be responsible for executing parts of the activity. In this model, accountable means end-to-end accountability for the process. Accountability should remain with the same person for all activities of a process.

The RACI chart in Table 6.1 shows the structure and power of RACI modelling. The rows represent a number of required activities and the columns identify the people who make the decisions, carry out the activities or provide input.

Whether RACI or some other tool or model is used, the important thing is to not just to leave the assignment of responsibilities to chance or leave it to the last minute to decide. For example, if there is a transfer of a service from one service provider to another, RACI models should be designed in the service design lifecycle stage, and tested and deployed in service transition. In service operation, people assigned to specific roles will perform the activities in the RACI matrix.

Further details on the RACI matrix are provided in Chapter 3 of *ITIL Service Design*.

6.6 COMPETENCE AND TRAINING

6.6.1 Competence and skills for service management

Delivering service successfully depends on personnel involved in service management having the appropriate education, training, skills and experience. People need to understand their role and how they contribute to the overall organization, services and processes to be effective and motivated. As changes are made, job requirements, roles, responsibilities and competencies should be updated if necessary.

Each service lifecycle stage depends on appropriate skills and experience of people and their knowledge to make key decisions. In many organizations, personnel will deliver tasks appropriate to more than one lifecycle stage. They may well find themselves allocated (fully or partially) from operational tasks to support a design exercise and then follow that service

Table 6.1 An example of a simple RACI matrix

	Director service management	Service level manager	Problem manager	Security manager	Procurement manager
Activity 1	AR	C	I	I	C
Activity 2	A	R	C	C	C
Activity 3	I	A	R	I	C
Activity 4	I	A	R	I	
Activity 5	I	R	A	C	I

through service transition. They may then, via early life support activities, move into support of the new or changed services that they have been involved in designing and implementing into the live environment.

The specific roles within ITIL service management all require specific skills, attributes and competences from the people involved to enable them to work effectively and efficiently. However, whatever the role, it is imperative that the person carrying out that role has the following attributes:

- Awareness of the business priorities, objectives and business drivers
- Awareness of the role IT plays in enabling the business objectives to be met
- Customer service skills
- Awareness of what IT can deliver to the business, including latest capabilities
- The competence, knowledge and information necessary to complete their role
- The ability to use, understand and interpret the best practice, policies and procedures to ensure adherence.

The following are examples of attributes required in many of the roles, dependent on the organization and the specific roles assigned:

- Management skills – both from a person management perspective and from the overall control of process
- Ability to handle meetings – organizing, chairing, and documenting meetings and ensuring that actions are followed up
- Communication skills – an important element of all roles is raising awareness of the processes in place to ensure buy-in and conformance. An ability to communicate at all levels within the organization will be imperative
- Articulateness – both written (e.g. for reports) and verbal
- Negotiation skills are required for several aspects, such as procurement and contracts
- An analytical mind – to analyse metrics produced from the activity.

Many people working in service management are involved with continual service improvement. *ITIL Continual Service Improvement* provides specific guidance on the skill levels needed for CSI activities.

6.6.2 Competence and skills framework

Standardizing job titles, functions, roles and responsibilities can simplify service management and human resource management. Many service providers use a common framework of reference for competence and skills to support activities such as skill audits, planning future skill requirements, organizational development programmes and resource allocation. For example, resource and cost models are simpler and easier to use if jobs and roles are standard.

The Skills Framework for the Information Age (SFIA) is an example of a common reference model for the identification of the skills needed to develop effective IT services, information systems and technology. SFIA defines seven generic levels at which tasks can be performed, with the associated professional skills required for each level. A second dimension defines core competencies that can be combined with the professional skills. SFIA is used by many IT service providers to identify career development opportunities.

More information on SFIA can be found at www.sfia.org.uk.

6.6.3 Training

Training in service management helps service providers to build and maintain their service management capability. Training needs must be matched to the requirements for competence and professional development.

The official ITIL qualification scheme enables organizations to develop the competence of their personnel through approved training courses. The courses help students to gain knowledge of ITIL best practices, develop their competencies and gain a recognized qualification. The scheme has four levels:

- Foundation level
- Intermediate level
- ITIL Expert
- ITIL Master.

More information on ITIL qualifications can be found at www.itil-officialsite.com

6.7 SERVICE TRANSITION RELATIONSHIP WITH OTHER LIFECYCLE STAGES

Service transition is presented as a discrete lifecycle stage, but this should not be taken to imply that it can stand alone. Service transition exists to deliver the concepts documented within service design through to service operation functions for day-to-day management, and so without design and operation it has no purpose.

6.7.1 Upstream relationships for service transition

6.7.1.1 Logical staff mobility

Service transition takes its shape and input from the strategy set by the organization and from the new or changed services it is charged with bringing into live operation, i.e. by the output of the service design stage. Its very nature is therefore dependent on its relationship with 'upstream areas'.

In most organizations, many staff will deliver tasks appropriate to more than one lifecycle stage. Indeed, the skills and experience accumulated by service transition and service operation staff will typically be valuable in the stages upstream of their nominal focus.

Specifically, service transition will depend on appropriate experience from skilled staff in the service operation functions to deliver much of the knowledge required to make key decisions, based on predicting likely successful practice based on previous behaviour of systems in similar situations, as shown in Figure 6.5. In this figure the CSI lifecycle stage is represented by the arrows, which include feedback and improvement suggestions.

When service design establishes the best transition approach, and when, within service transition, the continued viability of that approach is assessed, service transition and service operation are best placed to play the role of subject matter experts, and provide input to the assessment and evaluation of the design's initial and ongoing viability.

Service operation staff will be involved in (design and) operation tasks directly via population of the service knowledge management system with precedents and experiences detected during service operation stages – e.g. through incident–problem–error cycles. This will drive informed and correct decision-making processes and facilitate more effective service transition.

In order to retain and make effective use of experience, staff may well find themselves allocated (fully or partially) from service operation functions to support a design exercise and then follow that service through service transition. They may then, via early life support activities, move into support of the new or changed services that they have been involved in designing and implementing into the live environment.

Expert advice on transition (as with design and operation) will also provide expert input to the development and maintenance of service strategy.

6.7.1.2 Process communications

Many of the capabilities of a service that require testing and acceptance with transition are established and approach and measures set within the service design stage of the lifecycle. As described above, this exercise is likely to have involved service transition staff, either through direct involvement (perhaps even formal secondment) or through consultation and expert advice.

6.7.2 Downstream process and procedure influence

Many elements initiated or perfected during service transition will be established and become key elements within service operation.

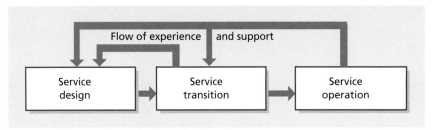

Figure 6.5 Flow of experience

During transition testing, incidents will be detected that reveal errors within the new or changed service. The nature and identified resolution of these errors will provide direct input to the service operation procedures for supporting the new or changed service in live use. Service transition input is likely to affect most areas of the service operation stage.

Testing will share processes with service operation, possibly with some variations in procedure, e.g. to accommodate the differing requirements and risk environments of analysing and rectifying errors in testing and live environments.

Where testing detects errors in a new or changed service that are not significant enough to prevent the release of the service, these errors are released into the live known error database, and notification is passed to continual service improvement, via the SKMS, which CSI will make extensive use of.

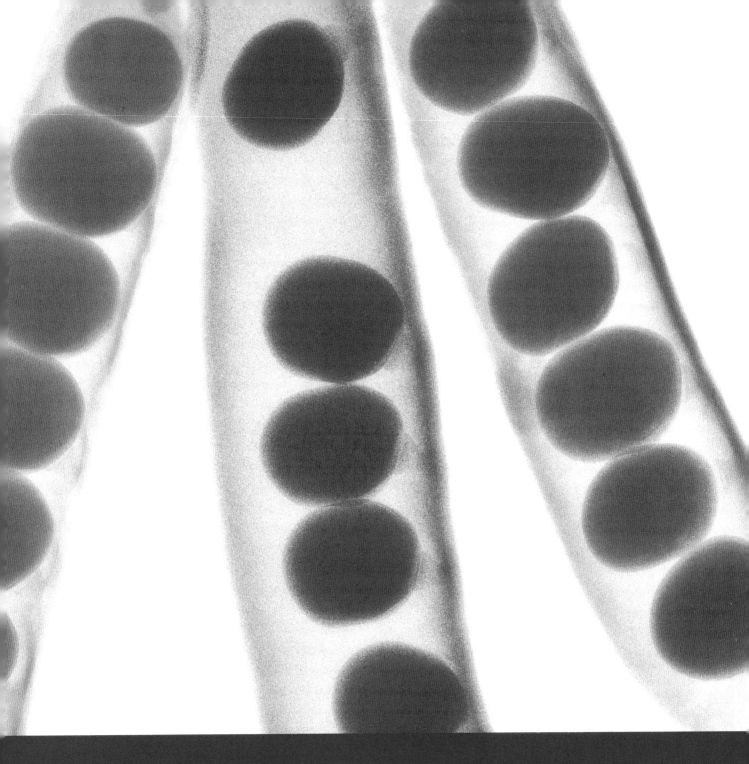

Technology considerations

7

7 Technology considerations

Technology has a major role to play in service transition. The use of supporting technology should be part of the design for service transition, and mechanisms for maintaining and maximizing benefit from that technology must be in place.

Selection and implementation of tools to support service transition should also consider wider issues such as:

■ Green IT and sustainability
■ The need to support future types of configuration item (CI) as well as those currently in use (see for example section 8.3 for a discussion of issues relating to virtual and cloud technologies).

There are two ways in which service transition is supported by technology:

■ Enterprise-wide tools that support the broader systems and processes within which service transition delivers support
■ Tools targeted more specifically at supporting service transition or parts of service transition.

The following systems, supporting the wider scope, will provide automated support for some elements of service transition management:

■ IT service management systems:
  ● Enterprise frameworks that provide integration capabilities to integrate and link in the configuration management system
  ● System, network and application management tools
  ● Service dashboards and reporting tools
■ Specific IT service management (ITSM) technology and tools that cover:
  ● Service knowledge management system (but note that this may use a generic knowledge management tool for the business, rather than a service management specific tool)
  ● Collaborative, content management, workflow tools
  ● Data-mining tools, to discover patterns and correlations in existing data
  ● Extract, transform and load data tools
  ● Measurement and reporting systems

● Test management and testing tools
● Database and test data management tools
● Copying and publishing tools
● Release and deployment management technology
● Deployment and logistics systems and tools.

There are many support tools that can assist change management, service asset and configuration management (SACM) and release and deployment management. These may come in a variety of combinations and include:

■ Configuration management systems and tools
■ Version control tools
■ Document management systems
■ Requirements analysis and design tools, systems architecture and computer-aided software engineering (CASE) tools, which can facilitate impact analysis from a business perspective
■ Database management audit tools to track physical databases
■ Distribution and installation tools
■ Comparison tools (software files, directories, databases)
■ Build and release tools (which provide listings of input and output CIs)
■ Installation and de-installation tools (which provide listings of CIs installed)
■ Compression tools (to save storage space)
■ Listing and configuration baseline tools (e.g. full directory listings with date–time stamps and check sums)
■ Discovery and audit tools (also called 'inventory' tools)
■ Detection and recovery tools (where the build is returned to a known state)
■ Visualization, mapping and graphical representations with drill-down
■ Reporting tools including those that access objects from several databases, providing integrated reports across systems.

7.1 KNOWLEDGE MANAGEMENT TOOLS

Knowledge management tools address an organization's need to manage the processing of information and promulgation of knowledge. Knowledge management tools address the requirements of maintaining records and documents electronically. Records are distinguished from documents by the fact that they function as evidence of activities, rather than evidence of intentions. Examples of documents include policy statements, plans, procedures, service level agreements and contracts.

- **Document management** Defines the set of capabilities to support the storage, protection, classification, searching, retrieval, maintenance, archiving and retirement of documents and information
- **Records management** Defines the set of capabilities to support the storage, protection, classification, searching, retrieval, maintenance, archiving and retirement of records
- **Content management** The capability that manages the storage, maintenance and retrieval of documents and information of a system or website. The result is often a knowledge asset represented in written words, figures, graphics and other forms of knowledge presentation. Examples of knowledge services that directly support content management are:
  - Web-publishing tools
  - Web conferencing, wikis, blogs etc.
  - Word processing
  - Data and financial analysis
  - Presentation tools
  - Flow-charting
  - Content management systems (codify, organize, version control, document architectures)
  - Publication and distribution.

7.2 COLLABORATION

Collaboration is the process of sharing tacit knowledge and working together to accomplish stated goals and objectives. The following is a list of knowledge services widely available today, which, when properly implemented, can significantly improve the productivity of people by streamlining and improving the way they collaborate:

- Shared calendars and tasks
- Threaded discussions
- Instant messaging
- White-boarding
- Video or teleconferencing
- Email.

7.2.1 Communities

Communities are rapidly becoming the method of choice for groups of people spread across time zones and country boundaries to communicate, collaborate and share knowledge. These communities are typically facilitated through an online medium such as an intranet or extranet, and the community often acts as the integration point for all knowledge services provided to its members. Well-run communities will typically elect a leader to manage and run the community and a group of subject matter experts to contribute and evaluate knowledge assets within the community. Examples of services and functions provided within the typical online community are:

- Community portals
- Email alias management
- Focus groups
- Intellectual property, best practice, work examples and template repository
- Online events and net shows.

Successful communities often implement a reward and recognition programme for their members. Such a programme is a means to acknowledge and reward the contribution of valuable knowledge assets. These assets are submitted by members of the community and are evaluated by the community leader and elected subject matter experts. The author(s) are then recognized within the community and meaningfully rewarded in some fashion for their contribution. This is a highly effective way to encourage members to share their knowledge and move past the old paradigm that knowledge is power and job security and therefore needs to be hoarded. In addition, it is highly recommended that senior management actively participates in these communities to foster a culture and environment that rewards knowledge-sharing and collaboration.

7.2.2 Workflow management

Workflow management is another broad area of knowledge services that provides systemic support for managing knowledge assets through a predefined workflow or process. Many knowledge assets today go through a workflow process that creates, modifies, augments, informs or approves aspects of the asset. For example, within the sphere of application management, a change record is a knowledge asset that moves through a workflow that creates it, modifies it, assesses it, estimates it, authorizes it and ultimately deploys it. Workflow applications provide the infrastructure and support necessary to implement a highly efficient process to accomplish these types of tasks. Typical workflow services provided within this services category include:

- Workflow design
- Routeing objects
- Event services
- Gate keeping at authorization checkpoints
- State transition services.

Many service management tools include workflow capability that can be configured to support these requirements.

7.3 CONFIGURATION MANAGEMENT SYSTEM

Many organizations have some form of configuration management in operation, but in some cases it is paper-based and not fit for purpose. For large and complex infrastructures, service asset and configuration management will operate more effectively when supported by a software tool that is capable of maintaining a CMS. The CMS contains details about the attributes and the history of each CI and details of the important relationships between CIs. Ideally, any configuration management database (CMDB) should be linked to the definitive media library (DML). Often, several tools need to be integrated to provide the fully automated solution across platforms, e.g. a federated CMDB.

The service asset and configuration management process should work with change management to prevent changes from being made to the IT infrastructure or service configuration baseline without valid authorization via change management. The authorization record should automatically 'drive' the change. As far as possible, all changes should be recorded on the CMS at least by the time that the change is implemented. The status (e.g. 'live', 'archive' etc.) of each CI affected by a change should be updated automatically if possible. Examples of ways in which this automatic recording of changes could be implemented include automatic updating of the CMS when software is moved between libraries (e.g. from 'acceptance test' to 'live', or from 'live' to an 'archive' library), when the service catalogue is changed, or when a release is distributed.

When designing a configuration management system you should consider whether you will need the following functionality:

- Ability to integrate multiple data sources, based on open standards or known interfaces and protocols
- Sufficient security controls to limit access on a need-to-know basis
- Support for CIs of varying complexity, e.g. entire systems, releases, single hardware items, software modules
- Hierarchical and networked relationships between CIs; by holding information on the relationships between CIs, SACM tools facilitate the impact assessment of requests for change (RFCs)
- Easy addition of new CIs and deletion of old CIs
- Automatic validation of input data (e.g. are all CI names unique?)
- Automatic determination of all relationships that can be automatically established when new CIs are added
- Support for CIs with different model numbers, version numbers, and copy numbers
- Automatic identification of other affected CIs when any CI is the subject of an incident report/record, problem record, known error record, change or release
- Integration of problem management data within the configuration management system, or at least an interface from the CMS to any separate problem management databases that may exist
- Automatic updating and recording of the version number of a CI if the version number of any component CI is changed

- Maintenance of a history of all CIs (both a historical record of the current version – such as installation date, records of changes, previous locations etc. – and of previous versions)
- Support for the management and use of configuration baselines (corresponding to definitive copies, versions etc.), including support for reversion to trusted versions
- Ease of interrogation of the CMS and good reporting facilities, including trend analysis (e.g. the ability to identify the number of RFCs affecting particular CIs)
- Ease of reporting of the CI inventory so as to facilitate configuration audits
- Flexible reporting tools to facilitate impact analyses
- The ability to show graphically the configuration models and maps of interconnected CIs, and to input information about new CIs via such maps
- The ability to show the hierarchy of relationships between 'parent' CIs and 'child' CIs.

For software, support tools should allow control to be maintained, for applications software, from the outset of systems analysis and design right through to live running. Ideally, organizations should use the same tool to control all stages of the lifecycle, although this may not be possible if all the platforms cannot be supported by one software tool. If this is not possible, then the ITSM infrastructure SACM tool should at least allow service asset and configuration management information to be transferred from a software development configuration management system into the CMS without the need for re-keying.

These individual tools and solutions may be integrated with the main service management system or the configuration management system where the effort of integration is beneficial. Otherwise, the integration may be undertaken at the procedural or data level.

Automating the initial discovery and configuration audits significantly increases the efficiency and effectiveness of SACM. These tools can determine what hardware and software is installed and how applications are mapped to the infrastructure.

This results in a greater coverage of audited CIs with the resources available, and staff can focus on handling the exceptions rather than doing the audits. If the DML is not integrated with the CMDB it may be worth automating the comparison of the DML contents with the CMDB.

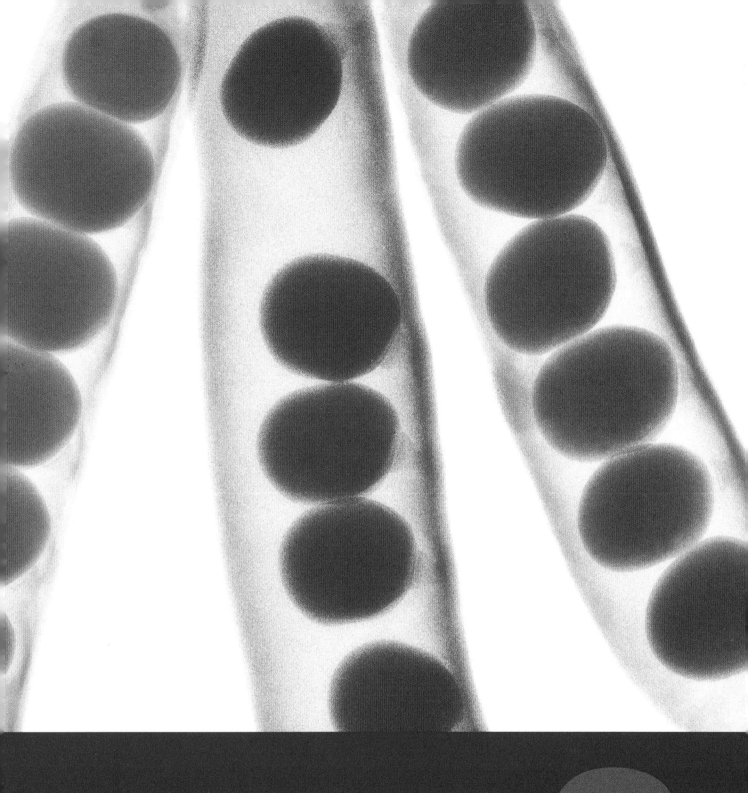

Implementing service transition

8 Implementing service transition

Implementing service transition in a green-field situation, i.e. a starting point where no service transition exists at all, would only be likely if a new service provider is being established. Therefore, the task for most service provider organizations will be one of service improvement, a matter of assessing their current approach to the service transition processes and establishing the most effective and efficient improvements to make, prioritized according to the business benefit that can be achieved. Considerable guidance on this topic is contained within *ITIL Continual Service Improvement*, but the cycle will be as illustrated in Figure 8.1.

Introducing new or improved service transition processes will mean a significant organizational change and an introduction of improved services delivered by the service provider. From that context, much of the guidance in this publication on delivering new or changed services is directly applicable to introducing service transition itself. Doing so is, in itself, a service transition exercise, since it is changing the services delivered by the service provider.

8.1 KEY ACTIVITIES IN THE INTRODUCTION OF SERVICE TRANSITION

The stages of introducing service transition will match that of other services, requiring a justification for the implementation (strategic considerations), design of the service transition components and then their introduction to the organization (service transition) before they can run in normal mode (service operation).

8.1.1 Justifying service transition

Service transition is a key contributor to the service provider's ability to deliver quality services to the business. Service transition is the delivery mechanism between the work of design, and the day-to-day care delivered by operations. However, the service transition processes are not always visible to the customers, and this can make financial justification difficult. When setting up service transition, attention needs to be paid to ways of quantifying and measuring the benefits, typically in terms of the balance between impact to the business (negative and positive) and cost (in terms of money/staff resources) and in terms

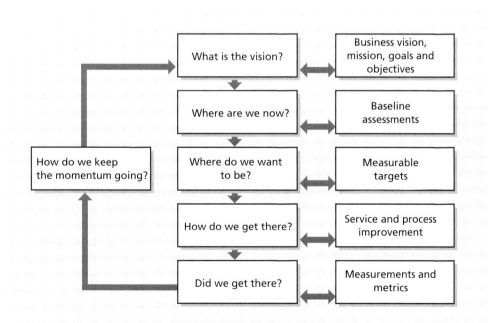

Figure 8.1 Steps to improving the service transition processes

of what would be prevented by applying resource to any specific transition, such as diverting staff or delaying implementation.

Gathering of evidence on the cost of current inadequate service transition is a valid and useful exercise, addressing such issues as:

- Cost of failed changes
- Extra cost of actual transition compared with budgeted costs
- Errors found in live running that could have been detected during test transition.

8.1.2 Designing service transition

Design of the service transition processes and how they fit within an organization are addressed throughout this publication. Useful factors to consider when designing service transition are described below.

8.1.2.1 Applicable standards and policies

Consider how agreed policies, standards and legislation will constrain the design of service transition. Factors might include requirements for independence and visible accountability, such as are commonly found controlling financial sector companies or within legislation such as Sarbanes-Oxley, health insurance portability and accountability (HIPPA) or the payment card industry (PCI).

8.1.2.2 Relationships

Other internal support services

In many situations service transition must work together with parts of the organization that are transitioning other elements of a business change, such as HR, facilities management, telecoms, production control, education and training. The processes will be designed to facilitate these relationships.

The aim should be to ensure that ownership for each component of the overall service is defined and that subsequent management responsibility is clear.

Programme and project management

Major transitions may be managed as programmes or projects, based on PRINCE2 or PMBOK, and service transition will deliver its role within the appropriate umbrella. Clear areas of delineation and collaboration between programmes, projects

and service transition will be required, and these need to be set out and agreed within the organization. To ensure that appropriate transition is delivered, service transition staff will be involved in agreeing key programme and project milestones and timelines, and service transition should be set up to adopt this role. For example if a project is due to deliver a major release at the end of the month, service transition must provide sufficient and timely resources to baseline and release the service, at the agreed time and according to approved quality levels.

To be effective, service transition needs to take a broader view across projects, combining transitions and releases to make the best use of available resources.

Service transition will set up and maintain (working through continual service improvement) an approach to dealing with an ongoing influx of tasks (service transitions) that must be delivered, scheduling, combining and sharing resources as appropriate. The strategy should seek to establish this role for service transition together with the delegated authority and escalation channels that enable it to deliver.

Internal development teams and external suppliers

Communication channels will need to deal with defects, risks and issues discovered during the transition process, e.g. errors found during testing. Channels both to internal teams and to external suppliers will need to be identified and maintained.

Customers/users

Communication with customers and users is important to ensure that the transitioned service will remain focused on current business requirements. The requirements at actual transition may evolve from the needs identified at design stage, and communication channels with the customer will be the source of identifying those changes. Effective communication will benefit from an agreed strategic stakeholder contact map (see section 5.3.2). In many circumstances this communication will be routed through business relationship management or service level management (SLM), but these channels need to be identified and designed into the service transition processes also.

Other stakeholders

Other stakeholders will need to interface with service transition, and these should be identified for all foreseeable circumstances, including in disaster recovery scenarios, and so liaison with IT service continuity management (ITSCM) should be catered for. Other possible considerations might include:

■ IT stakeholders, e.g. networks, IT security, data management
■ Stakeholders outside IT but within the organization, e.g. facilities management, HR, physical security
■ Stakeholders outside the organization, e.g. landlords and regulatory bodies.

8.1.2.3 Budget and resources

The tasks required to deliver service transition should provide an overall net benefit to the organization (or they should be revisited and revised) but nonetheless they do require funding, and the service transition strategy should address the source and control of financial provision.

Funding approach

A mechanism for controlling the funding of the transition infrastructure must be established, including:

■ **Testing environments** In many organizations testing groups (including specialist testing aspects such as usability testing) are not under the direct control of transition. The relationship and authority to engage and allocate resources needs to be established, understood, maintained and managed.
■ **Configuration management system (CMS) and service knowledge management system (SKMS)** These will specifically require funding for the technology and skills essential to their effectiveness.

The costing of transition objectives must be an integral part of design. This applies whatever the funding mechanism may be, and will involve serviced transition and customers working with design. Typically, the transition options will be costed and a business risk-based decision reached.

Resources

Similarly to the options and issues faced when considering funding, supply and control of other resources will need to be addressed within the service transition strategy, for example:

■ Staff – for example, the allocation of project resource to transition activities
■ Central infrastructure – for example:
  ● Central test data – a compromise between data that is broadly applicable and re-usable as against that which is focused on individual services/features
  ● Network resources for distribution of software, documentation and for testing of networked elements of services to be transitioned.

Test environment management is a major item of expenditure and a significant resource element in many organizations. Under-funding and/or under-resourcing in this respect (either through lack of numbers or lack of requisite skills) can cause expensive errors and problems in supporting live services and have severe detrimental effects on an organization's overall business capability.

8.1.3 Impact of introducing service transition on existing projects

Experience shows that it is not advisable to attempt to retrofit a new transition's practices onto projects that are under way; the benefits from the improved (and still unproven) practices are unlikely to outweigh the disruption caused by changing horses in midstream. If a particular transition is especially problematical, and it may be relevant to force a change of attitude, then an exception could be justified.

One technique that has worked in organizations is capturing 'in-flight' initiatives and bringing them into line with the new approach. This involves adjusting projects currently going through design/transition and adjusting their planning to fit in with the new procedures, typically at acceptance test/go-live stage. For this to be successful, conversion strategies form 'old transition routes' to the new procedures should be considered, designed (and tested where possible) as part of the design responsibility.

8.1.4 Cultural change aspects

Even formalization of mostly existing procedures will deliver cultural change; if implementing service transition into an organization involves installing formal processes that were not there before, the cultural change will be significant. Experience shows that staff working in change management, and even those evangelizing change among others, are potentially as resistant to change in their own areas as anyone else.

While it is important to focus on gaining the support of service transition staff working directly in service transition, it is equally important that those supporting, and being supported by, service transition understand why the changes to procedures are being made, the benefits to themselves and to the organization, and their changed roles. The cultural change programme should address all stakeholders and should continue throughout and after transition, to ensure that the changed attitudes are firmly embedded and not seen as a fashion accessory that can be dispensed with after the initial high profile has faded.

Considerably more information on cultural change can be found in Chapter 5.

8.1.5 Risk and value

As with all transitions, decisions around transitioning should not be made without adequate understanding of the expected risks and benefits. In this specific situation the risks might include:

- Alienation of support staff
- Excessive costs to the business
- Unacceptable delays to business benefits.

The risks and beneficial values require a baseline of the current situation, if the changes are to be measurable. Measures of the added value from service transition might include:

- Customer and user satisfaction
- Reduced incident and failure rates for transitioned services
- Reduced cost of transitioning.

8.2 AN INTEGRATED APPROACH TO SERVICE TRANSITION PROCESSES

The processes involved in the service transition stage of the service lifecycle are not independent of each other. The relationships between them are complex and it is not possible to design and implement them separately.

Figure 8.2 shows an example of the steps that might be required for a single service transition. This is a greatly simplified flowchart, showing major steps only. Each service provider will need to plan and design service management processes based on a full understanding of how they will fit together to support the overall goals of the organization.

An integrated plan for introduction or improvement of service transition processes should be based on an understanding of how the processes fit together; the roles and responsibilities of all the people involved; and matching the inputs, outputs and triggers of each process step with the corresponding steps in other processes.

This integrated plan should result in an integrated set of processes, with:

- A clear understanding of how the processes will work together in practice for different types of transition
- Each required input being the output of another process step
- Each activity having roles that are accountable and responsible, and people that fill those roles
- An integrated set of critical success factors (CSFs), key performance indicators (KPIs) and metrics that support the objectives of the organization
- An integrated improvement plan to ensure that planned changes to each process will work correctly with planned changes to other processes.

8.3 IMPLEMENTING SERVICE TRANSITION IN A VIRTUAL OR CLOUD ENVIRONMENT

Organizations that are implementing virtualization or cloud architectures must consider the impact of these on the design, implementation and operation of service transition. These environments can be very dynamic, often requiring the rapid

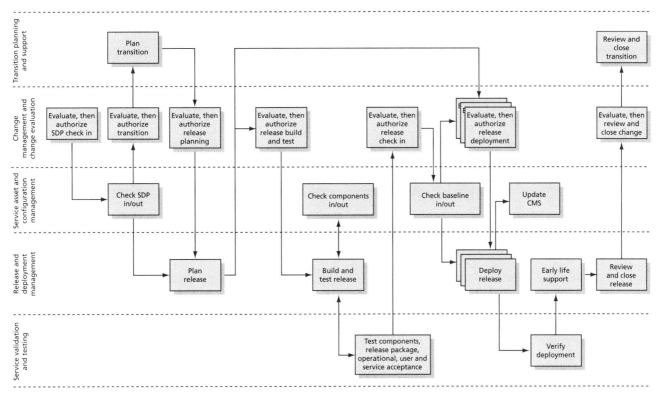

Figure 8.2 An example of a path through the processes that might be required for a single service transition

provisioning of new virtual servers or migration of virtual servers between hosts to support changing workloads. In order to get maximum value from the architecture, it is likely that many activities will be automated – for example:

■ Creation, deployment and retirement of virtual servers

■ Adding physical resources to provide greater capacity to an existing virtual server

■ Moving a virtual server from a physical server that requires maintenance to a different physical server.

This automation can lead both to difficulties and to opportunities in implementing effective service transition processes, and the service provider must understand these and provide robust processes that are able to function effectively in this environment. This will often require tools that are more sophisticated than those used in a traditional environment, and these tools will need to be integrated with the tools used for automation.

In some organizations there may be an increased need for configuration information to manage the dynamic nature of the configurations. The service provider may need to document all

allowed configurations and identify preferred configurations for use by incident management, problem management, change management and other processes. In other organizations it may be sufficient to document the configuration at a higher level and rely on discovery tools to identify the current state when needed. The decision as to which of these approaches is appropriate will depend on many different factors, including the agreed warranty for the service and the need to meet specific service levels.

The virtualization or cloud architecture may require the creation of new configuration item (CI) types, release models, change models and standard changes. It is likely that the tools, activities, authorities, roles and responsibilities for creating and managing virtual servers will be completely different from those used for deploying and managing physical servers. Often these activities will be carried out by different organizations or service units and the relationship between them will be managed by a contract, service level agreement (SLA) or operational level agreement (OLA). The change management and release and deployment management processes must be designed to work seamlessly across both physical and virtual servers, and the configuration management system must be able to reflect the complexity of the relationships. The scope of service transition must be well defined, and understood by everyone who might be involved. Roles and responsibilities must be defined to work across all internal and external parties involved. End-to-end supply chain agreements and an integrated supplier management process must be in place, linked to data in the CMS and in the service catalogue.

In a different context, an organization that moves its services from a traditional insourced data centre to a public cloud may find that its service asset and configuration management needs are greatly simplified, since the underlying complexity is now managed by an external service provider. There is still a need to carry out service asset and configuration management, but the CIs are likely to be at a much higher level.

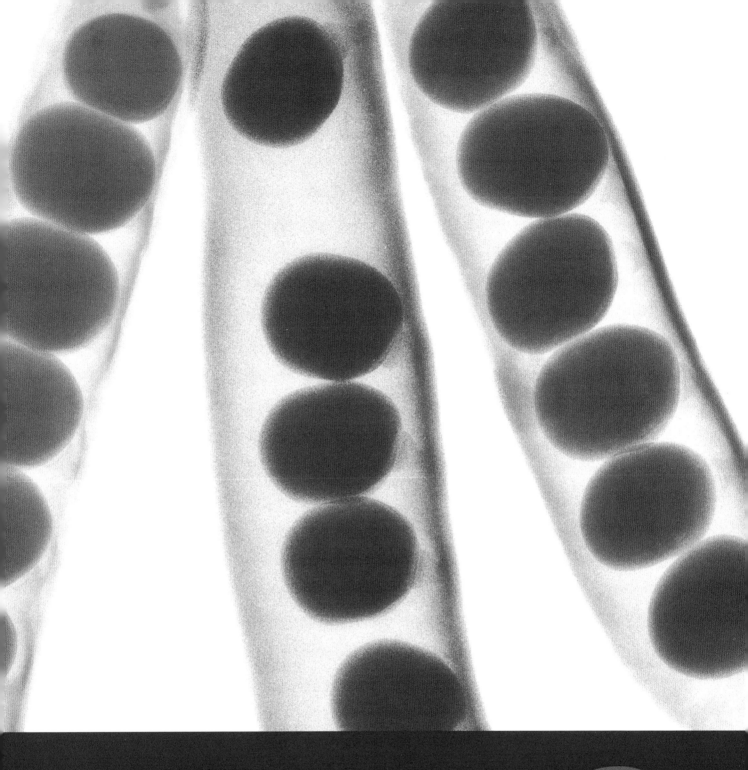

Challenges, critical success factors and risks

9

9 Challenges, critical success factors and risks

9.1 CHALLENGES

The complexity of services across the supply chain is increasing, and this leads to challenges for any service provider that implements new services or changes existing services. IT within e-business not only *supports* the primary business processes, but is *part of* the primary business processes.

This prime position brings a wide range of challenges to successful service transition such as:

- Enabling almost every business process and service in IT, resulting in a large customer and stakeholder group that is involved and impacted by service transition
- Managing many contacts, interfaces and relationships through service transition, including a variety of different customers, users, programmes, projects, suppliers and partners
- There being little harmonization and integration of the processes and disciplines that impact service transition, e.g. finance, engineering, human resource management etc.
- There being inherent differences among the legacy systems, new technology and human elements that result in unknown dependencies and are risky to change
- Achieving a balance between maintaining a stable live environment and being responsive to the business needs for changing the services
- Achieving a balance between pragmatism and bureaucracy
- Creating an environment that fosters standardization, simplification and knowledge sharing
- Being an enabler of business change and, therefore, an integral component of the business change programmes
- Establishing leaders to champion the changes and improvements
- Establishing 'who is doing what, when and where' and 'who should be doing what, when and where'

- Developing a culture that encourages people to collaborate and work effectively together and an atmosphere that fosters the cultural shifts necessary to get buy-in from people
- Developing standard performance measures and measurement methods across projects and suppliers
- Ensuring that the quality of delivery and support matches the business use of new technology
- Ensuring that the service transition time and budget are not impacted by events earlier in the service lifecycle (e.g. budget cuts)
- Understanding the different stakeholder perspectives that underpin effective risk management within an organization
- Understanding, and being able to assess, the balance between managing risk and taking risks as this affects the overall strategy of the organization, and potential mismatch between project risks and business risk
- Evaluating the effectiveness of reporting in relation to risk management and corporate governance, including provision of reporting required by Sarbanes-Oxley, ISO/IEC 20000, ISO/IEC 38500 and COBIT if these are applicable.

9.2 CRITICAL SUCCESS FACTORS

Service provision, in all organizations, needs to be matched to current and rapidly changing business demands. The objective is to continually improve the quality of service, aligned to the business requirements, cost-effectively. To meet this objective, the following critical success factors need to be considered for service transition:

- Understanding and managing the different stakeholder perspectives that underpin effective risk management within an organization and establishing and maintaining stakeholder 'buy-in' and commitment
- Having clearly defined relationships and interfaces with programme and project management

- Maintaining the contacts and managing all the relationships during service transition
- Integrating with the other service lifecycle stages, processes and disciplines that impact service transition
- Understanding the inherent dependencies among the legacy systems, new technology and human elements that result in unknown dependencies and are risky to change
- Automating processes to eliminate errors and reduce the cycle time
- Creating and maintaining new and updated knowledge in a form that people can find and use
- Developing good-quality systems, tools, processes and procedures required to manage a service transition practice
- Good service management and IT infrastructure tools and technology
- Being able to appreciate and exploit the cultural and political environment
- Being able to understand the service and technical configurations and their dependencies
- Developing a thorough grasp of the hard factors (processes and procedures) and soft factors (skills and competencies) required to manage a service transition practice
- Developing a workforce with the necessary knowledge and skills, appropriate training and the right service culture
- Defining clear accountabilities, roles and responsibilities
- Establishing a culture that enables knowledge to be shared freely and willingly
- Demonstrating improved cycle time to deliver change and less variation in time, cost and quality predictions during and after transition
- Demonstrating improved customer and user satisfaction ratings during service transition
- Demonstrating that the benefits of establishing and improving the service transition practice and processes outweigh the costs (across the organization and services)
- Being able to communicate the organization's attitude to risk and approach to risk management more effectively during service transition activities
- Building a thorough understanding of risks that have impacted or may impact successful service transition of services in the service portfolio.

9.3 RISKS

Implementing the service transition practice should not be made without recognizing the potential risk to services currently in transition and those releases that are planned. A baseline assessment of current service transitions and planned projects will help service transition to identify implementation risks.

These risks might include:

- Change in accountabilities, responsibilities and practices of existing projects that de-motivate the workforce
- Alienation of some key support and operations staff
- Additional unplanned costs to services in transition
- Resistance to change and circumvention of the processes due to perceived bureaucracy.

Other implementation risks include:

- Excessive costs to the business generated by overly risk-averse service transition practices and plans
- Knowledge sharing (the wrong people may have access to information)
- Lack of maturity and integration of systems and tools resulting in people 'blaming' technology for other shortcomings
- Poor integration between the processes causing process isolation and a silo approach to delivering IT service management (ITSM)
- Loss of productive hours, higher costs, loss of revenue or perhaps even business failure as a result of poor service transition processes.

9.4 SERVICE TRANSITION UNDER DIFFICULT CONDITIONS

In some circumstances, service transitions will be required under atypical or difficult conditions, such as:

- Short timescale
- Restricted finances
- Restricted resource availability – not enough people or lack of test environments, inadequate tools etc.
- Absence of anticipated skill sets
- Internal political difficulty, staff disincentives such as:

- Redundancy/outsourcing or similar threats
- Difficult corporate culture or confrontational management style
- Internal rivalries and competitiveness
■ External difficulties such as weather, political instability, post-disaster, legislation.

Clearly, some of these circumstances overlap with continuity planning, and many of the approaches set out in *ITIL Service Design* will be relevant to successful transition in difficult circumstances.

If the difficulties are anticipated, then alleviating measures will be identified and form part of the service, planning the route through transition within the transition model, as would any foreseen factors likely to influence transition.

It is quite possible, however, that the difficulties will be unanticipated, perhaps due to changed circumstances, and will require 'on the fly' adaptation. This section sets out some of the constraining circumstances that might require adaptation, modification or compromise, and elements of approach that would aid success. A key element common to most (if not all) of these situations is having a clear understanding of what will constitute success. When circumstances are difficult, priorities are often focused on specific aspects of service, customer base etc.; in this situation, delivery of accepted priorities in the constrained circumstances will often require compromises in other areas.

9.4.1 When speed is more important than accuracy or smoothness

In time-critical situations, implementation of a new or changed service may be more important than a degree of disruption. This is effectively a risk management decision, and general risk management principles apply. Some of the key factors that assist with delivering success in this context are:

■ Empowerment – with staff given the authority to take appropriate levels of risk. In volatile industries, service transition must act in a way that reflects the corporate risk culture and not suppress or undermine business risk decisions.
■ A need to know the absolute cut-off date/time that service transition must deliver by – too often either 'safety margins' are built in (meaning a product that could have been improved is delivered too early), or people

assume there is some leeway when there isn't (meaning critical deadlines are missed). It is often better to be totally open and trust key staff.
■ Knowing which components of the transitioned service must be available at the cut-off date, and which could be added later.
■ How separable are the components and what are the dependencies? What elements might be required although not initially on the 'essentials' list?
■ Which users/customers/locations etc. must be in place at the cut-off date?
■ What actually happens if you fail? Again, honesty is often the best policy here. Consider:
  - Business impact
  - Money
  - Life, health and safety
  - Political embarrassment
  - Reputation.

Understanding crisis management can be very helpful in coping with a difficult situation – especially understanding that the rules for crisis management are different from those for everyday management. Just being aware of the following rules of crisis management can help to reassure people that the situation is survivable:

■ **Rule 1** Don't panic.
■ **Rule 2** A good crisis manager makes decisions instantly and acts on them. If they later turn out to have been correct, so much the better, but speed is often more important than efficiency in a crisis situation.
■ **Rule 3** Accept that decisions won't be perfect and that people should not be blamed for making the best decision they can under difficult circumstances.

Success in these circumstances depends on:

■ Empowerment and subsequent support, and a belief in that support. Staff must be aware of their empowerment levels and actually believe that the organization will support their choices, without being in fear of a 'court martial' approach.
■ Authorization channels and those channels being open and rapid. There must be agreed actions if the channels don't function – for example, increased delegated authority, escalation, alternative support channels.

■ Following the procedures, realizing there is risk, and no blame afterwards – if not, the required flexibility and speed of response is constrained.

9.4.2 Restricted resources

When resources are in short supply, a key aspect is deciding what to measure and sticking to that decision and the framework for delivery, e.g.:

■ What is the important parameter – speed, or low cost or whatever? And knowing that this factor will still be the measure of importance afterwards – e.g. there will be no blame for it being expensive when the understanding was 'Get it in by 3 p.m. whatever the cost.'

■ Establish an applicable hierarchy of measures – e.g. (i) speed, (ii) money (iii) full functionality – with some subordinate items having absolute limits (e.g. 'as quickly as possible, but not more that £12,500'; or 'as cheaply as possible but must be in by 30 September'). This requires involving budget holders, business decision makers etc. to ensure that the correct parameters are built in.

■ Awareness and documentation. All relevant staff need to be aware of requirements; a mechanism for keeping staff informed quickly about changes to those requirements is essential.

9.4.3 Safety-critical services and high-risk environments

Ever increasingly, IT services directly support or actually deliver services on which lives depend, such as hospital services, emergency services call-taking, flood control and aircraft 'fly-by-wire'. Extra security and foolproof approaches are required in these circumstances, with features such as:

■ Appropriate documentation, which is essential and often includes counter-signatures and extra checks on stage approval. However, excessive documentation can be counter-productive; high risk can often be found in conjunction with time-restricted situations (e.g. emergency services coordination) meaning careful balancing of safety and speed is required; in such circumstances skill and experience and/or extensive training is a major factor

■ Accuracy typically taking priority over speed

■ More rigorous testing, longer time periods and more detailed data collected and maintained within the configuration management system (CMS)

■ Measures of safety accurately assessed by an accepted authority – e.g. what constitutes acceptable levels, such as safe radiation doses within X-ray or radioactive environments

■ Setting the sign-off authority, and ensuring that those responsible are not overly influenced by inappropriate pressures such as concern about company profit or staff bonuses as opposed to risking human lives

■ In extreme circumstances ensuring that more than one individual must be involved for certain actions to be taken (e.g. typically the procedures for launching nuclear weapons require simultaneous confirmation by two trained officers)

■ Consider 'veto' rights for sub-groupings whereby those controlling any key component of the service can stop implementation – as a 'no-go' from one of a dozen teams can stop a launch of a the space shuttle.

9.4.4 Working with difficult customers

Of course, there is no such thing as a bad customer, really, but often there are customers who are unclear of their role as a customer and so act in a way that prevents rather than supports successful implementation. Examples include customers who:

■ Feel the need to get too involved in the detail of how things are done, instead of judging by the service delivered

■ Are not able to deliver the decisions and choose options to suit their business needs

■ Do not make staff and resources available to facilitate effective service transition, for example by providing data and staff to assess the transitioned service or to effect user testing.

These kinds of situation can often be improved by awareness and education of:

■ Customers
■ Users
■ Transition staff (e.g. development of patience and diplomacy skills)
■ Business relationship management working with the customers to reassure customers and ascertain their requirements

- Careful budgetary control, so that customers can see the value returning from their investment of staff time and other resources.

Some activities that can help in these conditions include:

- Identifying appropriate customer contacts at multiple levels (operational, tactical and strategic)
- Ensuring that customer personnel are fully aware of all their responsibilities
- Agreeing communication and reporting requirements with the customer
- Providing the customer with sufficient information to enable them to make quick and effective decisions.

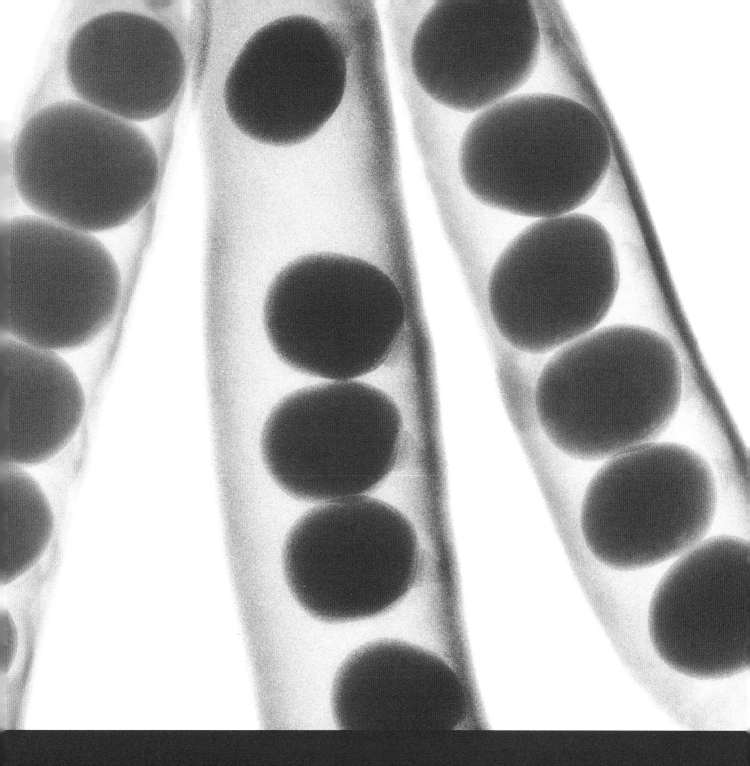

Afterword

Afterword

This publication is part of the ITIL series that sets out best practice and sound advice for organizations that recognize the importance of service management to their overall success.

This publication, like the others, offers good general advice, but this – in itself – is not enough. The advice must be understood in the context of a particular organization.

IT service managers must manage services according to the circumstances in which they find themselves – for some, safety will be the pre-eminent concern; others will consider speed, profitability, usability or some other factor to be their prime driver. Delivering effective service transition is a challenge for all; delivering effective service transition in any specific organization requires a sound appreciation of the service transition principle and an understanding of the business that is being supported and of the services being introduced, changed or retired.

This publication has been written to supply a foundation for IT service management professionals to implement solid and effective services to support their customers in their businesses, and to continue doing that in the longer term.

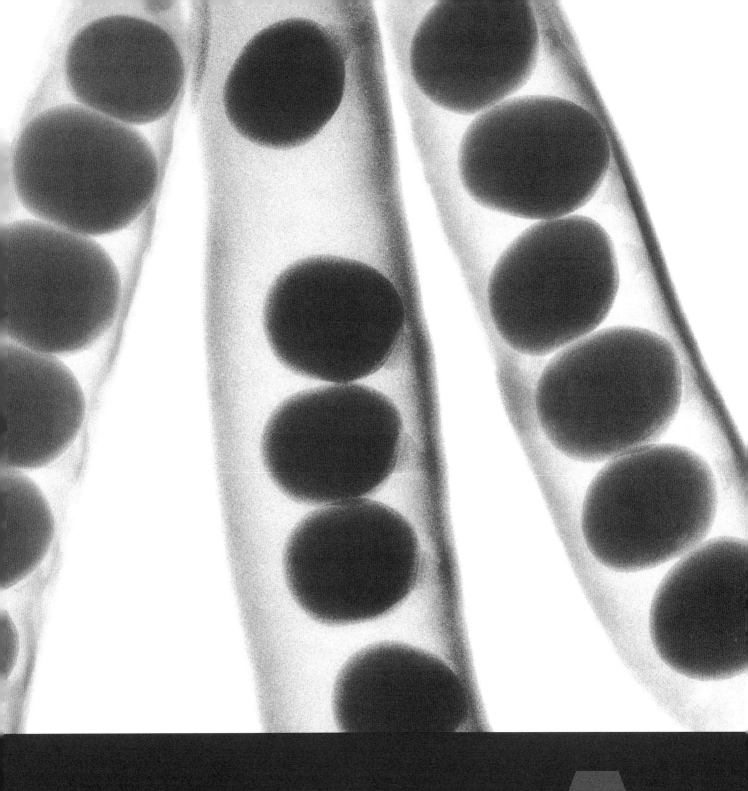

Appendix A: Description of asset types

A

Appendix A: Description of asset types

A.1 MANAGEMENT

Management is a system that includes leadership, administration, policies, performance measures and incentives. This layer cultivates, coordinates and controls all other asset types. Management includes idiosyncratic elements such as philosophy, core beliefs, values, decision-making style and perceptions of risk. It is also the most distinctive and inimitable type of asset which is deeply rooted in the organization.

The term organization is used here to refer to the enterprise or firm rather than the organization asset type. The most likely manner in which management assets can be partially extracted from an organization is by the poaching of key individuals who were instrumental in defining and developing a particular management system.

Service management itself is a type of specialized management asset like others such as project management, research and development, and manufacturing management.

A.2 ORGANIZATION

Organization assets are active configurations of people, processes, applications and infrastructure that carry out all organizational activities through the principles of specialization and coordination (see section 2.4.1). This category of assets includes the functional hierarchies, social networks of groups, teams and individuals, as well as the systems they use to work together towards shared goals and incentives. Organization assets include the patterns that people, applications, information and infrastructure deploy, either by design or by self-adaptive process, to maximize the creation of value for stakeholders. Some service organizations are superior to others simply by virtue of their organization – for example, networks of wireless access points, storage systems, point-of-sale terminals, databases, hardware stores and remote backup facilities. Strategic location of assets by itself is a basis for superior performance and competitive advantage.

A.3 PROCESS

Process assets are made of algorithms, methods, procedures and routines that direct the execution and control of activities and interactions. There is a great diversity in process assets, which are specialized to various degrees from generic management processes to sophisticated low-level algorithms embedded in software applications and other forms of automation. Process assets are the most dynamic of asset types. They signify action and transformation. Some of them are also the means by which organization and management assets coordinate and control each other and interact with the business environment. Process, people and application assets execute them; knowledge and information assets enrich them; and applications and infrastructure assets enable them. Examples of process assets are order fulfilment, accounts receivable, incident management, change management and testing.

A.4 KNOWLEDGE

Knowledge assets are accumulations of awareness, experience, information, insight and intellectual property that are associated with actions and context. Management, organization, process and applications assets use and store knowledge assets. People assets store tacit knowledge in the form of experience, skills and talent. Such knowledge is primarily acquired through experience, observation and training. Movement of teams and individuals is an effective way to transfer tacit knowledge within and across organizations (Argote, 2000). Knowledge assets in tacit form are hard for rivals to replicate but easy for owners to lose. Organizations seek to protect themselves from loss by codifying tacit knowledge into explicit forms such as knowledge embedded in process, applications and infrastructure assets. Knowledge assets are difficult to manage but can be highly leveraged with increasing returns and virtually zero opportunity costs (Lev, 2001). Knowledge assets include policies, plans, designs, configurations, architectures, process definitions, analytical methods, service definitions, analyses, reports and surveys. They may be owned as intellectual property and protected by copyrights, patents and trademarks. Knowledge assets can also be rented for use under licensing arrangements and service contracts.

A.5 PEOPLE

The value of people assets is the capacity for creativity, analysis, perception, learning, judgement, leadership, communication, coordination, empathy and trust. Such capacity is in teams and individuals within the organization, due to knowledge, experience and skills. Skills can be conceptual, technical and social. People assets are also the most convenient absorbers and carriers of all forms of knowledge. They are the most versatile and potent of all asset types because of their ability to learn and adapt. People assets represent an organization's capabilities and resources. If capabilities are the capacity for action, people assets are the actors. From the capabilities' perspective, people assets are the only type that can create, combine and consume all other asset types. Their tolerance of ambiguity and uncertainty also compensates for the limitations of processes, applications and infrastructure. Because of their enormous potential, people assets are often the most expensive in terms of development, maintenance and motivation. They are also assets that can be hired or rented but cannot be owned. Customers highly value services that enhance the productivity or potential of people assets.

People assets are also resources with productive capacity. Units of cost, time and effort measure their capacity as teams and individuals. They are mobile, multi-purpose and highly adaptive with the innate ability to learn. Staffing contracts, software agents and customers using self-service options augment the capacity of people assets.

A.6 INFORMATION

Information assets are collections, patterns and meaningful abstractions of data applied in contexts such as customers, contracts, services, events, projects and operations. They are useful for various purposes including communication, coordination and control of business activities. Information assets exist in various forms such as documents, records, messages and graphs. All asset types produce them but management, processes,

knowledge, people and applications primarily consume them. The value of information assets can vary with time, location and format, and depreciate very quickly. Some services create value by processing information and making it available as needed by management, processes, people and applications assets. The criteria of effectiveness, efficiency, availability, integrity, confidentiality, reliability and compliance can be used to evaluate the quality of information assets (ITGI, 2005).

A.7 APPLICATIONS

Applications assets are diverse in type and include artefacts, automation and tools used to support the performance of other asset types. Applications are composed of software, hardware, documents, methods, procedures, routines, scripts and instructions. They automate, codify, enable, enhance, maintain or mimic the properties, functions and activities of management, organization, processes, knowledge, people and information assets. Applications derive their value in relation to these other assets. Process assets in particular commonly exist inside applications. Applications assets consume, produce and maintain knowledge and information assets. They can be of various types such as general purpose, multi-purpose and special purpose. Some applications are analogous to industrial tools, machinery and equipment because they enhance the performance of processes. Others are analogous to office equipment and consumer appliances because they enhance the personal productivity of people assets. Examples of applications are accounting software, voicemail, imaging systems, encryption devices, process control, inventory tracking, electronic design automation, mobile phones and bar code scanners. Applications are themselves supported by infrastructure, people and process assets. One of the most powerful attributes of applications is that they can be creatively combined and integrated with other asset types, particularly other applications to create valuable new assets.

A.8 INFRASTRUCTURE

Infrastructure assets have the peculiar property of existing in the form of layers defined in relation to the assets they support, especially people and applications. They include information technology assets such as software applications, computers, storage systems, network devices, telecommunication equipment, cables, wireless links, access control devices and monitoring systems. This category of assets also includes traditional facilities such as buildings, electricity, heating, ventilation and air conditioning (HVAC) and water supply, without which it would be impossible for people, applications and other infrastructure assets to operate. Infrastructure assets by themselves may be composed mostly of applications and other infrastructure assets. Assets viewed as applications at one level can be utilized as infrastructure at another. This is an important principle that allows service orientation of assets.

A.9 FINANCIAL CAPITAL

Financial assets are required to support the ownership or use of all types of assets. They also measure the economic value and performance. Financial assets include cash, cash equivalents and other assets such as marketable securities, and receivables that are convertible into cash with degrees of certainty and ease. Adequacy of financial assets is an important concern for all organizations including government agencies and non-profit organizations. The promise and potential of other assets are not realized in full without financial assets.

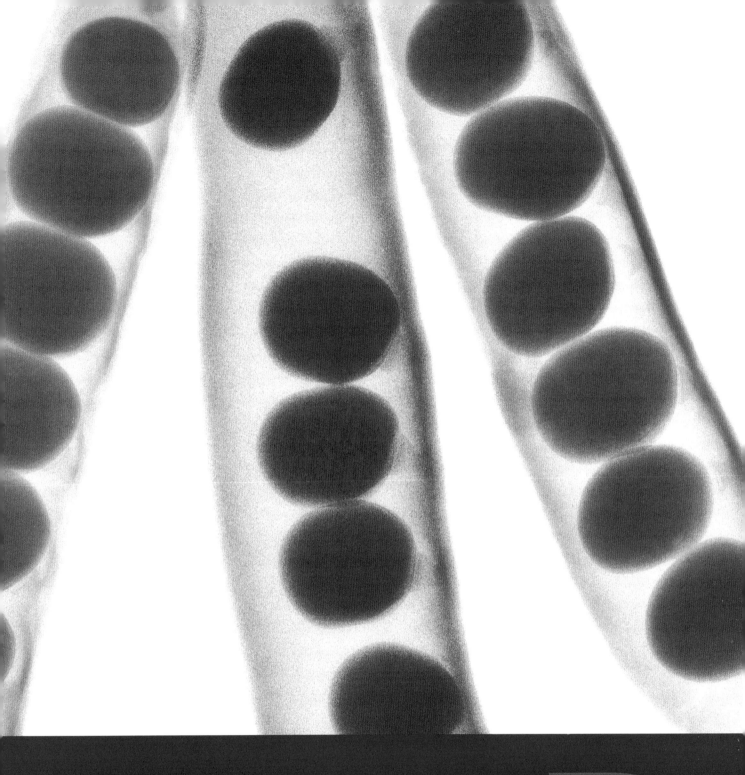

Appendix B:
Risk assessment
and management

B

Appendix B: Risk assessment and management

This appendix contains basic information about several broadly known and used approaches to the assessment and management of risk. It is not intended to be a comprehensive study of the subject, but rather to provide an awareness of some of the methods in use.

B.1 DEFINITION OF RISK AND RISK MANAGEMENT

Risk may be defined as uncertainty of outcome, whether a positive opportunity or negative threat. It is the fact that there is uncertainty that creates the need for attention and formal management of risk. After all, if an organization were absolutely certain that a negative threat would materialize, there would be little difficulty in determining an appropriate course of action. Likewise, if an organization could be guaranteed that the positive opportunity would be realized, then its path would be clear. Managing risks requires the identification and control of the exposure to those risks which may have an impact on the achievement of an organization's business objectives.

Every organization manages its risk, but not always in a way that is visible, repeatable and consistently applied to support decision-making. The purpose of formal risk management is to enable better decision-making based on a sound understanding of risks and their likely impact on the achievement of objectives. An organization can gain this understanding by ensuring that it makes cost-effective use of a risk framework that has a series of well-defined steps. Decision-making should include determining any appropriate actions to take to manage the risks to a level deemed to be acceptable by the organization.

A number of different methodologies, standards and frameworks have been developed for risk management. Some focus more on generic techniques widely applicable to different levels and needs, while others are specifically concerned with risk management relating to important assets used by the organization in the pursuit of its objectives.

Each organization should determine the approach to risk management that is best suited to its needs and circumstances, and it is possible that the approach adopted will leverage the ideas reflected in more than one of the recognized standards and/or frameworks.

In this appendix the following approaches to managing risks are briefly explained:

■ Management of Risk (M_o_R)
■ ISO 31000
■ ISO/IEC 27001
■ Risk IT.

B.2 MANAGEMENT OF RISK (M_o_R)

Management of Risk (M_o_R) is intended to help organizations put in place an effective framework for risk management. This will help them take informed decisions about the risks that affect their strategic, programme, project and operational objectives.

M_o_R provides a route map of risk management, bringing together principles, an approach, a process with a set of interrelated steps and pointers to more detailed sources of advice on risk management techniques and specialisms. It also provides advice on how these principles, approach and process should be embedded, reviewed and applied differently depending on the nature of the objectives at risk.

The M_o_R framework is illustrated in Figure B.1.

The M_o_R framework is based on four core concepts:

■ **M_o_R principles** Principles are essential for the development and maintenance of good risk management practice. They are informed by corporate governance principles and the international standard for risk management, ISO 31000: 2009. They are high-level and universally applicable statements that provide

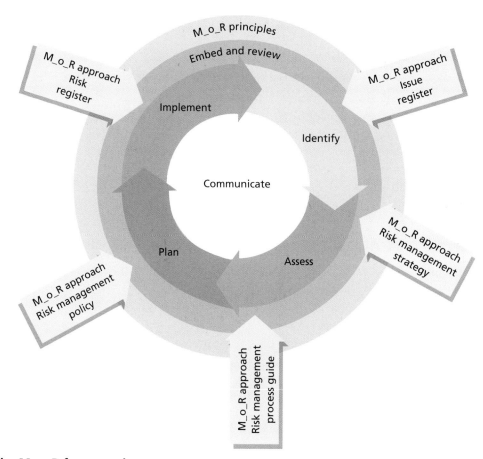

Figure B.1 The M_o_R framework

guidance to organizations as they design an appropriate approach to risk management as part of their internal controls.

■ **M_o_R approach** Principles need to be adapted and adopted to suit each individual organization. An organization's approach to the principles needs to be agreed and defined within a risk management policy, process guide and strategies.

■ **M_o_R process** The process is divided into four main steps: identify, assess, plan and implement. Each step describes the inputs, outputs, tasks and techniques involved to ensure that the overall process is effective.

■ **Embedding and reviewing M_o_R** Having put in place an approach and process that satisfy the principles, an organization should ensure that they are consistently applied across the organization and that their application undergoes continual improvement in order for them to be effective.

There are several common techniques which support risk management, including a summary risk profile. A summary risk profile is a graphical representation of information normally found in an existing risk register, and helps to increase the visibility of risks. For more information on summary risk profiles and other M_o_R techniques, see *Management of Risk: Guidance for Practitioners* (OGC, 2010).

B.3 ISO 31000

ISO 31000 was published in November 2009 and is the first set of international guidelines for risk management, intended to be applicable and adaptable for 'any public, private or community enterprise, association, group or individual.' ISO 31000 is a process-oriented rather than a control-oriented approach to risk management, and provides guidance on a broader, more conceptual basis, rather than specifying all aspects of an organization's risk assessment and management approach. For example, ISO 31000 does not

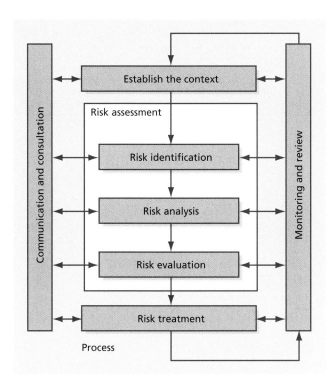

Figure B.2 ISO 31000 risk management process flow

define how an organization will create risk data or measure risk, nor does it ensure that an organization will include a review of all risk areas relevant to the achievement of their objectives. ISO 31000 was published as a standard without certification.

ISO 31000 defines risk as 'the effect of uncertainty on objectives'. Risk management should be performed within a framework that provides the foundations and provisions which will embed the management of risk throughout all levels of the organization. ISO 31000 identifies the necessary components of such a framework as:

- Mandate and commitment
- Design of framework for managing risk
- Understanding the organization and its context
- Establishing risk management policy
- Accountability
- Integration into organizational processes
- Resources
- Establishing internal communication and reporting mechanisms
- Establishing external communication and reporting mechanisms
- Implementing risk management
- Monitoring and review of the framework

- Continual improvement of the framework.

Within this context the risk management process is seen at a high level in Figure B.2.

Once the framework has been established and the context understood, risk assessment is undertaken. This consists of three steps: risk identification, risk analysis and risk evaluation. The risk identification step is intended to create a comprehensive list of risks based on those events that might create, enhance, prevent, degrade, accelerate or delay the achievement of the organization's objectives. Risk analysis involves developing a full understanding of the risks as an input to risk evaluation and the decisions regarding the plan for treating the risks. Risk evaluation is to make decisions about which risks require treatment and the relative priorities amongst them.

Risk treatment involves the modification of risks using one or more approaches. These approaches are not necessarily mutually exclusive and may include:

- Avoiding the risk by deciding not to start or continue with the activity that gives rise to the risk
- Taking or increasing the risk in order to pursue an opportunity
- Removing the risk source
- Changing the likelihood
- Changing the consequences
- Sharing the risk with another party or parties (including contracts and risk financing)
- Retaining the risk by informed decision.

The approach described in ISO 31000 provides broad scope for each organization to adopt the high-level principles and adapt them to their specific needs and circumstances.

B.4   ISO/IEC 27001

ISO/IEC 27001 was published in October 2005 and is an information security management system (ISMS) standard which formally specifies a management system that is intended to bring information security under explicit management control. While ISO/IEC 27001 is a security standard, not a risk management standard, it mandates specific requirements for security, including requirements relating to risk management. The risk management methods described in this context may be applied to general risk management activities as well.

ISO/IEC 27001 requires that management:

- Systematically examines the organization's information security risks, taking account of the threats, vulnerabilities and impacts
- Designs and implements a coherent and comprehensive suite of information security controls and/or other forms of risk treatment (such as risk avoidance or risk transfer) to address those risks that are deemed unacceptable
- Adopts an overarching management process to ensure that the information security controls continue to meet the organization's information security needs on an ongoing basis.

The key risk management-related steps described in ISO/IEC 27001 include:

- Define the risk assessment approach of the organization
- Identify a risk assessment methodology that is suited to the ISMS, and the identified business information security, legal and regulatory requirements
- Develop criteria for accepting risks and identify acceptable levels of risk
- Identify the risks
- Identify the assets within the scope of the ISMS, and the owners of these assets
- Identify the threats to these assets
- Identify the vulnerabilities that might be exploited by the threats
- Identify the impact that losses of confidentiality, integrity and availability may have on these assets
- Analyse and evaluate the risks
- Assess the business impacts on the organization that might result from security failures, taking into account the consequences of a loss of confidentiality, integrity or availability of the assets
- Assess the realistic likelihood of security failures occurring in the light of prevailing threats and vulnerabilities, and impacts associated with these assets, and the controls currently implemented
- Estimate the levels of risk

- Determine whether the risks are acceptable or require treatment using the previously established criteria for accepting risks
- Identify and evaluate options for the treatment of risks. Possible actions may include:
  - Applying appropriate controls
  - Knowingly and objectively accepting risks, providing they clearly satisfy the organization's policies and the criteria for accepting risks
  - Avoiding risks
  - Transferring the associated business risks to other parties, e.g. insurers, suppliers
- Select control objectives and controls for the treatment of risks
- Obtain management approval of the proposed residual risks
- Obtain management authorization to implement and operate the ISMS.

During the implementation and operation of the ISMS, a plan for risk treatment is formulated (identifying the appropriate management action, resources, responsibilities and priorities for managing information security risks) and implemented. ISO/IEC 27001 also calls for the ongoing monitoring and reviewing of the risks and risk treatment and the formal maintenance of the ISMS to ensure that the organization's goals are met.

This approach is focused specifically on the assets involved in organizational information security, but the general principles can be applied to overall service provision.

B.5 RISK IT

Risk IT is part of the IT governance product portfolio of ISACA that provides a framework for effective governance and management of IT risk, based on a set of guiding principles. Risk IT is about IT risk, including business risk related to the use of IT. The publications in which Risk IT is documented include *The Risk IT Framework* (ISACA, 2009) and *The Risk IT Practitioner Guide* (ISACA, 2009) (available from www.isaca.org).

The key principles in Risk IT are that effective enterprise governance and management of IT risk:

- Always connect to the business objectives
- Align the management of IT-related business risk with overall enterprise risk management

- Balance the costs and benefits of managing IT risk
- Promote fair and open communication of IT risk
- Establish the right tone from the top while defining and enforcing personal accountability for operating within acceptable and well-defined tolerance levels
- Are continuous processes and part of daily activities.

The framework provides for three domains, each containing three processes, as shown in Figure B.3. *The Risk IT Framework* describes the key activities of each process, the responsibilities for the process, information flows between the processes and the performance management of each process.

Risk governance ensures that IT risk management practices are embedded in the enterprise, enabling it to secure optimal risk-adjusted return. Risk evaluation ensures that IT-related risks and opportunities are identified, analysed and presented in business terms. Risk response ensures that IT-related risk issues, opportunities and events are addressed in a cost-effective manner and in line with business priorities.

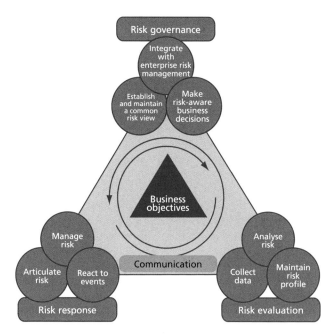

Figure B.3 ISACA Risk IT process framework

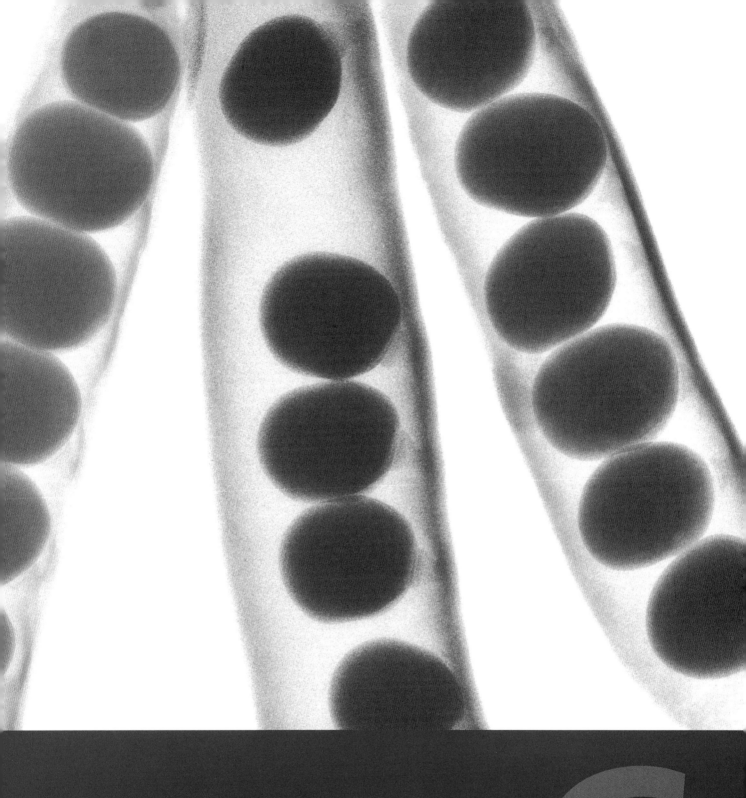

Appendix C:
Related guidance

Appendix C: Related guidance

This is a common appendix across the ITIL core publications. It includes frameworks, best practices, standards, models and quality systems that complement and have synergy with the ITIL service lifecycle.

Section 2.1.7 describes the role of best practices in the public domain and references some of the publications in this appendix. Each core publication references this appendix where relevant.

Related guidance may also be referenced within a single ITIL core publication where the topic is specific to that publication.

C.1 ITIL GUIDANCE AND WEB SERVICES

ITIL is part of the Best Management Practice (BMP) portfolio of best-practice guidance (see section 1.3). BMP products present flexible, practical and effective guidance, drawn from a range of the most successful global business experiences. Distilled to its essential elements, the guidance can then be applied to every type of business and organization.

The BMP website (www.best-management-practice.com) includes news, reviews, case studies and white papers on ITIL and all other BMP best-practice guidance.

The ITIL official website (www.itil-officialsite.com) contains reliable, up-to-date information on ITIL – including information on accreditation and the ITIL software scheme for the endorsement of ITIL-based tools.

Details of the core publications are as follows:

- Cabinet Office (2011). *ITIL Service Strategy*. TSO, London.
- Cabinet Office (2011). *ITIL Service Design*. TSO, London.
- Cabinet Office (2011). *ITIL Service Transition*. TSO, London.
- Cabinet Office (2011). *ITIL Service Operation*. TSO, London.
- Cabinet Office (2011). *ITIL Continual Service Improvement*. TSO, London.

The full ITIL glossary, in English and other languages, can be accessed through the ITIL official site at:

www.itil-officialsite.com/InternationalActivities/ITILGlossaries.aspx

The range of translated glossaries is always growing, so check this website for the most up-to-date list.

Details of derived and complementary publications can be found in the publications library of the Best Management Practice website at:

www.best-management-practice.com/Publications-Library/IT-Service-Management-ITIL/

C.2 QUALITY MANAGEMENT SYSTEM

Quality management focuses on product/service quality as well as the quality assurance and control of processes to achieve consistent quality. Total Quality Management (TQM) is a methodology for managing continual improvement by using a quality management system. TQM establishes a culture involving all people in the organization in a process of continual monitoring and improvement.

ISO 9000:2005 describes the fundamentals of quality management systems that are applicable to all organizations which need to demonstrate their ability to consistently provide products that meet customer and applicable statutory and regulatory requirements. ISO 9001:2008 specifies generic requirements for a quality management system.

Many process-based quality management systems use the methodology known as 'Plan-Do-Check-Act' (PDCA), often referred to as the Deming Cycle, or Shewhart Cycle, that can be applied to all processes. PDCA can be summarized as:

- **Plan** Establish the objectives and processes necessary to deliver results in accordance with customer requirements and the organization's policies.
- **Do** Implement the processes.
- **Check** Monitor and measure processes and product against policies, objectives and

requirements for the product and report the results.

■ **Act** Take actions to continually improve process performance.

There are distinct advantages of tying an organization's ITSM processes, and service operation processes in particular, to its quality management system. If an organization has a formal quality management system that complies with ISO 9001, then this can be used to assess progress regularly and drive forward agreed service improvement initiatives through regular reviews and reporting.

Visit www.iso.org for information on ISO standards.

See www.deming.org for more information on the W. Edwards Deming Institute and the Deming Cycle for process improvement.

C.3   RISK MANAGEMENT

A number of different methodologies, standards and frameworks have been developed for the assessment and management of risk. Some focus more on generic techniques widely applicable to different levels and needs, while others are specifically concerned with risk management relating to important assets used by the organization in the pursuit of its objectives. Each organization should determine the approach to risk management that is best suited to its needs and circumstances. It is possible that the approach adopted will leverage the ideas reflected in more than one of the recognized standards and/or frameworks.

Appendix B gives more information on risk management. See also:

■ Office of Government Commerce (2010). *Management of Risk: Guidance for Practitioners*. TSO, London.
■ ISO 31000:2009 Risk management – principles and guidelines.
■ ISO/IEC 27001: 2005 Information technology – security techniques – information security management systems – requirements.
■ ISACA (2009). *The Risk IT Framework* (based on COBIT, see section C.5).

C.4   GOVERNANCE OF IT

Corporate governance refers to the rules, policies, processes (and in some cases, laws) by which businesses are operated, regulated and controlled. These are often defined by the board or shareholders, or the constitution of the organization; but they can also be defined by legislation, regulation or consumer groups.

ISO 9004 (Managing for the sustained success of an organization – a quality management approach) provides guidance on governance for the board and executive of an organization.

The standard for corporate governance of IT is ISO/IEC 38500. The purpose of this standard is to promote effective, efficient and acceptable use of IT in all organizations by:

■ Assuring stakeholders (including consumers, shareholders and employees) that, if the standard is followed, they can have confidence in the organization's corporate governance of IT
■ Informing and guiding directors in governing the use of IT in their organization
■ Providing a basis for objective evaluation of the corporate governance of IT.

Typical examples of regulations that impact IT include: financial, safety, data protection, privacy, software asset management, environment management and carbon emission targets.

Further details are available at www.iso.org

ITIL Service Strategy references the concepts of ISO/IEC 38500 and how the concepts can be applied.

C.5   COBIT

The Control OBjectives for Information and related Technology (COBIT) is a governance and control framework for IT management created by ISACA and the IT Governance Institute (ITGI).

COBIT is based on the analysis and harmonization of existing IT standards and good practices and conforms to generally accepted governance principles. It covers five key governance focus areas: strategic alignment, value delivery, resource management, risk management and performance management. COBIT is primarily aimed at internal and external stakeholders within an enterprise who wish to generate value from IT investments; those who provide IT services; and those who have a control/risk responsibility.

COBIT and ITIL are not 'competitive', nor are they mutually exclusive – on the contrary, they can be used in conjunction as part of an organization's overall governance and management framework. COBIT is positioned at a high level, is driven by business requirements, covers the full range of IT activities, and concentrates on *what* should be achieved rather than *how* to achieve effective governance, management and control. ITIL provides an organization with best-practice guidance on *how* to manage and improve its processes to deliver high-quality, cost-effective IT services. The following COBIT guidance supports strategy management and continual service improvement (CSI):

■ COBIT maturity models can be used to benchmark and drive improvement.
■ Goals and metrics can be aligned to the business goals for IT and used to create an IT management dashboard.
■ The COBIT 'monitor and evaluate' (ME) process domain defines the processes needed to assess current IT performance, IT controls and regulatory compliance.

Further details are available at www.isaca.org and www.itgi.org.

C.6 ISO/IEC 20000 SERVICE MANAGEMENT SERIES

ISO/IEC 20000 is an internationally recognized standard for ITSM covering service providers who manage and deliver IT-enabled services to internal or external customers. ISO/IEC 20000-1 is aligned with other ISO management systems standards such as ISO 9001 and ISO/IEC 27001.

One of the most common routes for an organization to achieve the requirements of ISO/IEC 20000 is by adopting ITIL best practices. ISO/IEC 20000-1 is based on a service management system (SMS). The SMS is defined as a management system to direct and control the service management activities of the service provider. ISO/IEC 20000 includes:

■ ISO/IEC 20000-1:2005 – Information technology – Service management – Part 1: Specification

■ ISO/IEC 20000-1:2011 – Information technology – Service management – Part 1: Requirements for a service management system (the most recent edition of the ISO/IEC 20000 standard)
■ ISO/IEC 20000-2:2005 – Information technology – Service management – Part 2: Code of practice (being updated to include guidance on the application of service management systems and to support ISO/IEC 20000-1:2011)
■ ISO/IEC 20000-3:2005 – Information technology – Service management – Part 3: Scope and applicability
■ ISO/IEC TR 20000-4 – Information technology – Service management – Part 4: Process reference model
■ ISO/IEC TR 20000-5:2010 – Information technology – Service management – Part 5: Exemplar implementation plan for ISO/IEC 20000-1.

A closely related publication that is under development is ISO/IEC TR 15504-8 – Process assessment model for IT service management.

Further details can be found at www.iso.org or www.isoiec20000certification.com.

Organizations using ISO/IEC 20000-1: 2005 for certification audits will transfer to the new edition, ISO/IEC 20000-1: 2011.

ITIL guidance supports organizations that are implementing service management practices to achieve the requirements of ISO/IEC 20000-1: 2005 and the new edition ISO/IEC 20000-1: 2011.

Other references include:

■ Dugmore, J. and Lacy, S. (2011). *Introduction to ISO/IEC 20000 Series: IT Service Management*. British Standards Institution, London.
■ Dugmore, J. and Lacy, S. (2011). *BIP 0005: A Manager's Guide to Service Management* (6th edition). British Standards Institution, London.

C.7 ENVIRONMENTAL MANAGEMENT AND GREEN/SUSTAINABLE IT

The transition to a low-carbon economy is a global challenge. Many governments have set targets to reduce carbon emissions or achieve carbon neutrality. IT is an enabler for environmental and cultural change that will help governments to achieve their targets – for example, through enabling tele- and video-conferencing, and remote and home working. However, IT is also a major user of energy and natural resources. Green IT refers to environmentally sustainable computing where the use and disposal of computers and printers are carried out in sustainable ways that do not have a negative impact on the environment.

Appendix E in *ITIL Service Design* includes further information on environmental architectures and standards. Appendix E in *ITIL Service Operation* also provides useful considerations for facilities management, including environmental aspects.

The ISO 14001 series of standards for an environment management system is designed to assure internal and external stakeholders that the organization is an environmentally responsible organization. It enables an organization of any size or type to:

■ Identify and control the environmental impact of its activities, products or services
■ Improve its environmental performance continually
■ Implement a systematic approach to setting and achieving environmental objectives and targets, and then demonstrating that they have been achieved.

Further details are available at www.iso.org.

C.8 ISO STANDARDS AND PUBLICATIONS FOR IT

ISO 9241 is a series of standards and guidance on the ergonomics of human system interaction that cover people working with computers. It covers aspects that impact the utility of a service (whether it is fit for purpose) such as:

■ ISO 9241-11:1999 Guidance on usability
■ ISO 9241-210:2010 Human-centred design for interactive systems
■ ISO 9241-151:2008 Guidance on world wide web user interfaces.

ISO/IEC JTC1 is Joint Technical Committee 1 of ISO and the International Electrotechnical Commission (IEC). It deals with information technology standards and other publications.

SC27 is a subcommittee under ISO/IEC JTC1 that develops ISO/IEC 27000, the information security management system (ISMS) family of standards. For further details, Appendix B includes information on

ISO/IEC 27001. SC7 is a subcommittee under ISO/IEC JTC1 that covers the standardization of processes, supporting tools and supporting technologies for the engineering of systems, services and software. SC7 publications include:

■ ISO/IEC 20000 Information technology – service management (see section C.6)
■ ISO/IEC 19770-1 Information technology – software asset management processes. ISO/IEC 19770-2:2009 establishes specifications for tagging software to optimize its identification and management
■ ISO/IEC 15288 Systems and software engineering – systems life cycle processes. The processes can be used as a basis for establishing business environments – e.g. methods, procedures, techniques, tools and trained personnel
■ ISO/IEC 12207 Systems and software engineering – software life cycle processes
■ ISO/IEC 15504 Process assessment series. Also known as SPICE (software process improvement and capability determination), it aims to ensure consistency and repeatability of the assessment ratings with evidence to substantiate the ratings. The series includes exemplar process assessment models (PAM), related to one or more conformant or compliant process reference model (PRM). ISO/IEC 15504-8 is an exemplar process assessment model for IT service management that is under development
■ ISO/IEC 25000 series – provides guidance for the use of standards named Software product Quality Requirements and Evaluation (SQuaRE)
■ ISO/IEC 42010 Systems and software engineering — recommended practice for architectural description of software-intensive systems.

SC7 is working on the harmonization of standards in the service management, software and IT systems domains. Further details are available at www.iso.org.

C.9 ITIL AND THE OSI FRAMEWORK

At around the time that ITIL V1 was being written, the International Standards Organization launched an initiative that resulted in the Open Systems Interconnection (OSI) framework. Since this initiative covered many of the same areas as ITIL V1, it is not surprising that there was considerable overlap.

However, it is also not surprising that they classified their processes differently, used different terminology, or used the same terminology in different ways. To confuse matters even more, it is common for different groups in an organization to use terminology from both ITIL and the OSI framework.

The OSI framework made significant contributions to the definition and execution of ITSM programmes and projects around the world. It has also caused a great deal of debate between teams that do not realize the origins of the terminology that they are using. For example, some organizations have two change management departments – one following the ITIL change management process and the other using the OSI installation, moves, additions and changes (IMAC) model. Each department is convinced that it is completely different from the other, and that it is performing a different role. Closer examination will reveal that there are several areas of commonality.

In service operation, the management of known errors may be mapped to fault management. There is also a section related to operational capacity management, which can be related to the OSI concept of performance management.

Information on the set of ISO standards for the OSI framework is available at: www.iso.org

C.10 PROGRAMME AND PROJECT MANAGEMENT

Large, complex deliveries are often broken down into manageable, interrelated projects. For those managing this overall delivery, the principles of programme management are key to delivering on time and within budget. Best management practice in this area is found in *Managing Successful Programmes* (MSP).

Guidance on effective portfolio, programme and project management is brought together in *Portfolio, Programme and Project Offices* (P3O), which is aimed at helping organizations to establish and maintain appropriate business support structures with proven roles and responsibilities.

Structured project management methods, such as PRINCE2 (PRojects IN Controlled Environments) or the Project Management Body of Knowledge

(PMBOK) developed by the Project Management Institute (PMI), can be used when improving IT services. Not all improvements will require a structured project approach, but many will, due to the sheer scope and scale of the improvement. Project management is discussed in more detail in *ITIL Service Transition*.

Visit www.msp-officialsite.com for more information on MSP.

Visit www.p3o-officialsite.com for more information on P3O.

Visit www.prince-officialsite.com for more information on PRINCE2.

Visit www.pmi.org for more information on PMI and PMBOK.

See also the following publications:

- Cleland, David I. and Ireland, Lewis R. (2006). *Project Management: Strategic Design and Implementation* (5th edition). McGraw-Hill Professional.
- Haugan, Gregory T. (2006). *Project Management Fundamentals*. Management Concepts.
- Office of Government Commerce (2009). *Managing Successful Projects with PRINCE2*. TSO, London.
- Cabinet Office (2011). *Managing Successful Programmes*. TSO, London.
- Office of Government Commerce (2008). *Portfolio, Programme and Project Offices*. TSO, London.
- The Project Management Institute (2008). *A Guide to the Project Management Body of Knowledge* (PMBOK Guide) (4th edition). Project Management Institute.

C.11 ORGANIZATIONAL CHANGE

There is a wide range of publications that cover organizational change including the related guidance for programme and project management referred to in the previous section.

Chapter 5 in this publication covers aspects of organizational change elements that are an essential part of, or a strong contributor towards, service transition. This publication and *ITIL Continual Service Improvement* refer to Kotter's 'eight steps for organizational change'.

Visit www.johnkotter.com for more information. See also the following publications:

- Kotter, John P. (1996). *Leading Change*. Harvard Business School Press.
- Kotter, John P. (1999) *What Leaders Really Do*. Harvard Business School Press.
- Kotter, J. P. (2000). Leading change: why transformation efforts fail. *Harvard Business Review* January–February.
- Kotter, John P. and Cohen, Dan S. (2002) *The Heart of Change: Real-Life Stories of How People Change their Organizations*. Harvard Business School Press.
- Kotter, J. P. and Schlesinger, L. C. (1979). Choosing strategies for change. *Harvard Business Review* Vol. 57, No. 2, p.106.
- Kotter, John P., Rathgeber, Holger, Mueller, Peter and Johnson, Spenser (2006). *Our Iceberg Is Melting: Changing and Succeeding Under Any Conditions*. St. Martin's Press.

C.12 SKILLS FRAMEWORK FOR THE INFORMATION AGE

The Skills Framework for the Information Age (SFIA) enables employers of IT professionals to carry out a range of human resource activities against a common framework including a skills audit, planning future skill requirements, development programmes, standardization of job titles and functions, and resource allocation.

SFIA provides a standardized view of the wide range of professional skills needed by people working in IT. SFIA is constructed as a simple two-dimensional matrix consisting of areas of work on one axis and levels of responsibility on the other. It uses a common language and a sensible, logical structure that can be adapted to the training and development needs of a very wide range of businesses.

Visit www.sfia.org.uk for further details.

C.13 CARNEGIE MELLON: CMMI AND ESCM FRAMEWORK

The Capability Maturity Model Integration (CMMI) is a process improvement approach developed by the Software Engineering Institute (SEI) of Carnegie Mellon University. CMMI provides organizations with the essential elements of effective processes. It can be used to guide process improvement across a project, a division or an entire organization. CMMI helps integrate traditionally separate organizational functions, sets process improvement goals and priorities, provides guidance for quality processes, and suggests a point of reference for appraising current processes. There are several CMMI models covering different domains of application.

The eSourcing Capability Model for Service Providers (eSCM-SP) is a framework developed by ITSqc at Carnegie Mellon to improve the relationship between IT service providers and their customers.

Organizations can be assessed against CMMI models using SCAMPI (Standard CMMI Appraisal Method for Process Improvement).

For more information, see www.sei.cmu.edu/cmmi/

C.14 BALANCED SCORECARD

A new approach to strategic management was developed in the early 1990s by Drs Robert Kaplan (Harvard Business School) and David Norton. They named this system the 'balanced scorecard'. Recognizing some of the weaknesses and vagueness of previous management approaches, the balanced scorecard approach provides a clear prescription as to what companies should measure in order to 'balance' the financial perspective. The balanced scorecard suggests that the organization be viewed from four perspectives, and it is valuable to develop metrics, collect data and analyse the organization relative to each of these perspectives:

- The learning and growth perspective
- The business process perspective
- The customer perspective
- The financial perspective.

Some organizations may choose to use the balanced scorecard method as a way of assessing and reporting their IT quality performance in general and their service operation performance in particular.

Further details are available through the balanced scorecard user community at www.scorecardsupport.com

C.15 SIX SIGMA

Six Sigma is a data-driven process improvement approach that supports continual improvement. It is business-output-driven in relation to customer specification. The objective is to implement a measurement-oriented strategy focused on process improvement and defects reduction. A Six Sigma defect is defined as anything outside customer specifications.

Six Sigma focuses on dramatically reducing process variation using statistical process control (SPC) measures. The fundamental objective is to reduce errors to fewer than 3.4 defects per million executions (regardless of the process). Service providers must determine whether it is reasonable to expect delivery at a Six Sigma level given the wide variation in IT deliverables, roles and tasks within IT operational environments.

There are two primary sub-methodologies within Six Sigma: DMAIC (Define, Measure, Analyse, Improve, Control) and DMADV (Define, Measure, Analyse, Design, Verify). DMAIC is an improvement method for existing processes for which performance does not meet expectations, or for which incremental improvements are desired. DMADV focuses on the creation of new processes. For more information, see:

- George, Michael L. (2003). *Lean Six Sigma for Service: How to Use Lean Speed and Six Sigma Quality to Improve Services and Transactions*. McGraw-Hill.
- Pande, Pete and Holpp, Larry (2001) *What Is Six Sigma?* McGraw-Hill.
- Pande, Peter S., Neuman, Robert P. and Cavanagh, Roland R. (2000). *The Six Sigma Way: How GE, Motorola, and Other Top Companies are Honing their Performance*. McGraw-Hill.

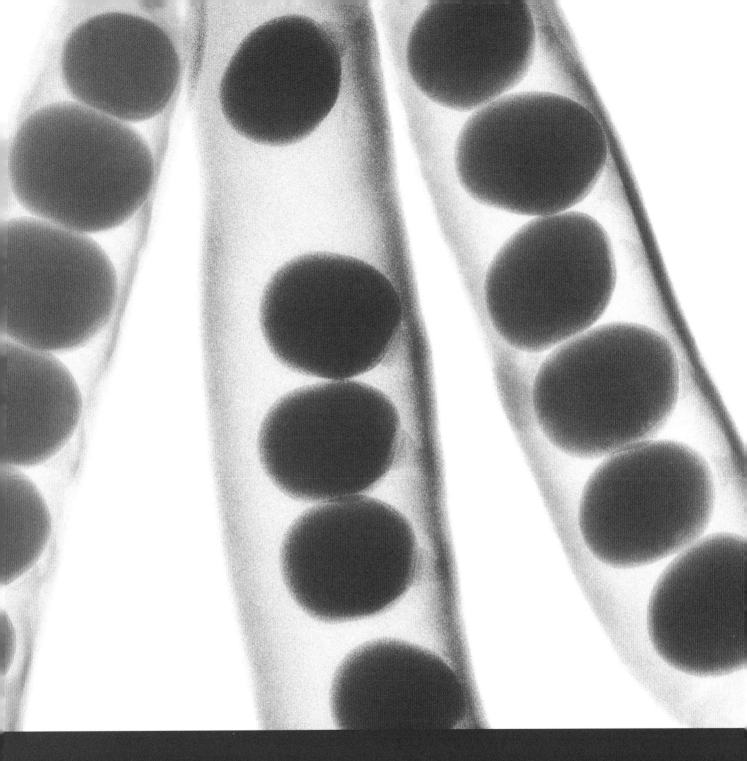

Appendix D:
Examples of inputs
and outputs across
the service lifecycle

D

Appendix D: Examples of inputs and outputs across the service lifecycle

This appendix identifies some of the major inputs and outputs between each stage of the service lifecycle. This is not an exhaustive list and is designed to help understand how the different lifecycle stages interact. See Table 3.1 for more detail on the inputs and outputs of the service transition stage.

Lifecycle stage	Examples of inputs from other service lifecycle stages	Examples of outputs to other service lifecycle stages
Service strategy	Information and feedback for business cases and service portfolio Requirements for strategies and plans Inputs and feedback on strategies and policies Financial reports, service reports, dashboards, and outputs of service review meetings Response to change proposals Service portfolio updates including the service catalogue Change schedule Knowledge and information in the service knowledge management system (SKMS)	Vision and mission Strategies, strategic plans and policies Financial information and budgets Service portfolio Change proposals Service charters including service packages, service models, and details of utility and warranty Patterns of business activity and demand forecasts Updated knowledge and information in the SKMS Achievements against metrics, KPIs and CSFs Feedback to other lifecycle stages Improvement opportunities logged in the CSI register
Service design	Vision and mission Strategies, strategic plans and policies Financial information and budgets Service portfolio Service charters including service packages, service models, and details of utility and warranty Feedback on all aspects of service design and service design packages Requests for change (RFCs) for designing changes and improvements Input to design requirements from other lifecycle stages Service reports, dashboards, and outputs of service review meetings Knowledge and information in the SKMS	Service portfolio updates including the service catalogue Service design packages, including: ■ Details of utility and warranty ■ Acceptance criteria ■ Updated service models ■ Designs and interface specifications ■ Transition plans ■ Operation plans and procedures Information security policies Designs for new or changed services, management information systems and tools, technology architectures, processes, measurement methods and metrics SLAs, OLAs and underpinning contracts RFCs to transition or deploy new or changed services Financial reports Updated knowledge and information in the SKMS Achievements against metrics, KPIs and CSFs Feedback to other lifecycle stages Improvement opportunities logged in the CSI register

Lifecycle stage	Examples of inputs from other service lifecycle stages	Examples of outputs to other service lifecycle stages
Service transition	Vision and mission Strategies, strategic plans and policies Financial information and budgets Service portfolio Change proposals, including utility and warranty requirements and expected timescales RFCs for implementing changes and improvements Service design packages, including: ■ Details of utility and warranty ■ Acceptance criteria ■ Service models ■ Designs and interface specifications ■ Transition plans ■ Operation plans and procedures Input to change evaluation and change advisory board (CAB) meetings Knowledge and information in the SKMS	New or changed services, management information systems and tools, technology architectures, processes, measurement methods and metrics Responses to change proposals and RFCs Change schedule Known errors Standard changes for use in request fulfilment Knowledge and information in the SKMS (including the configuration management system) Financial reports Updated knowledge and information in the SKMS Achievements against metrics, KPIs and CSFs Feedback to other lifecycle stages Improvement opportunities logged in the CSI register
Service operation	Vision and mission Strategies, strategic plans and policies Financial information and budgets Service portfolio Service reports, dashboards, and outputs of service review meetings Service design packages, including: ■ Details of utility and warranty ■ Operations plans and procedures ■ Recovery procedures Service level agreements (SLAs), operational level agreements (OLAs) and underpinning contracts Known errors Standard changes for use in request fulfilment Information security policies Change schedule Patterns of business activity and demand forecasts Knowledge and information in the SKMS	Achievement of agreed service levels to deliver value to the business Operational requirements Operational performance data and service records RFCs to resolve operational issues Financial reports Updated knowledge and information in the SKMS Achievements against metrics, KPIs and CSFs Feedback to other lifecycle stages Improvement opportunities logged in the CSI register
Continual service improvement	Vision and mission Strategies, strategic plans and policies Financial information and budgets Service portfolio Achievements against metrics, key performance indicators (KPIs) and critical success factors (CSFs) from each lifecycle stage Operational performance data and service records Improvement opportunities logged in the CSI register Knowledge and information in the SKMS	RFCs for implementing improvements across all lifecycle stages Business cases for significant improvements Updated CSI register Service improvement plans Results of customer and user satisfaction surveys Service reports, dashboards, and outputs of service review meetings Financial reports Updated knowledge and information in the SKMS Achievements against metrics, KPIs and CSFs Feedback to other lifecycle stages

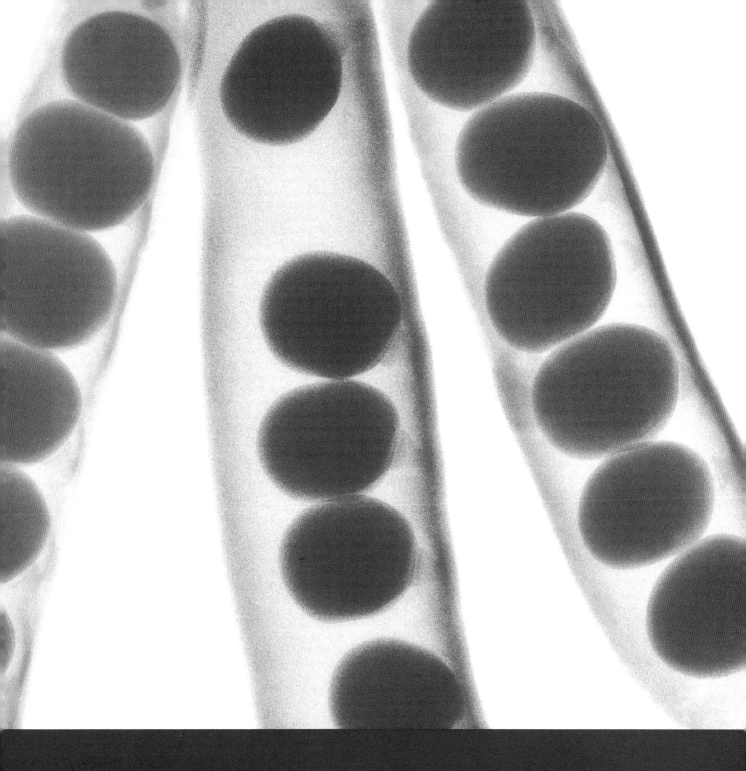

References and further reading

References and further reading

Note that this list does not include the publications in the Best Management Practice (BMP) portfolio which are cited in full in Appendix C.

Argote, L. (2000). Knowledge transfer: a basis for competitive advantage in firms. *Organizational Behaviour and Human Decision Processes*. Vol. 82, No. 1, pp. 150–69.

BSI (2003). *Managing Culture and Knowledge: A Guide to Good Practice*. Committee KMS/1, Rob Young (Chairman), PD 7501. British Standards Institution, London.

BSI (2003). *Guide to Measurements in Knowledge Management*. Committee KMS/1, Rob Young (Chairman), PD 7502. British Standards Institution, London.

BSI (2001). *Knowledge Management: A Guide to Good Practice*. British Standards Institution, London.

Drake, P. (2005a). *Communicative Action in Information Security Systems: An Application of Social Theory in a Technical Domain*. Hull Business School, University of Hull.

Drake, P. (2005b). Socialising the domain of information security. *OR Insight*, Vol. 18, No. 3, pp. 15–23. Operational Research Society, University of Hull.

Duck, J. D. (2000). Managing change: the art of balancing. *Harvard Business Review*, November–December.

Dugmore, J. and Lacy, S. (2006). *Achieving ISO/IEC 20000*. British Standards Institution, London.

Hackman, J. R. and Oldham, G. R. (1980). *Work Redesign (Organization Development)*. Addison-Wesley, Reading, MA.

Hambling, B. (ed.) with Morgan, P., Samaroo, A., Thompson, G. and Williams, P. (2007). *Software Testing: An ISEB Foundation*. British Computer Society, Swindon.

Institute of Internal Auditors (2005). *Global Technology Audit Guide 2: Change and Patch Management Controls: Critical for Organizational Success*. Institute of Internal Auditors, Altamonte Springs, Florida.

ISO/IEC TR 9294:2005. *Information Technology: Guidelines for the Management of Software Documentation*.

ITGI (2005). *COBIT 4.0: Control OBjectives, Management Guidelines and Maturity Models*. IT Governance Institute.

Kanter, R. M. (2001). *Evolve! Succeeding in the Digital Culture of Tomorrow*. Harvard Business School Press, Boston, MA.

Kotter, J. P. and Schlesinger, L. C. (1979). Choosing strategies for change. *Harvard Business Review* Vol. 57, No. 2, p.106.

Lev, B. (2001). *Intangibles: Management, Measurement and Reporting*. The Brookings Institution.

Magretta, J. (2002). *What Management Is: How it Works and Why it's Everyone's Business*. The Free Press, New York.

Peters, T. and Waterman, R. (1982). *In Search of Excellence (McKinsey 7S model)*. Harper & Row, New York.

Sirkin, H. L., Keenan, P. and Jackson, A. (2005). The hard side of change management. *Harvard Business Review*, October.

Szulanski, G. (1992). *Sticky Knowledge: Barriers to Knowing in the Firm*. Sage Publication, London.

Szulanski, G. (1996). Exploring internal stickiness: impediments to the transfer of best practice within the firm. *Strategic Management Journal*, 17 (summer special issue), pp. 27–43.

Vogel, D. (2005). *Effective Regulatory Compliance Requires IT Configuration Management*. Gartner Inc. Research ID: G00127752. Gartner Inc., Stamford, CT.

Whitmore, J. (1992). *Coaching for Performance*. Nicholas Brealey Publishing, London.

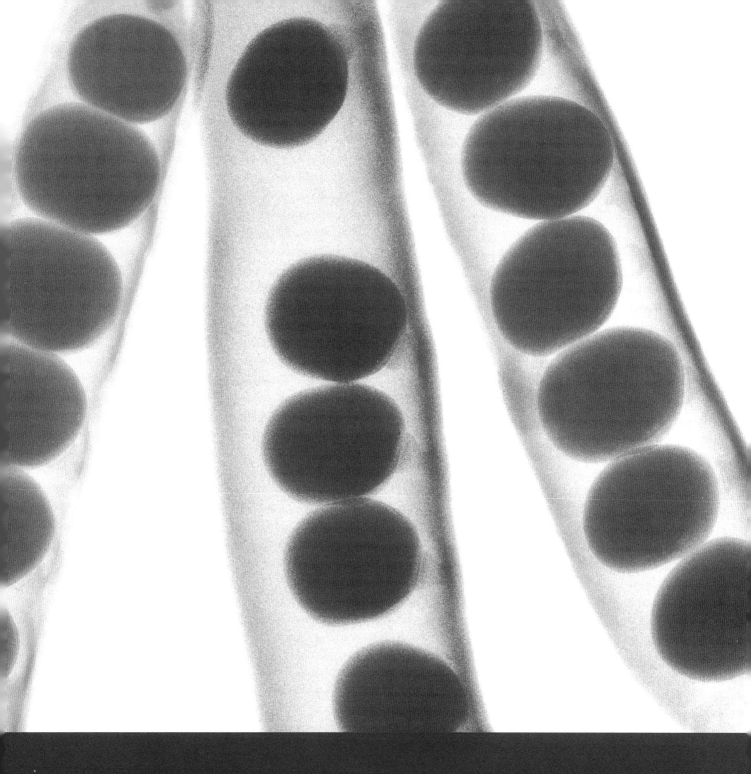

Abbreviations and
glossary

Abbreviations

ACD	automatic call distribution	eSCM-CL	eSourcing Capability Model for Client Organizations
AM	availability management	eSCM-SP	eSourcing Capability Model for Service Providers
AMIS	availability management information system	FTA	fault tree analysis
ASP	application service provider	IRR	internal rate of return
AST	agreed service time	ISG	IT steering group
BCM	business continuity management	ISM	information security management
BCP	business continuity plan	ISMS	information security management system
BIA	business impact analysis		
BMP	Best Management Practice	ISO	International Organization for Standardization
BRM	business relationship manager		
BSI	British Standards Institution	ISP	internet service provider
CAB	change advisory board	IT	information technology
CAPEX	capital expenditure	ITSCM	IT service continuity management
CCM	component capacity management	ITSM	IT service management
CFIA	component failure impact analysis	itSMF	IT Service Management Forum
CI	configuration item	IVR	interactive voice response
CMDB	configuration management database	KEDB	known error database
CMIS	capacity management information system	KPI	key performance indicator
		LOS	line of service
CMM	capability maturity model	MIS	management information system
CMMI	Capability Maturity Model Integration	M_o_R	Management of Risk
CMS	configuration management system	MTBF	mean time between failures
COBIT	Control OBjectives for Information and related Technology	MTBSI	mean time between service incidents
		MTRS	mean time to restore service
COTS	commercial off the shelf	MTTR	mean time to repair
CSF	critical success factor	NPV	net present value
CSI	continual service improvement	OLA	operational level agreement
CTI	computer telephony integration	OPEX	operational expenditure
DIKW	Data-to-Information-to-Knowledge-to-Wisdom	PBA	pattern of business activity
		PDCA	Plan-Do-Check-Act
DML	definitive media library	PFS	prerequisite for success
ECAB	emergency change advisory board	PIR	post-implementation review
ELS	early life support		

PMBOK	Project Management Body of Knowledge
PMI	Project Management Institute
PMO	project management office
PRINCE2	PRojects IN Controlled Environments
PSO	projected service outage
QA	quality assurance
QMS	quality management system
RACI	responsible, accountable, consulted and informed
RCA	root cause analysis
RFC	request for change
ROA	return on assets
ROI	return on investment
RPO	recovery point objective
RTO	recovery time objective
SAC	service acceptance criteria
SACM	service asset and configuration management
SAM	software asset management
SCM	service capacity management
SCMIS	supplier and contract management information system
SDP	service design package
SFA	service failure analysis
SIP	service improvement plan
SKMS	service knowledge management system
SLA	service level agreement
SLM	service level management
SLP	service level package
SLR	service level requirement
SMART	specific, measurable, achievable, relevant and time-bound
SMIS	security management information system
SMO	service maintenance objective
SoC	separation of concerns
SOP	standard operating procedure
SOR	statement of requirements
SOX	Sarbanes-Oxley (US law)
SPI	service provider interface
SPM	service portfolio management
SPOF	single point of failure
TCO	total cost of ownership
TCU	total cost of utilization
TO	technical observation
TOR	terms of reference
TQM	total quality management
UC	underpinning contract
UP	user profile
VBF	vital business function
VOI	value on investment
WIP	work in progress

Glossary

The core ITIL publications (*ITIL Service Strategy*, *ITIL Service Design*, *ITIL Service Operation*, *ITIL Service Transition*, *ITIL Continual Service Improvement*) referred to in parentheses at the beginning of a definition indicate where a reader can find more information. Terms without such a reference may either be used generically across all five core publications, or simply may not be explained in any greater detail elsewhere in the ITIL series. In other words, readers are only directed to other sources where they can expect to expand on their knowledge or to see a greater context.

acceptance

Formal agreement that an IT service, process, plan or other deliverable is complete, accurate, reliable and meets its specified requirements. Acceptance is usually preceded by change evaluation or testing and is often required before proceeding to the next stage of a project or process. *See also* service acceptance criteria.

access management

(*ITIL Service Operation*) The process responsible for allowing users to make use of IT services, data or other assets. Access management helps to protect the confidentiality, integrity and availability of assets by ensuring that only authorized users are able to access or modify them. Access management implements the policies of information security management and is sometimes referred to as rights management or identity management.

accounting

(*ITIL Service Strategy*) The process responsible for identifying the actual costs of delivering IT services, comparing these with budgeted costs, and managing variance from the budget.

accredited

Officially authorized to carry out a role. For example, an accredited body may be authorized to provide training or to conduct audits.

activity

A set of actions designed to achieve a particular result. Activities are usually defined as part of processes or plans, and are documented in procedures.

agreement

A document that describes a formal understanding between two or more parties. An agreement is not legally binding, unless it forms part of a contract. *See also* operational level agreement; service level agreement.

alert

(*ITIL Service Operation*) A notification that a threshold has been reached, something has changed, or a failure has occurred. Alerts are often created and managed by system management tools and are managed by the event management process.

application

Software that provides functions which are required by an IT service. Each application may be part of more than one IT service. An application runs on one or more servers or clients. *See also* application management; application portfolio.

application management

(*ITIL Service Operation*) The function responsible for managing applications throughout their lifecycle.

application portfolio

(*ITIL Service Design*) A database or structured document used to manage applications throughout their lifecycle. The application portfolio contains key attributes of all applications. The application portfolio is sometimes implemented as part of the service portfolio, or as part of the configuration management system.

architecture

(*ITIL Service Design*) The structure of a system or IT service, including the relationships of components to each other and to the environment they are in. Architecture also includes the standards and guidelines that guide the design and evolution of the system.

assembly

(*ITIL Service Transition*) A configuration item that is made up of a number of other CIs. For example, a server CI may contain CIs for CPUs, disks, memory etc.; an IT service CI may contain many hardware, software and other CIs. *See also* build; component CI.

assessment

Inspection and analysis to check whether a standard or set of guidelines is being followed, that records are accurate, or that efficiency and effectiveness targets are being met. *See also* audit.

asset

(*ITIL Service Strategy*) Any resource or capability. The assets of a service provider include anything that could contribute to the delivery of a service. Assets can be one of the following types: management, organization, process, knowledge, people, information, applications, infrastructure or financial capital. *See also* customer asset; service asset; strategic asset.

asset management

(*ITIL Service Transition*) A generic activity or process responsible for tracking and reporting the value and ownership of assets throughout their lifecycle. *See also* service asset and configuration management; fixed asset management; software asset management.

asset register

(*ITIL Service Transition*) A list of fixed assets that includes their ownership and value. *See also* fixed asset management.

attribute

(*ITIL Service Transition*) A piece of information about a configuration item. Examples are name, location, version number and cost. Attributes of CIs are recorded in a configuration management database (CMDB) and maintained as part of a configuration management system (CMS). *See also* relationship; configuration management system.

audit

Formal inspection and verification to check whether a standard or set of guidelines is being followed, that records are accurate, or that efficiency and effectiveness targets are being met. An audit may be carried out by internal or external groups. *See also* assessment; certification.

authority matrix

See RACI.

availability

(*ITIL Service Design*) Ability of an IT service or other configuration item to perform its agreed function when required. Availability is determined by reliability, maintainability, serviceability, performance and security. Availability is usually calculated as a percentage. This calculation is often based on agreed service time and downtime. It is best practice to calculate availability of an IT service using measurements of the business output.

availability management (AM)

(*ITIL Service Design*) The process responsible for ensuring that IT services meet the current and future availability needs of the business in a cost-effective and timely manner. Availability management defines, analyses, plans, measures and improves all aspects of the availability of IT services, and ensures that all IT infrastructures, processes, tools, roles etc. are appropriate for the agreed service level targets for availability. *See also* availability management information system.

availability management information system (AMIS)

(*ITIL Service Design*) A set of tools, data and information that is used to support availability management. *See also* service knowledge management system.

availability plan

(*ITIL Service Design*) A plan to ensure that existing and future availability requirements for IT services can be provided cost-effectively.

back-out

(*ITIL Service Transition*) An activity that restores a service or other configuration item to a previous baseline. Back-out is used as a form of remediation when a change or release is not successful.

backup

(*ITIL Service Design*) (*ITIL Service Operation*) Copying data to protect against loss of integrity or availability of the original.

balanced scorecard

(*ITIL Continual Service Improvement*) A management tool developed by Drs Robert Kaplan (Harvard Business School) and David Norton. A balanced scorecard enables a strategy to be broken down into key performance indicators. Performance against the KPIs is used to demonstrate how well the strategy is being achieved. A balanced scorecard has four major areas, each of which has a small number of KPIs. The same four areas are considered at different levels of detail throughout the organization.

baseline

(*ITIL Continual Service Improvement*) (*ITIL Service Transition*) A snapshot that is used as a reference point. Many snapshots may be taken and recorded over time but only some will be used as baselines. For example:

- An ITSM baseline can be used as a starting point to measure the effect of a service improvement plan
- A performance baseline can be used to measure changes in performance over the lifetime of an IT service
- A configuration baseline can be used as part of a back-out plan to enable the IT infrastructure to be restored to a known configuration if a change or release fails.

See also benchmark.

benchmark

(*ITIL Continual Service Improvement*) (*ITIL Service Transition*) A baseline that is used to compare related data sets as part of a benchmarking exercise. For example, a recent snapshot of a process can be compared to a previous baseline of that process, or a current baseline can be compared to industry data or best practice. *See also* benchmarking; baseline.

benchmarking

(*ITIL Continual Service Improvement*) The process responsible for comparing a benchmark with related data sets such as a more recent snapshot, industry data or best practice. The term is also used to mean creating a series of benchmarks over time, and comparing the results to measure progress or improvement. This process is not described in detail within the core ITIL publications.

Best Management Practice (BMP)

The Best Management Practice portfolio is owned by the Cabinet Office, part of HM Government. Formerly owned by CCTA and then OGC, the BMP functions moved to the Cabinet Office in June 2010. The BMP portfolio includes guidance on IT service management and project, programme, risk, portfolio and value management. There is also a management maturity model as well as related glossaries of terms.

best practice

Proven activities or processes that have been successfully used by multiple organizations. ITIL is an example of best practice.

British Standards Institution (BSI)

The UK national standards body, responsible for creating and maintaining British standards. See www.bsi-global.com for more information. *See also* International Organization for Standardization.

budget

A list of all the money an organization or business unit plans to receive, and plans to pay out, over a specified period of time. *See also* budgeting; planning.

budgeting

The activity of predicting and controlling the spending of money. Budgeting consists of a periodic negotiation cycle to set future budgets (usually annual) and the day-to-day monitoring and adjusting of current budgets.

build

(*ITIL Service Transition*) The activity of assembling a number of configuration items to create part of an IT service. The term is also used to refer to a release that is authorized for distribution – for example, server build or laptop build. *See also* configuration baseline.

build environment

(*ITIL Service Transition*) A controlled environment where applications, IT services and other builds are assembled prior to being moved into a test or live environment.

business

(*ITIL Service Strategy*) An overall corporate entity or organization formed of a number of business units. In the context of ITSM, the term includes public sector and not-for-profit organizations, as well as companies. An IT service provider provides IT services to a customer within a business. The IT service provider may be part of the same business as its customer (internal service provider), or part of another business (external service provider).

business capacity management

(*ITIL Continual Service Improvement*) (*ITIL Service Design*) In the context of ITSM, business capacity management is the sub-process of capacity management responsible for understanding future business requirements for use in the capacity plan. *See also* service capacity management; component capacity management.

business case

(*ITIL Service Strategy*) Justification for a significant item of expenditure. The business case includes information about costs, benefits, options, issues, risks and possible problems. *See also* cost benefit analysis.

business continuity management (BCM)

(*ITIL Service Design*) The business process responsible for managing risks that could seriously affect the business. Business continuity management safeguards the interests of key stakeholders, reputation, brand and value-creating activities. The process involves reducing risks to an acceptable level and planning for the recovery of business processes should a disruption to the business occur. Business continuity management sets the objectives, scope and requirements for IT service continuity management.

business continuity plan (BCP)

(*ITIL Service Design*) A plan defining the steps required to restore business processes following a disruption. The plan also identifies the triggers for invocation, people to be involved, communications etc. IT service continuity plans form a significant part of business continuity plans.

business customer

(*ITIL Service Strategy*) A recipient of a product or a service from the business. For example, if the business is a car manufacturer, then the business customer is someone who buys a car.

business impact analysis (BIA)

(*ITIL Service Strategy*) Business impact analysis is the activity in business continuity management that identifies vital business functions and their dependencies. These dependencies may include suppliers, people, other business processes, IT services etc. Business impact analysis defines the recovery requirements for IT services. These requirements include recovery time objectives, recovery point objectives and minimum service level targets for each IT service.

business objective

(*ITIL Service Strategy*) The objective of a business process, or of the business as a whole. Business objectives support the business vision, provide guidance for the IT strategy, and are often supported by IT services.

business operations

(*ITIL Service Strategy*) The day-to-day execution, monitoring and management of business processes.

business perspective

(*ITIL Continual Service Improvement*) An understanding of the service provider and IT services from the point of view of the business, and an understanding of the business from the point of view of the service provider.

business process

A process that is owned and carried out by the business. A business process contributes to the delivery of a product or service to a business customer. For example, a retailer may have a purchasing process that helps to deliver services to its business customers. Many business processes rely on IT services.

business relationship management

(*ITIL Service Strategy*) The process responsible for maintaining a positive relationship with customers. Business relationship management identifies customer needs and ensures that the service provider is able to meet these needs with an appropriate catalogue of services. This process has strong links with service level management.

business relationship manager (BRM)

(*ITIL Service Strategy*) A role responsible for maintaining the relationship with one or more customers. This role is often combined with the service level manager role.

business service

A service that is delivered to business customers by business units. For example, delivery of financial services to customers of a bank, or goods to the customers of a retail store. Successful delivery of business services often depends on one or more IT services. A business service may consist almost entirely of an IT service – for example, an online banking service or an external website where product orders can be placed by business customers. *See also* customer-facing service.

business service management

The management of business services delivered to business customers. Business service management is performed by business units.

business unit

(*ITIL Service Strategy*) A segment of the business that has its own plans, metrics, income and costs. Each business unit owns assets and uses these to create value for customers in the form of goods and services.

call

(*ITIL Service Operation*) A telephone call to the service desk from a user. A call could result in an incident or a service request being logged.

capability

(*ITIL Service Strategy*) The ability of an organization, person, process, application, IT service or other configuration item to carry out an activity. Capabilities are intangible assets of an organization. *See also* resource.

Capability Maturity Model Integration (CMMI)

(*ITIL Continual Service Improvement*) A process improvement approach developed by the Software Engineering Institute (SEI) of Carnegie Mellon University, US. CMMI provides organizations with the essential elements of effective processes. It can be used to guide process improvement across a project, a division or an entire organization. CMMI helps integrate traditionally separate organizational functions, set process improvement goals and priorities, provide guidance for quality processes, and provide a point of reference for appraising current processes. See www.sei.cmu.edu/cmmi for more information. *See also* maturity.

capacity

(*ITIL Service Design*) The maximum throughput that a configuration item or IT service can deliver. For some types of CI, capacity may be the size or volume – for example, a disk drive.

capacity management

(*ITIL Continual Service Improvement*) (*ITIL Service Design*) The process responsible for ensuring that the capacity of IT services and the IT infrastructure is able to meet agreed capacity- and performance-related requirements in a cost-effective and timely manner. Capacity management considers all resources required to deliver an IT service, and is concerned with meeting both the current and future capacity and performance needs of the business. Capacity management includes three sub-processes: business capacity management, service capacity management, and component capacity management. *See also* capacity management information system.

capacity management information system (CMIS)

(*ITIL Service Design*) A set of tools, data and information that is used to support capacity management. *See also* service knowledge management system.

capacity plan

(*ITIL Service Design*) A plan used to manage the resources required to deliver IT services. The plan contains details of current and historic usage of IT services and components, and any issues that need to be addressed (including related improvement activities). The plan also contains scenarios for different predictions of business demand and costed options to deliver the agreed service level targets.

category

A named group of things that have something in common. Categories are used to group similar things together. For example, cost types are used to group similar types of cost. Incident categories are used to group similar types of incident, while CI types are used to group similar types of configuration item.

certification

Issuing a certificate to confirm compliance to a standard. Certification includes a formal audit by an independent and accredited body. The term is also used to mean awarding a certificate to provide evidence that a person has achieved a qualification.

change

(*ITIL Service Transition*) The addition, modification or removal of anything that could have an effect on IT services. The scope should include changes to all architectures, processes, tools, metrics and documentation, as well as changes to IT services and other configuration items.

change advisory board (CAB)

(*ITIL Service Transition*) A group of people that support the assessment, prioritization, authorization and scheduling of changes. A change advisory board is usually made up of representatives from: all areas within the IT service provider; the business; and third parties such as suppliers.

change evaluation

(*ITIL Service Transition*) The process responsible for formal assessment of a new or changed IT service to ensure that risks have been managed and to help determine whether to authorize the change.

change history

(*ITIL Service Transition*) Information about all changes made to a configuration item during its life. Change history consists of all those change records that apply to the CI.

change management

(*ITIL Service Transition*) The process responsible for controlling the lifecycle of all changes, enabling beneficial changes to be made with minimum disruption to IT services.

change model

(*ITIL Service Transition*) A repeatable way of dealing with a particular category of change. A change model defines specific agreed steps that will be followed for a change of this category. Change models may be very complex with many steps that require authorization (e.g. major software release) or may be very simple with no requirement for authorization (e.g. password reset). *See also* change advisory board; standard change.

change proposal

(*ITIL Service Strategy*) (*ITIL Service Transition*) A document that includes a high level description of a potential service introduction or significant change, along with a corresponding business case and an expected implementation schedule. Change proposals are normally created by the service portfolio management process and are passed to change management for authorization.

Change management will review the potential impact on other services, on shared resources, and on the overall change schedule. Once the change proposal has been authorized, service portfolio management will charter the service.

change record

(*ITIL Service Transition*) A record containing the details of a change. Each change record documents the lifecycle of a single change. A change record is created for every request for change that is received, even those that are subsequently rejected. Change records should reference the configuration items that are affected by the change. Change records may be stored in the configuration management system, or elsewhere in the service knowledge management system.

change request

See request for change.

change schedule

(*ITIL Service Transition*) A document that lists all authorized changes and their planned implementation dates, as well as the estimated dates of longer-term changes. A change schedule is sometimes called a forward schedule of change, even though it also contains information about changes that have already been implemented.

change window

(*ITIL Service Transition*) A regular, agreed time when changes or releases may be implemented with minimal impact on services. Change windows are usually documented in service level agreements.

charging

(*ITIL Service Strategy*) Requiring payment for IT services. Charging for IT services is optional, and many organizations choose to treat their IT service provider as a cost centre. *See also* charging process; charging policy.

charging policy

(*ITIL Service Strategy*) A policy specifying the objective of the charging process and the way in which charges will be calculated. *See also* cost.

charging process

(*ITIL Service Strategy*) The process responsible for deciding how much customers should pay (pricing) and recovering money from them (billing). This process is not described in detail within the core ITIL publications.

charter

(*ITIL Service Strategy*) A document that contains details of a new service, a significant change or other significant project. Charters are typically authorized by service portfolio management or by a project management office. The term charter is also used to describe the act of authorizing the work required to complete the service change or project. *See also* change proposal; service charter; project portfolio.

CI type

(*ITIL Service Transition*) A category that is used to classify configuration items. The CI type identifies the required attributes and relationships for a configuration record. Common CI types include hardware, document, user etc.

classification

The act of assigning a category to something. Classification is used to ensure consistent management and reporting. Configuration items, incidents, problems, changes etc. are usually classified.

client

A generic term that means a customer, the business or a business customer. For example, client manager may be used as a synonym for business relationship manager. The term is also used to mean:

- A computer that is used directly by a user – for example, a PC, a handheld computer or a work station
- The part of a client server application that the user directly interfaces with – for example, an email client.

closed

(*ITIL Service Operation*) The final status in the lifecycle of an incident, problem, change etc. When the status is closed, no further action is taken.

closure

(*ITIL Service Operation*) The act of changing the status of an incident, problem, change etc. to closed.

COBIT

(*ITIL Continual Service Improvement*) Control OBjectives for Information and related Technology (COBIT) provides guidance and best practice for the management of IT processes. COBIT is published by ISACA in conjunction with the IT Governance Institute (ITGI). See www.isaca.org for more information.

code of practice

A guideline published by a public body or a standards organization, such as ISO or BSI. Many standards consist of a code of practice and a specification. The code of practice describes recommended best practice.

commercial off the shelf (COTS)

(*ITIL Service Design*) Pre-existing application software or middleware that can be purchased from a third party.

compliance

Ensuring that a standard or set of guidelines is followed, or that proper, consistent accounting or other practices are being employed.

component

A general term that is used to mean one part of something more complex. For example, a computer system may be a component of an IT service; an application may be a component of a release unit. Components that need to be managed should be configuration items.

component capacity management (CCM)

(*ITIL Continual Service Improvement*) (*ITIL Service Design*) The sub-process of capacity management responsible for understanding the capacity, utilization and performance of configuration items. Data is collected, recorded and analysed for use in the capacity plan. *See also* business capacity management; service capacity management.

component CI

(*ITIL Service Transition*) A configuration item that is part of an assembly. For example, a CPU or memory CI may be part of a server CI.

confidentiality

(*ITIL Service Design*) A security principle that requires that data should only be accessed by authorized people.

configuration

(*ITIL Service Transition*) A generic term used to describe a group of configuration items that work together to deliver an IT service, or a recognizable part of an IT service. Configuration is also used to describe the parameter settings for one or more configuration items.

configuration baseline

(*ITIL Service Transition*) The baseline of a configuration that has been formally agreed and is managed through the change management process. A configuration baseline is used as a basis for future builds, releases and changes.

configuration control

(*ITIL Service Transition*) The activity responsible for ensuring that adding, modifying or removing a configuration item is properly managed – for example, by submitting a request for change or service request.

configuration identification

(*ITIL Service Transition*) The activity responsible for collecting information about configuration items and their relationships, and loading this information into the configuration management database. Configuration identification is also responsible for labelling the configuration items themselves, so that the corresponding configuration records can be found.

configuration item (CI)

(*ITIL Service Transition*) Any component or other service asset that needs to be managed in order to deliver an IT service. Information about each configuration item is recorded in a configuration record within the configuration management system and is maintained throughout its lifecycle by service asset and configuration management.

Configuration items are under the control of change management. They typically include IT services, hardware, software, buildings, people and formal documentation such as process documentation and service level agreements.

configuration management

See service asset and configuration management.

configuration management database (CMDB)

(*ITIL Service Transition*) A database used to store configuration records throughout their lifecycle. The configuration management system maintains one or more configuration management databases, and each database stores attributes of configuration items, and relationships with other configuration items.

configuration management system (CMS)

(*ITIL Service Transition*) A set of tools, data and information that is used to support service asset and configuration management. The CMS is part of an overall service knowledge management system and includes tools for collecting, storing, managing, updating, analysing and presenting data about all configuration items and their relationships. The CMS may also include information about incidents, problems, known errors, changes and releases. The CMS is maintained by service asset and configuration management and is used by all IT service management processes. *See also* configuration management database.

configuration record

(*ITIL Service Transition*) A record containing the details of a configuration item. Each configuration record documents the lifecycle of a single configuration item. Configuration records are stored in a configuration management database and maintained as part of a configuration management system.

configuration structure

(*ITIL Service Transition*) The hierarchy and other relationships between all the configuration items that comprise a configuration.

continual service improvement (CSI)

(*ITIL Continual Service Improvement*) A stage in the lifecycle of a service. Continual service improvement ensures that services are aligned with changing business needs by identifying and implementing improvements to IT services that support business processes. The performance of the IT service provider is continually measured and improvements are made to processes, IT services and IT infrastructure in order to increase efficiency, effectiveness and cost effectiveness. Continual service improvement includes the seven-step improvement process. Although this process is associated with continual service improvement, most processes have activities that take place across multiple stages of the service lifecycle. *See also* Plan-Do-Check-Act.

contract

A legally binding agreement between two or more parties.

control

A means of managing a risk, ensuring that a business objective is achieved or that a process is followed. Examples of control include policies, procedures, roles, RAID, door locks etc. A control is sometimes called a countermeasure or safeguard. Control also means to manage the utilization or behaviour of a configuration item, system or IT service.

Control OBjectives for Information and related Technology

See COBIT.

control perspective

(*ITIL Service Strategy*) An approach to the management of IT services, processes, functions, assets etc. There can be several different control perspectives on the same IT service, process etc., allowing different individuals or teams to focus on what is important and relevant to their specific role. Examples of control perspective include reactive and proactive management within IT operations, or a lifecycle view for an application project team.

core service

(*ITIL Service Strategy*) A service that delivers the basic outcomes desired by one or more customers. A core service provides a specific level of utility and warranty. Customers may be offered a choice of utility and warranty through one or more service options. *See also* enabling service; enhancing service; IT service; service package.

cost

The amount of money spent on a specific activity, IT service or business unit. Costs consist of real cost (money), notional cost (such as people's time) and depreciation.

cost benefit analysis

An activity that analyses and compares the costs and the benefits involved in one or more alternative courses of action. *See also* business case; internal rate of return; net present value; return on investment; value on investment.

cost element

(*ITIL Service Strategy*) The middle level of category to which costs are assigned in budgeting and accounting. The highest-level category is cost type. For example, a cost type of 'people' could have cost elements of payroll, staff benefits, expenses, training, overtime etc. Cost elements can be further broken down to give cost units. For example, the cost element 'expenses' could include cost units of hotels, transport, meals etc.

cost model

(*ITIL Service Strategy*) A framework used in budgeting and accounting in which all known costs can be recorded, categorized and allocated to specific customers, business units or projects. *See also* cost type; cost element; cost unit.

cost type

(*ITIL Service Strategy*) The highest level of category to which costs are assigned in budgeting and accounting – for example, hardware, software, people, accommodation, external and transfer. *See also* cost element; cost unit.

cost unit

(*ITIL Service Strategy*) The lowest level of category to which costs are assigned, cost units are usually things that can be easily counted (e.g. staff numbers, software licences) or things easily measured (e.g. CPU usage, electricity consumed). Cost units are included within cost elements. For example, a cost element of 'expenses' could include cost units of hotels, transport, meals etc. *See also* cost type.

countermeasure

Can be used to refer to any type of control. The term is most often used when referring to measures that increase resilience, fault tolerance or reliability of an IT service.

course corrections

Changes made to a plan or activity that has already started to ensure that it will meet its objectives. Course corrections are made as a result of monitoring progress.

crisis management

Crisis management is the process responsible for managing the wider implications of business continuity. A crisis management team is responsible for strategic issues such as managing media relations and shareholder confidence, and decides when to invoke business continuity plans.

critical success factor (CSF)

Something that must happen if an IT service, process, plan, project or other activity is to succeed. Key performance indicators are used to measure the achievement of each critical success factor. For example, a critical success factor of 'protect IT services when making changes' could be measured by key performance indicators such as 'percentage reduction of unsuccessful changes', 'percentage reduction in changes causing incidents' etc.

CSI register

(*ITIL Continual Service Improvement*) A database or structured document used to record and manage improvement opportunities throughout their lifecycle.

culture

A set of values that is shared by a group of people, including expectations about how people should behave, their ideas, beliefs and practices. *See also* vision.

customer

Someone who buys goods or services. The customer of an IT service provider is the person or group who defines and agrees the service level targets. The term is also sometimes used informally to mean user – for example, 'This is a customer-focused organization.'

customer asset

Any resource or capability of a customer. *See also* asset.

customer agreement portfolio

(*ITIL Service Strategy*) A database or structured document used to manage service contracts or agreements between an IT service provider and its customers. Each IT service delivered to a customer should have a contract or other agreement that is listed in the customer agreement portfolio. *See also* customer-facing service; service catalogue; service portfolio.

customer portfolio

(*ITIL Service Strategy*) A database or structured document used to record all customers of the IT service provider. The customer portfolio is the business relationship manager's view of the customers who receive services from the IT service provider. *See also* customer agreement portfolio; service catalogue; service portfolio.

customer-facing service

(*ITIL Service Design*) An IT service that is visible to the customer. These are normally services that support the customer's business processes and facilitate one or more outcomes desired by the customer. All live customer-facing services, including those available for deployment, are recorded in the service catalogue along with customer-visible information about deliverables, prices, contact points, ordering and request processes. Other information such as relationships to supporting services and other CIs will also be recorded for internal use by the IT service provider.

dashboard

(*ITIL Service Operation*) A graphical representation of overall IT service performance and availability. Dashboard images may be updated in real time, and can also be included in management reports and web pages. Dashboards can be used to support service level management, event management and incident diagnosis.

Data-to-Information-to-Knowledge-to-Wisdom (DIKW)

(*ITIL Service Transition*) A way of understanding the relationships between data, information, knowledge and wisdom. DIKW shows how each of these builds on the others.

definitive media library (DML)

(*ITIL Service Transition*) One or more locations in which the definitive and authorized versions of all software configuration items are securely stored. The definitive media library may also contain associated configuration items such as licences and documentation. It is a single logical storage area even if there are multiple locations. The definitive media library is controlled by service asset and configuration management and is recorded in the configuration management system.

deliverable

Something that must be provided to meet a commitment in a service level agreement or a contract. It is also used in a more informal way to mean a planned output of any process.

demand management

(*ITIL Service Design*) (*ITIL Service Strategy*) The process responsible for understanding, anticipating and influencing customer demand for services. Demand management works with capacity management to ensure that the service provider has sufficient capacity to meet the required demand. At a strategic level, demand management can involve analysis of patterns of business activity and user profiles, while at a tactical level, it can involve the use of differential charging to encourage customers to use IT services at less busy times, or require short-term activities to respond to unexpected demand or the failure of a configuration item.

Deming Cycle

See Plan-Do-Check-Act.

dependency

The direct or indirect reliance of one process or activity on another.

deployment

(*ITIL Service Transition*) The activity responsible for movement of new or changed hardware, software, documentation, process etc. to the live environment. Deployment is part of the release and deployment management process.

depreciation

(*ITIL Service Strategy*) A measure of the reduction in value of an asset over its life. This is based on wearing out, consumption or other reduction in the useful economic value.

design

(*ITIL Service Design*) An activity or process that identifies requirements and then defines a solution that is able to meet these requirements. *See also* service design.

design coordination

(*ITIL Service Design*) The process responsible for coordinating all service design activities, processes and resources. Design coordination ensures the consistent and effective design of new or changed IT services, service management information systems, architectures, technology, processes, information and metrics.

detection

(*ITIL Service Operation*) A stage in the expanded incident lifecycle. Detection results in the incident becoming known to the service provider. Detection can be automatic or the result of a user logging an incident.

development

(*ITIL Service Design*) The process responsible for creating or modifying an IT service or application ready for subsequent release and deployment. Development is also used to mean the role or function that carries out development work. This process is not described in detail within the core ITIL publications.

diagnosis

(*ITIL Service Operation*) A stage in the incident and problem lifecycles. The purpose of diagnosis is to identify a workaround for an incident or the root cause of a problem.

diagnostic script

(*ITIL Service Operation*) A structured set of questions used by service desk staff to ensure they ask the correct questions, and to help them classify, resolve and assign incidents. Diagnostic scripts may also be made available to users to help them diagnose and resolve their own incidents.

document

Information in readable form. A document may be paper or electronic – for example, a policy statement, service level agreement, incident record or diagram of a computer room layout. *See also* record.

downtime

(*ITIL Service Design*) (*ITIL Service Operation*) The time when an IT service or other configuration item is not available during its agreed service time. The availability of an IT service is often calculated from agreed service time and downtime.

driver

Something that influences strategy, objectives or requirements – for example, new legislation or the actions of competitors.

early life support (ELS)

(*ITIL Service Transition*) A stage in the service lifecycle that occurs at the end of deployment and before the service is fully accepted into operation. During early life support, the service provider reviews key performance indicators, service levels and monitoring thresholds and may implement improvements to ensure that service targets can be met. The service provider may also provide additional resources for incident and problem management during this time.

economies of scale

(*ITIL Service Strategy*) The reduction in average cost that is possible from increasing the usage of an IT service or asset. *See also* economies of scope.

economies of scope

(*ITIL Service Strategy*) The reduction in cost that is allocated to an IT service by using an existing asset for an additional purpose. For example, delivering a new IT service from an existing IT infrastructure. *See also* economies of scale.

effectiveness

(*ITIL Continual Service Improvement*) A measure of whether the objectives of a process, service or activity have been achieved. An effective process or activity is one that achieves its agreed objectives. *See also* key performance indicator.

efficiency

(*ITIL Continual Service Improvement*) A measure of whether the right amount of resource has been used to deliver a process, service or activity. An efficient process achieves its objectives with the minimum amount of time, money, people or other resources. *See also* key performance indicator.

emergency change

(*ITIL Service Transition*) A change that must be introduced as soon as possible – for example, to resolve a major incident or implement a security patch. The change management process will normally have a specific procedure for handling emergency changes. *See also* emergency change advisory board.

emergency change advisory board (ECAB)

(*ITIL Service Transition*) A subgroup of the change advisory board that makes decisions about emergency changes. Membership may be decided at the time a meeting is called, and depends on the nature of the emergency change.

enabling service

(*ITIL Service Strategy*) A service that is needed in order to deliver a core service. Enabling services may or may not be visible to the customer, but they are not offered to customers in their own right. *See also* enhancing service.

enhancing service

(*ITIL Service Strategy*) A service that is added to a core service to make it more attractive to the customer. Enhancing services are not essential to the delivery of a core service but are used to encourage customers to use the core services or to differentiate the service provider from its competitors. *See also* enabling service; excitement factor.

enterprise financial management

(*ITIL Service Strategy*) The function and processes responsible for managing the overall organization's budgeting, accounting and charging requirements. Enterprise financial management is sometimes referred to as the 'corporate' financial department. *See also* financial management for IT services.

environment

(*ITIL Service Transition*) A subset of the IT infrastructure that is used for a particular purpose – for example, live environment, test environment, build environment. Also used in the term 'physical environment' to mean the accommodation, air conditioning, power system etc. Environment is used as a generic term to mean the external conditions that influence or affect something.

error

(*ITIL Service Operation*) A design flaw or malfunction that causes a failure of one or more IT services or other configuration items. A mistake made by a person or a faulty process that impacts a configuration item is also an error.

escalation

(*ITIL Service Operation*) An activity that obtains additional resources when these are needed to meet service level targets or customer expectations. Escalation may be needed within any IT service management process, but is most commonly associated with incident management, problem management and the management of customer complaints. There are two types of escalation: functional escalation and hierarchic escalation.

eSourcing Capability Model for Client Organizations (eSCM-CL)

(*ITIL Service Strategy*) A framework to help organizations in their analysis and decision-making on service sourcing models and strategies. It was developed by Carnegie Mellon University in the US. *See also* eSourcing Capability Model for Service Providers.

eSourcing Capability Model for Service Providers (eSCM-SP)

(*ITIL Service Strategy*) A framework to help IT service providers develop their IT service management capabilities from a service sourcing perspective. It was developed by Carnegie Mellon University in the US. *See also* eSourcing Capability Model for Client Organizations.

estimation

The use of experience to provide an approximate value for a metric or cost. Estimation is also used in capacity and availability management as the cheapest and least accurate modelling method.

event

(*ITIL Service Operation*) A change of state that has significance for the management of an IT service or other configuration item. The term is also used to mean an alert or notification created by any IT service, configuration item or monitoring tool. Events typically require IT operations personnel to take actions, and often lead to incidents being logged.

event management

(*ITIL Service Operation*) The process responsible for managing events throughout their lifecycle. Event management is one of the main activities of IT operations.

excitement attribute

See excitement factor.

excitement factor

(*ITIL Service Strategy*) An attribute added to something to make it more attractive or more exciting to the customer. For example, a restaurant may provide a free drink with every meal. *See also* enhancing service.

external customer

A customer who works for a different business from the IT service provider. *See also* external service provider; internal customer.

external metric

A metric that is used to measure the delivery of IT service to a customer. External metrics are usually defined in service level agreements and reported to customers. *See also* internal metric.

external service provider

(*ITIL Service Strategy*) An IT service provider that is part of a different organization from its customer. An IT service provider may have both internal and external customers. *See also* outsourcing; Type III service provider.

facilities management

(*ITIL Service Operation*) The function responsible for managing the physical environment where the IT infrastructure is located. Facilities management includes all aspects of managing the physical environment – for example, power and cooling, building access management, and environmental monitoring.

failure

(*ITIL Service Operation*) Loss of ability to operate to specification, or to deliver the required output. The term may be used when referring to IT services, processes, activities, configuration items etc. A failure often causes an incident.

fault

See error.

fault tolerance

(*ITIL Service Design*) The ability of an IT service or other configuration item to continue to operate correctly after failure of a component part. *See also* countermeasure; resilience.

financial management

(*ITIL Service Strategy*) A generic term used to describe the function and processes responsible for managing an organization's budgeting, accounting and charging requirements. Enterprise financial management is the specific term used to describe the function and processes from the perspective of the overall organization. Financial management for IT services is the specific term used to describe the function and processes from the perspective of the IT service provider.

financial management for IT services

(*ITIL Service Strategy*) The function and processes responsible for managing an IT service provider's budgeting, accounting and charging requirements. Financial management for IT services secures an appropriate level of funding to design, develop and deliver services that meet the strategy of the organization in a cost-effective manner. *See also* enterprise financial management.

financial year

(*ITIL Service Strategy*) An accounting period covering 12 consecutive months. A financial year may start on any date (for example, 1 April to 31 March).

fit for purpose

(*ITIL Service Strategy*) The ability to meet an agreed level of utility. Fit for purpose is also used informally to describe a process, configuration item, IT service etc. that is capable of meeting its objectives or service levels. Being fit for purpose requires suitable design, implementation, control and maintenance.

fit for use

(*ITIL Service Strategy*) The ability to meet an agreed level of warranty. Being fit for use requires suitable design, implementation, control and maintenance.

fixed asset

(*ITIL Service Transition*) A tangible business asset that has a long-term useful life (for example, a building, a piece of land, a server or a software licence). *See also* service asset; configuration item.

fixed asset management

(*ITIL Service Transition*) The process responsible for tracking and reporting the value and ownership of fixed assets throughout their lifecycle. Fixed asset management maintains the asset register and is usually carried out by the overall business, rather than by the IT organization. Fixed asset management is sometimes called financial asset management and is not described in detail within the core ITIL publications.

fulfilment

Performing activities to meet a need or requirement – for example, by providing a new IT service, or meeting a service request.

function

A team or group of people and the tools or other resources they use to carry out one or more processes or activities – for example, the service desk. The term also has two other meanings:

- An intended purpose of a configuration item, person, team, process or IT service. For example, one function of an email service may be to store and forward outgoing mails, while the function of a business process may be to despatch goods to customers.
- To perform the intended purpose correctly, as in 'The computer is functioning.'

gap analysis

(*ITIL Continual Service Improvement*) An activity that compares two sets of data and identifies the differences. Gap analysis is commonly used to compare a set of requirements with actual delivery. *See also* benchmarking.

governance

Ensures that policies and strategy are actually implemented, and that required processes are correctly followed. Governance includes defining roles and responsibilities, measuring and reporting, and taking actions to resolve any issues identified.

guideline

A document describing best practice, which recommends what should be done. Compliance with a guideline is not normally enforced. *See also* standard.

high availability

(*ITIL Service Design*) An approach or design that minimizes or hides the effects of configuration item failure from the users of an IT service. High availability solutions are designed to achieve an agreed level of availability and make use of techniques such as fault tolerance, resilience and fast recovery to reduce the number and impact of incidents.

identity

(*ITIL Service Operation*) A unique name that is used to identify a user, person or role. The identity is used to grant rights to that user, person or role. Example identities might be the username SmithJ or the role 'change manager'.

impact

(*ITIL Service Operation*) (*ITIL Service Transition*) A measure of the effect of an incident, problem or change on business processes. Impact is often based on how service levels will be affected. Impact and urgency are used to assign priority.

incident

(*ITIL Service Operation*) An unplanned interruption to an IT service or reduction in the quality of an IT service. Failure of a configuration item that has not yet affected service is also an incident – for example, failure of one disk from a mirror set.

incident management

(*ITIL Service Operation*) The process responsible for managing the lifecycle of all incidents. Incident management ensures that normal service operation is restored as quickly as possible and the business impact is minimized.

incident record

(*ITIL Service Operation*) A record containing the details of an incident. Each incident record documents the lifecycle of a single incident.

indirect cost

(*ITIL Service Strategy*) The cost of providing an IT service which cannot be allocated in full to a specific customer – for example, the cost of providing shared servers or software licences. Also known as overhead. *See also* direct cost.

information security management (ISM)

(*ITIL Service Design*) The process responsible for ensuring that the confidentiality, integrity and availability of an organization's assets, information, data and IT services match the agreed needs of the business. Information security management supports business security and has a wider scope than that of the IT service provider, and includes handling of paper, building access, phone calls etc. for the entire organization. *See also* security management information system.

information security management system (ISMS)

(*ITIL Service Design*) The framework of policy, processes, functions, standards, guidelines and tools that ensures an organization can achieve its information security management objectives. *See also* security management information system.

information security policy

(*ITIL Service Design*) The policy that governs the organization's approach to information security management.

information system

See management information system.

information technology (IT)

The use of technology for the storage, communication or processing of information. The technology typically includes computers, telecommunications, applications and other software. The information may include business data, voice, images, video etc. Information technology is often used to support business processes through IT services.

infrastructure service

A type of supporting service that provides hardware, network or other data centre components. The term is also used as a synonym for supporting service.

insourcing

(*ITIL Service Strategy*) Using an internal service provider to manage IT services. The term insourcing is also used to describe the act of transferring the provision of an IT service from an external service provider to an internal service provider. *See also* service sourcing.

integrity

(*ITIL Service Design*) A security principle that ensures data and configuration items are modified only by authorized personnel and activities. Integrity considers all possible causes of modification, including software and hardware failure, environmental events, and human intervention.

internal customer

A customer who works for the same business as the IT service provider. *See also* external customer; internal service provider.

internal metric

A metric that is used within the IT service provider to monitor the efficiency, effectiveness or cost effectiveness of the IT service provider's internal processes. Internal metrics are not normally reported to the customer of the IT service. *See also* external metric.

internal rate of return (IRR)

(*ITIL Service Strategy*) A technique used to help make decisions about capital expenditure. It calculates a figure that allows two or more alternative investments to be compared. A larger internal rate of return indicates a better investment. *See also* net present value; return on investment.

internal service provider

(*ITIL Service Strategy*) An IT service provider that is part of the same organization as its customer. An IT service provider may have both internal and external customers. *See also* insourcing; Type I service provider; Type II service provider.

International Organization for Standardization (ISO)

The International Organization for Standardization (ISO) is the world's largest developer of standards. ISO is a non-governmental organization that is a network of the national standards institutes of 156 countries. See www.iso.org for further information about ISO.

International Standards Organization

See International Organization for Standardization.

invocation

(*ITIL Service Design*) Initiation of the steps defined in a plan – for example, initiating the IT service continuity plan for one or more IT services.

ISO 9000

A generic term that refers to a number of international standards and guidelines for quality management systems. See www.iso.org for more information. *See also* International Organization for Standardization.

ISO 9001

An international standard for quality management systems. *See also* ISO 9000; standard.

ISO/IEC 20000

An international standard for IT service management.

ISO/IEC 27001

(*ITIL Continual Service Improvement*) (*ITIL Service Design*) An international specification for information security management. The corresponding code of practice is ISO/IEC 27002. *See also* standard.

IT infrastructure

All of the hardware, software, networks, facilities etc. that are required to develop, test, deliver, monitor, control or support applications and IT services. The term includes all of the information technology but not the associated people, processes and documentation.

IT operations

(*ITIL Service Operation*) Activities carried out by IT operations control, including console management/operations bridge, job scheduling, backup and restore, and print and output management. IT operations is also used as a synonym for service operation.

IT operations control

(*ITIL Service Operation*) The function responsible for monitoring and control of the IT services and IT infrastructure. *See also* operations bridge.

IT operations management

(*ITIL Service Operation*) The function within an IT service provider that performs the daily activities needed to manage IT services and the supporting IT infrastructure. IT operations management includes IT operations control and facilities management.

IT service

A service provided by an IT service provider. An IT service is made up of a combination of information technology, people and processes. A customer-facing IT service directly supports the business processes of one or more customers and its service level targets should be defined in a service level agreement. Other IT services, called supporting services, are not directly used by the business but are required by the service provider to deliver customer-facing services. *See also* core service; enabling service; enhancing service; service; service package.

IT service continuity management (ITSCM)

(*ITIL Service Design*) The process responsible for managing risks that could seriously affect IT services. IT service continuity management ensures that the IT service provider can always provide minimum agreed service levels, by reducing the risk to an acceptable level and planning for the recovery of IT services. IT service continuity management supports business continuity management.

IT service continuity plan

(*ITIL Service Design*) A plan defining the steps required to recover one or more IT services. The plan also identifies the triggers for invocation, people to be involved, communications etc. The IT service continuity plan should be part of a business continuity plan.

IT service management (ITSM)

The implementation and management of quality IT services that meet the needs of the business. IT service management is performed by IT service providers through an appropriate mix of people, process and information technology. *See also* service management.

IT service provider

(*ITIL Service Strategy*) A service provider that provides IT services to internal or external customers.

ITIL

A set of best-practice publications for IT service management. Owned by the Cabinet Office (part of HM Government), ITIL gives guidance on the provision of quality IT services and the processes, functions and other capabilities needed to support them. The ITIL framework is based on a service lifecycle and consists of five lifecycle stages (service strategy, service design, service transition, service operation and continual service improvement), each of which has its own supporting publication. There is also a set of complementary ITIL publications providing guidance specific to industry sectors, organization types, operating models and technology architectures. See www.itil-officialsite.com for more information.

job description

A document that defines the roles, responsibilities, skills and knowledge required by a particular person. One job description can include multiple roles – for example, the roles of configuration manager and change manager may be carried out by one person.

key performance indicator (KPI)

(*ITIL Continual Service Improvement*) (*ITIL Service Design*) A metric that is used to help manage an IT service, process, plan, project or other activity. Key performance indicators are used to measure the achievement of critical success factors. Many metrics may be measured, but only the most important of these are defined as key performance indicators and used to actively manage and report on the process, IT service or activity. They should be selected to ensure that efficiency, effectiveness and cost effectiveness are all managed.

knowledge base

(*ITIL Service Transition*) A logical database containing data and information used by the service knowledge management system.

knowledge management

(*ITIL Service Transition*) The process responsible for sharing perspectives, ideas, experience and information, and for ensuring that these are available in the right place and at the right time. The knowledge management process enables informed decisions, and improves efficiency by reducing the need to rediscover knowledge. *See also* Data-to-Information-to-Knowledge-to-Wisdom; service knowledge management system.

known error

(*ITIL Service Operation*) A problem that has a documented root cause and a workaround. Known errors are created and managed throughout their lifecycle by problem management. Known errors may also be identified by development or suppliers.

known error database (KEDB)

(*ITIL Service Operation*) A database containing all known error records. This database is created by problem management and used by incident and problem management. The known error database may be part of the configuration management system, or may be stored elsewhere in the service knowledge management system.

known error record

(*ITIL Service Operation*) A record containing the details of a known error. Each known error record documents the lifecycle of a known error, including the status, root cause and workaround. In some implementations, a known error is documented using additional fields in a problem record.

lifecycle

The various stages in the life of an IT service, configuration item, incident, problem, change etc. The lifecycle defines the categories for status and the status transitions that are permitted. For example:

- The lifecycle of an application includes requirements, design, build, deploy, operate, optimize
- The expanded incident lifecycle includes detection, diagnosis, repair, recovery and restoration
- The lifecycle of a server may include: ordered, received, in test, live, disposed etc.

live

(*ITIL Service Transition*) Refers to an IT service or other configuration item that is being used to deliver service to a customer.

live environment

(*ITIL Service Transition*) A controlled environment containing live configuration items used to deliver IT services to customers.

maintainability

(*ITIL Service Design*) A measure of how quickly and effectively an IT service or other configuration item can be restored to normal working after a failure. Maintainability is often measured and reported as MTRS. Maintainability is also used in the context of software or IT service development to mean ability to be changed or repaired easily.

major incident

(*ITIL Service Operation*) The highest category of impact for an incident. A major incident results in significant disruption to the business.

manageability

An informal measure of how easily and effectively an IT service or other component can be managed.

management information

Information that is used to support decision making by managers. Management information is often generated automatically by tools supporting the various IT service management processes. Management information often includes the values of key performance indicators, such as 'percentage of changes leading to incidents' or 'first-time fix rate'.

management information system (MIS)

(*ITIL Service Design*) A set of tools, data and information that is used to support a process or function. Examples include the availability management information system and the supplier and contract management information system. *See also* service knowledge management system.

Management of Risk (M_o_R)

M_o_R includes all the activities required to identify and control the exposure to risk, which may have an impact on the achievement of an organization's business objectives. See www.mor-officialsite.com for more details.

management system

The framework of policy, processes, functions, standards, guidelines and tools that ensures an organization or part of an organization can achieve its objectives. This term is also used with a smaller scope to support a specific process or activity – for example, an event management system or risk management system. *See also* system.

market space

(*ITIL Service Strategy*) Opportunities that an IT service provider could exploit to meet the business needs of customers. Market spaces identify the possible IT services that an IT service provider may wish to consider delivering.

maturity

(*ITIL Continual Service Improvement*) A measure of the reliability, efficiency and effectiveness of a process, function, organization etc. The most mature processes and functions are formally aligned to business objectives and strategy, and are supported by a framework for continual improvement.

mean time to repair (MTTR)

The average time taken to repair an IT service or other configuration item after a failure. MTTR is measured from when the configuration item fails until it is repaired. MTTR does not include the time required to recover or restore. It is sometimes incorrectly used instead of mean time to restore service.

mean time to restore service (MTRS)

The average time taken to restore an IT service or other configuration item after a failure. MTRS is measured from when the configuration item fails until it is fully restored and delivering its normal functionality. *See also* maintainability; mean time to repair.

metric

(*ITIL Continual Service Improvement*) Something that is measured and reported to help manage a process, IT service or activity. *See also* key performance indicator.

mission

A short but complete description of the overall purpose and intentions of an organization. It states what is to be achieved, but not how this should be done. *See also* vision.

model

A representation of a system, process, IT service, configuration item etc. that is used to help understand or predict future behaviour.

modelling

A technique that is used to predict the future behaviour of a system, process, IT service, configuration item etc. Modelling is commonly used in financial management, capacity management and availability management.

monitoring

(*ITIL Service Operation*) Repeated observation of a configuration item, IT service or process to detect events and to ensure that the current status is known.

near-shore

(*ITIL Service Strategy*) Provision of services from a country near the country where the customer is based. This can be the provision of an IT service, or of supporting functions such as a service desk. *See also* offshore; onshore.

net present value (NPV)

(*ITIL Service Strategy*) A technique used to help make decisions about capital expenditure. It compares cash inflows with cash outflows. Positive net present value indicates that an investment is worthwhile. *See also* internal rate of return; return on investment.

normal change

(*ITIL Service Transition*) A change that is not an emergency change or a standard change. Normal changes follow the defined steps of the change management process.

objective

The outcomes required from a process, activity or organization in order to ensure that its purpose will be fulfilled. Objectives are usually expressed as measurable targets. The term is also informally used to mean a requirement.

off the shelf

See commercial off the shelf.

Office of Government Commerce (OGC)

OGC (former owner of Best Management Practice) and its functions have moved into the Cabinet Office as part of HM Government. See www. cabinetoffice.gov.uk

offshore

(*ITIL Service Strategy*) Provision of services from a location outside the country where the customer is based, often in a different continent. This can be the provision of an IT service, or of supporting functions such as a service desk. *See also* near-shore; onshore.

onshore

(*ITIL Service Strategy*) Provision of services from a location within the country where the customer is based. *See also* near-shore; offshore.

operate

To perform as expected. A process or configuration item is said to operate if it is delivering the required outputs. Operate also means to perform one or more operations. For example, to operate a computer is to do the day-to-day operations needed for it to perform as expected.

operation

(*ITIL Service Operation*) Day-to-day management of an IT service, system or other configuration item. Operation is also used to mean any predefined activity or transaction – for example, loading a magnetic tape, accepting money at a point of sale, or reading data from a disk drive.

operational

The lowest of three levels of planning and delivery (strategic, tactical, operational). Operational activities include the day-to-day or short-term planning or delivery of a business process or IT service management process. The term is also a synonym for live.

operational level agreement (OLA)

(*ITIL Continual Service Improvement*) (*ITIL Service Design*) An agreement between an IT service provider and another part of the same organization. It supports the IT service provider's delivery of IT services to customers and defines the goods or services to be provided and the responsibilities of both parties. For example, there could be an operational level agreement:

■ Between the IT service provider and a procurement department to obtain hardware in agreed times
■ Between the service desk and a support group to provide incident resolution in agreed times.

See also service level agreement.

operations bridge

(*ITIL Service Operation*) A physical location where IT services and IT infrastructure are monitored and managed.

operations control

See IT operations control.

operations management

See IT operations management.

opportunity cost

(*ITIL Service Strategy*) A cost that is used in deciding between investment choices. Opportunity cost represents the revenue that would have been generated by using the resources in a different way. For example, the opportunity cost of purchasing a new server may include not carrying out a service improvement activity that the money could have been spent on. Opportunity cost analysis is used as part of a decision-making process, but opportunity cost is not treated as an actual cost in any financial statement.

optimize

Review, plan and request changes, in order to obtain the maximum efficiency and effectiveness from a process, configuration item, application etc.

organization

A company, legal entity or other institution. The term is sometimes used to refer to any entity that has people, resources and budgets – for example, a project or business unit.

outcome

The result of carrying out an activity, following a process, or delivering an IT service etc. The term is used to refer to intended results as well as to actual results. *See also* objective.

outsourcing

(*ITIL Service Strategy*) Using an external service provider to manage IT services. *See also* service sourcing.

overhead

See indirect cost.

Pareto principle

(*ITIL Service Operation*) A technique used to prioritize activities. The Pareto principle says that 80% of the value of any activity is created with 20% of the effort. Pareto analysis is also used in problem management to prioritize possible problem causes for investigation.

partnership

A relationship between two organizations that involves working closely together for common goals or mutual benefit. The IT service provider should have a partnership with the business and with third parties who are critical to the delivery of IT services. *See also* value network.

pattern of business activity (PBA)

(*ITIL Service Strategy*) A workload profile of one or more business activities. Patterns of business activity are used to help the IT service provider understand and plan for different levels of business activity. *See also* user profile.

performance

A measure of what is achieved or delivered by a system, person, team, process or IT service.

performance management

Activities to ensure that something achieves its expected outcomes in an efficient and consistent manner.

pilot

(*ITIL Service Transition*) A limited deployment of an IT service, a release or a process to the live environment. A pilot is used to reduce risk and to gain user feedback and acceptance. *See also* change evaluation; test.

plan

A detailed proposal that describes the activities and resources needed to achieve an objective – for example, a plan to implement a new IT service or process. ISO/IEC 20000 requires a plan for the management of each IT service management process.

Plan-Do-Check-Act (PDCA)

(*ITIL Continual Service Improvement*) A four-stage cycle for process management, attributed to Edward Deming. Plan-Do-Check-Act is also called the Deming Cycle. **Plan** – design or revise processes that support the IT services; **Do** – implement the plan and manage the processes; **Check** – measure the processes and IT services, compare with objectives and produce reports; **Act** – plan and implement changes to improve the processes.

planned downtime

(*ITIL Service Design*) Agreed time when an IT service will not be available. Planned downtime is often used for maintenance, upgrades and testing. *See also* change window; downtime.

planning

An activity responsible for creating one or more plans – for example, capacity planning.

policy

Formally documented management expectations and intentions. Policies are used to direct decisions, and to ensure consistent and appropriate development and implementation of processes, standards, roles, activities, IT infrastructure etc.

post-implementation review (PIR)

A review that takes place after a change or a project has been implemented. It determines if the change or project was successful, and identifies opportunities for improvement.

practice

A way of working, or a way in which work must be done. Practices can include activities, processes, functions, standards and guidelines. *See also* best practice.

PRINCE2

See PRojects IN Controlled Environments.

priority

(*ITIL Service Operation*) (*ITIL Service Transition*) A category used to identify the relative importance of an incident, problem or change. Priority is based on impact and urgency, and is used to identify required times for actions to be taken. For example, the service level agreement may state that Priority 2 incidents must be resolved within 12 hours.

problem

(*ITIL Service Operation*) A cause of one or more incidents. The cause is not usually known at the time a problem record is created, and the problem management process is responsible for further investigation.

problem management

(*ITIL Service Operation*) The process responsible for managing the lifecycle of all problems. Problem management proactively prevents incidents from happening and minimizes the impact of incidents that cannot be prevented.

problem record

(*ITIL Service Operation*) A record containing the details of a problem. Each problem record documents the lifecycle of a single problem.

procedure

A document containing steps that specify how to achieve an activity. Procedures are defined as part of processes. *See also* work instruction.

process

A structured set of activities designed to accomplish a specific objective. A process takes one or more defined inputs and turns them into defined outputs. It may include any of the roles, responsibilities, tools and management controls required to reliably deliver the outputs. A process may define policies, standards, guidelines, activities and work instructions if they are needed.

process control

The activity of planning and regulating a process, with the objective of performing the process in an effective, efficient and consistent manner.

process manager

A role responsible for the operational management of a process. The process manager's responsibilities include planning and coordination of all activities required to carry out, monitor and report on the process. There may be several process managers for one process – for example, regional change managers or IT service continuity managers for each data centre. The process manager role is often assigned to the person who carries out the process owner role, but the two roles may be separate in larger organizations.

process owner

The person who is held accountable for ensuring that a process is fit for purpose. The process owner's responsibilities include sponsorship, design, change management and continual improvement of the process and its metrics. This role can be assigned to the same person who carries out the process manager role, but the two roles may be separate in larger organizations.

production environment

See live environment.

programme

A number of projects and activities that are planned and managed together to achieve an overall set of related objectives and other outcomes.

project

A temporary organization, with people and other assets, that is required to achieve an objective or other outcome. Each project has a lifecycle that typically includes initiation, planning, execution, and closure. Projects are usually managed using a formal methodology such as PRojects IN Controlled Environments (PRINCE2) or the Project Management Body of Knowledge (PMBOK). *See also* charter; project management office; project portfolio.

Project Management Body of Knowledge (PMBOK)

A project management standard maintained and published by the Project Management Institute. See www.pmi.org for more information. *See also* PRojects IN Controlled Environments (PRINCE2).

Project Management Institute (PMI)

A membership association that advances the project management profession through globally recognized standards and certifications, collaborative communities, an extensive research programme, and professional development opportunities. PMI is a not-for-profit membership organization with representation in many countries around the world. PMI maintains and publishes the Project Management Body of Knowledge (PMBOK). See www.pmi.org for more information. *See also* PRojects IN Controlled Environments (PRINCE2).

project management office (PMO)

(*ITIL Service Design*) (*ITIL Service Strategy*) A function or group responsible for managing the lifecycle of projects. *See also* charter; project portfolio.

project portfolio

(*ITIL Service Design*) (*ITIL Service Strategy*) A database or structured document used to manage projects throughout their lifecycle. The project portfolio is used to coordinate projects and ensure that they meet their objectives in a cost-effective and timely manner. In larger organizations, the project portfolio is typically defined and maintained by a project management office. The project portfolio is important to service portfolio management as new services and significant changes are normally managed as projects. *See also* charter.

projected service outage (PSO)

(*ITIL Service Transition*) A document that identifies the effect of planned changes, maintenance activities and test plans on agreed service levels.

PRojects IN Controlled Environments (PRINCE2)

The standard UK government methodology for project management. See www.prince-officialsite.com for more information. *See also* Project Management Body of Knowledge (PMBOK).

qualification

(*ITIL Service Transition*) An activity that ensures that the IT infrastructure is appropriate and correctly configured to support an application or IT service. *See also* validation.

quality

The ability of a product, service or process to provide the intended value. For example, a hardware component can be considered to be of high quality if it performs as expected and delivers the required reliability. Process quality also requires an ability to monitor effectiveness and efficiency, and to improve them if necessary. *See also* quality management system.

quality assurance (QA)

(*ITIL Service Transition*) The process responsible for ensuring that the quality of a service, process or other service asset will provide its intended value. Quality assurance is also used to refer to a function or team that performs quality assurance. This process is not described in detail within the core ITIL publications. *See also* service validation and testing.

quality management system (QMS)

(*ITIL Continual Service Improvement*) The framework of policy, processes, functions, standards, guidelines and tools that ensures an organization is of a suitable quality to reliably meet business objectives or service levels. *See also* ISO 9000.

quick win

(*ITIL Continual Service Improvement*) An improvement activity that is expected to provide a return on investment in a short period of time with relatively small cost and effort. *See also* Pareto principle.

RACI

(*ITIL Service Design*) A model used to help define roles and responsibilities. RACI stands for responsible, accountable, consulted and informed.

record

A document containing the results or other output from a process or activity. Records are evidence of the fact that an activity took place and may be paper or electronic – for example, an audit report, an incident record or the minutes of a meeting.

recovery

(*ITIL Service Design*) (*ITIL Service Operation*) Returning a configuration item or an IT service to a working state. Recovery of an IT service often includes recovering data to a known consistent state. After recovery, further steps may be needed before the IT service can be made available to the users (restoration).

redundancy

(*ITIL Service Design*) Use of one or more additional configuration items to provide fault tolerance. The term also has a generic meaning of obsolescence, or no longer needed.

relationship

A connection or interaction between two people or things. In business relationship management, it is the interaction between the IT service provider and the business. In service asset and configuration management, it is a link between two configuration items that identifies a dependency or connection between them. For example, applications may be linked to the servers they run on, and IT services have many links to all the configuration items that contribute to that IT service.

release

(*ITIL Service Transition*) One or more changes to an IT service that are built, tested and deployed together. A single release may include changes to hardware, software, documentation, processes and other components.

release and deployment management

(*ITIL Service Transition*) The process responsible for planning, scheduling and controlling the build, test and deployment of releases, and for delivering new functionality required by the business while protecting the integrity of existing services.

release identification

(*ITIL Service Transition*) A naming convention used to uniquely identify a release. The release identification typically includes a reference to the configuration item and a version number – for example, Microsoft Office 2010 SR2.

release package

(*ITIL Service Transition*) A set of configuration items that will be built, tested and deployed together as a single release. Each release package will usually include one or more release units.

release record

(*ITIL Service Transition*) A record that defines the content of a release. A release record has relationships with all configuration items that are affected by the release. Release records may be in the configuration management system or elsewhere in the service knowledge management system.

release unit

(*ITIL Service Transition*) Components of an IT service that are normally released together. A release unit typically includes sufficient components to perform a useful function. For example, one release unit could be a desktop PC, including hardware, software, licences, documentation etc. A different release unit may be the complete payroll application, including IT operations procedures and user training.

release window

See change window.

reliability

(*ITIL Continual Service Improvement*) (*ITIL Service Design*) A measure of how long an IT service or other configuration item can perform its agreed function without interruption. Usually measured as MTBF or MTBSI. The term can also be used to state how likely it is that a process, function etc. will deliver its required outputs. *See also* availability.

remediation

(*ITIL Service Transition*) Actions taken to recover after a failed change or release. Remediation may include back-out, invocation of service continuity plans, or other actions designed to enable the business process to continue.

repair

(*ITIL Service Operation*) The replacement or correction of a failed configuration item.

request for change (RFC)

(*ITIL Service Transition*) A formal proposal for a change to be made. It includes details of the proposed change, and may be recorded on paper or electronically. The term is often misused to mean a change record, or the change itself.

request fulfilment

(*ITIL Service Operation*) The process responsible for managing the lifecycle of all service requests.

requirement

(*ITIL Service Design*) A formal statement of what is needed – for example, a service level requirement, a project requirement or the required deliverables for a process. *See also* statement of requirements.

resilience

(*ITIL Service Design*) The ability of an IT service or other configuration item to resist failure or to recover in a timely manner following a failure. For example, an armoured cable will resist failure when put under stress. *See also* fault tolerance.

resolution

(*ITIL Service Operation*) Action taken to repair the root cause of an incident or problem, or to implement a workaround. In ISO/IEC 20000, resolution processes is the process group that includes incident and problem management.

resource

(*ITIL Service Strategy*) A generic term that includes IT infrastructure, people, money or anything else that might help to deliver an IT service. Resources are considered to be assets of an organization. *See also* capability; service asset.

responsiveness

A measurement of the time taken to respond to something. This could be response time of a transaction, or the speed with which an IT service provider responds to an incident or request for change etc.

restore

(*ITIL Service Operation*) Taking action to return an IT service to the users after repair and recovery from an incident. This is the primary objective of incident management.

retire

(*ITIL Service Transition*) Permanent removal of an IT service, or other configuration item, from the live environment. Being retired is a stage in the lifecycle of many configuration items.

return on investment (ROI)

(*ITIL Continual Service Improvement*) (*ITIL Service Strategy*) A measurement of the expected benefit of an investment. In the simplest sense, it is the net profit of an investment divided by the net worth of the assets invested. *See also* net present value; value on investment.

return to normal

(*ITIL Service Design*) The phase of an IT service continuity plan during which full normal operations are resumed. For example, if an alternative data centre has been in use, then this phase will bring the primary data centre back into operation, and restore the ability to invoke IT service continuity plans again.

review

An evaluation of a change, problem, process, project etc. Reviews are typically carried out at predefined points in the lifecycle, and especially after closure. The purpose of a review is to ensure that all deliverables have been provided, and to identify opportunities for improvement. *See also* change evaluation; post-implementation review.

rights

(*ITIL Service Operation*) Entitlements, or permissions, granted to a user or role – for example, the right to modify particular data, or to authorize a change.

risk

A possible event that could cause harm or loss, or affect the ability to achieve objectives. A risk is measured by the probability of a threat, the vulnerability of the asset to that threat, and the impact it would have if it occurred. Risk can also be defined as uncertainty of outcome, and can be used in the context of measuring the probability of positive outcomes as well as negative outcomes.

risk assessment

The initial steps of risk management: analysing the value of assets to the business, identifying threats to those assets, and evaluating how vulnerable each asset is to those threats. Risk assessment can be quantitative (based on numerical data) or qualitative.

risk management

The process responsible for identifying, assessing and controlling risks. Risk management is also sometimes used to refer to the second part of the overall process after risks have been identified and assessed, as in 'risk assessment and management'. This process is not described in detail within the core ITIL publications. *See also* risk assessment.

role

A set of responsibilities, activities and authorities assigned to a person or team. A role is defined in a process or function. One person or team may have multiple roles – for example, the roles of configuration manager and change manager may be carried out by a single person. Role is also used to describe the purpose of something or what it is used for.

root cause

(*ITIL Service Operation*) The underlying or original cause of an incident or problem.

root cause analysis (RCA)

(*ITIL Service Operation*) An activity that identifies the root cause of an incident or problem. Root cause analysis typically concentrates on IT infrastructure failures. *See also* service failure analysis.

Sarbanes-Oxley (SOX)

US law that regulates financial practice and corporate governance.

scalability

The ability of an IT service, process, configuration item etc. to perform its agreed function when the workload or scope changes.

scope

The boundary or extent to which a process, procedure, certification, contract etc. applies. For example, the scope of change management may include all live IT services and related configuration items; the scope of an ISO/IEC 20000 certificate may include all IT services delivered out of a named data centre.

second-line support

(*ITIL Service Operation*) The second level in a hierarchy of support groups involved in the resolution of incidents and investigation of problems. Each level contains more specialist skills, or has more time or other resources.

security

See information security management.

security management

See information security management.

security management information system (SMIS)

(*ITIL Service Design*) A set of tools, data and information that is used to support information security management. The security management information system is part of the information security management system. *See also* service knowledge management system.

security policy

See information security policy.

server

(*ITIL Service Operation*) A computer that is connected to a network and provides software functions that are used by other computers.

service

A means of delivering value to customers by facilitating outcomes customers want to achieve without the ownership of specific costs and risks. The term 'service' is sometimes used as a synonym for core service, IT service or service package. *See also* utility; warranty.

service acceptance criteria (SAC)

(*ITIL Service Transition*) A set of criteria used to ensure that an IT service meets its functionality and quality requirements and that the IT service provider is ready to operate the new IT service when it has been deployed. *See also* acceptance.

service asset

Any resource or capability of a service provider. *See also* asset.

service asset and configuration management (SACM)

(*ITIL Service Transition*) The process responsible for ensuring that the assets required to deliver services are properly controlled, and that accurate and reliable information about those assets is available when and where it is needed. This information includes details of how the assets have been configured and the relationships between assets. *See also* configuration management system.

service capacity management (SCM)

(*ITIL Continual Service Improvement*) (*ITIL Service Design*) The sub-process of capacity management responsible for understanding the performance and capacity of IT services. Information on the resources used by each IT service and the pattern of usage over time are collected, recorded and analysed for use in the capacity plan. *See also* business capacity management; component capacity management.

service catalogue

(*ITIL Service Design*) (*ITIL Service Strategy*) A database or structured document with information about all live IT services, including those available for deployment. The service catalogue is part of the service portfolio and contains information about two types of IT service: customer-facing services that are visible to the business; and supporting services required by the service provider to deliver customer-facing services. *See also* customer agreement portfolio; service catalogue management.

service catalogue management

(*ITIL Service Design*) The process responsible for providing and maintaining the service catalogue and for ensuring that it is available to those who are authorized to access it.

service change

See change.

service charter

(*ITIL Service Design*) (*ITIL Service Strategy*) A document that contains details of a new or changed service. New service introductions and significant service changes are documented in a charter and authorized by service portfolio management. Service charters are passed to the service design lifecycle stage where a new or modified service design package will be created. The term charter is also used to describe the act of authorizing the work required by each stage of the service lifecycle with respect to the new or changed service. *See also* change proposal; service portfolio; service catalogue.

service continuity management

See IT service continuity management.

service contract

(*ITIL Service Strategy*) A contract to deliver one or more IT services. The term is also used to mean any agreement to deliver IT services, whether this is a legal contract or a service level agreement. *See also* customer agreement portfolio.

service culture

A customer-oriented culture. The major objectives of a service culture are customer satisfaction and helping customers to achieve their business objectives.

service design

(*ITIL Service Design*) A stage in the lifecycle of a service. Service design includes the design of the services, governing practices, processes and policies required to realize the service provider's strategy and to facilitate the introduction of services into supported environments. Service design includes the following processes: design coordination, service catalogue management, service level management, availability management, capacity management, IT service continuity management, information security management, and supplier management. Although these processes are associated with service design, most processes have activities that take place across multiple stages of the service lifecycle. *See also* design.

service design package (SDP)

(*ITIL Service Design*) Document(s) defining all aspects of an IT service and its requirements through each stage of its lifecycle. A service design package is produced for each new IT service, major change or IT service retirement.

service desk

(*ITIL Service Operation*) The single point of contact between the service provider and the users. A typical service desk manages incidents and service requests, and also handles communication with the users.

service failure analysis (SFA)

(*ITIL Service Design*) A technique that identifies underlying causes of one or more IT service interruptions. Service failure analysis identifies opportunities to improve the IT service provider's processes and tools, and not just the IT infrastructure. It is a time-constrained, project-like activity, rather than an ongoing process of analysis.

service hours

(*ITIL Service Design*) An agreed time period when a particular IT service should be available. For example, 'Monday–Friday 08:00 to 17:00 except public holidays'. Service hours should be defined in a service level agreement.

service improvement plan (SIP)

(*ITIL Continual Service Improvement*) A formal plan to implement improvements to a process or IT service.

service knowledge management system (SKMS)

(*ITIL Service Transition*) A set of tools and databases that is used to manage knowledge, information and data. The service knowledge management system includes the configuration management system, as well as other databases and information systems. The service knowledge management system includes tools for collecting, storing, managing, updating, analysing and presenting all the knowledge, information and data that an IT service provider will need to manage the full lifecycle of IT services. *See also* knowledge management.

service level

Measured and reported achievement against one or more service level targets. The term is sometimes used informally to mean service level target.

service level agreement (SLA)

(*ITIL Continual Service Improvement*) (*ITIL Service Design*) An agreement between an IT service provider and a customer. A service level agreement describes the IT service, documents service level targets, and specifies the responsibilities of the IT service provider and the customer. A single agreement may cover multiple IT services or multiple customers. *See also* operational level agreement.

service level management (SLM)

(*ITIL Service Design*) The process responsible for negotiating achievable service level agreements and ensuring that these are met. It is responsible for ensuring that all IT service management processes, operational level agreements and underpinning contracts are appropriate for the agreed service level targets. Service level management monitors and reports on service levels, holds regular service reviews with customers, and identifies required improvements.

service level package (SLP)

See service option.

service level requirement (SLR)

(*ITIL Continual Service Improvement*) (*ITIL Service Design*) A customer requirement for an aspect of an IT service. Service level requirements are based on business objectives and used to negotiate agreed service level targets.

service level target

(*ITIL Continual Service Improvement*) (*ITIL Service Design*) A commitment that is documented in a service level agreement. Service level targets are based on service level requirements, and are needed to ensure that the IT service is able to meet business objectives. They should be SMART, and are usually based on key performance indicators.

service lifecycle

An approach to IT service management that emphasizes the importance of coordination and control across the various functions, processes and systems necessary to manage the full lifecycle of IT services. The service lifecycle approach considers the strategy, design, transition, operation and continual improvement of IT services. Also known as service management lifecycle.

service management

A set of specialized organizational capabilities for providing value to customers in the form of services.

service manager

A generic term for any manager within the service provider. Most commonly used to refer to a business relationship manager, a process manager or a senior manager with responsibility for IT services overall.

service model

(*ITIL Service Strategy*) A model that shows how service assets interact with customer assets to create value. Service models describe the structure of a service (how the configuration items fit together) and the dynamics of the service (activities, flow of resources and interactions). A service model can be used as a template or blueprint for multiple services.

service operation

(*ITIL Service Operation*) A stage in the lifecycle of a service. Service operation coordinates and carries out the activities and processes required to deliver and manage services at agreed levels to business users and customers. Service operation also manages the technology that is used to deliver and support services. Service operation includes the following processes: event management, incident management, request fulfilment, problem management, and access management. Service operation also includes the following functions: service desk, technical management, IT operations management, and application management. Although these processes and functions are associated with service operation, most processes and functions have activities that take place across multiple stages of the service lifecycle. *See also* operation.

service option

(*ITIL Service Design*) (*ITIL Service Strategy*) A choice of utility and warranty offered to customers by a core service or service package. Service options are sometimes referred to as service level packages.

service owner

(*ITIL Service Strategy*) A role responsible for managing one or more services throughout their entire lifecycle. Service owners are instrumental in the development of service strategy and are responsible for the content of the service portfolio. *See also* business relationship management.

service package

(*ITIL Service Strategy*) Two or more services that have been combined to offer a solution to a specific type of customer need or to underpin specific business outcomes. A service package can consist of a combination of core services, enabling services and enhancing services. A service package provides a specific level of utility and warranty. Customers may be offered a choice of utility and warranty through one or more service options. *See also* IT service.

service pipeline

(*ITIL Service Strategy*) A database or structured document listing all IT services that are under consideration or development, but are not yet available to customers. The service pipeline provides a business view of possible future IT services and is part of the service portfolio that is not normally published to customers.

service portfolio

(*ITIL Service Strategy*) The complete set of services that is managed by a service provider. The service portfolio is used to manage the entire lifecycle of all services, and includes three categories: service pipeline (proposed or in development), service catalogue (live or available for deployment), and retired services. *See also* customer agreement portfolio; service portfolio management.

service portfolio management (SPM)

(*ITIL Service Strategy*) The process responsible for managing the service portfolio. Service portfolio management ensures that the service provider has the right mix of services to meet required business outcomes at an appropriate level of investment. Service portfolio management considers services in terms of the business value that they provide.

service provider

(*ITIL Service Strategy*) An organization supplying services to one or more internal customers or external customers. Service provider is often used as an abbreviation for IT service provider. *See also* Type I service provider; Type II service provider; Type III service provider.

service provider interface (SPI)

(*ITIL Service Strategy*) An interface between the IT service provider and a user, customer, business process or supplier. Analysis of service provider interfaces helps to coordinate end-to-end management of IT services.

service reporting

(*ITIL Continual Service Improvement*) Activities that produce and deliver reports of achievement and trends against service levels. The format, content and frequency of reports should be agreed with customers.

service request

(*ITIL Service Operation*) A formal request from a user for something to be provided – for example, a request for information or advice; to reset a password; or to install a workstation for a new user. Service requests are managed by the request fulfilment process, usually in conjunction with the service desk. Service requests may be linked to a request for change as part of fulfilling the request.

service sourcing

(*ITIL Service Strategy*) The strategy and approach for deciding whether to provide a service internally, to outsource it to an external service provider, or to combine the two approaches. Service sourcing also means the execution of this strategy. *See also* insourcing; internal service provider; outsourcing.

service strategy

(*ITIL Service Strategy*) A stage in the lifecycle of a service. Service strategy defines the perspective, position, plans and patterns that a service provider needs to execute to meet an organization's business outcomes. Service strategy includes the following processes: strategy management for IT services, service portfolio management, financial management for IT services, demand management, and business relationship management. Although these processes are associated with service strategy, most processes have activities that take place across multiple stages of the service lifecycle.

service transition

(*ITIL Service Transition*) A stage in the lifecycle of a service. Service transition ensures that new, modified or retired services meet the expectations of the business as documented in the service strategy and service design stages of the lifecycle. Service transition includes the following processes: transition planning and support, change management, service asset and configuration management, release and deployment management, service validation and testing, change evaluation, and knowledge management. Although these processes are associated with service transition, most processes have activities that take place across multiple stages of the service lifecycle. *See also* transition.

service validation and testing

(*ITIL Service Transition*) The process responsible for validation and testing of a new or changed IT service. Service validation and testing ensures that the IT service matches its design specification and will meet the needs of the business.

seven-step improvement process

(*ITIL Continual Service Improvement*) The process responsible for defining and managing the steps needed to identify, define, gather, process, analyse, present and implement improvements. The performance of the IT service provider is continually measured by this process and improvements are made to processes, IT services and IT infrastructure in order to increase efficiency, effectiveness and cost effectiveness. Opportunities for improvement are recorded and managed in the CSI register.

shared service unit

See Type II service provider.

shift

(*ITIL Service Operation*) A group or team of people who carry out a specific role for a fixed period of time. For example, there could be four shifts of IT operations control personnel to support an IT service that is used 24 hours a day.

single point of contact

(*ITIL Service Operation*) Providing a single consistent way to communicate with an organization or business unit. For example, a single point of contact for an IT service provider is usually called a service desk.

SMART

(*ITIL Continual Service Improvement*) (*ITIL Service Design*) An acronym for helping to remember that targets in service level agreements and project plans should be specific, measurable, achievable, relevant and time-bound.

snapshot

(*ITIL Continual Service Improvement*) (*ITIL Service Transition*) The current state of a configuration item, process or any other set of data recorded at a specific point in time. Snapshots can be captured by discovery tools or by manual techniques such as an assessment. *See also* baseline; benchmark.

software asset management (SAM)

(*ITIL Service Transition*) The process responsible for tracking and reporting the use and ownership of software assets throughout their lifecycle. Software asset management is part of an overall service asset and configuration management process. This process is not described in detail within the core ITIL publications.

source

See service sourcing.

specification

A formal definition of requirements. A specification may be used to define technical or operational requirements, and may be internal or external. Many public standards consist of a code of practice and a specification. The specification defines the standard against which an organization can be audited.

stakeholder

A person who has an interest in an organization, project, IT service etc. Stakeholders may be interested in the activities, targets, resources or deliverables. Stakeholders may include customers, partners, employees, shareholders, owners etc. *See also* RACI.

standard

A mandatory requirement. Examples include ISO/IEC 20000 (an international standard), an internal security standard for Unix configuration, or a government standard for how financial records should be maintained. The term is also used to refer to a code of practice or specification published by a standards organization such as ISO or BSI. *See also* guideline.

standard change

(*ITIL Service Transition*) A pre-authorized change that is low risk, relatively common and follows a procedure or work instruction – for example, a password reset or provision of standard equipment to a new employee. Requests for change are not required to implement a standard change, and they are logged and tracked using a different mechanism, such as a service request. *See also* change model.

statement of requirements (SOR)

(*ITIL Service Design*) A document containing all requirements for a product purchase, or a new or changed IT service. *See also* terms of reference.

status

The name of a required field in many types of record. It shows the current stage in the lifecycle of the associated configuration item, incident, problem etc.

status accounting

(*ITIL Service Transition*) The activity responsible for recording and reporting the lifecycle of each configuration item.

strategic

(*ITIL Service Strategy*) The highest of three levels of planning and delivery (strategic, tactical, operational). Strategic activities include objective setting and long-term planning to achieve the overall vision.

strategic asset

(*ITIL Service Strategy*) Any asset that provides the basis for core competence, distinctive performance or sustainable competitive advantage, or which allows a business unit to participate in business opportunities. Part of service strategy is to identify how IT can be viewed as a strategic asset rather than an internal administrative function.

strategy

(*ITIL Service Strategy*) A strategic plan designed to achieve defined objectives.

strategy management for IT services

(*ITIL Service Strategy*) The process responsible for defining and maintaining an organization's perspective, position, plans and patterns with regard to its services and the management of those services. Once the strategy has been defined, strategy management for IT services is also responsible for ensuring that it achieves its intended business outcomes.

supplier

(*ITIL Service Design*) (*ITIL Service Strategy*) A third party responsible for supplying goods or services that are required to deliver IT services. Examples of suppliers include commodity hardware and software vendors, network and telecom providers, and outsourcing organizations. *See also* supply chain; underpinning contract.

supplier and contract management information system (SCMIS)

(*ITIL Service Design*) A set of tools, data and information that is used to support supplier management. *See also* service knowledge management system.

supplier management

(*ITIL Service Design*) The process responsible for obtaining value for money from suppliers, ensuring that all contracts and agreements with suppliers support the needs of the business, and that all suppliers meet their contractual commitments. *See also* supplier and contract management information system.

supply chain

(*ITIL Service Strategy*) The activities in a value chain carried out by suppliers. A supply chain typically involves multiple suppliers, each adding value to the product or service. *See also* value network.

support group

(*ITIL Service Operation*) A group of people with technical skills. Support groups provide the technical support needed by all of the IT service management processes. *See also* technical management.

supporting service

(*ITIL Service Design*) An IT service that is not directly used by the business, but is required by the IT service provider to deliver customer-facing services (for example, a directory service or a backup service). Supporting services may also include IT services only used by the IT service provider. All live supporting services, including those available for deployment, are recorded in the service catalogue along with information about their relationships to customer-facing services and other CIs.

system

A number of related things that work together to achieve an overall objective. For example:

- A computer system including hardware, software and applications
- A management system, including the framework of policy, processes, functions, standards, guidelines and tools that are planned and managed together – for example, a quality management system
- A database management system or operating system that includes many software modules which are designed to perform a set of related functions.

tactical

The middle of three levels of planning and delivery (strategic, tactical, operational). Tactical activities include the medium-term plans required to achieve specific objectives, typically over a period of weeks to months.

technical management

(*ITIL Service Operation*) The function responsible for providing technical skills in support of IT services and management of the IT infrastructure. Technical management defines the roles of support groups, as well as the tools, processes and procedures required.

technical support

See technical management.

terms of reference (TOR)

(*ITIL Service Design*) A document specifying the requirements, scope, deliverables, resources and schedule for a project or activity.

test

(*ITIL Service Transition*) An activity that verifies that a configuration item, IT service, process etc. meets its specification or agreed requirements. *See also* acceptance; service validation and testing.

test environment

(*ITIL Service Transition*) A controlled environment used to test configuration items, releases, IT services, processes etc.

third party

A person, organization or other entity that is not part of the service provider's own organization and is not a customer – for example, a software supplier or a hardware maintenance company. Requirements for third parties are typically specified in contracts that underpin service level agreements. *See also* underpinning contract.

third-line support

(*ITIL Service Operation*) The third level in a hierarchy of support groups involved in the resolution of incidents and investigation of problems. Each level contains more specialist skills, or has more time or other resources.

threat

A threat is anything that might exploit a vulnerability. Any potential cause of an incident can be considered a threat. For example, a fire is a threat that could exploit the vulnerability of flammable floor coverings. This term is commonly used in information security management and IT service continuity management, but also applies to other areas such as problem and availability management.

threshold

The value of a metric that should cause an alert to be generated or management action to be taken. For example, 'Priority 1 incident not solved within four hours', 'More than five soft disk errors in an hour', or 'More than 10 failed changes in a month'.

throughput

(*ITIL Service Design*) A measure of the number of transactions or other operations performed in a fixed time – for example, 5,000 e-mails sent per hour, or 200 disk I/Os per second.

total cost of ownership (TCO)

(*ITIL Service Strategy*) A methodology used to help make investment decisions. It assesses the full lifecycle cost of owning a configuration item, not just the initial cost or purchase price. *See also* total cost of utilization.

total cost of utilization (TCU)

(*ITIL Service Strategy*) A methodology used to help make investment and service sourcing decisions. Total cost of utilization assesses the full lifecycle cost to the customer of using an IT service. *See also* total cost of ownership.

total quality management (TQM)

(*ITIL Continual Service Improvement*) A methodology for managing continual improvement by using a quality management system. Total quality management establishes a culture involving all people in the organization in a process of continual monitoring and improvement.

transaction

A discrete function performed by an IT service – for example, transferring money from one bank account to another. A single transaction may involve numerous additions, deletions and modifications of data. Either all of these are completed successfully or none of them is carried out.

transition

(*ITIL Service Transition*) A change in state, corresponding to a movement of an IT service or other configuration item from one lifecycle status to the next.

transition planning and support

(*ITIL Service Transition*) The process responsible for planning all service transition processes and coordinating the resources that they require.

trend analysis

(*ITIL Continual Service Improvement*) Analysis of data to identify time-related patterns. Trend analysis is used in problem management to identify common failures or fragile configuration items, and in capacity management as a modelling tool to predict future behaviour. It is also used as a management tool for identifying deficiencies in IT service management processes.

tuning

The activity responsible for planning changes to make the most efficient use of resources. Tuning is most commonly used in the context of IT services and components. Tuning is part of capacity management, which also includes performance monitoring and implementation of the required changes. Tuning is also called optimization, particularly in the context of processes and other non-technical resources.

Type I service provider

(*ITIL Service Strategy*) An internal service provider that is embedded within a business unit. There may be several Type I service providers within an organization.

Type II service provider

(*ITIL Service Strategy*) An internal service provider that provides shared IT services to more than one business unit. Type II service providers are also known as shared service units.

Type III service provider

(*ITIL Service Strategy*) A service provider that provides IT services to external customers.

underpinning contract (UC)

(*ITIL Service Design*) A contract between an IT service provider and a third party. The third party provides goods or services that support delivery of an IT service to a customer. The underpinning contract defines targets and responsibilities that are required to meet agreed service level targets in one or more service level agreements.

unit cost

(*ITIL Service Strategy*) The cost to the IT service provider of providing a single component of an IT service. For example, the cost of a single desktop PC, or of a single transaction.

urgency

(*ITIL Service Design*) (*ITIL Service Transition*) A measure of how long it will be until an incident, problem or change has a significant impact on the business. For example, a high-impact incident may have low urgency if the impact will not affect the business until the end of the financial year. Impact and urgency are used to assign priority.

usability

(*ITIL Service Design*) The ease with which an application, product or IT service can be used. Usability requirements are often included in a statement of requirements.

use case

(*ITIL Service Design*) A technique used to define required functionality and objectives, and to design tests. Use cases define realistic scenarios that describe interactions between users and an IT service or other system.

user

A person who uses the IT service on a day-to-day basis. Users are distinct from customers, as some customers do not use the IT service directly.

user profile (UP)

(*ITIL Service Strategy*) A pattern of user demand for IT services. Each user profile includes one or more patterns of business activity.

utility

(*ITIL Service Strategy*) The functionality offered by a product or service to meet a particular need. Utility can be summarized as 'what the service does', and can be used to determine whether a service is able to meet its required outcomes, or is 'fit for purpose'. The business value of an IT service is created by the combination of utility and warranty. *See also* service validation and testing.

validation

(*ITIL Service Transition*) An activity that ensures a new or changed IT service, process, plan or other deliverable meets the needs of the business. Validation ensures that business requirements are met even though these may have changed since the original design. *See also* acceptance; qualification; service validation and testing; verification.

value chain

(*ITIL Service Strategy*) A sequence of processes that creates a product or service that is of value to a customer. Each step of the sequence builds on the previous steps and contributes to the overall product or service. *See also* value network.

value for money

An informal measure of cost effectiveness. Value for money is often based on a comparison with the cost of alternatives. *See also* cost benefit analysis.

value network

(*ITIL Service Strategy*) A complex set of relationships between two or more groups or organizations. Value is generated through exchange of knowledge, information, goods or services. *See also* partnership; value chain.

value on investment (VOI)

(*ITIL Continual Service Improvement*) A measurement of the expected benefit of an investment. Value on investment considers both financial and intangible benefits. *See also* return on investment.

variance

The difference between a planned value and the actual measured value. Commonly used in financial management, capacity management and service level management, but could apply in any area where plans are in place.

verification

(*ITIL Service Transition*) An activity that ensures that a new or changed IT service, process, plan or other deliverable is complete, accurate, reliable and matches its design specification. *See also* acceptance; validation; service validation and testing.

verification and audit

(*ITIL Service Transition*) The activities responsible for ensuring that information in the configuration management system is accurate and that all configuration items have been identified and recorded. Verification includes routine checks that are part of other processes – for example, verifying the serial number of a desktop PC when a user logs an incident. Audit is a periodic, formal check.

version

(*ITIL Service Transition*) A version is used to identify a specific baseline of a configuration item. Versions typically use a naming convention that enables the sequence or date of each baseline to be identified. For example, payroll application version 3 contains updated functionality from version 2.

vision

A description of what the organization intends to become in the future. A vision is created by senior management and is used to help influence culture and strategic planning. *See also* mission.

vulnerability

A weakness that could be exploited by a threat – for example, an open firewall port, a password that is never changed, or a flammable carpet. A missing control is also considered to be a vulnerability.

warranty

(*ITIL Service Strategy*) Assurance that a product or service will meet agreed requirements. This may be a formal agreement such as a service level agreement or contract, or it may be a marketing message or brand image. Warranty refers to the ability of a service to be available when needed, to provide the required capacity, and to provide the required reliability in terms of continuity and security. Warranty can be summarized as 'how the service is delivered', and can be used to determine whether a service is 'fit for use'. The business value of an IT service is created by the combination of utility and warranty. *See also* service validation and testing.

work instruction

A document containing detailed instructions that specify exactly what steps to follow to carry out an activity. A work instruction contains much more detail than a procedure and is only created if very detailed instructions are needed.

work order

A formal request to carry out a defined activity. Work orders are often used by change management and by release and deployment management to pass requests to technical management and application management functions.

workaround

(*ITIL Service Operation*) Reducing or eliminating the impact of an incident or problem for which a full resolution is not yet available – for example, by restarting a failed configuration item. Workarounds for problems are documented in known error records. Workarounds for incidents that do not have associated problem records are documented in the incident record.

workload

The resources required to deliver an identifiable part of an IT service. Workloads may be categorized by users, groups of users, or functions within the IT service. This is used to assist in analysing and managing the capacity, performance and utilization of configuration items and IT services. The term is sometimes used as a synonym for throughput.

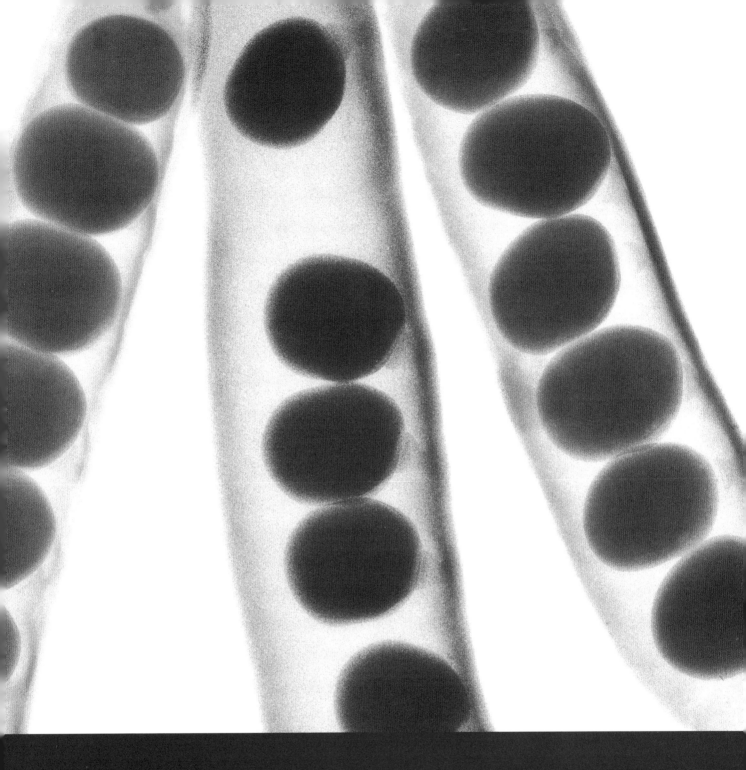

Index

Index

Page numbers in *italic* refer to figures and tables.

application management 25
applications assets 268
asset management 97–9
asset types
   applications 268
   financial capital 269
   information 268
   infrastructure 268
   knowledge 267
   management 267
   organization 267
   people 268
   process 267
assets 22, 267–9

balanced scorecard 286
bar-coding 63
Best Management Practice (BMP) 8–9
best practices 20–2, 37–45
build and test authorization 78–9
build and test coordination 79
build and test environment managers 231
build and test planning 124–7
business change 57, 210–11
   processes 85–6

CAB (change advisory board) 80–2, 228–9
capabilities 22, *23*
Capability Maturity Model Integration (CMMI) 286
capacity management 87
challenges 255
change advisory board 80–2, 228–9
change authorities 228
change deployment authorization 79
change documentation *72–3*
change evaluation 75–6, 175–81
   challenges 181
   critical success factors 180–1
   effect of changes 176–8
   information management 180
   inputs 180
   interfaces 180
   key performance indicators 180–1
   key terms *176*
   outputs 180

   performance evaluation 178–9
   plans 176
   policies 175
   practitioners 233
   principles 175–6
   process *177*
   process managers 233
   process owners 232–3
   purpose and objectives 175
   reports 180
   risk management 179
   risks 181
   scope 175
   test plans 179
   test results 179
   triggers 180
change initiators 228
change logging 72–4
change management 60–89
   assessment and evaluation of changes 73–8
   build and test authorization 78–9
   build and test coordination 79
   business change processes 85–6
   business value 62–3
   capacity management 87
   challenges 89
   change advisory board 80–2
   change deployment authorization 79
   change documentation *72–3*
   change evaluation 75–6
   change logging 72–4
   change models 66–7
   change proposals 67
   change records 65
   change records review and closure 79–80
   change requests 65, 69–73
   changes 65
   critical success factors 88–9
   demand management 87
   design and planning considerations 64–5
   emergency changes 82–4
   information management 88
   information security management 87
   inputs 85
   interfaces 85–6
   IT service continuity management 87
   key performance indicators 88–9

change management *continued*
  organizational management 86
  outputs 85
  planning and scheduling 76–8
  policies 63–4, 152
  priorities *76*
  priority allocation 76
  problem management 87
  process activities, methods and techniques
    68–84
  process flow for changes *70*
  process managers 228
  process owners 227–8
  programme management 86
  project management 86
  purpose and objectives 61
  release and deployment management 147
  remediation planning 68, 78
  RFCs 65, 73
  risk assessment 74–5
  risks 89
  scope 61–2
  service asset and configuration management 86,
    87
  service management 86–7
  service portfolio management 87
  service validation and testing 232
  seven Rs 74
  sourcing and partnering 86
  stakeholder management 86
  standard changes 67–8
  standard deployment requests 69, *71*
  triggers 84–5
change models 66–7
change practitioners 228
change proposals 67
change records 65, 79–80
change requests 65, *66,* 69–73
CIs *see* configuration items
cloud environments 250–2
CMDB (configuration management database) 92,
  95–6, 111, 184–5
CMMI (Capability Maturity Model Integration) 286
CMS (configuration management systems) 92,
  94–7, 184–5, 243–4
COBIT 282–3
collaboration 242–3
communications 199–203
communities 242
competence 234–5
compliance testing 164
configuration analysts 229–30

configuration baselines 96, 107, *108*
configuration breakdowns *103*
configuration control 109
configuration documentation 105, *106*
configuration identification 100–7
configuration items 92, 93–4, 101–5, 132
configuration librarians 230
configuration management *see* service asset and
  configuration management
configuration management database 92, 95–6,
  111, 184–5
configuration management systems 92, 94–7,
  184–5, 243–4
configuration models 92, *93*
configuration records 92, 110
content management 242
continual service improvement 7, 8, *33,* 158
contract and regulation testing 163–4
Control OBjectives for Information and related
  Technology (COBIT) 282–3
core services 16
corporate governance of IT 282
course corrections 42
critical success factors 60, 255–6
cultural change 250
customer assets 22
customer-facing services 26
customers
  difficult 258–9

data layers 189
data mining 190
Data-to-Information-to-Knowledge-to-Wisdom
  structure 183–4
decommissioning assets 98–9
definitive hardware spares 98
definitive media libraries 98, *99*
delivery plans 128–9
demand management 87
departments 24
deployment 137–46
  options 119–21
  planning 127–8
  practitioners 231
  review and closure 145–6
  verification 142–5
design 248–9
design constraints 153, *154*
difficult customers 258–9
DIKW (Data-to-Information-to-Knowledge-to-
  Wisdom structure) 183–4
discussion forums 188

divisions 24
DMLs (definitive media libraries) 98, *99*
document management 242

early life support practitioners 231
embedding and reviewing M_o_R 274
emergency changes 82–4
emergency-room syndrome 200
employee shock 210
enabling services 16
enhancing services 16
environmental management 283–4

financial assets 269
functions 221

governance 27, 282
green IT 283–4
groups 24

implementation 247–52
information architecture 189–90
information assets 268
information integration layers 189–90
information management 59–60, 88
information security management 87
infrastructure assets 268–9
inputs by lifecycle stage *46, 291–2*
integrated planning 56
integrated plans 250, *251*
ISO 9000:2005 281
ISO 9001:2008 281
ISO 9004 282
ISO 9241 284
ISO 14001 series 284
ISO 31000 274–5
ISO/IEC 12207 284
ISO/IEC 15288 284
ISO/IEC 15504 284
ISO/IEC 19770-1 284
ISO/IEC 20000 283
ISO/IEC 25000 series 284
ISO/IEC 27001 275–6
ISO/IEC 38500 282
ISO/IEC 42010 284
ISO/IEC 20000 29–30
ISO/IEC JTC1 284
ITIL
    guidance 281
    overview 3
    success of 10
    web services 281

ITIL Continual Service Improvement 7, 8
ITIL Service Design 7, *31*
ITIL Service Operation 8, 31
ITIL Service Strategy 7, *31*
ITIL Service Transition 8, 10–11, *31*
ITSM (IT service management) *see* service
    management

journals 188
justification 247–8

knowledge assets 267–8
knowledge creators 234
knowledge management 26, 181–95
    business value 182–3
    challenges 195
    configuration management database 184–5
    critical success factors 194
    data 189
    Data-to-Information-to-Knowledge-to-Wisdom
        structure 183–4
    evaluation and improvement 191
    information 189
    information architecture 189–90
    information management 193–4
    inputs 193
    interfaces 193
    key performance indicators 194
    knowledge transfer 186–8, 195
    outputs 193
    policies 183
    practitioners 233
    procedures 190–1
    process managers 233
    process owners 233
    purpose and objectives 181–2
    risks 195
    scope 182
    service knowledge management systems 184–5,
        191–2
    strategy 185–6
    tools 242
    triggers 193
knowledge processing layers 190
knowledge transfer 186–8, 195
knowledge visualization 187
Kotter, J. P. *213*

lifecycle stages 55
location change 211
logical staff mobility 236

management asset 267
Management of Portfolios (MoP) 9
Management of Risk (M_o_R) 9, 273–4
Management of Value (MoV) 9
management systems 27–30
Managing Successful Programmes (MSP) 9–10
Managing Successful Projects with PRINCE2 10
media libraries 98, *99,* 106
metadata management 190
metrics 45–6
M_o_R approach 274
M_o_R principles 273–4
M_o_R process 274
motivation 203

newsletters 188

Open Systems Interconnection (OSI) framework
    284–5
operational changes 84–5
operational tests 164
operations management 24–5
organization 221–37
    assets 267
    context 222–3
    functions 221
    interfaces *224*
    structures 221, *222*
organizational change 204–15, 285–6
    business change 210–11
    emotional impact 204–5
    employee shock 210
    location change 211
    methods 212–15
    planning and implementation 208
    practices 212–15
    products 208–9
    progress monitoring 209–10
    readiness assessment *210*
    resistance to 214–15
    roles and responsibilities 205
    service transition 205–7
    sourcing strategy 211–12
    strategies 212–14
    strategy and design 207
    techniques 212–15
    tips *212*
    transformation steps *213*
organizational culture 25, 206–7
organizational management 86
OSI framework 284–5
outcomes 15

outputs by lifecycle stage *46, 291–2*
outsourcing 203

PDCA (Plan-Do-Check-Act) cycle 29, 281–2
people assets 268
performance indicators 60
performance optimization 45
pilots 129–30
Plan-Do-Check-Act (PDCA) cycle 29, 281–2
planning 56–8
    see also transition planning and support
Portfolio, Programme and Project Offices (P3O) 10
preparation activities 55–6
presentation layers 190
principles for service transition 37–45
problem management 87
process assets 267
process communications 236
process managers 226
process model *23*
process owners 226, 227
process practitioners 226–7
process support 58
processes 22–4
product documentation 188
programme management 56–7, 86, 285
progress monitoring and reporting 58
project management 56–7, 86, 285
projected service outages (PSOs) 77
public frameworks 21–2

quality management systems 281–2

RACI (Responsible, Accountable, Consulted,
    Informed) matrix *209,* 234
records management 242
regression testing 164
release and deployment management 114–50
    build and test planning 124–7
    challenges 149
    change management 147
    configuration items 132
    critical success factors 148
    delivery plans 128–9
    deployment 137–42
        options 119–21
        planning 127–8
        review and closure 145–6
        verification 142–5
    documentation 131–2
    financial/commercial planning 130–1
    information management 147–8

inputs 146
interfaces 147
key performance indicators 148
logistics 128
models 122
outputs 146–7
phases of 122–3
pilots 129–30
planning 123–30
process managers 230
process owners 230
release and deployment models 122
release packages 132–3
risks 149–50
service asset and configuration management 147
service design coordination 147
service rehearsals 135–6
service testing 133–5, *134*
service validation and testing 147
test environments 133
transition planning and support 147
triggers 146
release packages 116–19, 126–7, 132–3
release packaging and build practitioners 230–1
release points
    responsibility matrix for *53*
release policy 52–4
release units 107, 116–19
release windows 118
remediation 68
remediation planning 78
requests for change 65, 73
resource restrictions 258
resources 22, *23*
responsibility matrix for release points *53*
retired services 26
retrofitting 249
RFCs (requests for change) 65, 73
risk assessment 74–5, 273–7
Risk IT 276–7
risk management 179, 273–7, 282
risks 256, 273
roles 25, 223–34

SACM *see* service asset and configuration management
safety-criticality 258
SAM (software asset management) 97
SC7 284
SC27 284
schema mapping 190

secure libraries 97
secure stores 98
seminars 188
service asset and configuration management 89–114
    activity model *101*
    business value 90–1
    challenges 114
    change management 86, *87*
    configuration control 109
    configuration identification 100–7
    critical success factors 113–14
    information management 113
    inputs 112
    interfaces 112
    key performance indicators 113–14
    management and planning 100
    outputs 112
    policies 91
    principles 91–2
    process managers 229
    purpose and objectives 89–90
    release and deployment management 147
    reports 110–11
    risks 114
    scope 90
    status accounting and reporting 109–11
    triggers 112
    verification and audit 111–12
service assets 22, 92
service assurance 153–4
service catalogues 26
service continuity management 87
service design coordination 147
service design packages 152–3
service desks 24, 202
service knowledge management systems 26, 92, 184–5
    architectural layers *28*
    business value 115
    data and information *186*
    implementation 191–2
    policies 115–16
    purpose and objectives 114–15
    scope 115
    use 191–2
service level testing 162
service lifecycle 30–3
    and continual service improvement *33*
    inputs and outputs *291–2*
    integration across *32*
service management 17–18

service management *continued*
 change management 86–7
 definition 17
 organization for 24–5
 stakeholders 19
 testing 164
service managers 224
service models 153
service operations 158
service owners 224–6
service pipelines 26
service portfolio management 87
service portfolios 25–6, *27*
service providers 17, 18–19
service quality policy 152
service rehearsals 135–6
service release policy *55*
service testing 133–5, *134*
service transition
 business value 6
 context 6–8
 inputs and outputs by lifecycle stage *46*
 overview 3–6
 policies 37–45
 processes 5
 purpose and objectives 4
 scope 4–5
service validation and testing 150–74
 business value 151
 challenges 174
 change management 232
 change management policy 152
 clean up and closure 170
 compliance testing 164
 continual service improvement 158
 contract and regulation testing 163–4
 critical success factors 173–4
 customers 232
 design considerations 159–61
 design verification 170
 developers 232
 evaluation 170
 information management 172–3
 inputs 171–2
 interfaces 172
 key performance indicators 173–4
 operational tests 164
 outputs 172
 plan verification 170
 planning and design 170
 policies 151–2
 practitioners 232

process managers 232
process owners 232
purpose and objectives 150
regression testing 164
release and deployment management 147
release policy 152
risk policy 152
risks 174
scope 150–1
service assurance 153–4
service design 232
service design packages 152–3
service level testing 162
service management testing 164
service operations 158
service quality policy 152
suppliers 232
test data 173
test environments 170, 173
test management 169–70
test models 156, *157*, 159
test performance 170
test strategies 154–6
testing
 types of 161–4
testing approaches 159
testing levels 158–9
testing perspectives 156–8
testing process *165–9*
triggers 171
usability testing 163
user testing 158
users 232
warranty and assurance tests 162–3
services 15–16, 19–20
seven Rs of change management 74
SFIA (Skills Framework for the Information Age) 235, 286
Six Sigma 287
Skills Framework for the Information Age (SFIA) 235, 286
SKMS *see* service knowledge management systems
snapshots 96–7
social media 188
software asset management 97
sourcing and partnering 86
stakeholder management 86, 215–18
stakeholders 19
standard changes 67–8
standard deployment requests 69, *71*
strategic changes 84
supporting services 26